Essential Microeconomics
Principles, Cases, Problems

Essential Microeconomics

Principles, Cases, Problems

EDWIN MANSFIELD

University of Pennsylvania

W. W. Norton & Company

NEW YORK ■ LONDON

Photos for Parts One, Two, and Five courtesy AP/Wide World Photos.
Photos for Parts Three and Four courtesy of the Warder Collection.

The text of this book is composed in Meridien
with the display set in various weights of Eras
Composition by New England Typographic Service
Manufactured by Courier
Book design by Martin Lubin Graphic Design

Library of Congress Cataloging-in-Publication Data

Mansfield, Edwin.
    Essential microeconomics: principles, cases, problems/Edwin
  Mansfield
        p.   cm.
    Includes index.
    1. Microeconomics.   I. Title.
  HB172.M349   1997
338.5—dc20   96-16023

ISBN 0-393-97040-X (pbk.)

W. W. Norton & Company, Inc., 500 Fifth Avenue, New York, N.Y. 10110 http://web.wwnorton.com
W. W. Norton & Company Ltd., 10 Coptic Street, London WC1A 1PU

1 2 3 4 5 6 7 8 9 0

CONTENTS

PREFACE ix

PART ONE
Market Demand and Firm Behavior

■ CHAPTER 1
Demand Theory 2

Essentials of Demand Theory 2
1. The Demand Side of a Market 2
2. The Price Elasticity of Demand 4
3. Determinants of the Price Elasticity of Demand 6
4. Price Elasticity and Total Money Expenditure 7
5. Income Elasticity of Demand and Cross Elasticity of Demand 9
6. A Model of Consumer Behavior 10
7. The Equilibrium Market Basket 13
Chapter Review 15

■ CHAPTER 2
Production Theory 20

Essentials of Production Theory 20
1. Motivation and Technology of the Firm 20
2. Fixed and Variable Inputs 21
3. The Law of Diminishing Marginal Returns 23
4. The Optimal Input Decision 24
5. Short-Run Total Costs 26
6. Average and Marginal Costs in the Short Run 28
7. The Long-Run Average Cost Function 30
Chapter Review 32

■ CHAPTER 3
Economics by the Glass, Can, or Keg 40

1. Introduction 40
2. Anheuser-Busch 41
3. Miller, Coors, and Stroh 42
4. How Beer Is Produced 43
5. Concentration in the Brewing Industry 43
6. Pricing 44
7. Advertising 45
8. Applying Economics: The Market for Beer 46
9. Applying Economics: Elasticities of Demand 49
10. Applying Economics: Economies of Scale and Advertising 51
11. Applying Economics: International Comparisons 53
12. Conclusion 53

PART TWO
Perfect Competition and Monopoly

■ CHAPTER 4
Perfect Competition 56

Essentials of Perfect Competition 56
1. What is Perfect Competition? 56
2. The Output of the Firm 57
3. Deriving the Market Supply Curve 62
4. Price and Output: The Short Run 64

5. Price and Output: The Long Run 66

Chapter Review 68

▪ CHAPTER 5

Monopoly 74

Essentials of Monopoly 74

1. Causes of Monopoly 74
2. Demand Curve and Marginal Revenue under Monopoly 76
3. Price and Output: The Short Run 78
4. Price and Output: The Long Run 82
5. Perfect Competition and Monopoly: A Comparison 82

Chapter Review 85

▪ CHAPTER 6

No Electricity, No Modern Civilization 91

1. Introduction 91
2. Public Regulation 91
3. Regulation and the Electric Industry 92
4. Does Regulation Affect Prices? 93
5. Effects of Regulation on Efficiency 93
6. The Dawn of a New Competitive Era 94
7. Should Indian Point 3 Be Shut Down? 95
8. Applying Economics: Electricity Demand 95
9. Applying Economics: Costs of Electricity 96
10. Applying Economics: The Pricing of Electricity 97
11. Applying Economics: Differences among Electric Utilities in Prices Charged 99
12. Applying Economics: The Tennessee Valley Authority 101
13. Conclusion 102

PART THREE

Oligopoly, Monopolistic Competition, and Antitrust Policy

▪ CHAPTER 7

Oligopoly and Monopolistic Competition 104

Essentials of Oligopoly and Monopolistic Competition 104

1. Oligopoly 104
2. The Kinked Oligopoly Demand Curve 105
3. Price and Output of a Cartel 106
4. The Theory of Contestable Markets 108
5. The Theory of Games 109
6. Comparison of Oligopoly with Perfect Competition 112
7. Monopolistic Competition 114
8. Comparisons with Perfect Competition and Monopoly 117

Chapter Review 118

▪ CHAPTER 8

Industrial Concentration and the Antitrust Laws 123

Essentials of Industrial Concentration and the Antitrust Laws 123

1. The Case against Monopoly 123
2. The Defense of Monopoly Power 126
3. Concentration of Economic Power 127
4. The Antitrust Laws 128
5. The Role of the Courts 130
6. The Role of the Justice Department 131

Chapter Review 133

▪ CHAPTER 9

Henry Ford Wouldn't Recognize the Auto Industry Today 136

1. Introduction 136
2. General Motors and Alfred P. Sloan 136
3. Problems of Small Firms: The Case of Studebaker 137
4. The Energy Crisis and the Chrysler Bailout 137
5. The Japanese Repudiation of Henry Ford 139
6. Import Restrictions on Japanese Autos 140

7. Japanese Transplants and Changes in the Structure of the U.S. Auto Industry **141**
8. Applying Economics: Auto Demand **142**
9. Applying Economics: Auto Production **144**
10. Applying Economics: Pricing and Rivalry **146**
11. Applying Economics: Government Regulation **148**
12. Conclusion **149**

PART FOUR

The Distribution of Income

■ CHAPTER 10

Wages 152

Essentials of Wages **152**
1. The Firm's Demand Curve for Labor **152**
2. Wages under Perfect Competition **154**
3. Wage Differentials **158**
4. Monopsony **159**
5. Labor Unions **160**
Chapter Review **164**

■ CHAPTER 11

Interest, Rent, and Profits 170

Essentials of Interest, Rent, and Profits **170**
1. The Demand and Supply of Loanable Funds **170**
2. Functions of the Interest Rate **173**
3. The Present Value of Future Income **175**
4. Rent: Nature and Significance **176**
5. Profits **177**
Chapter Review **179**

■ CHAPTER 12

A Woman's Work Is Never Done 183

1. The Growing Role of Women in the Labor Force **183**

2. Sex Discrimination **183**
3. Affirmative Action **184**
4. Comparable Worth **185**
5. Applying Economics: Female Participation in the Labor Force **186**
6. Applying Economics: The Effect of Taxes and Subsidies on Female Labor Force Participation **187**
7. Applying Economics: Poverty and Age-Earnings Profiles **188**
8. Applying Economics: Affirmative Action and Comparable Worth **190**
9. Conclusion **191**

PART FIVE

Resource Allocation and the Government

■ CHAPTER 13 (Optional)

Optimal Resource Allocation 194

Essentials of Optimal Resource Allocation **194**
1. Welfare Economics **194**
2. Conditions for Optimal Resource Allocation **195**
3. Optimal Resource Allocation: A Case Study **197**
4. Perfect Competition and Welfare Maximization **198**
Chapter Review **200**

■ CHAPTER 14

The Economic Role of the Government 202

Essentials of the Economic Role of the Government **202**
1. The United States: A Mixed Capitalist System **202**
2. What Functions Should the Government Perform? **204**
3. Providing Public Goods **207**
4. Externalities **208**
5. Size and Nature of Government Activities **210**
6. What the Federal, State, and Local Governments Receive in Taxes **211**
Chapter Review **212**

▪ CHAPTER 15

Will Pollution Make Caviar Extinct? 216

1. The Plight of the Beluga **216**
2. Why Environmental Pollution? **216**
3. Direct Regulation by Government **217**
4. Effluent Fees **218**
5. Transferable Emissions Permits **219**
6. Tax Credits for Pollution-Control Equipment **219**
7. How Clean Should the Environment Be? **220**
8. A Goal of Zero Pollution? **221**

9. The Ban on Ocean Dumping **221**
10. Global Warming **222**
11. Applying Economics: Global Warming **223**
12. Applying Economics: Water Pollution **225**
13. Applying Economics: Air Pollution **226**
14. Applying Economics: Tax Relief, Economic Development, and the Environment **227**
15. Conclusion **228**

ANSWERS TO ODD-NUMBERED NUMERICAL PROBLEMS **230**

GLOSSARY OF TERMS **238**

INDEX **244**

PREFACE

Economics, while not an easy subject for many students, is not as difficult—or as dry—as it sometimes appears. The key, it seems to many teachers, is to provide students with rich and interesting material that illustrates and tests their understanding of the basic principles they are learning and that relates these principles to problems of public policy and business decision making that are of interest to them. This is the view that underlies this new book.

The topics ordinarily taken up in an elementary course in microeconomics are included here. What is different is that a much larger proportion of the text is devoted to questions of various kinds that the student is expected to answer. Indeed, five of the book's fifteen chapters are devoted to

areas where the student is asked to apply the material he or she has learned in previous parts of the book. These chapters are: "Economics by the Glass, Can, or Keg," "No Electricity, No Modern Civilization," "Henry Ford Wouldn't Recognize the Auto Industry Today," "A Woman's Work Is Never Done," and "Will Pollution Make Caviar Extinct?" Also, a large part of each of the other chapters is designed to get the student to *do* some economics, not just *read about* it.

My thanks go to Ed Parsons, Richard Rivellese, and Carol Loomis of W. W. Norton & Company for their work on this book. Also, my wife has helped in countless ways.

Edwin Mansfield

Essential Microeconomics
Principles, Cases, Problems

PART ONE

Market Demand and Firm Behavior

CHAPTER 1

Demand Theory

Essentials of **Demand Theory**

■ The demand curve for a commodity shows the amount buyers would demand at various prices.

■ The price elasticity of demand is used to measure how sensitive the quantity demanded is to changes in price.

■ Consumers allocate their income among commodities; the collection of commodities chosen by the consumer is called a market basket.

■ The optimal market basket maximizes the satisfaction of the consumer.

1 ■ The Demand Side of a Market

Every market has a demand side and a supply side. The demand side can be represented by a **market demand curve,** which shows the amount of the commodity buyers would like to purchase at various prices. Consider Figure 1.1, which shows the demand curve for wheat in the U.S. market during the early 1990s. The figure shows that about 2.4 billion bushels of wheat will be demanded annually if the farm price is $2.80 per bushel, about 2.5 billion bushels will be demanded annually if the farm price is $2.40 per bushel, and about 2.6 billion bushels will be demanded annually if the farm price is $2.00 per bushel. The total demand for wheat is for several types to produce bread and other food products for domestic use, as well as for feed use, for export purposes, and for industrial uses. The demand curve in Figure 1.1 shows the total demand—including all these components—at each price. Any demand curve pertains to a particular period of time, and the shape and position of the demand curve depend on the length of this period.

Take a good look at the demand curve for wheat in Figure 1.1. This simple, innocent-looking curve influences a great many people's lives.

After all, wheat is the principal grain used for direct human consumption in the United States. To states like Kansas, North Dakota, Oklahoma,

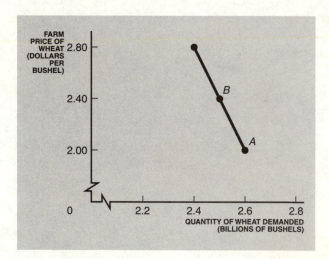

■ **FIGURE 1.1**

Market Demand Curve for Wheat, Early 1990s

The curve shows the amount of wheat buyers would demand at various prices. At $2.00 per bushel, about 8 percent more wheat can be sold than at $2.80 per bushel.

Montana, Washington, Nebraska, Texas, Illinois, Indiana, and Ohio, wheat is a mighty important cash crop. Note that the demand curve for wheat slopes downward to the right. In other words, the quantity of wheat demanded increases as the price falls. This is true of the demand curve for most commodities: they almost always slope downward to the right. This makes sense; one would expect increases in a good's price to result in a smaller quantity demanded.

Any demand curve is based on the assumption that the tastes, incomes, and number of consumers, as well as the prices of other commodities, are held constant. Changes in any of these factors are likely to shift the position of a commodity's demand curve, as indicated below.

CONSUMER TASTES If consumers show an increasing preference for a product, the demand curve will shift to the right; that is, at each price, consumers will desire to buy more than previously. On the other hand, if consumers show a decreasing preference for a product, the demand curve will shift to the left, since, at each price, consumers will desire to buy less than previously.

INCOME LEVEL OF CONSUMERS For some types of products, the demand curve shifts to the right if per capita income increases; whereas for other types of commodities, the demand curve shifts to the left if per capita income rises. Economists can explain why some goods fall into one category and other goods fall into the other, but, at present, this need not concern you. All that is important here is that changes in per capita income affect the demand curve, the size and direction of this effect varying from product to product.

NUMBER OF CONSUMERS IN THE MARKET Compare Austria's demand for wheat with the United States's. Austria is a small country with a population of less than 8 million; the United States is a huge country with a population of over 200 million. Clearly, at a given price of wheat, the quantity demanded by U.S. consumers will greatly exceed the quantity demanded by Austrian consumers. Even if consumer tastes, income and other factors were held constant, this would still be true simply because the United States has so many more consumers in the relevant market.

LEVEL OF OTHER PRICES A commodity's demand curve can be shifted by a change in the price of other commodities. Whether an increase in the price of good B will shift the demand curve for good A to the right or the left depends on the relationship between the two goods. If they are substitutes, such an increase will shift the demand curve for good A to the right. Consider the case of corn and wheat. If the price of corn goes up, more wheat will be demanded since it will be profitable to substitute wheat for corn. If the price of corn drops, less wheat will be demanded since it will be profitable to substitute corn for wheat. Thus, increases in the price of corn will shift the demand curve for wheat to the right, and decreases in the price of corn will shift it to the left.

 TEST YOUR UNDERSTANDING

True or false?

_____ **1** The consumer almost always responds to an increase in a commodity's price by reducing the amount of it he consumes.

_____ **2** Since the market demand curve reflects what consumers want and are willing to pay for, when the market demand curve for wheat shifts upward to the right, this indicates that consumers want more wheat at the existing price.

_____ **3** If a consumer buys three pieces of pizza on August 1 when the price per piece is 70 cents, and if she buys four pieces on September 3 when the price per piece is 60 cents, a change in her demand for pizzas must have occurred between August 1 and September 3.

2 ■ The Price Elasticity of Demand

The quantity demanded of some commodities is fairly sensitive to changes in the commodity's price. That is, changes in price result in significant changes in quantity demanded. On the other hand, the quantity demanded of other commodities is very insensitive to changes in the price. Large changes in price result in small changes in the quantity demanded.

To promote unambiguous discussion of this subject, we must have some measure of the sensitivity of quantity demanded to changes in price. The measure customarily used for this purpose is the **price elasticity of demand,** *defined as the percentage change in quantity demanded resulting from a 1 percent change in price.*[1] For example, suppose that a 1 percent reduction in the price of slingshots results in a 2 percent increase in quantity demanded. Then, using this definition, the price elasticity of demand for slingshots is 2. (Convention dictates that we give the elasticity a positive sign even though the change in price is negative and the change in quantity is positive.) The price elasticity of demand is likely to vary

from one point to another on the market demand curve. For example, the price elasticity of demand for slingshots may be higher when a slingshot costs $1.00 than when it costs $.25.

Note that the price elasticity of demand is expressed in terms of *relative*—that is, proportional or percentage—changes in price and quantity demanded, not *absolute* changes in price and quantity demanded. Thus, in studying the slingshot market, look at the *percentage* change in quantity demanded resulting from a 1 *percent* change in price. This is because absolute changes depend on the units in which price and quantity are measured. Consider good Y. A cut in the price of good Y from $100 to $99 results in an increase in the quantity demanded from 200 to 210 pounds per month. If price is measured in dollars, the quantity demanded of good Y seems quite sensitive to price changes, since a decrease in price of 1 results in an increase in quantity demanded of 10. On the other hand, if price is measured in cents, the quantity demanded of good Y seems quite insensitive to price changes, since a decrease in price of 100 results in an increase in quantity demanded of 10. By using relative changes, we do not encounter this problem. Relative changes do not depend on the units of measurement. Thus the percentage reduction in the price of good Y is 1 percent, regardless of whether price is measured in dollars or cents. And the percentage increase in the quantity de-

---

[1] What if price does not change by 1 percent? Then the price elasticity of demand is defined as the *percentage change in quantity demanded divided by the percentage change in price.* This definition will be used below. Put in terms of symbols, the price elasticity of demand equals $-\Delta Q/\Delta P \times P/Q$, where P is price, ΔP is change in price, Q is quantity demanded, and ΔQ is change in the quantity demanded.

manded of good Y is 5 percent, regardless of whether it is measured in pounds or tons.

CALCULATING THE PRICE ELASTICITY OF DEMAND

The price elasticity of demand is a very important concept and one that economists use often, so it is worthwhile to spend some time explaining exactly how it is computed. Suppose that you have a table showing various points on a market demand curve. For example, Table 1.1 shows the quantity of wheat demanded at various prices, as estimated by Professor Karl Fox of Iowa State University during the early 1960s.[2] Given these data, how do you go about computing the price elasticity of demand for wheat? Since the price elasticity of demand for any product generally varies from point to point on its market demand curve, you must first determine at what point on the demand curve you want to measure the price elasticity of demand.

Let us assume that you want to estimate the price elasticity of demand for wheat when the price of wheat is between $2.00 and $2.20 per

▪ **TABLE 1.1**

Market Demand for Wheat, Early 1960s

FARM PRICE OF WHEAT (dollars per bushel)	QUANTITY OF WHEAT DEMANDED (millions of bushels)
1.00	1,500
1.20	1,300
1.40	1,100
1.60	900
1.80	800
2.00	700
2.20	675

SOURCE: K. Fox, V. Ruttan, and L. Witt, *Farming, Farmers, and Markets for Farm Goods* (New York: Committee for Economic Development, 1962).

[2] Note that Table 1.1 pertains to the early 1960s whereas Figure 1.1 pertains to the early 1990s. Consequently, the demand curves are quite different, as you can see.

bushel. To do this, you can use the following formula:

$$\text{price elasticity} = \frac{\text{percentage change in quantity demanded}}{} \div \frac{\text{percentage change in price}}{}$$

$$= \frac{\text{change in quantity demanded}}{\text{original quantity demanded}} \div \frac{\text{change in price}}{\text{original price}}.$$

Table 1.1 shows that the quantity demanded equals 700 million bushels when the price is $2.00, and that it equals 675 million bushels when the price is $2.20. But should we use $2.00 and 700 million bushels as the original price and quantity? Or should we use $2.20 and 675 million bushels as the original price and quantity? If we choose the former,

$$\text{price elasticity} = -\frac{675 - 700}{700} \div \frac{2.20 - 2.00}{2.00} = 0.36.$$

The price elasticity of demand is estimated to be 0.36. (The minus sign at the beginning of this equation is due to the fact, noted above, that convention dictates that the elasticity be given a positive sign.)

But you could just as well have used $2.20 and 675 million bushels as the original price and quantity. If this had been your choice, the answer would be

$$\text{price elasticity} = -\frac{700 - 675}{675} \div \frac{2.00 - 2.20}{2.20} = 0.41,$$

which is somewhat different from the answer in the previous paragraph.

To get around this difficulty, the generally accepted procedure is to use the average values of price and quantity as the original price and quantity. In other words, use as an estimate of the price elasticity of demand:

$$\text{price elasticity} = \frac{\text{change in quantity demanded}}{\text{sum of quantities}/2} \div \frac{\text{change in price}}{\text{sum of prices}/2}$$

$$= -\frac{(675 - 700)}{(675 + 700)/2} \div \frac{2.20 - 2.00}{(2.20 + 2.00)/2} = 0.38.$$

This is the answer to the problem.

TEST YOUR UNDERSTANDING

True or false?

_____ **1** The price elasticity of demand is expressed in terms of relative, not absolute, changes in price and quantity demanded.

_____ **2** The price elasticity of demand is a measure of the sensitivity of quantity demanded to the price of other commodities.

Exercises

1 Suppose that the relationship between the price of aluminum and the quantity of aluminum demanded is as follows:

PRICE (dollars)	QUANTITY
1	8
2	7
3	6
4	5
5	4

What is the elasticity of demand when price is between $1 and $2? Between $4 and $5?

2 Professor Kenneth Warner of the University of Michigan has estimated that a 10 percent increase in the price of cigarettes results in a 4 percent decline in the quantity of cigarettes consumed. For teenagers, he estimated that a 10 percent price increase results in a 14 percent decline in cigarette consumption. Based on his estimates, what is the price elasticity of demand for cigarettes? Among teenagers, what is the price elasticity of demand? Why is the price elasticity different among teenagers than for the public as a whole?

3 ■ Determinants of the Price Elasticity of Demand

Many studies have been made of the price elasticity of demand for particular commodities. For example, the estimated price elasticity of demand for women's hats is about 3.00, whereas for cotton it is only about 0.12. The following factors are important determinants of whether the price elasticity of demand is high or low.

NUMBER AND CLOSENESS OF AVAILABLE SUBSTITUTES
If a commodity has many close substitutes, its demand is likely to be highly elastic; that is, the price elasticity is likely to be high. If the price of the product increases, a large proportion of its buyers will turn to the close substitutes that are available. If its price decreases, a great many buyers of substitutes will switch to this product. Naturally, the

closeness of the substitutes depends on how narrowly the commodity is defined. In general, one would expect that, as the definition of the product becomes narrower and more specific, the product has more close substitutes and its price elasticity of demand is higher. Thus the demand for a particular brand of oil is more price elastic than the overall demand for oil, and the demand for oil is more price elastic than the demand for fuel as a whole. If a commodity is defined so that it has perfect substitutes, its price elasticity of demand approaches infinity. Thus, if one farmer's wheat is exactly like that grown by other farmers and if the farmer raises the price slightly (to a point above the market level), the farmer's sales will be reduced to nothing.

IMPORTANCE IN CONSUMERS' BUDGETS It is often asserted that the price elasticity of demand for a commodity is likely to depend on the importance of the commodity in consumers' budgets. The elasticity of demand for commodities like pepper and salt may be quite low. Typical consumers spend a very small portion of their income on pepper and salt, and the quantity they demand may not be influenced much by changes in price within a reasonable range. However, although a tendency of this sort is often hypothesized, there is no guarantee that it always exists.

LENGTH OF THE PERIOD Every market demand curve pertains, you will recall, to a certain time interval. In general, *demand is likely to be more sensitive to price over a long period than over a short one*. The longer the period, the easier it is for consumers and business firms to substitute one good for another. If, for example, the price of oil should decline relative to other fuels, oil consumption in the month after the price decline would probably increase very little. But over a period of several years, people would have an opportunity to take account of the price decline in choosing the type of fuel to be used in new and renovated houses and businesses. In the longer period of several years, the price decline would have a greater effect on the consumption of oil than in the shorter period of one month.[3]

 TEST YOUR UNDERSTANDING

True or false?

____ **1** The demand for an appendectomy is likely to be less price elastic than the demand for aspirin.

____ **2** Demand is likely to be more sensitive to price over a short period than a long period.

Exercise

1 Suppose that each of the four corners of an intersection contains a gas station, and that the gasoline is essentially the same. Do you think that the price elasticity of demand for each station's gasoline is above or below 1? Why? Do you think that it is less than or greater than the price elasticity of demand for all gasoline in the United States?

---

4 ▪ Price Elasticity and Total Money Expenditure

The price elasticity of demand determines the effect of a price change on the total amount spent on a commodity. To see this, you must understand three terms: price elastic, price inelastic, and unitary elasticity. The demand for a commodity is **price elastic** if the price elasticity of demand is *greater than* 1. The demand for a commodity is **price inelastic** if the price elasticity of demand is *less than* 1. And the demand for a commodity is of **unitary elasticity** if the price elasticity of demand *equals* 1. As indicated below,

the effect of a price change on the total amount spent on a commodity depends on whether the demand for the commodity is price elastic, price

---

[3] For durable goods like automobiles, the price elasticity of demand may be smaller over a long period than over a short one. If the price of autos increases, the quantity demanded is likely to fall substantially because many people will postpone buying a new car. But as time goes on, the quantity of autos demanded will tend to rise as old autos wear out.

inelastic, or of unitary elasticity. Consider each case.

CASE 1: DEMAND IS PRICE ELASTIC

In this case, if the price of the commodity is *reduced*, the total amount spent on the commodity will *increase*. To see why, suppose that the price elasticity of demand for compact discs is 2 and that the price of the compact discs is reduced by 1 percent. Because the price elasticity of demand is 2, the 1 percent reduction in price results in a 2 percent increase in quantity of compact discs demanded. Since the total amount spent on compact discs equals the quantity demanded times the price, the 1 percent reduction in price will be more than offset by the 2 percent increase in quantity demanded. The result of the price cut will be an increase in the total amount spent on compact discs.

On the other hand, if the price of the commodity is *increased*, the total amount spent on the commodity will *fall*. For example, if the price of compact discs is raised by 1 percent, this will reduce the quantity demanded by 2 percent. The 2 percent reduction in the quantity demanded will more than offset the 1 percent increase in price, the result being a decrease in the total amount spent on compact discs.

CASE 2: DEMAND IS PRICE INELASTIC

In this case, if the price is *reduced*, the total amount spent on the commodity will *decrease*. To see why, suppose that the price elasticity of demand for corn is 0.5 and the price of corn is reduced by 1 percent. Because the price elasticity of demand is 0.5, the 1 percent price reduction results in a 0.5 percent increase in the quantity demanded of corn. Since the total amount spent on corn equals the quantity demanded times the price, the 0.5 percent increase in the quantity demanded will be more than offset by the 1 percent reduction in price. The result of the price cut will be a decrease in the total amount spent on corn.

On the other hand, if the price of the commodity is *increased*, the total amount spent on the commodity will *increase*. For example, if the price of corn is raised by 1 percent, this will reduce quantity demanded by 0.5 percent. The 1 percent price increase will more than offset the 0.5 percent reduction in quantity demanded, the result being an increase in the total amount spent on corn.

CASE 3: DEMAND IS OF UNITARY ELASTICITY

In this case, a price increase or decrease results in no difference in the total amount spent on the commodity. Why? Because a price decrease (increase) of a certain percentage always results in a quantity increase (decrease) of the same percentage, so that the product of the price and quantity is unaffected.

 TEST YOUR UNDERSTANDING

True or false?

_____ **1** If the demand for a commodity is price elastic, an increase in its price will lead to an increase in the total amount spent by consumers on the commodity.

_____ **2** The demand for a commodity is price elastic if the price elasticity of demand is less than 1.

_____ **3** If the demand for the commodity is price elastic, an increase in its price will lead to a decrease in the total amount spent by consumers on the commodity.

_____ **4** The demand for a commodity is price inelastic if the price elasticity of demand is greater than 1.

Exercise

1 On the basis of the following table, if the price of each of these commodities is increased, which ones will experience an increase in the total amount spent by consumers on them?

COMMODITY	PRICE ELASTICITY
Gasoline	0.30
Sugar	0.31
Corn	0.49
Cotton	0.12
Hay	0.43
Potatoes	0.31
Oats	0.56
Barley	0.39
Buckwheat	0.99
Refrigerators	1.40
Airline travel	2.40
Radio and TV sets	1.20
Legal services	0.50
Pleasure boats	1.30
Canned tomatoes	2.50
Newspapers	0.10
Tires	0.60
Beef	0.92
Shoes	0.40

5 ▪ Income Elasticity of Demand and Cross Elasticity of Demand

So far this chapter has dealt almost exclusively with the effect of a commodity's price on the quantity demanded of it in the market. But price is not, of course, the only factor that influences the quantity demanded of the commodity. Another important factor is the level of money income among the consumers in the market. The sensitivity of the quantity demanded to the total money income of all the consumers in the market is measured by the **income elasticity of demand,** *which is defined as the percentage change in the quantity demanded resulting from a 1 percent increase in total money income (all prices being held constant).*

A commodity's income elasticity of demand may be positive or negative. For many commodities, increases in income result in increases in the amount demanded. Such commodities, like steak or caviar, have positive income elasticities of demand. For other commodities, increases in income result in decreases in the amount demanded. These commodities, like margarine and poor grades of vegetables, have negative income elasticities of demand. However, be careful to note that the income elasticity of demand of a commodity is likely to vary with the level of income under consideration. For example, if only families at the lowest income levels are considered, the income elasticity of demand for margarine may be positive.

Luxury items tend to have bigger income elasticities of demand than necessities. Indeed, one way to define luxuries and necessities is to say that luxuries are commodities with high income elasticities of demand, and necessities are commodities with low income elasticities of demand.

The **cross elasticity of demand,** *defined as the percentage change in the quantity demanded of one commodity resulting from a 1 percent change in the price of another commodity, is used to measure the sensitivity of the former commodity's quantity demanded to changes in the latter commodity's price.*

Pairs of commodities are classified as **substitutes** or **complements,** depending on the sign of the cross elasticity of demand. *If the cross elasticity of demand is positive, two commodities are substitutes.* Butter and margarine are substitutes because a decrease in the price of butter will re-sult in a decrease in the quantity demanded of margarine—many margarine eaters really prefer the "higher-priced spread." *On the other hand, if the cross elasticity of demand is negative, two commodities are complements.* For example, gin and tonic may be complements since a decrease in the price of gin may increase the quantity demanded of tonic. The reduction in the price of gin will increase the quantity demanded of gin, and thus increase the quantity demanded of tonic since gin and tonic tend to be used together.

 TEST YOUR UNDERSTANDING

True or false?

_____ **1** An increase in the price of fishing licenses will reduce the total amount spent on fishing poles.

_____ **2** A commodity's income elasticity of demand may be positive or negative.

_____ **3** The income elasticity of demand for food is very high.

Exercises

1 Is each of the following statements true, partly true, or false? Explain.
   a. If a good's income elasticity of demand is less than 1, an increase in the price of the good will increase the amount spent on it.
   b. The income elasticity of demand will have the same sign regardless of the level of income at which it is measured.
   c. If Mr. Miller spends all his income on steak (regardless of his income or the price of steak), Mr. Miller's cross elasticity of demand between steak and any other good is 0.

2 Give the sign of the cross elasticity of demand for each of the following pairs of commodities:
   a. Tea and coffee
   b. Tennis rackets and tennis balls
   c. Whiskey and gin

3 According to the U.S. Department of Agriculture, the income elasticity of demand for coffee is about 0.23. If incomes rose by 1 percent, what effect would this have on the quantity demanded of coffee?

---

6 ▪ A Model of Consumer Behavior

Why do consumers spend their money the way they do? The economist answers this question with the aid of a **model of consumer behavior,** which is useful both for analysis and decision making. To construct this model, the economist obviously must consider the tastes of the consumer. As Henry Adams put it, "Everyone carries his own inch-rule of taste, and amuses himself by applying it, triumphantly, wherever he travels." Certainly one would expect that the amount a consumer purchases of a particular commodity is influenced by his or her tastes. Some people like beef; others like pork. Some people like the opera; others would trade a ticket to hear Luciano

Pavarotti for a ticket to a Dallas Cowboys game any day of the week. Three assumptions, which seem reasonable for most purposes, underlie the economist's model of consumer preferences.

1 Assume that *consumers, when confronted with two alternative market baskets, can decide whether they prefer the first to the second, prefer the second to the first, or are indifferent between them.* For example, suppose Joan Martin is confronted with a choice between a market basket containing three chocolate bars and a ticket to a Broadway show and another market basket containing two chocolate bars and an air ticket to Chicago. Assume that she can somehow decide whether she prefers the first market basket to the second, prefers the second market basket to the first, or is indifferent between them.

2 Assume that *the consumer's preferences are transitive.* The meaning of "transitive" in this context is simple enough. Suppose that Joan Martin prefers a week's vacation on Cape Cod to a week's vacation in Florida, and that she prefers a week's vacation in California to a week's vacation on Cape Cod. Then, if her preferences are transitive, she must prefer a week's vacation in California to a week's vacation in Florida. The reason for this assumption is clear. If the consumer's preferences were not transitive, the consumer would have inconsistent or contradictory preferences. Although some people may have preferences that are not transitive, this assumption seems to be a reasonable first approximation—for the noninstitutionalized part of the population at least.

3 Assume that *the consumer always prefers more of a commodity to less.* For example, if one market basket contains three bars of soap and two monkey wrenches and a second contains three bars of soap and three monkey wrenches, it is assumed that the second market basket is preferred to the first. To a large extent, this assumption is justified by the definition of a commodity as something the consumer desires. This does not mean that certain things are not a nuisance. If one market basket contains three bars of soap and two rattlesnakes, you would not be at all surprised if the consumer did *not* prefer this market basket to one

containing three bars of soap and no rattlesnakes. But to such a consumer, a rattlesnake would not be desired—and thus would not be a commodity. Instead, the absence of a rattlesnake would be desired—and would be a commodity.

TOTAL UTILITY

For simplicity, assume that there are only two goods, food and clothing. This is an innocuous assumption, since the results you will obtain can be generalized to include cases in which any number of goods exists. For simplicity, food is measured in pounds, and clothing is measured in number of pieces of clothing.

Consider Joan Martin. Undoubtedly, she regards certain market baskets—that is, certain combinations of food and clothing (the only commodities)—to be more desirable than others. She certainly regards 2 pounds of food and 1 piece of clothing to be more desirable than 1 pound of food and 1 piece of clothing. For simplicity, suppose that it is possible to measure the amount of satisfaction that she gets from each market basket by its utility. A **utility** *is a number that represents the level of satisfaction that the consumer derives from a particular market basket.* For example, the utility attached to the market basket containing 2 pounds of food and 1 piece of clothing may be 10 utils, and the utility attached to the market basket containing 1 pound of food and 1 piece of clothing may be 6 utils. (A util is the traditional unit in which utility is expressed.)

MARGINAL UTILITY

It is important to distinguish between total utility and marginal utility. The total utility of a market basket is the number described in the previous paragraph, whereas *the **marginal utility** measures the additional satisfaction derived from an additional unit of a commodity.* To see how marginal utility is obtained, take a close look at Table 1.2. The total utility that Joan Martin derives from the consumption of various amounts of food is given in the middle column of this table. (For simplicity, assume for the moment that she consumes only food.) The marginal utility, shown in the right-

▪ **TABLE 1.2**

Total Utility and Marginal Utility Derived by Joan Martin from Consuming Various Amounts of Food per Day[a]

POUNDS OF FOOD	TOTAL UTILITY	MARGINAL UTILITY
0	0	
		3 (= 3 − 0)
1	3	
		4 (= 7 − 3)
2	7	
		2 (= 9 − 7)
3	9	
		1 (= 10 − 9)
4	10	

[a]This table assumes that no clothing is consumed. If a nonzero amount of clothing is consumed, the figures in this table will probably be altered since the marginal utility of a certain amount of food is likely to depend on the amount of clothing consumed.

hand column, is the extra utility derived from each amount of food over and above the utility derived from 1 less pound of food. Thus it equals the difference between the total utility of a certain amount of food and the total utility of 1 less pound of food.

For example, as shown in Table 1.2, the *total* utility of 3 pounds of food is 9 utils, which is a measure of the total amount of satisfaction that Joan Martin gets from this much food. In contrast, the *marginal* utility of 3 pounds of food is the extra utility obtained from the third pound of food; that is, the total utility of 3 pounds of food less the total utility of 2 pounds of food. Specifically, as shown in Table 1.2, it is 2 utils. Similarly, the *total* utility of 2 pounds of food is 7

utils, which is a measure of the total amount of satisfaction that she gets from this much food. In contrast, the *marginal* utility of 2 pounds of food is the extra utility from the second pound of food; that is, the total utility of 2 pounds of food less the total utility of 1 pound of food. Specifically, as shown in Table 1.2, it is 4 utils.

THE LAW OF DIMINISHING MARGINAL UTILITY

Economists generally assume that, as a person consumes more and more of a particular commodity, there is, beyond some point, a decline in the extra satisfaction derived from the last unit of the commodity consumed. For example, if Joan Martin consumes 2 pounds of food in a particular period of time, it may be just enough to meet her basic physical needs. If she consumes 3 pounds of food in the same period of time, the third pound of food is likely to yield her less satisfaction than the second. If she consumes 4 pounds of food in the same period of time, the fourth pound of food is likely to yield her less satisfaction than the third. And so on.

This assumption or hypothesis is often called the **law of diminishing marginal utility.** This law states that, *as a person consumes more and more of a given commodity (the consumption of other commodities being held constant), the marginal utility of the commodity eventually will tend to decline.* The figures concerning Joan Martin in Table 1.2 are in accord with this law. Once the consumption of food exceeds about $1\frac{1}{2}$ pounds, the marginal utility of food declines.

 TEST YOUR UNDERSTANDING

True or false?

_____ **1** If the total utility from consuming hot dogs is proportional to the number of hot dogs consumed, the law of diminishing marginal utility may or may not be violated, depending on the number of utils received per hot dog.

Exercise

1 Suppose that the total utility attached by Ms. Johnson to various quantities of hamburgers consumed (per day) is as follows:

NUMBERS OF HAMBURGERS	TOTAL UTILITY (utils)
0	0
1	5
2	12
3	15
4	17
5	18

Between 3 and 4 hamburgers, what is the marginal utility of a hamburger? Between 4 and 5 hamburgers, what is the marginal utility of a hamburger? Do these results conform to the law of diminishing marginal utility?

7 ▪ The Equilibrium Market Basket

Preferences alone do not determine the consumer's actions. *Besides knowing the consumer's preferences, you must also know his or her income and the prices of commodities to predict which market basket he or she will buy.* The consumer's money income is the amount of money he or she can spend per unit of time. A consumer's choice of a market basket is constrained by the size of his or her money income. For example, although a man regards a Burberry as his favorite suit, he may not buy it because he may have insufficient funds (as the bankers delicately put it). Also, the market basket the consumer chooses is influenced by the prices of commodities. If the Burberry suit were offered by a discount store at $100, rather than its list price of $795, the man might purchase it after all.

Given the consumer's tastes, economists assume that he or she attempts to maximize utility. In other words, *consumers are assumed to be rational in the sense that they choose the market basket—or more generally, the course of action—that is most to their liking.* As previously noted, consumers cannot choose whichever market baskets they please. Instead, they must maximize their utilities subject to the constraints imposed by the sizes of their money incomes and by commodity prices.

The optimal market basket, the one that maximizes utility subject to these constraints, is the one for which the consumer's income is allocated among commodities so that, for every commodity purchased, the marginal utility of the commodity is proportional to its price. For example, consider Joan Martin. For her, the optimal market basket is the one for which

$$\frac{MU_F}{P_F} = \frac{MU_C}{P_C}, \tag{1.1}$$

where MU_F is the marginal utility of food, MU_C is the marginal utility of clothing, P_F is the price of a pound of food, and P_C is the price of a piece of clothing.

WHY IS THIS RULE CORRECT?

To understand why the rule in Equation (1.1) is correct, it is convenient to begin by pointing out that $MU_F \div P_F$ is the marginal utility of the *last dollar's worth* of food and that $MU_C \div P_C$ is the marginal utility of the *last dollar's worth* of clothing. To see why this is so, take the case of food. Since MU_F is the extra utility of the last pound of food bought, and since P_F is the price of this *last pound,* the extra utility of the *last dollar's worth* of food must be $MU_F \div P_F$. For example, if the last pound of food results in an extra utility of 4 utils and costs $2, then the extra utility from the last dollar's worth of food must be $4 \div 2$, or 2 utils. In other words, the marginal utility of the last dollar's worth of food is 2 utils.

Since $MU_F \div P_F$ is the marginal utility of the last dollar's worth of food and $MU_C \div P_C$ is the marginal utility of the last dollar's worth of clothing, what Equation (1.1) really says is that *the rational consumer will choose a market basket for which the marginal utility of the last dollar spent on all commodities purchased is the same.* To see why this must be so, consider the numerical example in Table 1.3, which shows the marginal utility Joan Martin derives from various amounts of food and clothing. Rather than being measured in physical units, food and clothing, they are measured in Table 1.3 in terms of the amount of money spent on them.

Given the information in Table 1.3, how much of each commodity should Joan Martin buy if her money income is only $4 (a ridiculous assumption but one that will help to make the point)? Clearly, the first dollar she spends should be on food since it will yield her a marginal utility of 20. The second dollar she spends should also be on food since a second dollar's worth of food has a marginal utility of 16. (Thus the total utility derived from the $2 of expenditure is 20 + 16 = 36.)[4] The marginal utility of the third dollar is 12 if it is spent on more food—and 12 too if it is spend on clothing. Suppose that she chooses more food. (The total utility derived from the $3 of expenditure is 20 + 16 + 12 = 48.) What about the final dollar? Its marginal utility is

[4] Since the marginal utility is the extra utility obtained from each dollar spent, the total utility from the total expenditure must be the sum of the marginal utilities of the individual dollars of expenditure.

▪ **TABLE 1.3**

Marginal Utility Derived by Joan Martin from Various Quantities of Food and Clothing (utils)

COMMODITY	DOLLARS WORTH				
	1	**2**	**3**	**4**	**5**
Food	20	16	12	10	7
Clothing	12	10	7	5	3

10 if it is spent on more food and 12 if it is spent on clothing; thus she will spend it on clothing. (The total utility derived from all $4 of expenditure is then 20 + 16 + 12 + 12 = 60.)

Thus Joan Martin, if she is rational, will allocate $3 of her income to food and $1 to clothing. This is the **equilibrium market basket,** the market basket that maximizes consumer satisfaction. The important thing to note is that this market basket demonstrates the principle set forth earlier in Equation (1.1). As shown in Table 1.3, the marginal utility derived from the last dollar spent on food is equal to the marginal utility derived from the last dollar spent on clothing. (Both are 12.) Thus this market basket has the characteristic described above: the marginal utility of the last dollar spent on all commodities purchased is the same. This will always be the case for market baskets that maximize the consumer's utility. If it were not true, the consumer could obtain a higher level of utility by changing the composition of his or her market basket.

 TEST YOUR UNDERSTANDING

True or false?

_____ **1** If the total utility from consuming hot dogs is 3 times the number of hot dogs consumed and the total utility from consuming hoagies is 4 times the number of hoagies consumed, the consumer should buy hoagies, not hot dogs.

Exercises

1 If Ms. Johnson is maximizing her satisfaction, and if the marginal utility of a hot dog is twice that of a bottle of beer, what must the price of a hot dog be if:

   a. The price of a bottle of beer is $.75?
   b. The price of a bottle of beer is $1?

(Assume that Ms. Johnson consumes both beer and hot dogs.)

2 "A good's price is related to its marginal utility, not its total utility. Thus a good like water or air may be cheap, even though its total utility is high." Comment and evaluate.

3 If the marginal utility of one good is 3 and its price is $1, while the marginal utility of another good is 6 and its price is $3, is the consumer maximizing his or her satisfaction, given that he or she is consuming both goods?

▪ CHAPTER REVIEW

KEY TERMS

market demand curve

price elasticity of demand

income elasticity of demand

cross elasticity of demand

substitutes

complements

utility

marginal utility

law of diminishing marginal utility

equilibrium market basket

COMPLETION QUESTIONS

1 When income increases from $80 billion to $81 billion, the quantity demanded of good X increases from 3,000 to 3,050. The income elasticity of demand for good X equals _____. When computing the income elasticity of demand, the price of good X is held _____.

2 The total amount spent on a good is not affected by its price if the price elasticity of demand equals _____. The total quantity demanded of a good is not affected by its price if the price elasticity of demand equals _____.

3 If the government imposes a $1 tax on a commodity, it will obtain the most revenue from the tax if the commodity's price elasticity of demand equals _____. The largest burden of the tax is borne by consumers if the price elasticity of demand equals _____.

4 Whether a price cut results in an increase in the total amount spent on a commodity depends on the _____.

5 The total amount spent on a commodity is the _____ times _____.

6 If the demand for a commodity is price inelastic, then the price elasticity of demand is _____.

7 The income elasticity of demand is the percentage change in the quantity demanded resulting from _____ increase in total _____.

ANSWERS TO COMPLETION QUESTIONS

1.3

constant

1

0

0

0

price elasticity of demand

quantity demanded   price

less than 1

a 1 percent   money income

8 If the cross elasticity of demand is positive, two commodities are _____ .

substitutes

9 The demand for a commodity is _____ when a price increase or decrease results in no difference in the total amount spent on the commodity.

of unitary elasticity

10 The _____ is the percentage change in quantity demanded resulting from a 1 percent change in price.

price elasticity of demand

11 During a (long, short) _____ period, demand is likely to be more sensitive to price than over a (long, short) _____ one. The longer the period, the (easier, harder) _____ it is for consumers and business firms to substitute one good for another.

long

short
easier

12 The demand curve for the output of a particular firm is generally (less, more) _____ price elastic than the market demand curve for the commodity, because the products of other firms in the industry are close (substitutes, complements) _____ for the product of this firm.

more

substitutes

NUMERICAL PROBLEMS

1 Suppose that the relationship between the price of aluminum and the quantity of aluminum demanded is as follows:

PRICE (dollars)	QUANTITY
1	8
2	7
3	6
4	5
5	4

What is the price elasticity of demand when price is between $1 and $2? Between $4 and $5?

2 Suppose that the price elasticity of demand for gasoline is 0.50. About how big a price increase will be required to reduce the consumption of gasoline by 1 percent?

3 Suppose that the income elasticity of demand for automobiles is 2.5 in the United States and 3.0 in the United Kingdom. If incomes in the United States rise by 2 percent next year and incomes in the United Kingdom rise by 1 percent, what will be the effect in each country on the quantity of automobiles purchased?

4 If a 1.5 percent reduction in the price of Nike running shoes results in a 3.0 percent reduction in the quantity demanded of New Balance running shoes, what is the cross elasticity of demand for these two commodities? Are they substitutes or complements?

5 Suppose that the market demand curve for sofas is as follows:

PRICE (dollars)	QUANTITY OF SOFAS
500	500
1,000	300
1,500	200
2,000	100

a What is the price elasticity of demand for sofas when the price is between $1,500 and $2,000?

b What is the price elasticity of demand when the price is between $500 and $1,000?

c According to this chapter, an increase in price results in increased total expenditures on a product if its price elasticity of demand is less than 1, and less total expenditure on a product if its price elasticity of demand is greater than 1. Show that this proposition is true if the price of sofas is raised from $500 to $1,000.

d Show that the proposition in part C is true if the price of sofas is raised from $1,500 to $2,000.

6 Suppose that there are only three people in the market for sailboats—Mary Smith, Bill Kennedy, and Martin Jones. Suppose their demand curves are as given below. Fill in the blank spaces for the market demand curve for sailboats.

PRICE OF A SAILBOAT (dollars)	QUANTITY DEMANDED			MARKET DEMAND
	SMITH	KENNEDY	JONES	
500	3	2	5	_____
1,000	2	1	4	_____
1,500	2	1	3	_____
2,000	1	0	2	_____

7 (Advanced) Prove that the price elasticity of demand at any price less than $5 will always be the same on D_1 as on D_2 in the following figure.

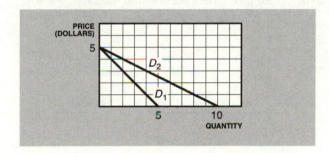

8 Tom and Jean buy beer for their social clubs. Every time the price of a sixpack falls by a dime, Tom runs out and buys 3 more sixpacks per week, but Jean runs out and buys 5 more. The price is now $1, and we observe Tom buying 25 sixpacks per week while Jean is buying 10 sixpacks.

a Draw each person's demand curve for beer.

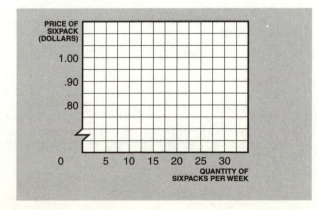

b Whose price elasticity of demand for beer is higher at the current price of a sixpack?

9 Suppose the price elasticity of demand for tables is unity when the price is $40. Suppose further that when the price is $40, 100 tables are sold each week in Sommersville. Assuming no change in the elasticity for a small rise in table prices, how many will be sold next week if price should rise to $42 per table?

10 Suppose that the Brazilian government destroys a substantial portion of its coffee harvest in order to increase its revenue from coffee exports. What conditions are essential in order to make this type of policy economically beneficial for the country? Why would the conditions you identify increase export revenues?

11 a On the basis of the diagram below, which of the following would be more expensive for the government?

(1) Set minimum wages at $2.50 per hour and hire all the people the market will not hire at that wage.

(2) Let the market determine an equilibrium wage ($1.50 per hour in the diagram) and pay everyone who works a subsidy of $1.00 to make up the difference between what the market will pay and what is deemed a fair wage ($2.50 per hour).

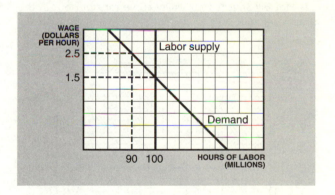

b Would the answer be different if the demand for labor were price elastic with the result that an increase in the wage rate to $2.50 cut the quantity of labor demanded to a greater extent than shown above? Why or why not?

12 A firm estimates that the demand curves for its two products are given by

$$Q_1 = 200 - 2P_1 - 3P_2 \quad \text{and} \quad Q_2 = 450 + 6P_1 - 2P_2,$$

where Q_1 is the quantity demanded of the first product, P_1 is its price, Q_2 is the quantity demanded of the second product, and P_2 is its price. Compute the following elasticities at $P_1 = \$2$ and $P_2 = \$2$:

a Price elasticity of demand for the first product

b Cross elasticity of demand for the second product with respect to variation in the price of the first product

13 Suppose that Bill Smith's utility can be regarded as measurable, and that the utility he gets from the consumption of various numbers of hot dogs per day is shown below:

HOT DOGS CONSUMED PER DAY	TOTAL UTILITY (utils)
0	0
1	5
2	11
3	16
4	20
5	23

a What is the marginal utility of the third hot dog per day to Bill Smith? What is the marginal utility of the fourth hot dog?

b Plot Bill Smith's total utility curve for hot dogs in the graph below:

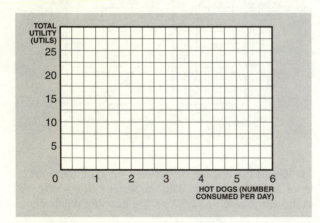

c Suppose that Bill Smith divides his income entirely between hot dogs and Hershey bars—on the advice of his (incompetent) physician. He allocates his income between these two commodities in such a way as to maximize his satisfaction. His marginal utility from an extra Hershey bar is 2 utils, and the price of a Hershey

bar is 20 cents. If the price of a hot dog is 40 cents, how many hot dogs does he consume per day?

d In part c how many hot dogs would he consume per day if the price of a hot dog were 30 cents?

e In part c how many hot dogs would he consume per day if the price of a hot dog were 50 cents?

14 The fact that each individual consumes many different goods supports the theory of diminishing marginal utility. Use an example to show that without diminishing marginal utility, people would allocate their incomes very differently than they do with this phenomenon.

15 "The markets for some goods must be truly strange! Why, just the other day I heard that some people actually buy more hamburger at $1.00 per pound than others do at $.75 per pound. Surely this violates the law of downward-sloping demand curves." Explain why it does or does not.

16 You are given the following information about Sue, who buys only clothing and food with her income of $700.

FOOD PRICE (dollars per unit)	QUANTITY (units)	
	FOOD	CLOTHING
40	5	_____
30	10	_____
10	20	_____

a Fill in the last column of the table. (Clothing costs $50 per unit.)

b Diagram three points on Sue's demand curve for food.

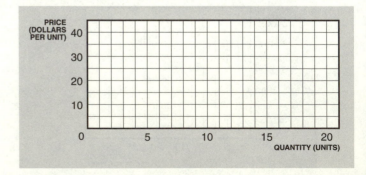

ANSWERS TO
TEST YOUR UNDERSTANDING

SECTION 1

TRUE OR FALSE: 1. True 2. True 3. False

EXERCISE

1. The demand curve is as follows:

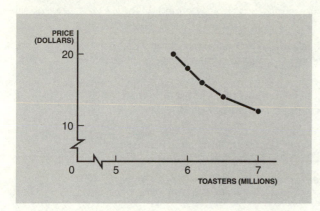

SECTION 2

TRUE OR FALSE: 1. True 2. False

EXERCISES

1. Elasticity $= -\dfrac{(7-8)}{7.5} \div \dfrac{(2-1)}{1.5} = 0.20.$

Elasticity $= -\dfrac{(4-5)}{4.5} \div \dfrac{(5-4)}{4.5} = 1.00.$

2. About 0.4. About 1.4. Teenagers have lower incomes than adults.

SECTION 3

TRUE OR FALSE: 1. True 2. False

EXERCISE

1. Above 1, because the gasolines provided by the four gas stations are very close substitutes. It will be greater than the price elasticity for all gasoline in the United States.

SECTION 4

TRUE OR FALSE: 1. False 2. False 3. True 4. False

EXERCISE

1. All but refrigerators, airline travel, radio and TV sets, pleasure boats, and canned tomatoes.

SECTION 5

TRUE OR FALSE: 1. True 2. True 3. False

EXERCISES

1. a. False b. Not true for some goods c. True.

2. a. Positive b. Negative c. Positive

3. It would increase by 0.23 percent.

SECTION 6

TRUE OR FALSE: 1. False

EXERCISE

1. 2 utils. 1 util. Yes.

SECTION 7

TRUE OR FALSE: 1. False

EXERCISES

1. a. $1.50. b. $2.00.

2. Air is cheap because its marginal utility is quite low. In general, people are willing to pay relatively high prices for commodities having high marginal utilities.

3. No.

■ CHAPTER 2

Production Theory

Essentials of **Production Theory**

- Economists usually assume that a firm attempts to maximize profits, which are defined as the difference between the firm's revenues and its costs.

- To produce goods and services, firms combine inputs like labor (the time of workers who perform productive tasks) and capital (the machinery and materials required to produce the good or service).

- The law of diminishing marginal returns states that, if equal increments of an input are added (the quantities of other inputs being held constant), the resulting increments of product will decrease beyond some point.

- Various combinations of inputs may be used to produce a given product; firms are assumed to choose the combination of inputs that minimizes cost.

- Economists use cost functions to show the minimum costs for a firm to produce various levels of output.

- Cost functions can be either short run (where at least one input is fixed) or long run (where no input is fixed).

1 ■ Motivation and Technology of the Firm

What determines the behavior of the business firm? As a first approximation, economists usually assume that firms attempt to maximize **profits,** which are defined as the difference between the firm's revenue and its costs. In other words, economists generally assume that firms try to make as much money as possible. This assumption certainly does not seem unreasonable; most business executives appear to be interested in making money. Nonetheless, the assumption of profit maximization oversimplifies the situation. Although business executives certainly want profits, they are interested in other things as well. Some firms claim that they want to promote better cultural activities or better racial relations in their community. At a less-lofty level, other firms say that their aim is to increase their share of the market. Whether or not one takes these self-proclaimed goals very seriously, it is clear that firms are not interested only in making money.

The decisions a firm should make in order to maximize its profits are determined by the current state of technology. Technology is the sum total of society's knowledge concerning the industrial arts. Just as consumers are limited by their incomes, firms are limited by the current state of technology. If the current state of technology is such that the firm does not know how to produce more than 40 bushels of corn per year from an acre of land if 2 workers are hired, then this is as much as the firm can produce from this combination of land and labor. In making its decisions, the firm must take this into account.

INPUTS

In constructing a model of the profit-maximizing firm, economists must somehow represent the state of technology and include it in their model. As a first step toward this end, it is necessary to define an **input.** Perhaps the simplest definition of an input is that it is anything the firm uses in its production process. Some of the inputs of a farm producing corn might be seed, land, labor, water, fertilizer, and various type of machinery, as well as the time of the people managing the farm.

PRODUCTION FUNCTION

The basic concept economists use to represent the state of technology is the production function. For any commodity, *the* **production function** *is the relationship between the quantities of various inputs used per period of time and the maximum quantity of the commodity that can be produced per period of time.* More specifically, the production function is a table, graph, or equation showing the maximum output rate that can be achieved from any specified set of usage rates of inputs. The production function summarizes the characteristics of existing technology at a given point in time. It reflects the technological constraints the firm must reckon with.

 TEST YOUR UNDERSTANDING

True or false?

_____ **1** Information concerning a firm's production function is often obtained from the firm's engineers, as well as its artisans and technicians.

Exercises

1 Which of the following are inputs in the steel industry?

a. Coke	b. Iron ore
c. Labor	d. Land
e. Capital	f. Water
g. Oxygen	h. Food eaten by Bethlehem Steel's workers

2 A small firm collects the following data regarding the relationship between the quantity of its output and the amount of labor it uses.

QUANTITY OF LABOR USED PER MONTH	OUTPUT PER MONTH
0	0
1	100
2	210
3	315
4	415
5	500

Is this a production function? Why or why not?

---

2 ▪ Fixed and Variable Inputs

A **fixed input** *is one whose quantity cannot change during the period of time under consideration.* This period will vary. It may be six months in one case, six years in another case. Among the most important inputs often included as fixed are the firm's plant and equipment; that is, its factory and office buildings, machinery, tooling, and transportation facilities.

A **variable input** *is one whose quantity can be changed during the relevant period.* It is generally possible to increase or decrease the number of workers engaged in a particular activity (although this is not always the case, since they may have long-term contracts). Similarly, it frequently is possible to alter the amount of raw material that is used.

Whether an input is considered variable or fixed depends on the length of the period under consideration. The longer the period, the more inputs are variable, not fixed. Although the length of the period varies from case to case, economists have found it very useful to focus special attention on two time periods: the short run and the long run. *The* **short run** *is defined as the period of time in which at least one of the firm's inputs is fixed.* More specifically, since the firm's plant and equipment are among the most difficult inputs to change quickly, *the short run is generally understood to mean the length of time during which the firm's plant and equipment are fixed.* On the other hand, *the* **long run** *is that period of time in which all inputs are variable.* In the long run, the firm can make a complete adjustment to any change in its environment.

A useful way to look at the long run is to consider it a *planning horizon.* While operating in the short run, the firm must continually be planning ahead and deciding its strategy in the long run. Its decisions concerning the long run determine the sort of short-run position the firm will occupy in the future. Before a firm makes the decision to add a new type of product to its line, the firm is in a long-run situation (with regard to the new product), since it can choose among a wide variety of types and sizes of equipment to produce the new product. But once the investment is made, the firm is confronted with a short-run situation, since the type and size of equipment is, to a considerable extent, frozen.

AVERAGE PRODUCT OF AN INPUT

In order to determine which production technique—that is, which combination of inputs—a firm should use, it is necessary to define the average product and marginal product of an input. *The* **average product** *of an input is the firm's total output divided by the amount of input used to produce*

■ **TABLE 2.1**

Average and Marginal Products of Labor, 1-Acre Wheat Farm

NUMBER OF UNITS OF LABOR	TOTAL OUTPUT (bushels per year)	MARGINAL PRODUCT (bushels per unit of labor)	AVERAGE PRODUCT (bushels per unit of labor)
0	0		—
		30	
1	30		30
		40	
2	70		35
		30	
3	100		33⅓
		25	
4	125		31¼
		20	
5	145		29

this amount of output. The average product of an input can be calculated from the production function. Consider the wheat farm in Table 2.1. The average product of labor is 30 bushels per unit of labor when 1 unit of labor is used, 35 bushels per unit of labor when 2 units are used, 33⅓ bushels per unit of labor when 3 units are used, and so forth.

MARGINAL PRODUCT OF AN INPUT

As the amount of labor used on the farm increases, so does the farm's output, but the amount of extra output from the addition of an extra unit of labor varies depending on how much labor is already being used. The extra output from the addition of the first unit of labor is $30 - 0 = 30$ bushels per unit of labor. The extra output due to the addition of the second unit of labor is $70 - 30 = 40$ bushels per unit of labor. And the extra output from the addition of the fifth unit of labor is $145 - 125 = 20$ bushels per unit of labor. *The* **marginal product** *of an input is the addition to total output due to the addition of the last unit of input used, the quantity of other inputs used being held constant.* Thus the marginal product of labor is 30 bushels when between 0 and 1 unit of labor are used, 40 bushels when between 1 and 2 units of labor are used, and so on. Table 2.1 shows the average and marginal products of labor at various levels of utilization of labor.

TEST YOUR UNDERSTANDING

True or false?

____ **1** If the average product of labor equals 6/L, where L is the number of units of labor employed per day, total output is the same regardless of how much labor is used per day.

____ **2** If the average product of labor equals 4 when the number of units of labor employed per day is between 1 and 6, the marginal product of labor also equals 4 when the amount of labor used is within this range.

____ **3** If the average product of labor equals 5L, where L is the number of units of labor employed per day, the law of diminishing marginal returns is violated.

____ **4** The long run refers to a period when all inputs are variable and none is fixed.

____ **5** The average product of an input is the addition to the total output due to the addition of the last unit of input used, the quantity of other inputs used being held constant.

Exercises

1 Suppose that a firm has the following production function:

HOURS OF LABOR PER YEAR (thousands)	OUTPUT PER YEAR (thousands)
0	0
1	2
2	8
3	12
4	14
5	15

Plot on a graph the marginal product of labor at various levels of utilization of labor.

2 Using the data in Exercise 1, plot the average product of labor at various levels of utilization of labor.

3 A tool and die shop has three types of inputs: labor, machines, and materials. It cannot obtain additional machines in less than six months. In the next month, do you think that labor is a fixed or variable input? Do you think that machines are a fixed or variable input? Explain.

3 ▪ The Law of Diminishing Marginal Returns

Perhaps the best-known—and certainly one of the least-understood—laws of economics is the so-called **law of diminishing marginal returns.** Put in a single sentence, this law states that *if equal increments of an input are added, the quantities of other inputs being held constant, the resulting increments of product will decrease beyond some point;* that is, the marginal product of the input will diminish.

Suppose that a small factory that manufactures a metal automobile component has eight machine tools. If this firm hires only one or two workers, total output per worker will be quite low. These workers will have a number of quite different tasks to perform, and the advantages of specialization will be sacrificed. Workers will spend considerable time switching from one machine to another, and many of the eight machine tools will be idle much of the time. What happens as the firm increases its work force? As more and more workers are added, the marginal product (that is, the extra product) of each will tend to rise, while the work force grows to the point where it can man the fixed amount of equipment effectively. However, if the firm continues to increase the number of workers, the marginal product of a worker will eventually begin to decrease. Why? Because workers will have to wait in line to use the fixed number of machine tools, and because the extra workers will have to be assigned to less and less important tasks: Eventually, if enough workers are hired (and utilized within the plant), they may get in each other's way to such an extent that production may grind to a halt.

The law of diminishing marginal returns plays a major part in determining the firm's optimal input combination and the shape of the firm's cost functions, as you will see below. To prevent misunderstanding and confusion, several points about this law should be stressed. First, *it is assumed that technology remains fixed*. If technology changes, the law of diminishing marginal returns cannot predict the effect of an additional unit of input. Second, *at least one input must be fixed in quantity*, since the law of diminishing marginal returns is not applicable to cases in which there is a proportional increase in all inputs. Third, *it must be possible to vary the proportions in which the various inputs are utilized*. This is generally possible in industry and agriculture.

 TEST YOUR UNDERSTANDING

True or false?

_____ **1** If technology changes, the law of diminishing marginal returns can predict the effect of an additional unit of input.

_____ **2** The law of diminishing marginal returns is not applicable to cases in which there is a proportional increase in all inputs.

_____ **3** If a nonzero amount of output results when no labor is used, this violates the law of diminishing marginal returns.

Exercises

1 On the wheat farm in Table 2.1, does the law of diminishing marginal returns hold? Why or why not?

2 In the small firm in Exercise 2 on page 21, does the law of diminishing returns hold? Why or why not?

3 A firm uses two inputs: capital and labor. The firm's chief engineer says that its output depends in the following way on the amount of labor and capital it uses:

$$Q = 3L + 4C,$$

where Q is the number of units of output produced per day, L is the number of units of labor used per day, and C is the amount of capital used per day. Does this relationship seem sensible? Why, or why not?

4 ■ The Optimal Input Decision

Given that a firm is going to produce a particular quantity of output, what production technique—that is, what combination of inputs—should it choose to maximize profits? Note first that if the firm maximizes its profits, it must minimize the cost of producing this quantity of output. This seems obvious enough. But what combination of inputs (that will produce the required quantity of output) will minimize the firm's costs?

A firm will minimize cost by combining inputs in such a way that the marginal product of a dollar's worth of any one input equals the marginal

▪ TABLE 2.2

Determination of Optimal Input Combination

AMOUNT OF INPUT USED		MARGINAL PRODUCT		MARGINAL PRODUCT ÷ PRICE OF INPUT		TOTAL COSTS (dollars)
LABOR (units)	LAND (acres)	LABOR	LAND	LABOR	LAND	
0.5	7.0	50	5	50 ÷ 8,000	5 ÷ 2,000	18,000
1.0	4.1	40	10	40 ÷ 8,000	10 ÷ 2,000	16,200
1.5	3.0	30	30	30 ÷ 8,000	30 ÷ 2,000	18,000
2.5	2.0	20	50	20 ÷ 8,000	50 ÷ 2,000	24,000

product of a dollar's worth of any other input used. Another way to say the same thing is: *The firm will minimize cost by combining inputs in such a way that, for every input used, the marginal product of the input is proportional to its price.* Why does this say the same thing? Because the marginal product of a dollar's worth of an input equals the marginal product of the input divided by its price. If the marginal product of a unit of labor is 40 units of output, and if the price of labor is $8,000 per unit, the marginal product of a dollar's worth of labor is 40 ÷ $8,000 = 0.005 units of output. Thus, if the firm is combining inputs so that the marginal product of a dollar's worth of any one input used equals the marginal product of a dollar's worth of any other input used, it must at the same time be combining inputs so that, for every input used, the marginal product of the input is proportional to its price.

Consider the wheat farm discussed earlier. Suppose that the farm can vary the amount of labor it uses. Table 2.2 shows the marginal product of each input when various combinations of inputs (all combinations being able to produce the specified quantity of output) are used. Sup-

pose that the price of labor is $8,000 per unit and that the annual price of using land is $2,000 per acre. (Assume that the firm takes the prices of inputs as given and that it can buy all it wants of the inputs at these prices.) For each combination of inputs, Table 2.2 shows the marginal product of each input divided by its price. The optimal input combination is 4.1 acres of land and 1 unit of labor, since this is the only combination (capable of producing the required output) where the marginal product of labor divided by the price of labor equals the marginal product of land divided by the price of land. (See Table 2.2)

Is this correct? Does it really result in a least-cost combination of inputs? Look at the cost of the various input combinations in Table 2.2. The first combination (0.5 units of labor and 7 acres of land) costs $18,000, the second combination (1.0 units of labor and 4.1 acres of land) costs $16,200, and so on. An examination of the total cost of each input combination shows that the input combination—1.0 units of labor and 4.1 acres of land—is indeed the least-cost input combination, the one for the profit-maximizing firm to use.

 TEST YOUR UNDERSTANDING

True or false?

_____ **1** If the price of a unit of capital is equal to the price of a unit of labor, a cost-minimizing firm will choose a combination of inputs for which the mar-

ginal product of capital minus the marginal product of labor equals zero.

____ **2** If the price of a unit of capital is double the price of a unit of labor, a cost-minimizing firm will choose a combination of inputs for which the marginal product of capital minus the marginal product of labor equals the marginal product of labor.

____ **3** If labor can be obtained free, a cost-minimizing firm will choose a combination of inputs for which the marginal product of capital minus the marginal product of labor equals the marginal product of capital.

Exercises

1 Suppose that a cost-minimizing firm in a perfectly competitive market uses two inputs: labor and capi-

tal. If the marginal product of capital is twice the marginal product of labor, and if the price of a unit of labor is $4, what must be the price of a unit of capital?

2 In Exercise 3 on page 24, suppose that the price of using a unit of labor per day is $50 and the price of using a unit of capital per day is $100. What is the optimal input combination for the firm if the relationship in Exercise 3 is valid? Does this seem reasonable? Why, or why not?

5 ▪ Short-Run Total Costs

The previous section discussed how the input combination that minimizes costs can be determined. But what does "costs" mean?

Although this question may seem foolishly simple, it is in fact tricky. *Fundamentally, the cost of a certain course of action is the value of the best alternative course of action that could have been adopted instead.* The cost of producing automobiles is the value of the goods and services that could be obtained from the resources used currently in automobile production if these resources were no longer used to produce automobiles. In general, the costs of inputs to a firm are their values in their most valuable alternative uses. This is the so-called **opportunity cost,** or **alternative cost,** doctrine.

SHORT-RUN COST FUNCTIONS

In Section 4, you learned how to determine the least-cost combination of inputs to produce any quantity of output. With this information, it is easy to determine the minimum cost of producing each quantity of output. *Knowing the (minimum) cost of producing each quantity of output, you can define and measure the firm's* **cost functions,** *which*

show how various types of costs are related to the firm's output. A firm's cost functions will vary, depending on whether they are based on the short or long run. In the short run, the firm cannot vary the quantities of plant and equipment it uses. These are the firm's fixed inputs, and they determine the scale of its operations.

TOTAL FIXED COST

Three kinds of costs are important in the short run—total fixed cost, total variable cost, and total cost. **Total fixed cost** *is the total expenditure per period of time by the firm for fixed inputs.* Since the quantity of the fixed inputs is unvarying (by definition), the total fixed cost will be the same whatever the firm's level of output. Among the firm's fixed costs in the short run are property taxes and interest on bonds issued in the past. If the firm has contracts with suppliers and workers that cannot be renegotiated (without dire consequences) in the short run, the expenses involved in meeting these contracts are also fixed costs. Table 2.3 shows that the Johnson Company's fixed costs are $300 per day.

▪ TABLE 2.3

Fixed, Variable, and Total Costs, Johnson Company

NUMBER OF UNITS OF OUTPUT PRODUCED PER DAY	TOTAL FIXED COST	TOTAL VARIABLE COST	TOTAL COST
		(dollars)	
0	300	0	300
1	300	60	360
2	300	110	410
3	300	160	460
4	300	200	500
5	300	260	560
6	300	360	660
7	300	510	810
8	300	710	1,010
9	300	1,060	1,360

TOTAL VARIABLE COST

Total variable cost *is the firm's total expenditure on variable inputs per period of time.* Since higher output rates require greater utilization of variable inputs, they mean a higher total variable cost. Thus, if the Johnson Company increases its daily production, it must increase the amount it spends per day on materials, labor, and other variable inputs. Table 2.3 shows the Johnson Company's total variable costs at various output rates.

TOTAL COST

Total cost *is the sum of total fixed cost and total variable cost.* Thus, to obtain the Johnson Company's total cost at a given output, you need only add its total fixed cost and its total variable cost at the output. The result is shown in Table 2.3.

 TEST YOUR UNDERSTANDING

True or false?

_____ **1** The total cost curve differs by a constant amount (equal to the total fixed cost) from the total variable cost curve.

_____ **2** Total variable cost equals total cost minus total fixed cost.

Exercises

1 Suppose that a firm's short-run total cost function is as follows:

OUTPUT (number of units per year)	TOTAL COST PER YEAR (dollars)
0	20,000
1	20,100
2	20,200
3	20,300
4	20,500
5	20,800

What are the firm's total fixed costs? What are its total variable costs when it produces 4 units per year?

2 A machine shop has the following relationship between cost and output:

OUTPUT (thousands of units of output per year)	TOTAL FIXED COST	TOTAL VARIABLE COST
	(dollars per year)	
0	64,000	0
400	64,000	20,000
440	64,000	23,000
480	64,000	27,000
520	64,000	32,000

a. Included in the fixed cost is $5,600 in interest on the owner's investment in the machine shop. If the owner owns the shop completely (and does not have to pay interest to anyone else), should this item still be included?

b. Suppose that the owner and his wife do all the work, and that the opportunity cost of their labor is the same, regardless of the shop's output. Is their labor cost a fixed or variable cost?

6 ▪ Average and Marginal Costs in the Short Run

The president of the Johnson Company unquestionably cares about average cost as well as total cost; so do economists. *Average cost tells you how much a product costs per unit of output.* There are three average cost functions, one corresponding to each of the three total cost functions.

AVERAGE FIXED COST

First consider **average fixed cost,** *which is simply the total fixed cost divided by the firm's output.* Table 2.4 shows the average fixed cost function for the Johnson Company. Average fixed cost must decline with increases in output, since it equals a constant—total fixed cost—divided by the output rate.

AVERAGE VARIABLE COST

The next type of average cost is **average variable cost,** *which is the total variable cost divided by output.* For the Johnson Company, the average variable cost function is shown in Table 2.4. At first, increases in the output rate result in decreases in average variable cost, but beyond a point, they result in higher average variable cost. This is because the law of diminishing marginal returns is in operation. As more and more of the

variable inputs are utilized, the extra output they produce declines beyond some point, so that the amount spent on variable input per unit of output tends to increase.

AVERAGE TOTAL COST

The third type of average cost is **average total cost,** *which is total cost divided by output.* For the Johnson Company, the average total cost function is shown in Table 2.4. At any level of output, *average total cost equals average fixed cost plus average variable cost.* This is easy to prove:

average total cost

$$= \frac{\text{total cost}}{\text{output}} = \frac{\text{total fixed cost} + \text{total variable cost}}{\text{output}}$$

since total cost = total fixed cost + total variable cost. Moreover,

$$\frac{\text{total fixed cost} + \text{total variable cost}}{\text{output}}$$

$$= \frac{\text{total fixed cost}}{\text{output}} + \frac{\text{total variable cost}}{\text{output}}$$

and the right-hand side of this equation equals average fixed cost plus average variable cost.

▪ TABLE 2.4
Average Fixed Cost, Average Variable Cost, and Average Total Cost, Johnson Company

NUMBER OF UNITS OF OUTPUT PRODUCED PER DAY	AVERAGE FIXED COST	AVERAGE VARIABLE COST	AVERAGE TOTAL COST
		(dollars)	
1	300 (= 300 ÷ 1)	60 (= 60 ÷ 1)	360 (= 360 ÷ 1)
2	150 (= 300 ÷ 2)	55 (= 110 ÷ 2)	205 (= 410 ÷ 2)
3	100 (= 300 ÷ 3)	53 (= 160 ÷ 3)	153 (= 460 ÷ 3)
4	75 (= 300 ÷ 4)	50 (= 200 ÷ 4)	125 (= 500 ÷ 4)
5	60 (= 300 ÷ 5)	52 (= 260 ÷ 5)	112 (= 560 ÷ 5)
6	50 (= 300 ÷ 6)	60 (= 360 ÷ 6)	110 (= 660 ÷ 6)
7	43 (= 300 ÷ 7)	73 (= 510 ÷ 7)	116 (= 810 ÷ 7)
8	38 (= 300 ÷ 8)	89 (= 710 ÷ 8)	126 (= 1,010 ÷ 8)
9	33 (= 300 ÷ 9)	118 (= 1,060 ÷ 9)	151 (= 1,360 ÷ 9)

MARGINAL COST IN THE SHORT RUN

No one can understand the operations of a business firm without understanding the concept of **marginal cost,** *the addition to total cost resulting from the addition of the last unit of output.* To see how marginal cost is calculated, look at Table 2.5, which shows the total cost function of the Johnson Company. When output is between 0 and 1 unit per day, the firm's marginal cost is $60, since this is the *extra cost* of producing the first unit of output per day. In other words, $60 equals marginal cost in this situation because it is the difference between the total cost of producing 1 unit of output per day ($360) and the total cost of producing 0 units of output per day ($300).

In general, marginal cost will vary depending on the firm's output level. Thus Table 2.5 shows that at the Johnson Company marginal cost is $50 when the firm produces between 1 and 2 units of output per day, $100 when the firm produces between 5 and 6 units of output per day, and $350 when the firm produces between 8 and 9 units of output per day. Table 2.5 indicates that marginal cost, after decreasing with increases in output at low output levels, increases with further increases in output. In other words, *beyond some point it becomes more and more costly for the firm to produce yet another unit of output.*

The reason why marginal cost increases be-

yond some output level is to be found in the law of diminishing marginal returns. *If (beyond some point) increases in variable inputs result in less and less extra output, it follows that a larger and larger quantity of variable inputs must be added to produce an extra unit of output. Thus the cost of producing an extra unit of output must increase.*

RELATIONSHIP BETWEEN MARGINAL COST AND AVERAGE COST FUNCTIONS

The relationship between the marginal cost function and the average cost functions must be noted. Figure 2.1 shows the marginal cost curve

TABLE 2.5

Calculation of Marginal Cost, Johnson Company

NUMBER OF UNITS OF OUTPUT PRODUCED PER DAY	TOTAL COST	MARGINAL COST
		(dollars)
0	300	
		60 (= 360 − 300)
1	360	
		50 (= 410 − 360)
2	410	
		50 (= 460 − 410)
3	460	
		40 (= 500 − 460)
4	500	
		60 (= 560 − 500)
5	560	
		100 (= 660 − 560)
6	660	
		150 (= 810 − 660)
7	810	
		200 (= 1,010 − 810)
8	1,010	
		350 (= 1,360 − 1,010)
9	1,360	

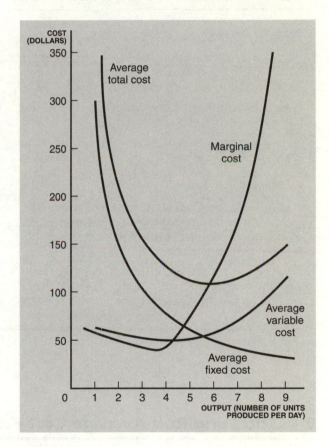

▪ **FIGURE 2.1**

Average Fixed Cost, Average Variable Cost, Average Total Cost, and Marginal Cost, Johnson Company

Note that the marginal cost curve intersects both the average variable cost curve and the average total cost curve at their minimum points.

together with the three average cost curves. *The marginal cost curve intersects both the average variable cost curve and the average total cost curve at their minimum points.* The reason for this is simple. If the extra cost of a unit of output is greater (less) than the average cost of the units of output already produced, the addition of an extra unit of output clearly must raise (lower) the average cost of

production. Thus, if marginal cost is greater (less) than average cost, average cost must be rising (falling). And if this is so, average cost can be a minimum only when it equals marginal cost. (The same reasoning holds for both average total cost and average variable cost, and for the short and long runs.)

 TEST YOUR UNDERSTANDING

True or false?

_____ **1** If average variable cost always equals $10 when output is less than 100 units, marginal cost is less than $10 when output is in this range.

_____ **2** Average fixed cost must increase in the short run with increases in output.

_____ **3** Average cost is at a minimum only when it is lower than marginal cost.

Exercises

1 In Exercise 1 on page 27, what is the firm's marginal cost when between 4 and 5 units are produced per year? Does marginal cost increase beyond some output level?

2 In Exercise 1 on page 27, what is the firm's average cost when it produces 1 unit per year? 2 units per year? 3 units per year?

3 Fill in the blanks below:

TOTAL OUTPUT	TOTAL FIXED COST	TOTAL VARIABLE COST	AVERAGE TOTAL COST	AVERAGE FIXED COST	AVERAGE VARIABLE COST
			(dollars)		
0	500	—			
1	—	20	—	—	—
2	—	—	300	—	—
3	—	—	—	—	133⅓
4	—	1,100	—	—	—

4 In Exercise 3, does marginal cost increase with increases in output? Explain.

---

7 ▪ The Long-Run Average Cost Function

A firm's **long-run average cost function** *shows the minimum average cost of producing each output level when any desired type or scale of plant can be built.* Unlike the cost functions discussed in the previous sections, this cost function pertains to the long run—*to a period long enough so that all*

inputs are variable and none is fixed. As pointed out in Section 2, a useful way to look at the long run is to consider it a *planning horizon.* The firm must continually be planning ahead and trying to decide its strategy in the long run.

What determines the shape of a long-run average cost function in a particular industry? Its shape must depend on the characteristics of the production function—specifically, on whether there are increasing, decreasing, or constant returns to scale. To understand what these terms mean, consider a long-run situation and suppose that the firm increases the amount of all inputs by the same proportion. What will happen to output? *If output increases by a larger proportion than each of the inputs, this is a case of* **increasing returns to scale.** *If output increases by a smaller proportion than each of the inputs, this is the case of* **decreasing returns to scale.** *If output increases by the same proportion as each of the inputs, this is a case of* **constant returns to scale.**

At first glance it may seem that constant returns should prevail: After all, if two factories are built with the same equipment and use the same type and number of workers, it would seem obvious that they can produce twice as much output as one such factory. But things are not that simple. If a firm doubles its scale, it may be able *to use techniques that could not be used at the smaller scale.* Some inputs are not available in small units; for example, you cannot install half a numerically controlled machine tool. Because of indivisibilities of this sort, increasing returns to scale may occur. Thus, although one could double a firm's size by simply building two small factories, this may be inefficient. One large factory may be more efficient than two smaller factories of the same total capacity because it is large enough to use certain techniques and inputs that the smaller factories cannot use.

Another reason for increasing returns to scale stems from certain *geometrical relations.* For example, since the volume of a box that is 3 × 3 × 3 feet is 27 times as great as the volume of a box that is 1 × 1 × 1 foot, the former box can carry 27 times as much as the latter box. But since the area of the six sides of the 3 × 3 × 3-foot box is 54 square feet and the area of the six sides of the 1 × 1 × 1-foot box is 6 square feet, the former box only requires 9 times as much wood as the latter. Greater *specialization* also can result in increasing returns to scale. As more men and machines are used, it is possible to subdivide tasks and allow various inputs to specialize.

Decreasing returns to scale can also occur; the most frequently cited reason is the *difficulty of coordinating a large enterprise.* It can be difficult even in a small firm to obtain the information required to make important decisions; in a large firm, the difficulties tend to be greater. It can be difficult even in a small firm to be certain that management's wishes are being carried out; in a larger firm these difficulties too tend to be greater. Although the advantages of a large organization seem to have captured the public fancy, there are often very great disadvantages as well.

Whether there are increasing, decreasing, or constant returns to scale in a particular situation must be settled case by case. Moreover, the answer is likely to depend on the particular range of output considered. There frequently are increasing returns to scale up to some level of output, then perhaps constant returns to scale up to a higher level of output, beyond which there may be decreasing returns to scale. This pattern is responsible for the U-shaped long-run average cost function in Figure 2.2. At relatively small output levels, there are increasing returns to scale, and long-run average cost decreases as output rises. At relatively high output levels, there are decreasing returns to scale and long-run average cost increases as output rises.

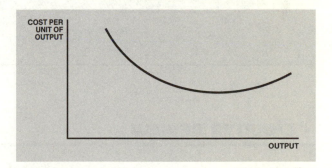

▪ **FIGURE 2.2**

Long-Run Average Cost Function

The long-run average cost function frequently is U-shaped.

TEST YOUR UNDERSTANDING

True or false?

____ **1** One of the principal determinants of the shape of the long-run average cost function is the law of diminishing marginal returns.

____ **2** In the long run a firm's fixed costs in industries like steel and autos may amount to tens of millions of dollars per year.

____ **3** When a firm is experiencing diminishing marginal returns to its variable input, there must be decreasing returns to scale.

Exercises

1 According to a study reported to the U.S. House of Representatives, the long-run average cost function of a firm providing cable television to households is as follows:

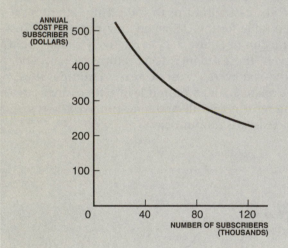

Do there appear to be economies of scale in the cable television business? In other words, does long-run average cost fall with increases in output?

2 Explain why each of the following statements is true, partly true, or false.

a. "Decreasing returns to scale occur when increased scale allows efficiencies of various sorts."

b. "The law of diminishing marginal returns is inconsistent with increasing returns to scale."

c. "John Maynard Keynes said, 'In the long run we are all dead.' He was right. What is important for the determination of the optimal number of firms in an industry is the short-run average cost function."

3 As the electronics industry has grown more mature and new technologies have been developed, the costs of many electronic products have fallen dramatically. Is this evidence that the long-run average cost curve slopes downward to the right? Explain.

▪ CHAPTER REVIEW

KEY TERMS

profit

input

production function

fixed input

variable input

short run

long run

average product of input

marginal product of input

law of diminishing marginal returns

opportunity cost

alternative cost

cost functions

total fixed cost

total variable cost

average variable cost

increasing returns to scale

total cost

average total cost

decreasing returns to scale

average fixed cost

marginal cost

constant returns to scale

COMPLETION QUESTIONS

1 The _____ of an input is the addition to total output due to the addition of the last unit of input.

2 A firm will minimize cost by combining inputs so that, for every input used, the _____ of the input is proportional to the input's _____ .

3 Marginal product must exceed average product when the latter is (decreasing, increasing) _____ , it must equal average product when the latter reaches a (maximum, minimum) _____ , and it must be less than average product when the latter is (decreasing, increasing) _____ .

4 An inefficient combination of inputs is one that includes (less, more) _____ of at least one input, and as much of the other inputs, as some other combination of inputs that can produce the same _____ . Inefficient combinations generally (can, cannot) _____ minimize costs or maximize profits.

5 The firm will minimize cost by combining inputs in such a way that the (average product, marginal product) _____ of a dollar's worth of any one input used equals the (average product, marginal product) _____ of a dollar's worth of any other input used.

6 If the marginal product of the first unit of labor equals 2 units of output, and if the marginal product of the second unit of labor equals 3 units of output, the total output produced with 2 units of labor equals _____ units of output. This answer will remain valid only if the quantities of the other _____ are held constant and if there is no change in _____ .

7 If the marginal product of the eighth unit of labor equals the marginal product of the ninth unit of labor, and if total output with 7 units of labor is 80 and total output with 9 units of labor is 90, the marginal product of the eighth unit of labor equals _____ .

8 The average product of labor equals 3L, where L is the number of units of labor employed per day. The total output produced per day if 4 units of labor are employed per day is _____ . The total output produced per day if 5 units of labor are employed per day is _____ . The marginal product of the fifth unit of labor employed per day is _____ .

ANSWERS TO COMPLETION QUESTIONS

marginal product

marginal product
price

increasing

maximum

decreasing

more

output
cannot

marginal product

marginal product

5
inputs
technology

5

48

75
27

9 If the average fixed cost is triple average variable cost, and if average total cost is $40, average fixed cost equals _____ and average variable cost equals _____. If marginal cost equals $20, average variable cost is (rising, falling) _____, and average total cost is (rising, falling) _____.

$30
$10
rising
falling

10 Total cost at a given output is the sum of _____ and _____.

total fixed cost   total variable cost

11 Average fixed cost is the firm's total fixed cost divided by its _____.

output

12 The addition to total cost resulting from the addition of the last unit of output is called _____.

marginal cost

13 To see whether a firm earns a positive profit, the firm's total revenue must be compared with its _____.

total costs

14 The social costs of producing a given commodity do not always equal the _____ costs. That is, the costs to _____ do not always equal the costs to the individual producer.

private
society

15 Total fixed cost is the total expenditure per period of time by the firm for _____ inputs. Since the quantity of the _____ inputs is unvarying (by definition), the total fixed cost will be (the same, different) _____ for various levels of the firm's output. Among the firm's fixed costs in the short run are _____ taxes and _____ on bonds issued in the past.

fixed
fixed
the same
property   interest

16 Total variable cost is the total expenditure per period of time on _____ inputs. Due to the law of diminishing marginal returns, total variable cost (decreases, increases) _____ first at a (decreasing, increasing) _____ rate, then at an (increasing, decreasing) _____ rate.

variable
increases
decreasing
increasing

17 Average total cost is total cost divided by _____. It equals average _____ cost plus average _____ cost; and beyond a point, it increases as output _____ because of the law of diminishing marginal returns.

output   fixed
variable
increases

18 Marginal cost is the addition to total cost resulting from the _____ of the last unit of output. Beyond a point, it _____ as output increases because of the law of diminishing marginal returns.

addition
increases

19 If the marginal cost of producing the first unit of output is $20, if the marginal cost of producing the second unit of output is $25, and if the marginal cost of producing the third unit of output is $30, the total variable cost of producing 3 units of output is _____. The average variable cost of producing two units of output is _____. Average variable

$75
$22.50

cost (rises, falls) _____ when output increases from 1 to 3 units.

20 If the average fixed cost of producing 10 units of output is $10, the average fixed cost of producing 20 units is _____. If the marginal cost of each of the first 20 units of output is $5, the average variable cost of producing 20 units is _____. And the average total cost of producing 20 units is _____.

rises

$5

$5
$10

NUMERICAL PROBLEMS

1 Suppose that the production function for a 1-acre wheat farm is as follows:

NUMBER OF PERSON-YEARS OF LABOR	BUSHELS OF WHEAT PRODUCED PER YEAR
1	50
2	90
3	120
4	145
5	165

a What is the average product of labor when 1 person-year of labor is used?

b What is the marginal product of labor when between 2 and 3 person-years of labor are used?

c Does the law of diminishing marginal returns seem to hold? Why or why not?

2 Suppose that the production function for a car wash is as follow:

HOURS OF LABOR PER DAY	CARS WASHED PER DAY	AVERAGE PRODUCT OF LABOR	MARGINAL PRODUCT OF LABOR
0	0	___	
1	2	___	___
2	5	___	___
3	7	___	___
4	8	___	___

a Fill in the blanks in the table above.

b Why isn't the average product of labor computed when there are 0 hours of labor?

3 Suppose that the marginal product of labor is as shown below:

QUANTITY OF LABOR PER DAY	MARGINAL PRODUCT OF LABOR	TOTAL OUTPUT PER DAY
0		0
1	3	—
2	5	—
3	8	—
4		23
5	2	—

a Fill in the blanks.

b Does this case conform to the law of diminishing marginal returns? Why or why not?

4 Suppose that the average product of capital is as shown below:

QUANTITY OF CAPITAL USED PER DAY	AVERAGE PRODUCT OF CAPITAL	MARGINAL PRODUCT OF CAPITAL
1	3	___
2	8	___
3	8	___
4	6	___
5	4	___

a Fill in the blanks.

b What is the maximum amount of capital that this firm will use per day? Why?

5 The average product of labor equals 6, regardless of how much labor is used.

a What is the marginal product of the first unit of labor?

b What is the marginal product of the fiftieth unit of labor?

c By how much will output increase if labor is increased by 200 units?

d By how much will output fall if labor is reduced by 100 units?

e Does this case confirm to the law of diminishing marginal returns? Why or why not?

f Does this case seem realistic? Why or why not?

6 A firm uses two inputs, labor and capital. The price of capital is $5 per unit, the price of labor is $7 per unit, and the marginal product of capital is 15.

a Is the firm minimizing cost if the marginal product of labor is 20? Why or why not?

b If the firm is not minimizing cost, should it use more or less labor relative to capital? Why?

c If the marginal product of labor is 23, is the firm minimizing cost? Why or why not?

d If the firm is not minimizing cost, should it use more or less labor relative to capital? Why?

e If the marginal product of labor is 21, is the firm minimizing cost? Why or why not?

7 A firm has two plants, A and B. Both produce the same product. The price of capital is the same at both plants, and the price of labor is the same at both plants. The marginal product of labor is 6 at plant A and 15 at plant B.

a Can you tell whether each plant is minimizing cost? Why or why not?

b If the marginal product of capital is 20 at plant A and 40 at plant B, is each plant minimizing cost? Why or why not?

c If the marginal product of capital is 40 at plant A, what must the marginal product of capital be at plant B if each plant is minimizing cost?

d If the marginal product of capital is 40 at plant A, and each plant is minimizing cost, can you tell what the price of capital and the price of labor are?

e If the marginal product of capital is 40 at plant A, what is the ratio of the price of labor to the price of capital?

8 Suppose that the Chicago plant of the Bolton Press Company has the following cost structure: (1) Its fixed costs are $1,000 per month. (2) Its variable costs are shown in the next column.

a Fill in the blanks below:

OUTPUT (presses per month)	TOTAL FIXED COST	TOTAL VARIABLE COST	TOTAL COST
		(dollars)	
0	_____	0	_____
1	_____	500	_____
2	_____	1,000	_____
3	_____	2,000	_____
4	_____	3,500	_____
5	_____	5,000	_____

b Fill in the blanks below. Each column shows an average cost function of the Chicago plant of the Bolton Press Company.

OUTPUT (presses per month)	AVERAGE FIXED COST	AVERAGE VARIABLE COST	AVERAGE TOTAL COST
		(dollars)	
1	_____	_____	_____
2	_____	_____	_____
3	_____	_____	_____
4	_____	_____	_____
5	_____	_____	_____

c Fill in the blanks below:

OUTPUT (presses per month)	MARGINAL COST (dollars)
0 to 1	_____
1 to 2	_____
2 to 3	_____
3 to 4	_____
4 to 5	_____

9 Suppose that the Wilson Press Company's short-run total cost function is as follows:

OUTPUT (number of units per year)	TOTAL COST (dollars per year)
0	20,000
1	20,100
2	20,200
3	20,300
4	20,500
5	20,800

a What are the firm's total fixed costs?

b What are its total variable costs when it produces 4 units per year?

c What is the firm's marginal cost when between 4 and 5 units are produced per year?

d Does the marginal cost increase beyond some output level? Why?

10 Farm *A* is a profit maximizing, perfectly competitive producer of wheat. It produces wheat using 1 acre of land (price = $1000) and varying inputs of labor (price = $500 per person-month). The production function is as follows:

NUMBER OF PERSON-MONTHS (per month)	OUTPUT PER MONTH (in truckloads)
0	0
1	1
3	2
7	3
12	4
18	5
25	6

Show that the production of Farm *A* is subject to Increasing marginal cost as output increases.

11 Suppose that firm *B* makes rugs, and that its fixed costs are $10,000 a month, while its average variable cost is $100 per rug. Suppose that it gets a price of $500 per rug.

a Plot the firm's total cost and total revenue against its output below:

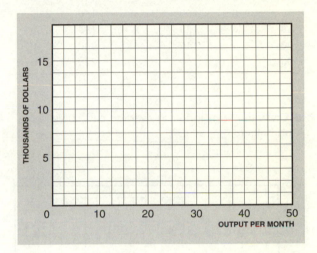

b How much must the firm produce to break even?

12 Suppose that you are given the production function, the price of the variable input, and the total fixed costs of the ABC Company. These data are shown below. (Price and costs are in dollars.) Fill in the blanks.

NUMBER OF UNITS OF VARIABLE INPUT	NUMBER OF UNITS OF OUTPUT PRODUCED	AVERAGE PRODUCT	MARGINAL PRODUCT	PRICE OF UNIT OF VARIABLE INPUT	TOTAL VARIABLE COST	AVERAGE VARIABLE COST	TOTAL FIXED COST	TOTAL COST	AVERAGE TOTAL COST	MARGINAL COST
0	0	—		2	—	—	100	—	—	
1	4	—	—	2	—	—	100	—	—	—
2	9	—	—	2	—	—	100	—	—	—
3	15	—	—	2	—	—	100	—	—	—
4	22	—	—	2	—	—	100	—	—	—
5	30	—	—	2	—	—	100	—	—	—
6	37	—	—	2	—	—	100	—	—	—
7	43	—	—	2	—	—	100	—	—	—
8	48	—	—	2	—	—	100	—	—	—
9	52	—	—	2	—	—	100	—	—	—

13 A firm can build plants of three types: D, E, and F. The short-run average cost curve with each type is given below:

TYPE D		TYPE E		TYPE F	
OUTPUT	AVERAGE COST (dollars)	OUTPUT	AVERAGE COST (dollars)	OUTPUT	AVERAGE COST (dollars)
20	10	80	6	140	3.00
40	8	100	4	160	2.00
60	6	120	2	180	0.50
80	4	140	1	200	0.40
100	6	160	1	220	0.75

a Draw the firm's long-run average cost curve in the graph below:

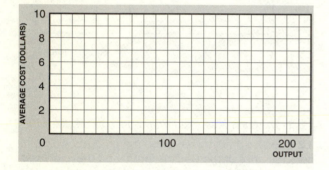

b What is the minimum price at which the firm will stay in the industry?

14 Firm S hires a consultant to estimate its long-run total cost function. The consultant, after a long study, concludes that for firm S long-run total cost equals $2 million + $4 × Q, where Q is annual output.

a What does this equation imply about the long-run total cost of producing nothing? Is this reasonable? Why or why not?

b What is the minimum value of long-run average cost?

c What size of plant results in the minimum value of long-run average cost? Is this reasonable? Why or why not?

15 Firm P's total cost curve is shown in the next column:

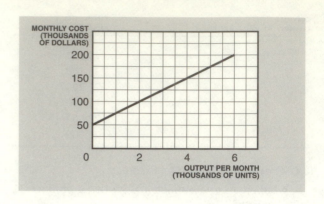

a Draw the firm's marginal cost function in the graph below.

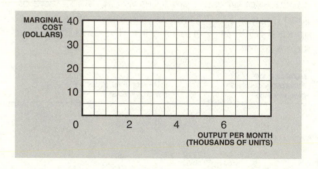

b Suppose that it is impossible for firm P to produce more than 6,000 units of output per month. What is marginal cost at outputs above 6,000?

16 On the basis of the graph in the previous problem, fill in the blanks in the table below for firm P.

OUTPUT (thousands)	AVERAGE FIXED COST	AVERAGE VARIABLE COST	AVERAGE TOTAL COST
		(dollars)	
1	———	———	———
2	———	———	———
3	———	———	———
4	———	———	———
5	———	———	———
6	———	———	———

ANSWERS TO
TEST YOUR UNDERSTANDING

SECTION 1

TRUE OR FALSE: 1. True

EXERCISES

1. All but h.

2. Yes.

SECTION 2

TRUE OR FALSE: 1. True   2. True   3. True   4. True
5. False

EXERCISES

1. and 2:

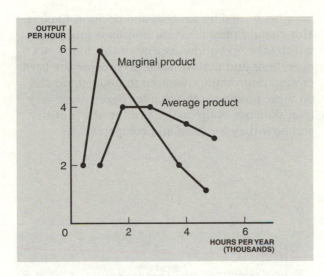

3. Probably a variable input.   A fixed input.

SECTION 3

TRUE OR FALSE: 1. False   2. True   3. False

EXERCISES

1. Yes.

2. Yes.

3. No. For one thing, it denies the existence of diminishing marginal returns in the short run.

SECTION 4

TRUE OR FALSE: 1. True   2. True   3. True

EXERCISES

1. The price of a unit of capital is $8.

2. The marginal product of labor is 3, and the marginal product of capital is 4. Thus, there is no input combination for which the ratio of the marginal products equals the ratio of the prices. The optimal input combination is that for which only labor is used; this does not seem reasonable.

SECTION 5

TRUE OR FALSE: 1. True   2. True

EXERCISES

1. $20,000. $500.

2. a. Yes, because if he sold this shop, he could lend out the proceeds and get $5,600 in interest. Thus, this is the opportunity cost of the owner's investment in the shop.

b. It is a fixed cost.

SECTION 6

TRUE OR FALSE: 1. False   2. False   3. False

EXERCISES

1. $300.   Yes.

2. $20,100. $10,100. $6,767.

3. The table is:

TOTAL OUTPUT	TOTAL FIXED COST	TOTAL VARIABLE COST	AVERAGE TOTAL COST	AVERAGE FIXED COST	AVERAGE VARIABLE COST
			(dollars)		
0	500	0			
1	500	20	520	500	20
2	500	100	300	250	50
3	500	400	300	$166\frac{2}{3}$	$133\frac{1}{3}$
4	500	1100	400	125	275

4. The marginal cost increases with output, since each extra unit of output increases total variable cost by more than the previous one does.

SECTION 7

TRUE OR FALSE: 1. False   2. False   3. False

EXERCISES

1. Yes.   Yes.

2. a. False; the statement describes increasing returns to scale.

b. False, the statement confuses the short run (decreasing marginal returns) with the long run (returns to scale).

c. False; what is important in determining the optimal number of firms in an industry is the shape of the long-run average cost function.

3. Not necessarily. The long-run average cost curve may have shifted downward.

CHAPTER 3

Economics by the Glass, Can, or Keg

1 ■ Introduction

Anyone who goes to a sports event, or watches one on television is likely to see or hear a beer advertisement. Anyone who goes to a college party is likely to be offered a beer, the origins of which go far back into history. In ancient Egypt, beer seems to have been the national beverage, which played a significant role in religious worship. During his reign, Ramses III is said to have distributed more than a half a million gallons of beer to the Egyptian populace. The Greeks learned brewing from the Egyptians, and the Romans learned it from the Greeks.

Returning from ancient times to the present, a depressing fact of life for the U.S. beer industry is that its sales have been relatively flat.[1] (In Germany and Japan too, there has been relatively little sales growth, as shown in Figure 3.1.) One reason for the lack of growth is that consumers, concerned about their health and appearance, have become more calorie conscious. Many people have turned from beer to other beverages that have fewer calories and less alcohol. Also, the increase in the national drinking age to 21 (which President Ronald Reagan signed into law in 1984) and the increased number and more rigorous enforcement of drunk-driving laws have probably reduced beer consumption in the United States.

The beer industry illustrates the many ways in which the principles of economics can be and

have been used by analysts and decision makers. This chapter presents eight multipart problems, which take up various aspects of this industry's operations and performance. To provide the background information required to understand and do these problems, the chapter begins with very brief sketches of the major firms in the industry, and how they function and compete.

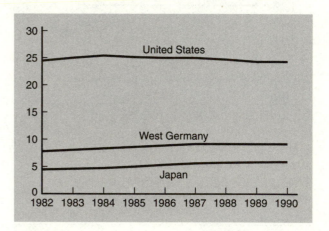

■ **FIGURE 3.1**

Annual Consumption of Beer, United States, Japan and West Germany, 1982–90

SOURCE: McKinsey Global Institute, *Manufacturing Productivity* (Washington, D.C.: McKinsey and Company, 1993).

---

[1] McKinsey Global Institute, *Manufacturing Productivity* (Washington, D.C.: McKinsey and Company, 1993).

2 ▪ Anheuser-Busch[2]

Anheuser-Busch, which sells almost half the beer in the United States, has deep midwestern roots. In 1860, Eberhard Anheuser, a soap manufacturer, assumed control of the Haymer and Urban Brewery in St. Louis, Missouri. Several years later, he asked his son-in-law, Adolphus Busch, to be a sales representative for the brewery. Busch eventually became president of the firm and its name was changed in 1879 to Anheuser-Busch Brewing Company. He was the first U.S. brewer to pasteurize beer, and in 1894 he and Carl Conrad developed a new beer, Budweiser, that was very successful. By 1901, sales of Anheuser-Busch exceeded a million barrels; since 1957, it has been the leading firm in the U.S. beer industry.

The president and chief executive officer of Anheuser-Busch has been August A. Busch, III, the fifth generation of the Busch brewing family. Born in 1937, he attended the University of Arizona and the Siebel Institute of Technology, a school in Chicago for brewers, and began his career by hauling beechwood chips out of the firm's aging tanks. When he took over as CEO in 1975, the firm had about 23 percent of the U.S. market; in 1990, it had about 45 percent. According to observers, he "transformed it from a large, loosely run company into a tightly run organization with an emphasis on the bottom line. Busch is known for his tough-mindedness and intensity, his highly competitive nature, and his attention to detail."[3]

Budweiser is not the only beer produced by Anheuser-Busch. In addition, it produces Bud Light, Michelob, Michelob Light, Michelob Classic Dark, Busch, Natural Light, LA, and others. In recent decades, the major brewers have introduced a variety of new brands, one purpose being to attract new customers. For example, Bud Light is targeted at young to middle-aged males. Natural Light is designed to go with good food, and LA is a low-alcohol beer aimed at health-conscious consumers. But Budweiser remains the company's flagship; it is still its biggest seller (with 53 percent of the firm's shipments in 1992).[4] Indeed, according to its advertising, it is the "King of Beers."

Anheuser-Busch is the most profitable firm in the brewing industry. As shown in Table 3.1, its after-tax annual earnings were about $900 million in the early 1990s. Since the equity of its shareholders was about $4 billion, the return on the owners' investment was over 20 percent per year. Anheuser-Busch has diversified into other businesses, such as food products and real estate (and the St. Louis Cardinals baseball club), but its primary business continues to be beer.

▪ **TABLE 3.1**

Income Statement, Anheuser-Busch, 1990–1992 (billions of dollars)

	1992	1991	1990
Net sales	11.4	11.0	10.7
Cost of goods sold	7.3	7.1	7.1
Selling and administrative expense	2.3	2.1	2.1
Interest and other costs	0.3	0.3	0.2
Income taxes	0.6	0.6	0.5
Net income	0.9	0.9	0.8

SOURCE: Disclosure Information Service, Compact d SEC, January 1994.

---

[2] This section has benefited from T. Wheelen and J. Gallagher, "Anheuser-Busch Companies, Inc. . . . August A. Busch, III," in T. Wheelen and J. D. Hunger (eds.), *Cases in Strategic Management* (3d ed.; Reading, Mass.: Addison-Wesley, 1990).

[3] Ibid., p. 222.

[4] *1993 Beer Industry Update* (West Nyack, N.Y.: Beer Marketer's Insights, 1993).

3 ▪ Miller, Coors, and Stroh

Anheuser-Busch's principal rival is Miller Brewing Company, founded in Milwaukee by Frederick Miller, a former German brewmaster, in 1855. In 1903, the firm held a contest to name its premium beer: the outcome was the name Miller High Life, and the slogan became the "champagne of bottled beer." The name (but not the slogan) still exists. In 1970, Philip Morris purchased Miller for about $200 million. The top officials of Philip Morris were convinced that the beer and cigarette industries were basically similar. Both are inexpensive consumer products made and packaged on high-speed equipment, and both are advertised in much the same way.

According to William Howell, president of Miller, "The change in the brewing industry began in October, 1971, when Philip Morris changed the management of Miller Brewing Company. But it took about two years for the change to show up as a real change in direction of the company and the industry. When the change was finally felt, beginning in 1973, it was explosive. Miller quickly shot up from seventh in the industry in 1972 to second place in 1977."[5] One reason was the phenomenal success of Miller's Lite Beer, one of the first low-calorie beers. According to Howell, "We have built our success by doing our homework, finding out what beer consumers want and then delivering it. . . . We have been innovators in product, merchandising and advertising. Our most visible competitive act has been to advertise on television. Those commercials have been called some of the highest quality in American advertising history."[6]

The Adolph Coors Company, the third largest brewer in the United States, is well behind Anheuser-Busch and Miller. Based in Colorado, it has emphasized that it uses "pure Rocky Mountain Spring Water." Confined to the western states up to 1970, it now has moved into the rest of the country. In 1979, after buying land in Virginia for a brewery, William Coors, the firm's chairman, indicated to a meeting of beer wholesalers that "you could make Coors from swamp water and it would be exactly the same."[7] In 1970, Coors only had about 6 percent of the market; in 1990, it had about 10 percent.

One reason for its rapid growth was the introduction in 1978 of Coors Light, which has been very successful. In 1992, Coors Light accounted for almost two-thirds of the firm's shipments, up from about half in 1987. In the early 1990s, Lee Kiely became the first president who was not a member of the Coors family. He faced the "significant challenge of generating earnings momentum as the number-three player with just a 10 percent share in a fiercely competitive market that isn't growing."[8]

The Stroh Brewing Company is in fourth place. In 1982, it purchased the Joseph Schlitz Brewing Company, which accounted for over 10 percent of the market in 1975, but which has slumped considerably. Stressing that its fire-brewed beer was of higher quality than steam-brewed beer, Stroh wanted to reach beyond its Midwest market. Unfortunately, Schlitz could not be resuscitated, and Stroh's market share fell in the late 1980s. In the early 1990s, Stroh's most successful branch was Old Milwaukee, which (together with Old Milwaukee Light) accounted for about half of its shipments, which declined in the late 1980s and early 1990s. Over three-quarters of Stroh's business is from its relatively low-priced brands. According to its president, Bill Henry, it was profitable in 1992, but "falling short of targets."[9]

---

[5] L. Byars and T. Neil, "Miller Brewing Company," in H. Bartlett (ed.), *Cases in Strategic Management of Business* (Chicago: Dryden Press, 1988), p. 255.

[6] Ibid., p. 260.

[7] D. Greer, "Beer: Causes of Structural Change," in L. Deutsch (ed.), *Industry Studies* (Englewood Cliffs, N.J.: Prentice-Hall, 1993), p. 97.

[8] *1993 Beer Industry Update*, pp. 175–76.

[9] Ibid., p. 181.

4 ▪ How Beer Is Produced

Beer is made primarily from four ingredients: (1) malt, which is barley that has been permitted to germinate and is dried, (2) yeast, (3) hops, which provide flavor, and (4) water. The production process lets the ingredients ferment until the desired alcohol content is attained, after which the resulting fluid is decanted, filtered (and sometimes diluted), pasteurized, and packaged in cans, bottles, or kegs. The machinery employed in brewing is highly specialized; this accounts for the fact that breweries ordinarily produce solely beer.

Beers vary in alcohol content. For example, Budweiser and Coors have a 4.6 to 5.0 percent alcohol by volume, whereas low-alcohol beers like LA have appreciably less. Also, beers vary in calorie content. Light beers have about 110 calories per 12 ounces, whereas regular beers have about 145 calories per 12 ounces. But holding such factors constant, the differences among mass-produced U.S. beers in the quality of the ingredients and of the brewing process tend to be rather small. (Microbrewers, with annual brewing productions under 15,000 barrels, are another story. They aim for higher quality levels than mass-produced beers.)

Although most beer drinkers are not able to reliably detect the difference between mass-produced U.S. beer brands, changes in a firm's production process can be risky. For example, in the early 1970s, Schlitz changed its mix of ingredients so as to reduce its raw materials' costs and shorten the brewing process from 20 to 15 days. Since these changes reduced the malt content, the taste of Schlitz changed. In 1974, David Kendall, head of the Flavor Sciences unit at Arthur D. Little, concluded, "Today's Schlitz isn't the same product as yesterday's."[10]

Further, the Schlitz brand underwent a reformulation in 1976, after which the new beer was shipped to customers at various locations. Although it tasted as expected, it turned cloudy when refrigerated, and customers reported that it had an unappealing appearance when poured into a glass. Apparently, this problem was not detected at Schlitz's Milwaukee brewery because temperatures there tended to be lower than in the South, where the difficulties surfaced. Despite the fact that Schlitz moved rapidly to replace the cloudy beer, this helped to trigger a substantial decline in the firm's sales.

5 ▪ Concentration in the Brewing Industry

One of the most striking characteristics of the beer industry is the increase in concentration in the past 40 years. As shown in Table 3.2 (next page), the top four brewers accounted for only about 17 percent of national output in 1947, in contrast to about 86 percent in 1990. This represents a transformation of the industry. In the 1940s there were hundreds of independent breweries scattered around the United States, each catering to a relatively narrow regional market. By the 1990s, there were only a few giants that dominated the industry from coast to coast, and Anheuser-Busch and Miller were clearly the leaders.

This does not mean that the beer industry used to be composed only of very small producers. In a particular regional market, there were generally only a small number of beers that were dominant. But the identity of these dominant firms varied from region to region. What has changed is that a few national beers are now dominant in many parts of the country. Wherever you go, Anheuser-

[10] J. D. Hunger, M. Schipper, D. Bellegante, D. Porter, and R. Wood, "Joseph Schlitz Brewing Company," in T. Wheelen and J. D. Hunger (eds.), *Cases in Strategic Management* (3d ed.; Reading, Mass.: Addison-Wesley), p. 333.

■ **TABLE 3.2**

Percent of National Output of Beer Produced by Largest Two, Four, and Eight Producers, United States, 1947–1990

YEAR	TWO LARGEST	FOUR LARGEST	EIGHT LARGEST
1947	8.8	17.1	26.0
1950	11.9	22.0	33.6
1955	13.3	22.1	36.3
1960	16.0	27.0	42.9
1965	20.1	34.4	52.1
1970	29.9	44.2	61.2
1975	38.8	57.7	76.7
1980	49.5	66.4	88.7
1985	58.9	80.8	96.7
1990	67.3	86.0	98.4

SOURCE: D. Greer, "Beer: Causes of Structural Change," in L. Deutsch (ed.), *Industry Studies* (Englewood Cliffs, N.J.: Prentice-Hall, 1993), p. 89.

Busch and Miller are likely to be among the leaders.

At the same time, concentration has increased considerably in many regional markets. For example, in California, the top two beer firms accounted for almost 70 percent of the market in 1989, up from about 30 percent in 1960. And in Texas, the top two beer firms accounted for about two-thirds of the market in 1989, up from about 40 percent in 1960. Clearly, the beer industry has become dominated by only a few firms. This increase in concentration was not due to mergers. Although there were many mergers of beer firms (for example, Stroh and Schlitz), the firms that merged have tended to lose market share. Instead, it has been due to the expansion of Anheuser-Busch, Miller, and Coors.

The fact that there were so many mergers does not mean that the federal government did not apply the antitrust laws. Consider, for example, Pabst Brewing Company, which set out to purchase Blatz Brewing Company in the 1960s. The Clayton Act, as amended by the Celler-Kefauver Anti-Merger Act, says that mergers that substantially "lessen competition or tend to create a monopoly" are illegal. Because the two firms together accounted for about 24 percent of the market in Wisconsin, the Justice Department challenged the merger. The district court, agreeing with Pabst and Blatz that Wisconsin should not be regarded as a distinct market, dismissed the government's complaint, but the district court's decision was reversed by the Superior Court. The merger was stopped.

6 ■ Pricing

Anheuser-Busch is generally regarded as the price leader for the industry. It usually announces its price increases in January; once Budweiser's price is set, other brewers generally establish a similar price for their premium brands. Super-premium brands like Michelob are priced above Budweiser; popular brands like Old Milwaukee, Busch, and Hamms are priced below Budweiser. How does Anheuser-Busch set its prices? In general, it seems to set them at the highest level it can, without falling short of its growth targets. Thus, if it wants to achieve a 5 percent growth rate of sales, and if this can be achieved only if its prices rise by 4 percent or less, it generally will establish a 4 percent price increase.

However, from time to time, Anheuser-Busch cuts prices to punish rivals that do not follow its lead or to meet competition. For example, in 1989, it announced price reductions because Miller and Coors "have been following a policy of continuous and deep discounting for at least the past 18 months. . . . We cannot permit a further slowing in our volume trend."[11] But such price reductions tend to be confined to particular re-

[11] Greer, "Beer: Causes of Structural Change," p. 102.

gions. The idea, of course, is to target them in areas where they hurt Anheuser-Busch's rivals much more than they do Anheuser-Busch itself. Thus, if Anheuser-Busch has a relatively low market share in a particular region, a price reduction there is likely to do less damage to Anheuser-Busch than to its rivals.

Price reductions tend to be more common for "popular-priced" beers like Meister Brau, Milwaukee's Best, Busch, and Natural Light than for premium or super-premium beers. For example, in the early 1980s, Miller, Stroh, Pabst, and Heileman (the fifth ranked firm in 1992) engaged in heavy price competition, in part, because Miller was trying to introduce Meister Brau and Milwaukee's Best. Some smaller firms claimed that Miller was pricing below its costs. According to some observers, Miller introduced Milwaukee's Best to attack Stroh's Old Milwaukee brand. To reduce the price of its Miller High Life would have risked High Life's image as a premium beer, so Miller introduced this new brand and priced it at a low level.

7 ▪ Advertising

Anyone who watches national television knows that beer companies spend a lot on advertising. But this was not always true. In the 1940s, beer companies devoted only about 3 percent of their sales revenue to advertising. But with the increase of package sales relative to tap sales and with the growth of national rather than regional beer firms, advertising increased considerably. And during the 1970s and 1980s there was an explosion of beer advertising; between 1970 and 1988, it more than doubled (in constant dollars).

Miller played a central role in causing this explosion. When Philip Morris took over Miller in 1970, it adopted the same sorts of marketing techniques that had worked well in the cigarette industry. Media spending more than tripled between 1970 and 1978. Much of the increase went to promote Miller Lite (introduced in 1975), which was hailed as "less filling and tastes great." The TV advertising featured well-known athletes who staged arguments over which of these characteristics was more important. Also, Miller spent large sums to change the image of Miller High Life from the "champagne" of beers to a beer that was right for the working stiff. These huge advertising outlays seemed to pay off handsomely: Miller's market share rose from 4 percent in 1970 to 19 percent in 1978.

Faced with this advertising blitz, Anheuser-Busch responded in kind. In 1985 it spent over $500 million on advertising, the bulk of which went for network television, sports television, and sports radio. It sponsored the 1984 Olympics and stressed patriotic themes in its advertising. For example, its ads proclaimed: "You make America work" and "This Bud's for you." In 1985, it spent $199 million on television ads, compared to Miller's $140 million. Nettled by Miller's boast that it soon would outsell Anheuser-Busch, August Busch told a reporter: "Tell Miller to come right along, but tell them to bring lots of money."[12] Between 1985 and 1990, Anheuser-Busch's market share increased from 38 to 45 percent, and there was no indication that Miller would overtake Anheuser-Busch any time soon.

Anheuser-Busch and Miller sometimes obtain "exclusives" when sponsoring live sports events on television. An "exclusive" allows a firm to ban its rivals from advertising on the same program. For example, if Anheuser-Busch has an exclusive on the Olympics, it can advertise any of its brands of beer on the television program showing the Olympics, but no other brewer is allowed to advertise on this program. Since sports fans are an important part of the market for beer, these exclusives are important competitive weapons. Smaller brewers find it difficult to obtain them.

In 1994, a study by the National Institute of

---

[12] Ibid., p. 106.

Alcohol Abuse and Alcoholism found that one result of intensive TV beer advertising during sports programs is that many children are exposed to these ads. Apparently, fifth graders can recite the slogans and brand names of various beers and say they want to drink plenty of beer when they grow up, since they link drinking with "romance, sociability, and relaxation."[13] The Beer Institute denies that there is any proof that advertising contributes to underage drinking, which has fallen since the 1970s, but the issue of advertising's impact on children remains controversial.

[13] *Philadelphia Inquirer*, February 11, 1994.

8 ▪ Applying Economics: The Market for Beer

The following three problems deal with the market for beer in the United States.

PROBLEM 3.1 According to the Simmons Market Research Bureau, the percent of all adults drinking beer declined from 1980 to 1992. Obviously, this was not good news in the beer industry. Also, males were more likely to drink beer than women, and young adults were more likely to be beer drinkers than older people. These and other data that Simmons compiled from interviews with 15,000 adults in 1980 and 19,000 adults in 1985 and 1992 are shown in Table 3.3.

a. Firms like Anheuser-Busch and Miller keep close tabs on the demographic characteristics of the population. Table 3.4 (next page) shows estimates by the U.S. Department of Commerce of the changes in the age distribution of the U.S. population between 1990 and 2000. Will these changes affect the market demand curve for beer? If so, will they shift it to the left or right, and why?

b. A Wall Street analyst issues a newsletter in which she predicts that the change in the age distribution of the population between 1990 and 2000 will reduce the percentage of adults drinking beer from about 40 percent to about 25 percent. On the basis of Tables 3.3 and 3.4, does this seem to be correct? Why or why not?

c. A marketing consultant says that the drop between 1985 and 1992 in the percent of all adults drinking beer was due entirely to the

▪ TABLE 3.3

Percentage of U.S. Adults Drinking Beer, by Sex, Age, and Race, 1980, 1985, and 1992

	1980	**1985**	**1992**
All adults	49	48	42
Males	62	60	53
Females	37	38	31
Age:			
18–24	58	57	48
25–34	59	57	51
35–44	53	51	47
45–54	47	47	39
55–64	40	41	34
65 or older	28	31	24
White	49	48	43
Black	47	49	34
Other	52	49	37

SOURCE: *1993 Beer Industry Update* (West Nyack, N.Y.,: Beer Marketer's Insights, 1993).

decrease in the proportion of adults under 35 years of age. On the basis of Table 3.3, does this appear to be true? Why or why not?

d. In 1992, because of increases in the minimum drinking age, beer consumption by people under 21 years of age was illegal in all states, whereas in 1985 this was not true in many states.[14] Did this affect the demand curve for

[14] *1993 Beer Industry Update*.

▪ **TABLE 3.4**

Age Distribution of U.S. Population, 1990 and 2000 (percent)

AGE GROUP	1990	2000
Under 5 years	7.7	6.6
5–14 years	14.2	14.3
15–19 years	6.8	7.1
20–24 years	7.4	6.4
25–29 years	8.6	6.5
30–34 years	8.8	7.1
35–39 years	8.0	8.1
40–44 years	7.2	8.2
45–49 years	5.6	7.4
50–54 years	4.6	6.5
55–64 years	8.4	8.9
65 years and over	12.7	13.0
Total	100.0	100.0

SOURCE: T. Wheelen and J. Gallagher, "Anheuser-Busch Companies, Inc.," in T. Wheelen and J. D. Hunger (eds.), *Cases in Strategic Management* (3d ed.; Reading, Mass.: Addison-Wesley, 1990), p. 237.

▪ **TABLE 3.5**

Percentage of U.S. Adults Drinking Various Types of Beer, by Sex, Age, and Race, 1983

	LIGHT	IMPORTED	MALT LIQUOR	ALE	DRAFT
All adults	24	16	8	9	26
Males	29	22	11	12	36
Females	21	10	6	6	18
AGE:					
18–24	29	27	15	14	36
25–34	31	21	11	11	36
35–44	28	16	7	8	27
45–54	24	14	6	7	23
55–64	17	8	4	6	17
65 or older	13	5	4	4	10
White	25	16	6	8	27
Black	19	14	25	10	16
Other	28	26	13	8	28

SOURCE: B. Callinicos and R. Levin, "The Golden Gate Brewing Company," in T. Wheelen and J. D. Hunger (eds.), *Cases in Strategic Management* (3d ed.; Reading, Mass.: Addison-Wesley, 1990), p. 183.

beer? If so, did it shift it to the left or right, and why? Does it help to explain some of the changes indicated in Table 3.3? If so, which changes?

e. According to a report published by the U.S. Department of Health and Human Services, about 90 percent of high school seniors in 1990 had consumed alcohol within the two weeks before they were interviewed. In general, high school students tend to drink beer, rather than wine or liquor. According to researchers at the National Bureau of Economic Research, increases in the tax on beer reduce consumption among high school students.[15] Do such tax increases affect the demand curve for

beer? If so, do they shift it to the left or the right, and why?

PROBLEM 3.2 Beer is by no means homogeneous; as you have seen, there is a wide variety of types of beer. Table 3.5 shows the percentage of U.S. adults in 1983 that drank each of five types of beer—light, imported, malt liquor, ale, and draft. Also, these data are broken down by sex, age, and race. The relative importance of these various types of beer can change considerably over time. For example, Budweiser fell from 65 percent of Anheuser-Busch's shipments in 1987 to 53 percent in 1992, whereas Bud Light increased from 11 percent to 16 percent during this period.[16]

a. Does the demand curve for light beer differ from the demand curve for imported beer?

[15] T. Yamada, M. Kendix, and T. Yamada, *The Impact of Alcohol Consumption and Marijuana Use on High School Graduation* (Cambridge, Mass.: National Bureau of Economic Research, 1993).

[16] *1993 Beer Industry Update.*

Why or why not? If so, can you tell from Table 3.5 which of these two demand curves is to the right of the other? Why or why not?

b. Does the demand curve for beer among females differ from the demand curve for beer among males? Why or why not? If beer producers want to increase their sales to women, what type of beer should they emphasize, on the basis of Table 3.5? Why?

c. In 1980, Heileman and Schlitz were the biggest sellers of malt liquor; together they accounted for about 67 percent of total sales.[17] If a firm produced and sold malt liquor, what segment of the population was a particularly important market, on the basis of Table 3.5?

d. In analyzing the market for beer, geography can be of relevance. Is it true, as the Supreme Court said in the case concerning the proposed merger of Pabst and Blatz, that Wisconsin, by itself, is "a distinguishable and economically significant market for the sale of beer"? (In answering this question, note that about one-fourth of the beer consumed in Wisconsin was not produced there, and that about three-fourths of the beer produced in Wisconsin was not consumed there.) Can you explain the price of beer in Wisconsin without considering the demand and supply in other states?

e. Brewing at home is legal and no permit is required, but quantities are limited to 200 gallons per year per household, and the beer cannot be sold.[18] The number of home brewers has increased by 30 percent per year recently. According to Lori Tullberg-Kelly, marketing director of the American Home Brewers Association in Boulder, Colorado, "home brewing is a way for [people] to tailor beer for their own taste. . . . I brewed 10 gallons of raspberry-flavored beer for my wedding last summer, and

there was none left. . . . It must have been good."[19] Does the fact that there was none left imply that, to the wedding guest who consumed the last glass of this beer, the marginal utility of this last glass of beer exceeded zero? Why or why not? Does it imply that this marginal utility exceeded the marginal utility of a glass of Budweiser beer? Why or why not?

PROBLEM 3.3 In 1968, J. D. McConnell published the results of a study he conducted to determine the effect of price on the perceived quality of beer. During a two-month period, he made 24 home deliveries of six-packs of beer to a large sample of beer drinkers. All the beer that was delivered was exactly the same, although the consumers did not know this because the labels were taken off and new ones (P, L, and M) were substituted. Beer labeled P was said to be a low-priced ("popular") brand; beer labeled L was said to be medium-priced ("premium") brand; and beer labeled M was said to be a high-priced ("super-premium") brand. After drinking and judging the beers over this two-month period, the sample of consumers assessed the beer with the M label as being of much higher quality than the others.[20]

a. Can you explain why this study turned out as it did? If so, provide your explanation in a few sentences.

b. Do the results of this study indicate that the demand curve for beer slopes *upward* to the right, rather than downward, as is generally assumed to be the case? Why or why not?

c. In the late 1970s and early 1980s, Stroh's changed the image of its beer. According to *Business Week*,

Stroh's had always been marketed as a popularly-priced brew with a six-pack selling for about 25 cents less than national premium

[17] K. Elzinga, "The Beer Industry," in W. Adams (ed.), *The Structure of Industry* (8th ed.; New York: Macmillan Co., 1990).

[18] *Philadelphia Inquirer*, March 7, 1994, p. MD4. Of course, laws may vary from place to place.

[19] Ibid.

[20] J. McConnell, "The Price-Quality Relationship in an Experimental Setting," *Journal of Marketing Research*, August 1968: 300–303.

brands. Its ads drilled home a monotonous message about the distinctive fire-brewed quality of the beer. "We always felt we had a quality product," says Peter Stroh. "But the marketing was saying, 'If you're so good, why don't you put your prices where your mouth is and go head-to-head with Budweiser!'" When Stroh moved into new markets, it did just that, promoting its premium-priced product as an "in" beer. . . . Stroh quickly captured 7% to 8% of its new markets.[21]

[21] *Business Week*, December 3, 1979, p. 91.

Did the higher price of Stroh's beer change its image in consumers' minds? If so, did it shift the demand curve for its beer?

d. Tom Kelly is a dairy farmer in Tyrone, Pennsylvania. If he increased the price of his milk, would consumers be led to believe that his milk was of above-average quality? If not, why is the situation different from that in the beer industry?

9 ▪ Applying Economics: Elasticities of Demand

The following two problems are concerned with the price, income, and cross elasticities of demand for beer in the United States.

PROBLEM 3.4 According to Thomas Fogarty and Kenneth Elzinga, the price elasticity of demand for beer in the United States is about 0.8.[22]

a. Is the demand curve shown below consis-

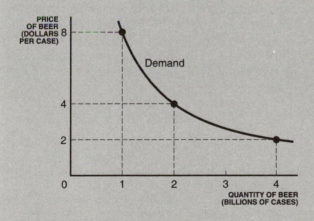

[22] T. Fogarty and K. Elzinga, "The Demand for Beer," *Review of Economics and Statistics*, May 1972.

tent with their findings? Why or why not?

b. If the price of a case of beer increases, will this result in an increase or decrease in the amount of money spent per year on beer? Why?

c. Holding the prices of other goods (and income) constant, do you think that the market demand curve for beer varies from month to month? From state to state? If so, why?

d. If Budweiser lowers the price of its beer by 1 percent, can it expect to increase the quantity it sells by 0.8 percent? Why or why not?

e. A number of years ago, Budweiser was selling for 58¢ per case more than its rivals in the St. Louis market and had 12 percent of the market. About a year later, Budweiser sold its beer at the same price as its rivals and had 39 percent of the market. Suppose that other brewers held their prices constant at $2 per case during this period, and that the total amount of beer sold in this market was constant during this period. What was the price elasticity of demand for Budweiser in the St. Louis market?

f. The Federal Trade Commission sued Anheuser-Busch after it lowered its price (in the situation described in part e) because its price in the St. Louis market was lower than elsewhere. Can selective price decreases of this sort be used to eliminate smaller rivals or enforce price leadership? If so, how? On the other hand, if a seller has to lower all its prices or none, won't this discourage price decreases? (In fact, Anheuser-Busch won the case.)[23]

PROBLEM 3.5 According to Fogarty and Elzinga, the income elasticity for beer in the United States is about 0.4.[24]

a. Table 3.6 shows estimates of the percentage of adults in various income categories who drank beer in 1992. If 34 percent of adults with incomes of $15,000 drink beer, and if 42 percent of those with incomes of $25,000 drink beer (and if, on the average, the amount drunk per person is the same in each income category), are these figures in accord with the finding of Fogarty and Elzinga? If not, how do they differ?

b. The Simmons Market Research Bureau reported that about 18 percent of adults with incomes of about $15,000 and about 22 percent of adults with incomes of about $25,000 drink light beer.[25] Does the income elasticity of demand for light beer seem to be positive?

c. Does the income elasticity of demand for beer seem to vary, depending on the level of income under consideration? If so, does this seem reasonable? Why or why not?

d. Can the data in Table 3.6 be used to determine how much U.S. beer consumption will change if total income in the United States goes up by 1 percent? Why or why not?

e. On the basis of the estimate by Fogarty and Elzinga (at the beginning of this problem),

▪ **TABLE 3.6**

Percentage of U.S. Adults Drinking Beer, by Household Income, 1992

HOUSEHOLD INCOME	PERCENTAGE DRINKING BEER
$40,000 or more	48
$30,000–$39,999	41
$20,000–$29,999	42
$10,000–$19,999	34
Under $10,000	30

SOURCE: *1993 Beer Industry Update.*

what will be the effect on the amount of money spent per year on beer if total consumer income increases by 15 percent while the price of beer remains constant?

f. Not all estimates of the income elasticity of demand for beer have been positive. For example, W. Niskanen concluded that it was zero, and T. McGuinness found it was negative.[26] If you were the chief economist of a beer firm and you were given the task of preparing a long-run forecast of total beer sales, what difference would it make whether this elasticity is positive, zero, or negative?

g. According to B. Lee and V. Tremblay, the cross elasticity of demand between beer and whiskey is about 0.4, and the cross elasticity of demand between beer and cola drinks is about 0.3.[27] Of what use might these estimates be in making the forecast in part f?

[23] Elzinga, "The Beer Industry."

[24] Fogarty and Elzinga, "The Demand for Beer."

[25] *1993 Beer Industry Update.*

[26] W. Niskanen, The Demand for Alcoholic Beverages, Unpublished Ph.D. Dissertation, University of Chicago, 1962; and T. McGuinness, "An Econometric Analysis of Total Demand for Alcoholic Beverages in the UK," *Journal of Industrial Economics* 29 (1980): 85–109.

[27] B. Lee and V. Tremblay, "Advertising and the U.S. Market Demand for Beer," *Applied Economics*, January 1992: 69–76.

10 ▪ Applying Economics: Economies of Scale and Advertising

The following two problems deal with economies of scale in the production of beer.

PROBLEM 3.6 In 1993, McKinsey and Company, the famous management consulting firm, carried out a study of the beer industry, in which it stressed that "In the beer industry, as in many other process industries, capital and scale are important determinants of profitability. Appropriate scale of the plant is crucial to being able to use efficient packaging technology. For example, a modern filling line processes 1,200 bottles per minute. Aluminum can filling lines operate at the speed of 2,000 12-oz. cans per minute. This is why the beer industry requires scale."[28]

a. According to F. M. Scherer and his coworkers, the long-run average cost curve is as shown below:[29]

About how large must a brewery be to realize fully all economies of scale?

b. From 1967 to 1987, the number of breweries with capabilities below 2 million barrels declined considerably. Is this what would be expected, given the above long-run average cost curve? Why or why not?

c. From 1967 to 1987, the number of breweries above 4 million barrels increased from 2 to 23. Is this what would be expected, given the above long-run average cost curve? Why or why not?

d. Besides economies of scale at the plant level, there are economies due to the operation of a number of beer plants. In particular, advertising on national network television is less costly than local spot television advertising because fewer contracts have to be negotiated and transactions costs are lower. The advertising

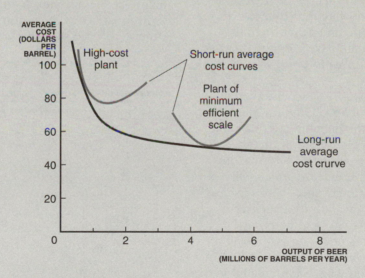

[28] McKinsey Global Institute, *Manufacturing Productivity*, p. 4.
[29] F. M. Scherer, A. Beckenstein, E. Kaufer, and R. Murphy, *The Economics of Multi-Plant Operation* (Cambridge, Mass.: Harvard University Press, 1975).

expenditures of Anheuser-Busch and Miller total nearly seven times more than those of their three smaller rivals—Coors, Stroh, and Heileman. According to Scherer and his colleagues, a "firm with three or four beer plants has a substantial advantage over a firm with only one plant because of these factors." If a beer plant has to have a capacity of 4.5 million barrels to be of minimum efficient size, and if a firm must have three or four plants to be of minimum efficient size, how big must a beer firm be to achieve minimum efficient size?

e. Are Anheuser-Busch and Miller above the minimum efficient scale? Are Coors and Stroh below the minimum efficient scale?

f. If annual beer production is about 190 million barrels, how many firms of minimum efficient scale can be supported in the United States? Can the existing level of concentration be explained by economies of scale alone?

PROBLEM 3.7 As stressed in earlier sections, beer producers spend enormous amounts on advertising. When Anheuser-Busch advertises that "This Bud's for you," it can hardly be regarded as solid evidence that Budweiser beer is better than its rivals, but Anheuser-Busch's managers and stockholders believe that it pays off. Similarly, beer producers spend large sums to sponsor sports events like the Olympics. In 1993, the two U.S. companies that spent the most on such sponsorships were Philip Morris (the owner of Miller Brewing Company) and Anheuser-Busch.[30]

a. In 1993, Anheuser-Busch spent $90 million to sponsor sports events. Suppose this resulted in the shift in the demand curve for Budweiser beer shown in Figure 3.2. If the price of Budweiser is X dollars per barrel (both before and after this expenditure), how much will Bud's sales go up because of these sponsorships?

b. If you were a consultant to Anheuser-Busch, and if you were asked to determine whether these sponsorships were profitable, would you be able to do so on the basis of the facts given here? If not, what additional information would you need?

c. Do you think that it is relatively easy to estimate the effects of sponsorships of this kind

[30] *Philadelphia Inquirer*, January 7, 1994, p. C1.

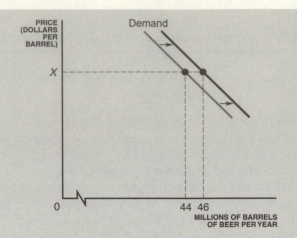

FIGURE 3.2

Effect of Sports Sponsorships on Demand Curve for Budweiser Beer

on the demand curve for Budweiser beer? If not, what are some of the principal difficulties?

d. If the relationship between Anheuser-Busch's advertising expenditures and its profit (before deducting the advertising expenditure) is as shown below, how much should Anheuser-Busch spend on advertising?

ADVERTISING EXPENDITURE	PROFIT BEFORE DEDUCTING ADVERTISING EXPENDITURE
(millions of dollars per year)	
550	1,300
600	1,380
650	1,440
700	1,500
750	1,540
800	1,580

e. Does advertising conform to the law of diminishing returns? Why or why not?

f. If advertising is so effective at increasing sales, why is it that total beer sales have been essentially constant (recall Figure 3.1) even though the advertising expenditures of the beer firms have gone through the roof?

11 ▪ Applying Economics: International Comparisons

This final problem is concerned with international differences in productivity in the brewing industry.

PROBLEM 3.8 McKinsey and Company, in the study cited previously, concluded that the average product of labor in 1990 was much higher in U.S. breweries than in those in Japan or Germany. (See Table 3.7.) Given that Germany and Japan are both regarded as efficient rivals of the United States in a variety of industries, it is interesting to look closely at the reasons for their relatively low productivity levels in beer production.

a. More than 1,000 firms produce beer in Germany. Practically all beer producers distribute their product within a 30-mile radius of their plant. German consumers prefer locally produced beer, and tradition dictates that beer be produced locally. The result is that the market for beer, which amounts to about 12.5 billion liters per year (Table 3.7), consists of a collection of local monopolies or near-monopolies. McKinsey estimates that a plant must produce about 170 million liters per year to be of minimum efficient size. Can you explain why output per hour of labor is lower in Germany than in the United States?

b. In Japan, there are only five companies producing beer. Kirin, the largest, accounts for about half the market, which is about 5.5 billion liters per year. Is the Japanese market too small to enable Japanese beer producers to realize economies of scale? Is this the rea-

▪ **TABLE 3.7**

Labor Productivity, Total Output, and Number of People in the Beer Industry, Germany, Japan, and the United States, 1990[a]

COUNTRY	LITERS OF BEER PRODUCED PER HOUR WORKED	ANNUAL TOTAL OUTPUT (billions of liters)	NUMBER OF PLANTS
Germany	193	12.5	1,128
Japan	300	5.5	37
United States	436	23.6	67

[a] Output and number of plants pertain to 1987.

SOURCE: McKinsey Global Institute, *Manufacturing Productivity* (Washington, D.C.: McKinsey and Company, 1993).

son why productivity is lower in Japan than in the United States?

c. The Japanese beer industry is regulated by the Ministry of Finance, which must grant permission for a company to build a plant or to open a new retail outlet. One effect of this government regulation is to encourage Japanese breweries to create more and more products aimed at smaller and smaller segments of the market. If a brewery produces a wide variety of beers, is this likely to reduce output per hour of labor? Why or why not?

d. In Japan, there has been a tradition among many firms to grant their employees lifetime employment. Could this help to explain the productivity difference between Japan and the United States? If so, how?

12 ▪ Conclusion

Let's return now from Anheuser-Busch and Miller (and their smaller rivals) to the classroom. The most important point for present purposes is that the economic concepts and techniques summarized in Chapters 1 and 2 are essential to understand how to manage a beer firm or how the beer industry is evolving. Such simple concepts as demand curve, price elasticity, income elasticity, economies of scale, average product, and diminishing returns are enormously useful and help managers and investors (and observers) to function more effectively.

PART TWO

Perfect Competition and Monopoly

CHAPTER 4

Perfect Competition

Essentials of **Perfect Competition**

- A perfectly competitive market has the following properties: (1) there are many sellers of identical products, (2) no one seller or buyer has control over the price, (3) firms may easily enter the market, and (4) resources can be switched readily from one use to another. Many agricultural markets are close to perfectly competitive.

- Economists use the model of perfect competition as a yardstick to assess the performance of markets under various conditions.

- The market supply curve, which relates the quantity of a good supplied to its price, generally slopes upward and to the right.

- Prices are determined by supply and demand. In the short run, the period during which each firm's plant and equipment are fixed, the intersection of the demand and supply curves gives the equilibrium price.

- There are no long-run economic profits under perfect competition.

1 ■ What Is Perfect Competition?

When business executives speak of a highly competitive market, they often mean one in which each firm is keenly aware of its rivalry with a few others and in which advertising, styling, packaging, and other such commercial weapons are used to attract business away from them. In contrast, the basic feature of the economist's definition of perfect competition is its *impersonality*. Because there are so many firms in the industry, no firm views another as a competitor, any more than one small tobacco farmer views another small tobacco farmer as a competitor. A market is perfectly competitive if it satisfies three conditions.

HOMOGENEITY OF PRODUCT The first condition is that *the product of any one seller must be the same as the product of any other seller*. This condition ensures that buyers do not care from which seller they purchase the goods, so long as the price is the same. This condition is met in many markets.

For example, farmer Brown's corn is likely to be essentially the same as farmer Smith's.

MANY BUYERS AND SELLERS The second condition is that there must be a large number of buyers and sellers. *Each participant in the market, whether buyer or seller, must be so small in relation to the entire market that he or she cannot affect the product's price.* That is, all buyers and sellers must be "price takers," not "price makers." A firm under perfect competition faces a *horizontal demand curve*, since variations in its output—within the range of its capabilities—will have no effect on market price.

MOBILITY OF RESOURCES The third condition is that *all resources must be able to switch readily from one use to another, and consumers, firms, and resource owners must have complete knowledge of all relevant economic and technological data*.

No industry in the real world, now or in the

past, satisfies all these conditions completely; thus no industry is perfectly competitive. Some agricultural markets may be reasonably close, but even they do not meet all the requirements. But this does not mean that it is useless to study the behavior of a perfectly competitive market. The conclusions derived from the model of perfect competition have proved very helpful in explaining and predicting behavior in the real world. Indeed, as you will see, they have permitted a reasonably accurate view of resource allocation in many important segments of our economy.

 TEST YOUR UNDERSTANDING

True or false?

____ **1** No industry, now or in the past, has met all of the requirements of perfect competition.

____ **2** Under perfect competition the product of any one seller must be the same as the product of any other seller.

2 ▪ The Output of the Firm

What determines the output rate in the short run of a perfectly competitive firm? Since the firm is perfectly competitive, it cannot affect the price of its product, and it can sell any amount it wants at this price. Since the question is about the short run, the firm can expand or contract its output rate by increasing or decreasing its utilization of its variable, but not its fixed, inputs. The situation in the long run will be reserved for a later section.

WHAT IS THE PROFIT AT EACH OUTPUT RATE?

To see how a firm determines its output rate, suppose that your aunt dies and leaves you her business, the Allegro Piano Company. Once you take over the business, your first problem is to decide how many pianos (each of which has a price of $1,000) the firm should produce per week. Having a good deal of economic intuition, you instruct your accountants to estimate the company's *total revenue* (defined as price times output) and total costs (as well as fixed and variable costs) at various output levels. They estimate the firm's total revenue at various output rates and its total cost function (as well as its total fixed cost function and total variable cost function), with the results shown in Table 4.1 (next page).

Subtracting the total cost at a given output rate from the total revenue at this output rate, you obtain the total profit at each output rate, which is shown in the last column of Table 4.1.

FINDING THE MAXIMUM-PROFIT OUTPUT RATE

As the output rate increases from 0 to 4 pianos per week, the total profit *rises. As* the output rate increases from 5 to 8 pianos per week, the total profit *falls*. Thus the *maximum* profit is achieved at an output rate between 4 and 5 pianos per week.[1] (Without more detailed data, one cannot tell precisely where the maximum occurs, but this is close enough for present purposes.) Since the maximum profit is obtained at an output of between 4 and 5 pianos per week, this is the output rate you choose.

Figure 4.1 gives a somewhat more vivid picture of the firm's situation by plotting the relationship between total revenue and total cost on the one hand and output on the other. At each output rate, the vertical distance between the total revenue curve and the total cost curve is the amount

---

[1] This assumes that the output rate can be varied continuously and that there is a single maximum. These are innocuous assumptions.

■ **TABLE 4.1**

Costs and Revenues, Allegro Piano Company

OUTPUT PER WEEK (pianos)	PRICE	TOTAL REVENUE (PRICE TIMES OUTPUT)	TOTAL FIXED COST	TOTAL VARIABLE COST	TOTAL COST	TOTAL PROFIT
			(dollars)			
0	1,000	0	1,000	0	1,000	−1,000
1	1,000	1,000	1,000	200	1,200	− 200
2	1,000	2,000	1,000	300	1,300	700
3	1,000	3,000	1,000	500	1,500	1,500
4	1,000	4,000	1,000	1,000	2,000	2,000
5	1,000	5,000	1,000	2,000	3,000	2,000
6	1,000	6,000	1,000	3,200	4,200	1,800
7	1,000	7,000	1,000	4,500	5,500	1,500
8	1,000	8,000	1,000	7,200	8,200	− 200

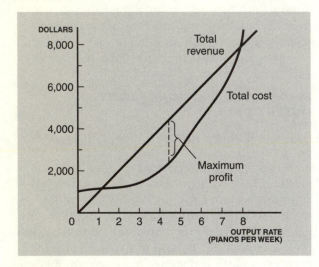

■ **FIGURE 4.1**

Costs, Revenues, and Profits, Allegro Piano Company

Profit equals the vertical distance between the total revenue curve and the total cost curve. This distance is maximized when the output rate is between 4 and 5 pianos per week. At this output rate, profit (measured by the vertical distance) is somewhat more than $2,000.

of profit the firm earns. Below an output rate of about 1 piano per week and above an output rate of about 8 pianos per week, the total revenue curve lies *below* the total cost curve, indicating that profits are negative; that is, there are losses. Both Table 4.1 and Figure 4.1 show that the output rate that will maximize the firm's profits is between 4 and 5 pianos per week. At this output rate, the firm will make a profit of over $2,000 per week, which is more than it can make at any other output rate.

There is an alternative way to analyze the firm's situation. Rather than looking at total revenue and total cost, let's look at price and marginal cost. Table 4.2 and Figure 4.2 show the product price and marginal cost of each output rate. It turns out that the maximum profit is achieved at the output rate where price equals marginal cost. In other words, both Table 4.2 and Figure 4.2 indicate that price equals marginal cost at the profit-maximizing output rate of between 4 and 5 pianos per week. This raises a question. Will price usually equal marginal cost at the profit-maximizing output rate, or is this merely a coincidence?

THE GOLDEN RULE OF OUTPUT DETERMINATION

Readers familiar with television scripts and detective stories will have recognized that the question just posed can only be answered in one way without ruining the plot. The equality of marginal cost and price at the profit-maximizing output

■ TABLE 4.2

Marginal Cost and Price, Allegro Piano Company

OUTPUT PER WEEK (pianos)	MARGINAL COST	PRICE
	(dollars)	
0		1,000
	200	
1		1,000
	100	
2		1,000
	200	
3		1,000
	500	
4		1,000
	1,000	
5		1,000
	1,200	
6		1,000
	1,300	
7		1,000
	2,700	
8		1,000

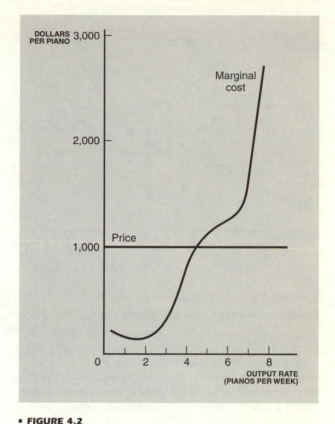

■ FIGURE 4.2

Marginal Cost and Price, Allegro Piano Company

At the profit-maximizing output rate of between 4 and 5 pianos per week, marginal cost (which is $1,000 when the output rate is between 4 and 5) equals price ($1,000). Note that marginal cost is plotted at the midpoint of the range of output to which it pertains.

rate is no mere coincidence. It will usually be true if the firm takes the price of its product as given. Indeed, the Golden Rule of Output Determination for a perfectly competitive firm is: *Choose the output rate at which marginal cost is equal to price.*

To determine the profit-maximizing output rate of a firm, compare the extra revenue with the extra cost of each additional unit of output. If the extra revenue (which equals price in the case of perfect competition) is greater than the extra cost (which equals marginal cost), the extra unit should be produced; otherwise, it should not be produced. For example, reconsider the Allegro Piano Company. Should this firm produce the first piano? Yes, because (according to Table 4.2) the extra revenue ($1,000) exceeds the cost ($200). Should it produce a second piano? Yes, because the extra revenue ($1,000) exceeds the extra cost ($100). Should it produce a sixth piano? No, because the extra revenue ($1,000) is less than the extra cost ($1,200).

To prove that a perfectly competitive firm will maximize profit by producing the output where price equals marginal cost, consider Figure 4.3 (next page) which shows a typical short-run marginal cost function. Suppose that the price is OP_1. At any output rate less than OQ_1, price is greater than marginal cost.[2] This means that increases in

[2] Except perhaps for an irrelevant range where marginal cost decreases with increases in output.

output will increase the firm's profits since they will add more to total revenues than to total costs. Why? Because, as you have seen, an extra unit of output adds an amount equal to price to total revenue and an amount equal to marginal cost to total cost. Thus, since price exceeds marginal cost, an extra unit of output adds more to total revenue than to total cost.

At any output rate above OQ_1, price is less than marginal cost. This means that decreases in output will increase the firm's profits since they will subtract more from total costs than from total revenue. This happens because 1 less unit of out-

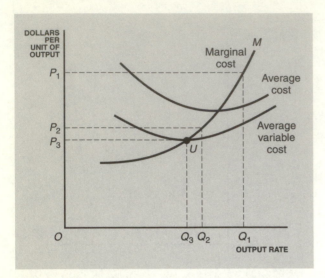

■ **FIGURE 4.3**

Short-Run Average and Marginal Cost Curves

If price is OP_1, the profit-maximizing output rate is OQ_1. If price is OP_2, the profit-maximizing output rate is OQ_2, even though the firm will incur a loss. If the price is below OP_3, the firm will discontinue production. (Note that, regardless of what the price is, the demand curve facing the firm is a horizontal line at this price.)

put subtracts an amount equal to price from total revenue and an amount equal to marginal cost from total cost. Thus, since price is less than marginal cost, 1 less unit of output subtracts more from total cost than from total revenue. (Such a case occurs when the Allegro Piano Company is producing 7 pianos per week. As shown in Table 4.2, the extra cost of producing the seventh piano is $1,300, while the extra revenue it brings in is $1,000. So it pays the Allegro Piano Company to produce less than 7 pianos per week.)

Since increases in output will increase profits if output is less than OQ_1, and decreases in output will increase profits if output is greater than OQ_1, it follows that profits must be maximized at OQ_1, the output rate at which price equals marginal cost. After all, if increases in output up to this output (OQ_1) result in increases in profit and further increases in output result in decreases in profit, OQ_1 must be the profit-maximizing output rate. For the Allegro Piano Company, this out-

put rate is between 4 and 5 pianos per week as before.

DOES IT PAY TO BE A DROPOUT?

All rules—even the Golden Rule just mentioned—have exceptions. Under some circumstances, the perfectly competitive firm will not maximize its profits if it sets marginal cost equal to price. Instead, it will maximize profits only if it becomes an economic dropout by discontinuing production. This is true because even if the firm is doing the best it can, it may not be able to earn a profit. If the price is OP_2 in Figure 4.3, short-run average cost exceeds the price, OP_2, at all possible output rates. Thus the firm cannot earn a profit whichever output it produces. Since the short run is too short for the firm to alter the scale of its plant, it cannot liquidate its plant in the short run. Its only choice is to produce at a loss or discontinue production.

Under which conditions will the firm produce at a loss, and under which conditions will it discontinue production? *If there is an output rate where price exceeds average variable cost, it will pay the firm to produce, even though price does not cover average total cost. If there is no such output rate, the firm is better off to produce nothing at all.* This is true because even if the firm produces nothing, it must pay its fixed cost. Thus, if the loss resulting from production is less than the firm's fixed cost, the firm is better off producing than not producing. On the other hand, if the loss resulting from production is greater than the firm's fixed cost, the firm is better off not to produce.

In other words, *the firm will find it advantageous to produce if total losses are less than total fixed cost.* Since

$$\text{total losses} = \text{total cost} - \text{total revenue,}$$

this will be the case if

$$\text{total cost} - \text{total revenue} < \text{total fixed cost.}$$

If you subtract total fixed cost from both sides of this inequality and add total revenue to both sides, you find that the firm is better off to produce if

$$\text{total cost} - \text{total fixed cost} < \text{total revenue.}$$

Dividing each side of this inequality by output (and recognizing that total revenue = price × output), you find that the firm is better off to produce if

$$\text{average variable cost} < \text{price,}$$

since average variable cost equals average total cost minus average fixed cost.

To repeat, the conclusion is that the firm will maximize profits by producing *nothing* if there is no output rate at which price exceeds average variable cost. If such an output rate does exist, the Golden Rule applies: The firm will set its output rate at the point where marginal cost equals price.

THE FIRM'S SUPPLY CURVE

Since the firm takes the price of its product as given (and can sell all it wants at that price), you know from the previous section that the firm will choose the output level at which price equals marginal cost. Or if the price is below the firm's average variable cost curve at every output level, the firm will produce nothing. These results are all that is needed to determine the firm's supply curve, which shows how much a firm will want to produce at each price.

Suppose that the firm's short-run cost curves are as shown in Figure 4.3. The marginal cost curve must intersect the average variable cost curve at the latter's minimum point, U. If the price of the product is less than OP_3, the firm will produce nothing, because there is no output level where price exceeds average variable cost. If the price of the product exceeds OP_3, the firm will set its output rate at the point where price equals marginal cost. Thus, if the price is OP_1, the firm will produce OQ_1; if the price is OP_2, the firm will produce OQ_2; and so forth. Consequently, *the firm's supply curve is exactly the same as the firm's marginal cost curve for prices above the minimum value of average variable cost* (OP_3). For prices at or below the minimum value of average variable cost, the firm's supply curve corresponds to the price axis, the desire to supply at these prices being uniformly zero. Thus the firm's supply curve is OP_3UM.

 TEST YOUR UNDERSTANDING

True or false?

_____ **1** The Golden Rule of Output Determination for a perfectly competitive firm is: Choose the output rate at which marginal cost is equal to price.

_____ **2** The firm will maximize profits by producing nothing if there is no output rate at which price exceeds average variable cost.

_____ **3** If firm X's marginal cost curve intersects its average variable cost curve at $4 per unit of output, firm X will shut down in the short run if the price of its product falls below $4 per unit.

Exercise

1 Agriculture has many of the characteristics of perfect competition. According to Daniel Suits, the average total cost curve (*ATC*), average variable cost curve (*AVC*), and marginal cost curve (*MC*) of a typical corn producer in the early 1970s were as follows:

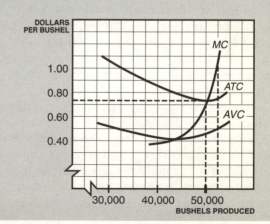

a. Assuming perfect competition, how many bushels of corn would this farmer produce if the price of corn were $1 per bushel?

b. Assuming perfect competition, how many bushels would this farmer produce if the price were $.40 per bushel?

c. If the price were $.70 per bushel, would this farmer be making a profit or a loss?

d. Suppose that every corn producer has the cost functions shown above, and that perfect competition prevails. If there are 100,000 corn producers, what would be the total supply of corn if the price were $1 per bushel?

e. If the price were $1 per bushel, would long-run equilibrium prevail? Why or why not?

3 ▪ Deriving the Market Supply Curve

The next step is to derive the market supply curve from the supply curves of the individual firms. If one assumption holds, the **market supply curve** *can be regarded as the horizontal summation of the supply curves of all the firms producing the product.* If there were three firms in the industry and their supply curves were shown in Figure 4.4, the market supply curve would be the horizontal summation of their three supply curves. Thus, since these three supply curves show that firm 1 would supply 25 units of output at a price of $2 per unit, that firm 2 would supply 40 units at this price, and that firm 3 would supply 55 units at this price, the market supply curve shows that 120 units of output will be supplied if the price is $2 per unit. Why? Because the market supply curve shows the *total* amount of the product that all the firms together would supply at this price, and 25 + 40 + 55 = 120. If there were only three firms, the market would not be perfectly competitive, but you can ignore this inconsistency. Figure 4.4 is designed to illustrate the fact that the market supply curve is the horizontal summation of the firm supply curves, at least under one important assumption.

The assumption underlying this construction of the short-run market supply curve is that *increases or decreases in output by all firms simultaneously do not affect input prices.* This is a convenient simplification, but it is not always true. Although changes in the output of one firm alone often cannot affect input prices, the simultaneous ex-

pansion or contraction of output by all firms may well alter input prices, so that the individual firm's cost curves—and supply curve—will shift. For instance, an expansion of the whole industry may bid up the price of certain inputs, with the

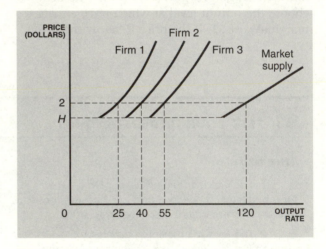

▪ **FIGURE 4.4**

Horizontal Summation of Short-Run Supply Curves of Firms

If each of the three firms' supply curves is as shown here (and if each firm supplies nothing if the price is below *OH*), the market supply curve is the horizontal summation of the firms' supply curves, assuming that input prices are not influenced by the output of the industry. If the price is $2, firm 1 will supply 25 units, firm 2 will supply 40 units, and firm 3 will supply 55 units; thus, the total amount supplied is 120 units.

result that the cost curves of the individual firms will be pushed upward. In the aerospace industry, a sudden expansion of the industry might well increase the price of certain inputs like the services of aerospace scientists and engineers.

If, contrary to the assumption underlying Figure 4.4, input prices *are* increased by the expansion of the industry, one can still derive the short-run market supply curve by seeing how much the industry will supply in the short run at each price of the product. But it is incorrect to assume that the market supply curve is the horizontal summation of the firm supply curves.

DETERMINANTS OF THE LOCATION AND SHAPE OF THE MARKET SUPPLY CURVE

On the basis of the previous discussion, you now can identify the basic determinants of the location and shape of a commodity's short-run market supply curve. If increases or decreases in output by all firms do not affect input prices, the short-run market supply curve is the horizontal summation of the firm supply curves. Thus its location and shape are derived from the location and shapes of the marginal cost curves of the firms in the industry, since these marginal cost curves determine the firm supply curves. From previous discussion, you know that the location and shape of each marginal cost curve depend on *the size of the firm's plants, the level of input prices, and the state of technology* in particular. Thus, these factors play a major role in determining the location and shape of the market supply curve. Also, its location and shape in the short run are determined by the *number of firms* in the industry. The market supply curve in Figure 4.4 would be located farther to the right if there were more firms in the industry. In addition, its location and shape are determined by *the effect of industry output on input prices.*

The short-run market supply curve generally slopes upward and to the right because marginal cost curves (in the relevant range) generally slope upward to the right. If industry output does not affect input prices, the market supply curve is the horizontal sum of the firm's marginal cost curves (in the range where they are rising). Consequently, since each of the marginal cost curves slopes upward and to the right (in this range), this is also true of their horizontal sum, the short-run market supply curve.

 TEST YOUR UNDERSTANDING

True or false?

_____ **1** If price is fixed, then increases in output will have little effect on the firm's profits.

_____ **2** Market supply curves tend to be more price elastic if the time period is short rather than long.

_____ **3** If we are dealing with a very short period, the supply of a product may be fixed; that is, the market supply curve may be perfectly inelastic. The price elasticity of supply will be zero, because the period is too short to produce any more of the product or transport it to the market.

Exercise

1 According to the U.S. Bureau of Mines, the quantity of mercury reserves in the United States at selected price levels of mercury is as follows:

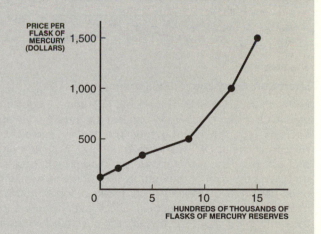

a. Is this the supply curve for mercury? Why or why not?

b. Does this curve show how much mercury will be supplied per period of time?

c. Why is the quantity of reserves sensitive to price?

d. Does it appear that, as price increases, beyond some point increasing price begins to lose its power to elicit substantially larger supplies? Is this reasonable? Why or why not?

4 ■ Price and Output: The Short Run

Turn now to the **short run,** *the period during which each firm's plant and equipment are fixed.* What determines the price and output of a good in a perfectly competitive market in the short run? The answer is the market demand and mar-

ket supply curves. In particular, the market supply curve in the short run will not be a vertical line; it will generally slope upward to the right, as in panel B of Figure 4.5. Thus, *in the short run, price influences, as well as rations, the amount sup-*

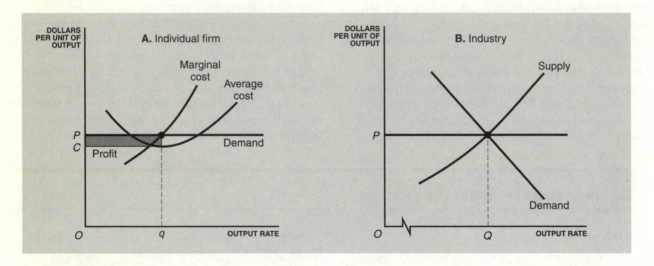

■ **FIGURE 4.5**

Short-Run Competitive Equilibrium

In the short-run, equilibrium price is *OP,* and the equilibrium output of the industry is *OQ,* since (as shown in panel B) the industry demand and supply curves intersect at this price and output. The demand curve facing the individual firm is a horizontal line at *OP* (as shown in panel A). Each firm produces *Oq* units of the product, since this is the output that maximizes its profits. The output of the industry (*OQ*) is the sum of the outputs (*Oq*) of the individual firms. In short-run equilibrium, firms may be making either profits or losses. In this particular case, the individual firm earns a profit equal to the shaded areas in panel A. [Why? Because the profit *per unit of output* equals the price (*OP*) minus average cost (*OC*), or the vertical distance *CP.* To obtain the firm's *total profit,* this distance must be multiplied by the firm's output (*Oq*), the result being the shaded area.] If firms were making losses rather than profits, the demand curve confronting each firm would intersect the marginal cost curve at a point below (rather than above) the average cost curve.

plied. In panel B of Figure 4.5, the equilibrium price and output in the short run are *OP* and *OQ*.

Panel A of Figure 4.5 shows the behavior of an individual firm in short-run equilibrium. Since *OP* is the price, the demand curve facing the firm is a horizontal line at *OP*, as shown in panel A. To maximize profit, the firm produces an output of *Oq*, because price equals marginal cost at this output. In short-run equilibrium, firms may be making either profits or losses. In the particular case described in panel A, the firm earns a profit equal to the shaded area shown there. Since the profit per unit of output equals *CP*, total profit equals *CP* multiplied by *Oq*, which is this shaded area.

Taken together, the two panels in Figure 4.5

bring out the following important point. To the *individual* firm, the price of the product is taken as given. If the price is *OP*, the firm in panel A reacts to this price by setting an output rate of *Oq* units. It cannot alter the price; it can only react to it. But *as a group* the reactions of the firms are a major determinant of the price of the product. The supply curve in panel B shows the total amount that the entire group of firms will supply at each price. It summarizes the reactions of the firms to various levels of the price. Put briefly, the equilibrium price is viewed by the individual firm as being beyond its control; yet the supply decisions of all firms taken as a group are a basic determinant of the equilibrium price.

 TEST YOUR UNDERSTANDING

True or false?

_____ **1** In the short run, price influences, but does not ration, the amount supplied.

Exercises

1 Suppose that the total costs of a perfectly competitive firm are as follows:

OUTPUT RATE	TOTAL COST (dollars)
0	40
1	60
2	90
3	130
4	180
5	240

If the price of the product is $50, what output rate should the firm choose?

2 Suppose that the firm in Exercise 1 experienced an increase of $30 in its fixed costs. What is its new total cost function? What effect will this increase in its fixed costs have on the output it will choose?

3 After the increase in fixed costs described in Exercise 2, what does the firm's marginal cost curve look like? Does it differ from what it was before the increase in fixed costs? Why or why not?

4 After the increase in fixed costs described in Exercise 2, what output rate would the firm choose if the price of its product were $40? $50? $60?

5 ■ Price and Output: The Long Run

In the **long run,** what determines the output and price of a good in a perfectly competitive market? In the long run, a firm can change its plant size; this means that established firms may *leave* an industry if it has below-average profits, or that new firms may *enter* an industry with above-average profits. Suppose that textile firms can earn up to (but no more than) a 15 percent rate of return by investing their resources in other industries. If they can earn only 12 percent by keeping these resources invested in the textile industry, they will leave the textile industry. On the other hand, if a rate of return of 18 percent can be earned by investing in the textile industry, firms in other industries, attracted by this relatively high return, will enter the textile industry.

EQUILIBRIUM: ZERO ECONOMIC PROFIT

Equilibrium is achieved in the long run when enough firms—no more, no less—are in the industry so that **economic profits**—*defined as the excess of a firm's profits over what it would make in other industries—are zero.* This condition is necessary for long-run equilibrium because, as you have seen, new firms will enter the industry if there are economic profits, and existing firms will leave if there are economic losses. This process of entry and exit is the key to long-run equilibrium. It is discussed repeatedly in this and subsequent sections.

Note that the existence of economic profits or losses in an industry brings about a shift in the industry's short-run supply curve. If there are economic profits, new firms will enter the industry, and so shift the short-run supply curve to the right. On the other hand, if there are economic losses in the industry (that is, if the industry's profits are less than could be obtained elsewhere), existing firms will leave the industry, and this will cause the short-run supply curve to shift to the left. Only if economic profits are zero will the number of firms in the industry—and the industry's short-run supply curve—be stable. Putting this equilibrium condition another way, *the long-*

run equilibrium position of the firm is at the point where its long-run average costs (that is, average total costs) equal price. If price exceeds average total costs, economic profits are being earned; and if price is less than average total costs, economic losses are being incurred.

EQUILIBRIUM: MAXIMUM ECONOMIC PROFIT

Going a step further, *long-run equilibrium requires that price equal the lowest value of long-run average total costs.* In other words, firms must be producing at the *minimum point* on their long-run average cost curves, because to maximize their profits they must operate where price equals long-run marginal costs, and at the same time they also have to operate where price equals long-run average cost.[3] But if both these conditions are satisfied, long-run marginal cost must equal long-run average cost, since both equal price. Long-run marginal cost equals long-run average cost only at the point at which long-run average cost is a minimum.[4] Consequently, if long-run marginal cost equals long-run average cost, the firm must be producing at the minimum point on the long-run average cost curve.

This equilibrium position is illustrated in Figure 4.6. When all adjustments are made, price equals *OP.* The equilibrium output of the firm is *Oq,* and its plant corresponds to the short-run average and marginal cost curves in Figure 4.6. At this output and with this plant, long-run marginal cost equals short-run marginal cost equals price. This ensures that the firm is maximizing profit. Also, long-run average cost equals short-run average cost equals price. This ensures that economic profits are zero. Since the long-run marginal cost and long-run average cost must be equal, the firm is producing at the minimum point on its long-run average cost curve.

[3] The reasons why marginal cost must be equal to price, if profits are to be maximized, are given in earlier sections of this chapter.

[4] The previous discussion of this in Chapter 2 concerned short-run cost functions, but the argument applies just as well to long-run cost functions.

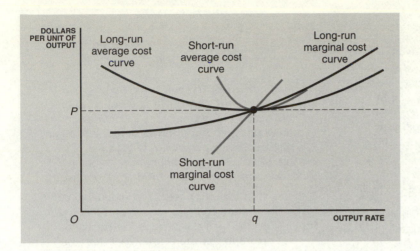

▪ **FIGURE 4.6**

Long-Run Equilibrium of a Perfectly Competitive Firm

In long-run equilibrium, output is Oq and the firm's plant corresponds to the short-run average and marginal cost curves shown in the figure. At Oq, long-run marginal cost equals short-run marginal cost equals price; also, long-run average cost equals short-run average cost equals price. These conditions ensure that the firm is maximizing profits and that economic profits are zero.

 TEST YOUR UNDERSTANDING

True or false?

_____ **1** Only if economic profits are zero will the number of firms in the industry be stable.

_____ **2** At all points where the total revenue curve lies below the total cost curve, profits will be negative.

_____ **3** A perfectly competitive firm in long-run equilibrium is earning normal profits (that is, profits equal to those obtainable elsewhere).

Exercises

1 Suppose that the demand and supply curves for apples are as shown below:

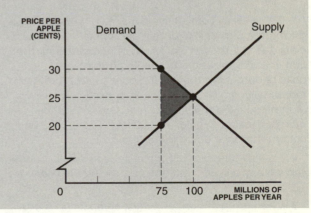

a. If 75 million apples are produced per year, how much would an additional apple cost to produce? How much would an additional apple be worth to consumers?

b. Under these circumstances, is it socially worthwhile to increase apple production? Why or why not?

c. If 100 million apples are produced per year, how much would an additional apple cost to produce? How much would an additional apple be worth to consumers?

d. If 100 million apples are produced, is it socially worthwhile to increase apple production? Explain.

e. How great is the loss to society if 75 million, rather than 100 million, apples are produced?

2 If the price elasticity of supply for corn is about 0.1 in the short run, as estimated by Marc Nerlove of the University of Maryland, a 1 percent increase in the price of corn would have approximately what impact on the quantity supplied?

3 In Exercise 1, suppose that 125 million apples are produced per year. Under these circumstances, is it socially desirable to reduce apple production? Explain.

4 Suppose that the demand curve for onions is $P = 10 - 3Q$, where P is the price of a pound of onions (in dollars) and Q is the quantity demanded (in millions of pounds). If the supply of onions is fixed at $3\frac{1}{6}$ million pounds (regardless of the price of onions), what is the equilibrium price of onions? What does the supply curve for onions look like?

5 In the short run, suppose that the demand curve for onions is as given in Exercise 4, and that the supply curve is $P = Q/3$. What is the equilibrium price of onions in the short run? What does the supply curve of onions look like in the short run?

■ CHAPTER REVIEW

KEY TERMS

market supply curve
short run

long run
economic profits

COMPLETION QUESTIONS

1 If a perfectly competitive firm's marginal cost of producing the Qth unit of output per month equals $5Q$ dollars, and if the price of a unit of output is $30, the firm, if it maximizes profit, should produce _____ units of output per month. If it does so, its profits per month will equal _____ if its fixed costs per month equal $100. If its fixed costs were $300 per month, the firm (would, would not) _____ be better off to shut down in the short run.

2 If a firm cannot affect the price of its product and it can sell any amount that it wants, the firm is said to be _____ .

3 Maximum profit under perfect competition is usu-

ANSWERS TO COMPLETION QUESTIONS

6

−$25

would not

perfectly competitive

ally achieved at the output rate where _____ equals _____ .

price
marginal cost

4 A firm's _____ shows how much it will desire to produce at each price.

supply curve

5 The _____ is the horizontal summation of the supply curves of all firms producing the product, assuming that industry output does not influence input prices.

market supply curve

6 If there is an output rate where price exceeds average _____ cost, it will pay the firm to produce, even though price does not cover average cost. If there is no such output rate, the firm is better off to produce _____ .

variable

nothing

7 Under perfect competition the firm's supply curve is exactly the same as the firm's _____ cost curve for prices above the minimum value of average _____ cost. For prices at or below the minimum value of average _____ cost, the firm's supply curve corresponds to the _____ axis, the desire to supply at these prices being uniformly _____ .

marginal

variable
variable
price
zero

8 The _____ of an item is the percentage change in quantity supplied as a result of a 1 percent change in _____ . For instance, suppose that 1 percent reduction in the price of an item results in a 1.3 percent reduction in the quantity supplied. The _____ for that item, at approximately the existing price, is _____ .

price elasticity of supply

price

price elasticity of supply
1.3

9 Market supply curves, like many market demand curves, tend to be (less, more) _____ price elastic if the time period is long rather than short. For instance, estimates of the short-run price elasticities of supply are about 0.2 for cotton and about 0.1 for corn; but in the long run, Marc Nerlove estimates the price elasticity of supply to be (higher, lower) _____ .

more

higher

10 In perfect competition, each firm has (no, little, much) _____ control over the price of its product.

no

11 If the supply of a good is fixed, its supply curve is _____ .

vertical

12 In the short run, _____ determines the amount of a product supplied. For instance, according to Hubert Risser of the University of Kansas, the short-run supply curve for bituminous coal is very price elastic when output is within the range of existing capacity. In other words, if output is less than existing capacity, small variations in price will result in (large, small) _____ variations in output.

price

large

13 Under perfect competition, long-run equilibrium requires that price equals the (highest, lowest) _____ value of long-run average total costs. In

lowest

other words, firms must be producing at the (maximum, minimum) _____ point on their long-run average cost curves, because to maximize their _____, they must operate where price equals long-run (average, marginal) _____ cost. Also, they must operate where price equals long-run _____ cost. But if both these conditions are satisfied, long-run _____ cost must equal long-run _____ cost, since both equal price. And you know that long-run _____ cost equals long-run _____ cost only at the point at which long-run average cost is a (maximum, minimum) _____.

> minimum
>
> profits
> marginal
>
> average
> marginal
> average
> marginal
> average
> minimum

14 Firm *X* is a perfectly competitive firm that is in long-run equilibrium. The price of its product is $10 more than the value of its economic profit; this means that the price of its product equals _____. Its long-run average cost (equals, exceeds, is less than) _____ $10. Its short-run marginal cost (equals, exceeds, is less than) _____ $10. In this situation firm *X*'s economic profit (does, does not) _____ equal its accounting profit.

> $10
> equals
>
> equals
> does not

NUMERICAL PROBLEMS

1 Suppose that the total costs of a perfectly competitive firm are as follows:

OUTPUT RATE	TOTAL COST (dollars)
0	40
1	60
2	90
3	130
4	180
5	240

Assume that the output rate can only assume integer values.

a If the price of the product is $50, what output rate should the firm choose?

b Draw on the following graph the short-run supply curve of the firm.

c Draw the firm's demand curve.

d Draw the firm's average total cost curve.

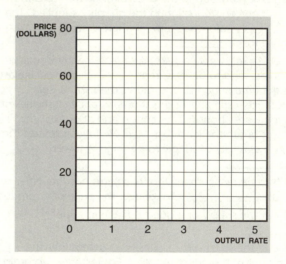

e What will be the firm's total profit?

2 Suppose that the price elasticity of supply of crude oil is 0.3. How much of a price increase will be required to obtain a 3 percent increase in the quantity supplied of crude oil?

3 You are the owner of a firm that is currently losing $1,000 per month, with fixed costs per month of $800. A management consultant advises you to cease production. Should you accept the advice? Why or why not?

4 Suppose that the total cost curve of the Rem Sofa Company is as follows:

OUTPUT (sofas per month)	TOTAL COST (dollars per month)
1	1,000
2	1,100
3	1,200
4	1,300
5	1,500
6	1,700
7	2,000
8	2,500

Assume that the output rate must be an integer amount per month.

a If the price of a sofa is $300, how many sofas should Rem produce per month?

b Suppose that Rem's fixed costs increase by $100 per month. What effect will this have on the optimal output?

c If its fixed costs increase by $100 per month, what will be the maximum profit rate that the Rem Sofa Company can earn?

d Does the Rem Sofa Company exhibit increasing marginal cost? What is the value of marginal cost when between 7 and 8 units of output are produced per month?

5 Data are provided below concerning the Allied Peanut Company, a firm producing peanut brittle.

a Supposing that this firm is a member of a perfectly competitive industry, complete the table below:

OUTPUT OF PEANUT BRITTLE PER DAY BY ALLIED (tons)	PRICE OF A TON OF PEANUT BRITTLE	TOTAL COST	TOTAL REVENUE	PROFIT	MARGINAL COST
			(dollars)		
0	200	100	____	____	
1	____	200	____	____	____
2	____	310	____	____	____
3	____	500	____	____	____
4	____	700	____	____	____
5	____	1,000	____	____	____

Assume that the output rate must equal an integer number of tons per day.

b If the price of a ton of peanut brittle falls to $50, will Allied continue producing, or will it shut down?

c What is the minimum price at which Allied will continue production (assuming that it cannot produce fractions of tons of output)?

d If the price of a ton of peanut brittle is $200, what output rate will Allied choose? Does price equal marginal cost at this output rate?

6 The following graph shows the total cost and total revenue curves of a hypothetical competitive firm:

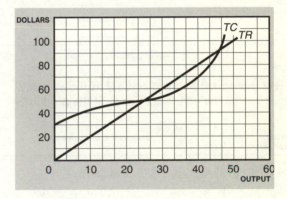

a How much is the price of the firm's product?

b How much is the firm's total fixed cost?

c At what output levels will the firm's profit be zero?

d At what output level will the firm's profit be a maximum?

7 Suppose that a perfectly competitive firm has the short-run total cost function shown below:

OUTPUT	TOTAL COST (dollars)
0	10
1	12
2	16
3	22
4	30
5	40

a If the firm can produce only integer amounts of output, what output level will it choose when the price of its product is (1) $3? (2) $5? (3) $7? (4) $9?

b What will be the firm's profits when the price of its product is (1) $3? (2) $5? (3) $7? (4) $9?

c If there are 1,000 firms in this industry, and all have the cost function shown above, the market supply curve is as follows. Fill in the blanks.

PRICE (dollars)	QUANTITY SUPPLIED
3	_____
5	_____
7	_____
9	_____

d If the market demand curve is as shown below, what will be the equilibrium price of the product?

PRICE (dollars)	QUANTITY DEMANDED
3	3,000
5	2,000
7	1,500
9	1,000

e What will be the output of each firm?

f How much profit will each firm make?

g Will firms enter or leave this industry in the long run?

8 As of midnight, December 13, American Agriculture, a recently formed farmers' lobby group, is calling for a nationwide strike by farmers. The goal is to raise the price of the crops enough to cover production costs and to provide some profit. Suppose that the current price of wheat is $1.50 per bushel, which is about half the cost of growing that bushel.

a Depict the current plight of a typical wheat farmer graphically. (Treat her as a perfect competitor.) Your diagram should correctly depict both variable and total costs relative to the assumed market price given the fact that the typical farmer is choosing to continue producing even while making losses.

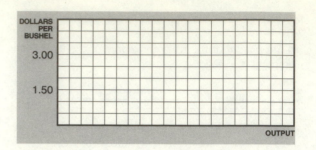

b In perfect competition no single firm has any market power. Suppose that by such an organization as American Agriculture all farmers could coordinate the selling of their produce. What would be the effect on the price of their produce? What would be the effect on the amount they would sell?

9 Assume that perfect competition exists. Assume that marginal cost increases with increases in output. In the table below you are to fill in all spaces that do not contain a number. An asterisk in a space means that ATC or AVC is at a minimum level at that output. *Treat each horizontal row in the table as a separate problem.* Enter in the last column one of the following responses:

NUMBER	RESPONSE
1	Firm is now at correct output.
2	Firm should increase price.
3	Firm should decrease price.
4	Firm should increase output.
5	Firm should decrease output.
6	Firm should shut down operations.

The symbols are as follows: P = Price, Q = Quantity, TR = Total Revenue, TC = Total Cost, TFC = Total Fixed Cost, TVC = Total Variable Cost, ATC = Average Total Cost, AVC = Average Variable Cost, MC = Marginal Cost.

P	Q	TR	TC	TFC	TVC	ATC	AVC	MC	RESPONSE
10	—	800	—	500	—	10	—	—	1
—	—	400	—	100	—	2	1	5	—
—	10	30	—	20	—	—	.30	.25	—
10	100	—	—	200	—	—	10	—	—
—	50	300	—	—	—	7	5	—	—

ANSWERS TO
TEST YOUR UNDERSTANDING

SECTION 1

TRUE OR FALSE: 1. True   2. True

SECTION 2

TRUE OR FALSE: 1. True   2. True   3. True

EXERCISE

1. a. 52,500.

b. Zero.

c. A loss.

d. 52,500 × 100,000 = 5,250 million bushels.

e. No. Price would not equal average total cost.

SECTION 3

TRUE OR FALSE: 1. False   2. False   3. True

EXERCISE

1. a. No. This curve shows how much mercury will be available (not produced) at various prices.

b. No.

c. Because, at higher mercury prices, it becomes profitable to obtain mercury from relatively high-cost sources, whereas at lower mercury prices this is not the case.

d. Yes. This is reasonable because beyond some point it becomes increasingly expensive to find and obtain an extra flask of mercury.

SECTION 4

TRUE OR FALSE: 1. False

EXERCISES

1. 3 or 4 units.

2. The new total cost function is:

OUTPUT RATE	TOTAL COST (dollars)
0	70
1	90
2	120
3	160
4	210
5	270

No effect.

3. The firm's marginal cost curve is not affected.

4. 2 or 3 units.   3 or 4 units.   4 or 5 units.

SECTION 5

TRUE OR FALSE: 1. True   2. True   3. True

EXERCISES

1. a. 20 cents, since the supply curve shows marginal cost. 30 cents, because the demand curve shows the maximum amount consumers would pay for an extra apple.

b. Yes, because the extra social cost of producing an extra apple is less than the extra social benefit from doing so. Consumers would be glad to pay producers to produce extra apples.

c. 25 cents. 25 cents.

d. No, since the extra social cost of producing an extra apple is no less than the maximum amount that consumers would pay for an extra apple. If private benefits and costs do not differ from social benefits and costs, 100 million apples is the optimal output level. It would not be socially worthwhile to exceed or fall short of it.

e. The vertical distance from the demand curve to the supply curve is the difference between the social benefit and the social cost of an *extra* apple. (For example, if 75 million apples are produced, the social benefit of an extra apple exceeds its social cost by 30 − 20 = 10 cents.) Thus the difference between the social benefit and social cost of the *extra 25 million apples* equals the sum of these vertical distances for all the extra apples. This sum equals the shaded area in the above diagram, which amounts to 25 million × 5 cents = $1.25 million. This is the loss to society.

2. A 0.1 percent increase.

3. Yes.

4. 50 cents per pound. The supply curve is vertical.

5. $1. The supply curve is linear, but not vertical.

■ CHAPTER 5

Monopoly

Essentials of **Monopoly**

- Under monopoly (where there is one and only one seller), the monopolist maximizes profit by setting its output rate at the point where marginal revenue equals marginal cost.

- Marginal revenue is the addition to total revenue attributable to the addition of 1 unit to sales; it will always be less than price if the firm's demand curve is downward sloping.

- If the product demand curve and the industry's cost functions are the same for a monopoly as for a perfectly competitive industry, the output of the monopoly tends to be less and the price tends to be higher than under perfect competition.

- Many economists believe that the allocation of resources is more socially desirable under perfect competition than under monopoly.

1 ■ Causes of Monopoly

A monopoly is a market where there exists one, and only one, seller. There are many reasons why monopolies or market structures that closely approximate monopoly may arise.

PATENTS   A firm may acquire a monopoly over the production of a good by having patents on the product or on certain basic processes used in its production. The patent laws of the United States give an inventor the exclusive right to make a certain product or to use a certain process for 20 years (from date of initial filing). The purpose of the patent system is to encourage invention and innovation and to discourage industrial secrecy. Many firms with monopoly power achieved it in considerable part through patents. For example, the United Shoe Machinery Company became the sole supplier of certain important kinds of shoemaking equipment through control of basic patents. United Shoe was free to dominate the market until 1954, when, after prosecution under the antitrust laws, the firm was ordered to license its patents. And in 1968,

when this remedy seemed insufficient, a divestiture program was agreed on.

CONTROL OF INPUT   A firm may become a monopolist by obtaining control over the entire supply of a basic input required to manufacture a product. The International Nickel Company of Canada controls about nine-tenths of the proven nickel reserves in the world. Since it is hard to produce nickel without nickel, the International Nickel Company obviously has a strong monopoly position. Similarly, the Aluminum Company of America (Alcoa) kept its dominant position for a long time by controlling practically all the sources of bauxite, the ore used to make aluminum. However, as you will see in Chapter 8, Alcoa's monopoly was broken in 1945 when the Supreme Court decided that Alcoa's control of practically all the industry's output violated the antitrust laws.

GOVERNMENT ACTION   A firm may become a monopolist because it is awarded a market franchise by a government agency. The government may give a particular firm the franchise to sell a particular product in a public facility. Or it may give a particular company the right to provide a service, such as telephone service, to people in a particular area. In exchange for this right, the firm agrees to allow the government to regulate certain aspects of its operation. The form of regulation does not matter here; the important point for now is that the monopoly is created by the government.

DECLINING COST OF PRODUCTION A firm may become a monopolist because the average costs of producing the product may reach a minimum at an output rate that is large enough to satisfy the entire market (at a price that is profitable). In a case like this, a firm obviously has an incentive to expand until it produces all the market wants of the good. (Its costs fall as it continues to expand.) Thus competition cannot be maintained in this case. If there are a number of firms in the industry, the result is likely to be economic warfare— and the survival of a single victor, the monopolist.

Cases in which costs behave like this are called **natural monopolies.** When an industry is a natural monopoly, the public often insists that its behavior be regulated by the government. The likelihood that the long-run average cost curve will decrease up to a point that satisfies the entire market depends on the size of the market. The smaller the market, the more likely it is. In Figure

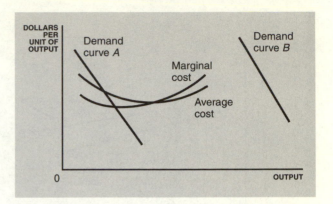

▪ **FIGURE 5.1**

Natural Monopoly

The industry is a natural monopoly if the demand curve is *A*, but not if it is *B*.

5.1, the industry is a natural monopoly if the demand curve is *A*, but not if it is *B*. In a large market like the United States, it is much less likely that an industry will be a natural monopoly than in a small market like Belgium or Denmark. One of the advantages claimed for the reduction in trade barriers among West European countries in 1992 was that it would create a larger market that could support more efficient production and more competitive industries. For now, the important point to recognize is that, just as stagnant marshes are the breeding ground for mosquitoes, so small, insulated markets are the breeding ground for monopoly.

 TEST YOUR UNDERSTANDING

True or false?

_____ **1** Many firms with monopoly power achieved it in considerable part through patents.

_____ **2** When an industry is a natural monopoly, the public often insists that its behavior be regulated by the government.

Exercise

1 An isolated town of 5,000 inhabitants in the Rocky Mountains is looking for a dentist. To simply matters, divide the town's inhabitants into two categories: the rich and the poor. The demand curve for dental care among each type of inhabitant is shown on the next page. Adding the two demand curves horizontally, you find that the total demand curve for dental care is *DAB*.

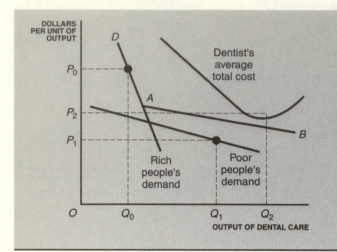

a. If a dentist charges the same price to all inhabitants (rich or poor), can the dentist cover his or her average total costs?

b. If the dentist charges the rich a higher price than the poor, can the dentist cover his or her average total cost?

c. **Price discrimination** occurs when a producer sells the same commodity or service at more than one price. Thus the dentist in b is engaging in price discrimination. In fact, do physicians and dentists engage in price discrimination?

d. In some instances, is it true that a good or service cannot be produced without price discrimination?

e. Is this always the case?

2 ■ Demand Curve and Marginal Revenue under Monopoly

Before we can make any statements about the behavior of a monopolistic market, we must point out certain important characteristics of the demand curve facing the monopolist. Since the monopolist is the only seller of the commodity, the demand curve it faces is the market demand curve for the product. Since the market demand curve is almost always downward sloping to the right, the monopolist's demand curve must also be downward sloping to the right. This is quite different from perfect competition, in which the firm's demand curve is horizontal. To illustrate the situation faced by a monopolist, consider the hypothetical case in Table 5.1. The price at which each quantity (shown in column 1) can be sold by the monopolist is shown in column 2. The firm's **total revenue**—its total dollar sales volume—is shown in column 3. Obviously, column 3 is the product of the first two columns. Column 4 contains the firm's **marginal revenue**, *defined as the addition to total revenue attributable to the addition of 1 unit to sales.* (Thus, if $R(q)$ is total revenue when q units are sold and $R(q - 1)$ is total revenue when $(q - 1)$ units are sold, the marginal

■ **TABLE 5.1**

Demand and Revenue of a Monopolist

QUANTITY	PRICE	TOTAL REVENUE	MARGINAL REVENUE
		(dollars)	
1	100	100	
			80
2	90	180	
			60
3	80	240	
			40
4	70	280	
			20
5	60	300	
			0
6	50	300	
			−20
7	40	280	
			−40
8	30	240	

revenue between q units and $(q - 1)$units is $R(q) - R(q - 1)$.)

Marginal revenue is very important to the monopolist. You can estimate it from the figures in the first three columns of Table 5.1. The marginal revenue between 1 and 2 units of output per day is $180 − $100, or $80; the marginal revenue

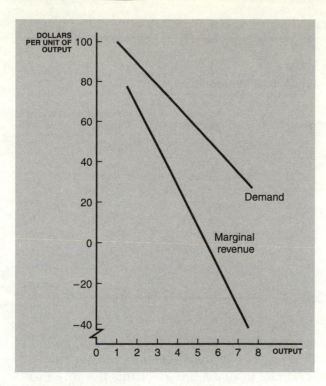

▪ **FIGURE 5.2**

Marginal Revenue and Demand Curves

The demand curve comes from Table 5.1. Each value of marginal revenue is plotted at the midpoint of the range of output to which it pertains. Since the demand curve is downward sloping, marginal revenue is always less than price, for reasons discussed in the text. Note that the value of marginal revenue is related to the price elasticity of demand. At outputs where demand is price elastic, marginal revenue is *positive*; at outputs where it is price inelastic, marginal revenue is *negative*; and at outputs where it is of unitary elasticity, *marginal revenue is zero*.

between 2 and 3 units of output per day is $240 − $180, or $60; the marginal revenue between 3 and 4 units of output per day is $280 − $240, or $40; and so on. The results are shown in column 4 of the table (and are plotted in Figure 5.2). Note that marginal revenue is analogous to marginal cost (and marginal utility and marginal product for that matter). Recall that marginal cost is the extra cost resulting from an extra unit of

production. Substitute "revenue" for "cost" and "sales" for "production" in the previous sentence, and what do you get? A perfectly acceptable definition of marginal revenue.

Marginal revenue will always be less than price if the firm's demand curve is downward sloping (as it is under monopoly and other market structures that are not perfectly competitive.) In Table 5.1, the extra revenue from the second unit of output is $80 whereas the price of this unit is $90. *The basic reason is that the firm must reduce the price of all units of output, not just the extra unit, in order to sell the extra unit.* Thus, in Table 5.1, the extra revenue from the second unit of output is $80 because, while the price of the second unit is $90, the price of the first unit must be reduced by $10 in order to sell the second one. Thus the extra revenue (that is, marginal revenue) from selling the second unit of output is $90 − $10, or $80, which is less than the price of the second unit.

Similarly, the marginal revenue from selling the third unit of output ($60, according to Table 5.1) is less than the price at which the third unit can be sold ($80, according to Table 5.1). Why? Because, to sell the third unit of output, the price of the first two units of output must be reduced by $10 each (that is, from $90 to $80). Thus the extra revenue (that is, marginal revenue) from selling the third unit is not $80, but $80 less the $20 reduction in the amount received for the first two units.

☑ **TEST YOUR UNDERSTANDING**

True or false?

_____ **1** If the demand curve is horizontal, marginal revenue equals price.

_____ **2** Marginal revenue is the addition to total revenue attributable to the addition of 1 unit to sales.

_____ **3** At outputs where demand is price elastic, marginal revenue is negative.

3 ■ Price and Output: The Short Run

You are now in a position to determine how output and price behave under monopoly. If the monopolist is free to maximize its profits, it will choose the price and output rate at which the difference between total revenue and total cost is greatest. Suppose that the firm's costs are as shown in Table 5.2 and that the demand curve it faces is as shown in Table 5.1. On the basis of the data in these two tables, the firm can calculate the profit that it will make at each output rate. To do so, it subtracts its total cost from its total revenue, as shown in Table 5.3. What output rate will maximize the firm's profit? According to Table 5.3, profit *rises* as its output rate increases from 1 to 3 units per day, and profit *falls* as its output rate increases from 4 to 8 units per day. Thus the *maximum* profit is achieved at an output rate between 3 and 4 units per day.[1] (Without more detailed data, you cannot tell precisely where the maximum occurs, but this is close enough for present purposes.) Figure 5.3 shows the same thing graphically.

■ **TABLE 5.2**

Costs of a Monopolist

QUANTITY	TOTAL VARIABLE COST	TOTAL FIXED COST	TOTAL COST	MARGINAL COST
		(dollars)		
0	0	100	100	
				40
1	40	100	140	
				30
2	70	100	170	
				40
3	110	100	210	
				40
4	150	100	250	
				50
5	200	100	300	
				60
6	260	100	360	
				90
7	350	100	450	
				100
8	450	100	550	

[1] This assumes that the output rate can vary continuously and that there is a single maximum. These are innocuous assumptions.

■ **TABLE 5.3**

Profits of a Monopolist

QUANTITY	TOTAL REVENUE	TOTAL COST	TOTAL PROFIT
		(dollars)	
1	100	140	−40
2	180	170	10
3	240	210	30
4	280	250	30
5	300	300	0
6	300	360	−60
7	280	450	−170
8	240	550	−310

What price will the monopolist charge? To maximize its profit, it must charge the price that results in its selling the profit-maximizing output, which in this case is between 3 and 4 units per day. Thus, according to Table 5.1, it must charge between $70 and $80 per unit. Why? Because if it charges $70, it will sell 4 units per day; and if it charges $80, it will sell 3 units per day. Consequently, to sell the profit-maximizing output of between 3 and 4 units per day, it must charge a price of between $70 and $80 per unit.

THE GOLDEN RULE OF OUTPUT DETERMINATION

In Chapter 4, you encountered the Golden Rule of Output Determination for a perfectly competitive firm. You can now formulate a Golden Rule of Output Determination for a monopolist: *set the output rate at the point where marginal revenue equals marginal cost*. Table 5.4 and Figure 5.4 show that this rule results in a maximum profit in this example. It is evident from Table 5.4 that marginal revenue equals marginal cost at the profit-maximizing output of between 3 and 4 units per day. Figure 5.4 shows the same thing graphically.

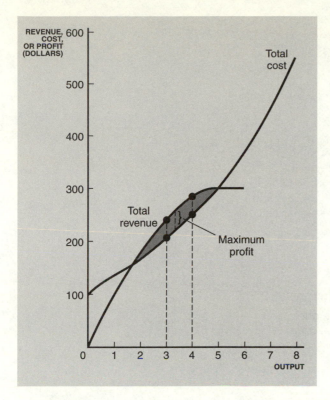

▪ **FIGURE 5.3**

Total Revenue, Cost, and Profit of a Monopolist

The output rate that will maximize the firm's profit is between 3 and 4 units per day. At this output rate, profit (which equals the vertical distance between the total revenue and total cost curves) is over $30 per day. On the basis of the demand curve for its product (shown in Table 5.1), the firm must set a price of between $70 and $80 to sell between 3 and 4 units per day.

▪ **TABLE 5.4**

Marginal Cost and Marginal Revenue of a Monopolist

QUANTITY	TOTAL PROFIT	MARGINAL COST	MARGINAL REVENUE
		(dollars)	
1	−40		
		30	80
2	10		
		40	60
3	30		
		40	40
4	30		
		50	20
5	0		
		60	0
6	−60		
		90	−20
7	−170		
		100	−40
8	−310		

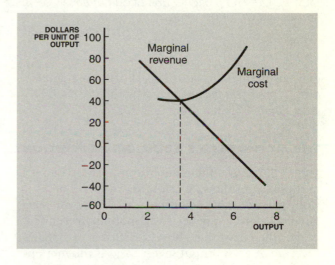

▪ **FIGURE 5.4**

Marginal Cost and Marginal Revenue of a Monopolist

At the profit-maximizing output rate of between 3 and 4 units per day, marginal cost (which is $40 between an output rate of 3 and 4 units per period) equals marginal revenue (which also is $40 between an output rate of 3 and 4 units per period). Both marginal cost and marginal revenue are plotted at the midpoints of the ranges of output to which they pertain. (See Figures 5.2 and 5.3.)

Why is this rule generally a necessary condition for profit maximization? At any output rate where marginal revenue *exceeds* marginal cost, profit can be increased by *increasing* output, since the extra revenue will exceed the extra cost. At any output rate where marginal revenue is *less than* marginal cost, profit can be increased by *reducing* output, since the decrease in cost will exceed the decrease in revenue. Thus, since profit will *not* be a maximum when marginal revenue

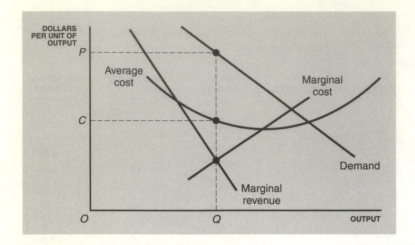

■ **FIGURE 5.5**

Equilibrium Position of a Monopolist

The monopolist sets its output rate at *OQ*, where the marginal revenue curve intersects the marginal cost curve. At this output, price must be *OP*. And profit per unit of output equals *CP*, since average cost equals *OC*.

exceeds marginal cost or falls short of marginal cost, *it must be a maximum only when marginal revenue equals marginal cost.*

THE MONOPOLIST'S EQUILIBRIUM POSITION

Figure 5.5 shows the equilibrium position of a monopolist in the short run. Short-run equilibrium will occur at the output *OQ*, where the marginal cost curve intersects the marginal revenue curve (the curve that shows the firm's marginal revenue at each output level). And if the monopolist is to sell *OQ* units per period of time, the demand curve shows that it must set a price of *OP*. Thus the equilibrium output and price are *OQ* and *OP*, respectively.

It is interesting to compare the Golden Rule of Output Determination for a monopolist (set the output rate at the point where marginal revenue equals marginal cost) with that for a perfectly competitive firm (set the output rate at the point where price equals marginal cost). The latter is really the same as the former because, *for a perfectly competitive firm, price equals marginal revenue.*

Since the perfectly competitive firm can sell all it wants at the market price, each additional unit sold increases the firm's total revenue by the amount of the price. Thus, *for both the monopolist and the perfectly competitive firm, profits are maximized by setting the output rate at the point where marginal revenue equals marginal cost.*

WHEN WILL A MONOPOLIST SHUT DOWN?

From Chapter 4, you know that perfectly competitive firms sometimes find it preferable to shut down rather than follow this rule. Is this true for monopolists as well? The answer is yes. *Just as perfectly competitive firms will discontinue production if they will lose more money by producing than by shutting down, so monopolists will do the same thing, and for the same reasons.* In other words, if there is no output such that price exceeds average variable cost, monopolists, like perfect competitors, will discontinue production. This makes sense. If by producing, monopolists incur greater losses than their fixed costs, they will "drop out," that is, produce nothing.

TWO MISCONCEPTIONS

Finally, note two misconceptions concerning monopoly behavior. First, it is sometimes said that monopolists will charge "as high a price as they can get." This is nonsense. The monopolist in Table 5.1 could charge a higher price than $70 to $80, but to do so would be foolish since it would result in lower profits. Second, it is sometimes said that monopolists will seek to maximize their profit per unit of output. This too is nonsense, since monopolists are interested in their total profits and their return on capital, not on the profit per unit of output. Rational monopolists will not sacrifice their total profits to increase their profit per unit of output.

 TEST YOUR UNDERSTANDING

True or False

____ **1** For monopolists, but not perfect competitors, profit is maximized by setting marginal revenue equal to marginal cost.

____ **2** A profit-maximizing monopolist will always set average revenue greater than average total cost in the short run.

____ **3** If a monopolist is not maximizing its profit per unit of output, it is not setting marginal cost equal to marginal revenue.

Exercises

1 If you were the president of a firm that has a monopoly on a certain product, would you choose an output level where demand for the product was price inelastic? Explain.

2 Suppose that a monopolist's demand curve is as follows:

QUANTITY DEMANDED (per year)	PRICE (dollars)
8	1,000
7	2,000
6	3,000
5	4,000
4	5,000
3	6,000
2	7,000
1	8,000

What is the firm's marginal revenue when output is between 7 and 8 units? When output is between 1 and 2 units?

3 Suppose that the monopolist in Exercise 2 has fixed costs of $10,000 and an average variable cost of $4,000. The average variable cost is the same for outputs of 1 to 10 units per year. What output rate will the firm choose? What price will it set?

4 Suppose that the firm in Exercise 3 experienced a 50 percent increase in both its fixed and average variable costs. If the demand curve in Exercise 2 remains valid, what effect will this cost increase have on the output rate and price that the firm will choose?

4 ▪ Price and Output: The Long Run

In contrast to the situation under perfect competition, the long-run equilibrium of a monopolistic industry may not be marked by the absence of economic profits. If a monopolist earns a short-run economic profit, it will not be confronted in the long run with competitors, unless the industry ceases to be a monopoly. The entrance of additional firms into the industry is incompatible with the existence of monopoly. Thus, the long-run equilibrium of an industry under monopoly may be characterized by economic profits.

On the other hand, if the monopolist incurs a short-run economic loss, it will be forced to look for other, more profitable uses for its resources.

One possibility is that the firm's existing plant is not optimal and that it can earn economic profits by appropriate alterations to its scale and characteristics. If so, the firm will make these alterations in the long run and remain in the industry. However, *if there is no scale of plant that will enable the firm to avoid economic losses, it will leave the industry in the long run*. The mere fact of having a monopoly over the production of a certain commodity does not mean that the firm must be profitable. A monopoly over the production of cut-glass spittoons would be unlikely to catapult a firm into financial glory, or even allow it to avoid losses.

 TEST YOUR UNDERSTANDING

True or False

_____ **1** The monopolist's long-run demand curve must always be horizontal.

_____ **2** A monopoly seeks to maximize profit per unit of output.

Exercises

1 Compare the long-run equilibrium of a perfectly competitive industry with that which would occur if all the firms were to be merged in a single monopolistic firm. Is there any reason for society to prefer one equilibrium over the other?

2 "No firm has a monopoly since every good competes to some extent with every other good. Thus there is no good that is completely sealed off from competition." Comment and evaluate.

3 "Firms with relatively high profits are bound to be monopolists. If they were competitive, the entry of new firms into the industry would drive economic profits down to zero. Thus the easiest and best way to determine whether a firm is a monopolist is to look at its profits." Comment and evaluate.

4 "According to the Council of Economic Advisers, "Although exit from an industry via bankruptcy is a normal characteristic of efficient competitive markets, the bankruptcy of a regulated firm tends to be viewed as a sign of regulatory failure." What problems are likely to result from this attitude?

5 ▪ Perfect Competition and Monopoly: A Comparison

A market's structure is likely to affect the behavior of the market; in other words, a market's structure influences how much is produced and the price that is set. If you could perform an ex-periment in which an industry was first operated under conditions of perfect competition and then under conditions of monopoly (assuming that the demand for the industry's product and the industry's cost functions would be the same in either case),[2] you would find that the equilibrium price and output would differ under the two sets of conditions.

HIGHER PRICE AND LESS OUTPUT UNDER MONOPOLY

Specifically, if the product demand curve and the industry's cost functions are the same, *the output of a perfectly competitive industry tends to be greater and the price tends to be lower than under monopoly.* We see this in Figure 5.6, which shows the perfectly competitive industry's demand and supply curves. Since price and output under perfect competition are given by the intersection of the demand and supply curves, OQ_C is the industry output and OP_C is the price. But what if all the competitive firms are bought up by a single firm,

which then operates as a pure monopolist? Under these conditions, what formerly was the industry's supply curve is now the monopolist's marginal cost curve.[3] And what formerly was the industry's demand curve is now the monopolist's demand curve. Since the monopolist chooses the output where marginal cost equals marginal revenue, the industry output will be OQ_M and the price will be OP_M. Clearly, OQ_M is less than OQ_C, and OP_M is greater than OP_C.

Of course, all this is in theory. But there is plenty of evidence that monopolists restrict output and charge higher prices than firms under

[2] The cost and demand curves need not be the same. For example, the monopolist may spend money on advertising, and thus shift the demand curve. It should be recognized that the assumption that the demand and cost curves are the same is stronger than it appears at first glance.

[3] The monopolist will operate the various plants that would be independent under perfect competition as branches of a single firm. The marginal cost curve of a multiplant monopoly is the horizontal sum of the marginal cost curves of the individual plants. (To see why, suppose that a monopoly has two plants, A and B. The total amount that the monopoly can produce at a particular marginal cost is the sum of (1) the amount plant A can produce at this marginal cost and (2) the amount plant B can produce at this marginal cost.) From the previous chapter, you know that this is also the supply curve of the industry if the plants are operated as separate firms under perfect competition.

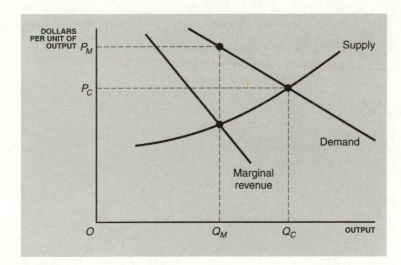

▪ FIGURE 5.6

Comparison of Long-Run Equilibria: Perfect Competition and Monopoly

Under perfect competition, OQ_C is the industry output and OP_C is the price. Under monopoly, OQ_M is the industry output and OP_M is the price. Clearly, output is higher and price is lower under perfect competition than under monopoly.

competition. Take the case of tungsten carbide, which sold for $50 per pound until a monopoly was established in 1927 by General Electric. The price went to between $225 and $453 per pound, until the monopoly was broken by the antitrust laws in 1945. The price then dropped back to between $27 and $45 per pound.[4] This case was extreme, but by no means unique. For centuries people have observed that when monopolies are formed, output tends to be restricted, and price tends to be driven up.

MONOPOLY AND RESOURCE ALLOCATION

Moreover, it has long been felt that the allocation of resources under perfect competition is socially more desirable than under monopoly. Society might be better off if more resources were devoted to producing the monopolized good in Figure 5.6, and if the competitive, not the mo-

[4] W. Adams, *The Structure of American Industry* (5th ed.; New York: Macmillian Co., 1977, p. 485.

nopolistic, output were produced. For example, in the *Wealth of Nations*, published about 200 years ago, Adam Smith stressed that when competitive forces are thwarted by "the great engine . . . of monopoly," the tendency for resources to be used "as nearly as possible in the proportion which is most agreeable to the interest of the whole society" is thwarted as well.

Why do so many economists believe that the allocation of resources under perfect competition is more socially desirable than that under monopoly? This is not a simple question, and like most hard questions can be answered at various levels of sophistication. Put most simply, many economists believe that firms under perfect competition are induced to produce quantities of goods that are more in line with consumer desires, and that firms under perfect competition are induced to use the least-costly methods of production. Chapter 8 provides a much more complete discussion of the pros and cons of monopoly and competition.

 TEST YOUR UNDERSTANDING

True or False

____ **1** For both the monopolist and the perfectly competitive firm, profits are maximized by setting the output rate at the point where price equals marginal cost.

____ **2** A monopolist will discontinue production if its losses have to exceed its fixed costs.

____ **3** A monopolist has to take into account the possibility that new firms might arise to challenge its monopoly if it attempted to extract conspicuously high profits. Thus, even the monopolist is subject to some restraint imposed by competitive forces.

Exercises

1 In Haverhill, Massachusetts, one newspaper had been published for over a century. Then, another newspaper was founded. In the Haverhill market, suppose that the market demand curve for the town's newspapers, and the demand curve facing each newspaper were as shown on the right. Also, each newspaper's cost curves and marginal revenue

curve are given below. (Note: In this special case, the firm's demand curve is the same as a monopolist's marginal revenue curve.)

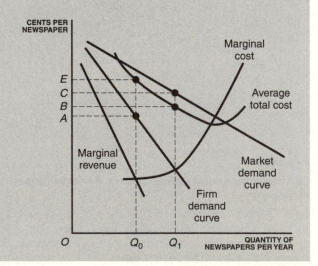

a. If both firms stay in business, how much will each lose?

b. If only one of them stays in business, can it make a profit? How big a profit?

c. Is this a case of natural monopoly?

d. If entry by one firm may drive the other out of business, is this illegal?

2 In this chapter, you have seen that the output rate that will result in an optimal allocation of resources (under the assumptions made here) is the one where price equals marginal cost. Economists have suggested that public utilities set their prices equal to their marginal costs. By so doing, it is argued, the allocation of resources will be improved. For example, consider an electric power plant that has the marginal cost curve shown on the right. Suppose that this plant's demand curve varies over time. For simplicity, assume that there is a peak period (when air conditioners are running and lights are on) and

an off-peak period. The demand curve during each period is as follows:

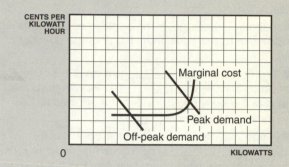

Should the electric power plant charge a higher price during the peak period than during the off-peak period?

■ CHAPTER REVIEW

KEY TERMS

natural monopolies

price discrimination
total revenue

marginal revenue

COMPLETION QUESTIONS

1 If the marginal revenue from the first unit of output is $5 and the marginal revenue from the second unit of output is $4, the total revenue from the first two units of output is _____. The average revenue when 1 unit of output is produced and sold equals _____. The average revenue when 2 units of output are produced and sold equals _____.

2 A monopolist can sell 12 units of output when it charges $10 a unit, 11 units of output when it charges $11 a unit, and 10 units of output when it charges $12 a unit. The marginal revenue from the eleventh unit of output equals _____. The marginal revenue from the twelfth unit of output equals _____.

3 For the monopolist, if demand is price _____, marginal revenue is positive; if demand is price _____, marginal revenue is negative.

ANSWERS TO COMPLETION QUESTIONS

$9

$5
$4.50

+$1
−$1

elastic

inelastic

4 The output of a perfectly competitive industry tends to be _____ and the price tends to be _____ than under monopoly.

greater
lower

5 A patent may result in a firm's becoming a _____ .

monopolist

6 A firm's _____ is the addition to total revenue attributable to the addition of 1 unit of the quantity sold.

marginal revenue

7 The firm under _____ has no direct competitors at all; it is the sole _____ . However, such a firm is not entirely free of rivals but it affected by certain indirect and potential forms of _____ .

monopoly
supplier

competition

8 A firm may become a monopolist because it is awarded a(n) _____ by a government agency. The government may give a particular firm the franchise to sell a particular product in a(n) _____ or the right to provide a(n) _____ , such as telephone service, to people in a particular area. In exchange for this right, the firm agrees to allow the government to _____ certain aspects of its operations.

market franchise

public facility
service

regulate

9 A firm may become a monopolist because the average costs of producing the product reach a(n) _____ at an output rate great enough to satisfy the entire market (at a price that is _____). Under such circumstances, the firm obviously has an incentive to _____ to the point where it produces all the market will buy of the good, because its costs (decrease, increase) _____ as it continues to expand. Competition cannot be maintained in such a case.

minimum
profitable

expand

decrease

10 A company's assets can be valued by _____ cost or _____ cost, that is, at what the company paid for them or at what it would cost to replace them. If the _____ does not change much, these two approaches are interchangeable. But if prices are rising, _____ cost will be greater than _____ cost.

historical
reproduction

price level

replacement   historical

11 If a monopolist's demand curve is of unitary elasticity, marginal revenue equals _____ . In such a case it would be (possible, impossible) _____ for the monopolist to set marginal cost equal to marginal revenue. The monopolist would try to make its output as _____ as possible, since _____ in output reduce its total cost but not its total revenue.

zero
impossible

small   decreases

12 If a monopolist's demand curve is price elastic, its marginal revenue is (positive, negative, zero) _____ . If a monopolist's demand curve is price inelastic, its marginal revenue is (positive, negative, zero) _____ . A monopolist will not operate at a point on its demand curve where demand is price (elastic, inelastic) _____ .

positive

negative

inelastic

NUMERICAL PROBLEMS

1 The demand curve for the product of a monopolist is as follows:

QUANTITY PER DAY	PRICE (dollars)
1	30
2	20
3	10
4	6
5	1

a Using these data fill in the following table for the monopolist:

QUANTITY PER DAY	TOTAL REVENUE (dollars)	MARGINAL REVENUE (dollars)
1	_____	
2	_____	_____
3	_____	_____
4	_____	_____
5	_____	_____

b Suppose that the monopolist has a horizontal marginal cost curve, its marginal cost being $9 per unit of output (see the following graph). Its fixed costs are zero. If its costs are as described, and if it is producing 1 unit of output, how much will a second unit of output add to its costs? How much will it add to its revenue? Is it profitable to produce a second unit?

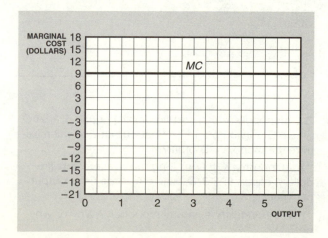

c On the basis of the data given above, what price should the monopolist charge?

d What output should it choose?

e What is the monopolist's profit if it produces at the optimal output rate?

f Suppose that its fixed costs are $10, rather than zero. Will this affect the optimal output rate? Will this affect the firm's profit? If so, how?

2 In a particular industry the minimum value of average cost is reached when a firm produces 1,000 units of output per month. At this output rate, average cost is $1 per unit of output. The demand curve for this product is as follows:

PRICE (dollars per unit of output)	QUANTITY (produced per month)
3.00	1,000
2.00	8,000
1.00	12,000
0.50	20,000

a Is this industry a natural monopoly? Why or why not?

b If the price is $2, how many firms, each of which is producing an output such that average cost is a minimum, can the market support?

3 The graph below pertains to a monopolist. One of the curves is its demand curve, one is its marginal revenue curve, and one is its marginal cost curve.

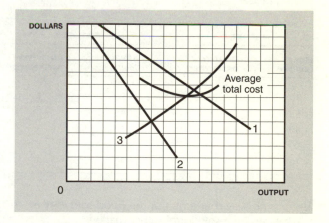

a Which is curve 1?

b Which is curve 2?

c Which is curve 3?

d Show the output rate that the monopolist will choose and the price it will set.

e Does the monopolist choose the output rate at which average total cost is a minimum? Do perfectly competitive firms choose such an output rate in the long run?

f In the graph above show the total profit earned by the monopolist.

g If the monopolist set price equal to marginal cost, what would be its output rate?

4 Suppose that a hypothetical monopoly has the following demand curve and total costs,

OUTPUT SOLD (per month)	PRICE	TOTAL REVENUE	TOTAL COST (per month)	AVERAGE TOTAL COST	MARGINAL COST	MARGINAL REVENUE	PROFIT
				(dollars)			
0	50	_____	40	_____		_____	_____
1	45	_____	50	_____		_____	_____
2	40	_____	70	_____		_____	_____
3	35	_____	95	_____		_____	_____
4	30	_____	125	_____		_____	_____
5	25	_____	165	_____		_____	_____
6	20	_____	225	_____		_____	_____

a Fill in the blanks of the preceding table.

b What output (or outputs) will maximize the monopolist's profits?

c What price will the monopolist choose?

5 Suppose that a monopolist has 5 units of output on hand. It can sell this output in one of two markets. The demand curve for the product in each market is shown below.

	MARKET A		MARKET B	
PRICE (dollars)	QUANTITY DEMANDED	PRICE (dollars)	QUANTITY DEMANDED
70	1	50	1
65	2	45	2
60	3	40	3
50	4	30	4
40	5	20	5

There is no way that a unit of the good sold in one market can be resold in the other market.

a Suppose that the monopolist is selling 4 units in market *A* and none in market *B*. Should it sell the fifth unit in market *A* or market *B*? Why?

b Suppose that the monopolist is selling 4 units in market *B* and none in market *A*. Should it sell the fifth unit in market *A* or market *B*? Why?

c Prove that the monopolist should allocate the goods between markets so that the marginal revenues in the two markets are equal.

6 A monopolist's demand curve is as follows:

PRICE (dollars)	QUANTITY DEMANDED
20	0
15	1
10	2
5	3

The monopolist's total cost (in dollars) equals $3 + 20Q$, where Q is its output rate. What output rate will maximize the monopolist's profit?

7 In industry *X*, a firm's long-run average cost (in dollars) equals $5 + 3/Q$, where Q is the firm's output per year.

a Is this industry a natural monopoly? Why or why not?

b If this industry is monopolized, and if the monopoly maximizes profit, what is the value of marginal revenue in the long run?

c In the long run under the circumstances described in part b, you can be sure that price exceeds a certain amount. What is this amount, and why does price exceed it?

8 A labor union can be viewed as a monopoly for supplying labor services. Use diagrammatic analysis

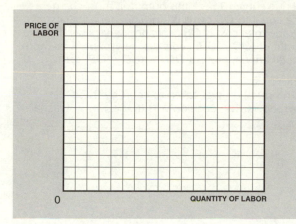

together with the concept of price elasticity of demand to apply what you have learned about monopoly to the way in which a union sets the wage. Your analysis should respond to two specific questions:

a How do the union-set wage and the wage that would be set by competition differ?

b Even though wages for each working union member might rise when the union sets the wage, show that it is possible that total wages to all members taken together might, in fact, fall when wages are raised to the union level.

9 Suppose a firm is a monopolist. The following information is given regarding the firm:

> Marginal revenue = $1{,}000 - 20Q$.
> Total revenue = $1{,}000Q - 10Q^2$.
> Marginal cost = $100 + 10Q$.

Q is the firm's output and P is the price it charges.

How many units of the good produced by this firm would be sold and at what price if:

a The firm sets price as a monopoly?

b The firm is broken up into many firms that behave perfectly competitively?

 ANSWERS TO
TEST YOUR UNDERSTANDING

SECTION 1

TRUE OR FALSE: 1. True 2. True

EXERCISE

1. a. No. The total demand curve lies below the average total cost curve. Thus, regardless of what output the dentist chooses, price would be less than average total cost.

b. Yes. If the dentist charges rich people a price of OP_0, he or she can sell OQ_0 units of dental care to them. If he or she charges poor people a price of OP_1, he or she can sell OQ_1 units of dental care to them. Thus the total output, which equals OQ_2, brings an average price of OP_2, which is greater than average total cost.

c. Yes

d. Yes, the situation depicted in the graph is an example. Without price discrimination, this dentist could not cover his or her costs.

e. No. It is important to note that price discrimination frequently occurs in situations in which the good or

service could be produced without it. Price discrimination is used in these situations to increase the profits of the producer. (From the point of view of society as a whole, price discrimination frequently is objectionable because it violates the conditions for optimal resource allocation described in Chapter 13.)

SECTION 2

TRUE OR FALSE: 1. True 2. True 3. False

SECTION 3

TRUE OR FALSE: 1. False 2. False 3. False

EXERCISES

1. No, because marginal revenue is negative when demand is price inelastic. Thus, a reduction in output will raise total revenue. Since it is also likely to reduce total costs, it will increase profits.

2. −$6,000. $6,000.

3. Marginal cost equals average variable cost over this range of output. Output will be between 2 and 3 units per year, and price will be between $6,000 and $7,000.

4. Output falls to between 1 and 2 units of output, and price increases to between $7,000 and $8,000.

SECTION 4

TRUE OR FALSE: 1. False   2. False

EXERCISES

1. Price would be likely to be lower and output would be likely to be higher under perfect competition. Yes.

2. A firm that is the sole producer of a good is a monopolist, even though it is not sealed off from competition.

3. Perfectly competitive firms can earn high accounting profits if they are more efficient than other firms. Also, in the short run, they may earn large profits.

4. Regulation may not allow firms to go bankrupt when they should do so.

SECTION 5

TRUE OR FALSE: 1. False   2. True   3. True

EXERCISES

1. a. Each firm will produce OQ_0 newspapers, since this is the output where marginal revenue equals marginal cost. To sell this output, each sets a price of OA, since this is the price on the firm's demand curve corresponding to the sale of OQ_0 newspapers. At an output of OQ_0 newspapers, each firm's average total cost equals OE. Thus it loses $(OE - OA)$ cents per newspaper sold, and since it sells OQ_0 newspapers per year, its total annual loss is $OQ_0 \times (OE - OA)$ cents.

b. The monopolist will produce OQ_1 newspapers, since this is the output where its marginal revenue equals marginal cost. (Recall that in this case the firm's demand curve is the same as the monopolist's marginal revenue curve.) To sell this output, it must charge a price equal to OC cents per newspaper. Since its average total cost is OB cents per newspaper, it makes a profit of $(OC - OB)$ cents per newspaper sold, and its total annual profit is $OQ_1 \times (OC - OB)$ cents.

c. Yes.

d. This question was taken to court by these newspapers. The decision was that it was not illegal.

2. Yes.

■ CHAPTER 6

No Electricity, No Modern Civilization

1 ■ Introduction

In the United States, households use a huge amount of electricity. The range of activities requiring electricity is vast, as illustrated vividly by power outages. When power goes out, so do heaters, refrigerators, radios, television sets, air conditioning, elevators, lights, and a host of other mechanisms that are at the core of modern living. Moreover, power is as important to the world's factories and offices as to its homes. Without power, automobile assembly lines, steel plants, airlines, and oil refineries, as well as most other industrial and agricultural units, could not function.

Over 3,000 entities distribute electricity at the retail level to over 100 million customers in the United States, but the bulk of the electricity (about 75 to 80 percent) is supplied by over 100 private investor-owned utilities. (The remainder is supplied by several thousand publicly or cooperatively owned entities.) Investor-owned utilities generally have owned and operated all the facilities required to generate, transmit, and distribute electricity to their retail customers. Also, investor-owned utilities have bought and sold electricity from one another.

2 ■ Public Regulation

Many investor-owned utilities have been monopolies. One way that society has attempted to reduce the harmful effects of monopoly is through **public regulation.** Suppose that the long-run cost curve in a particular industry is such that competition is not feasible. In such a case, society may permit a monopoly to be established, but a commission or some other public body is established to regulate the monopoly's behavior. Among the many such regulatory commissions in the United States are the Federal Energy Regulatory Commission, the Federal Communications Commission, and the Interstate Commerce Commission. They regulate the behavior of firms with monopoly power in the electric power, communication, transportation, and other industries.

Regulatory commissions often set the price or the maximum price at the level at which it equals average total cost, including a "fair" rate of return on the firm's investment. In Figure 6.1 (next page), the price would be established by the commission at *OP*, where the demand curve intersects the average total cost curve (which includes what the commission regards as a fair profit per unit of output). Needless to say, there has been considerable controversy over what constitutes a fair rate of return. Frequently, commissions have settled on 8 to 10 percent. In addition, there has been a good

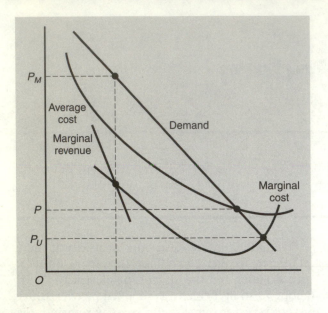

■ **FIGURE 6.1**

Regulation of Monopoly

The price established by a commission might be OP, where the demand curve intersects the average total cost curve. (Costs here include what the commission regards as fair profit per unit of output.) In the absence of regulation, the monopolist would set a price of OP_M (because it would set its output at the point where marginal revenue equals marginal cost). Since OP is less than OP_M, regulation has reduced price in this instance, but not to the point where price equals marginal cost (as in perfect competition). For price to equal marginal cost, price would have to equal OP_U.

deal of controversy over what should be included in the company's "investment" on which the fair rate of return is to be earned. A company's assets can be valued at **historical cost** or at **reproduction cost**—at what the company paid for them or at what it would cost to replace them. If the price level does not change much, these two ap-proaches yield much the same answer. But if prices are rising—as they have been during most of the past 40 years—replacement cost will be greater than historical cost, with the result that the company will be allowed higher profits and rates if replacement cost is used. Most commissions now use historical cost.

3 ■ Regulation of the Electric Industry

From its inception, the electric industry has been regulated, but this regulation has taken various forms. In the latter part of the nineteenth century, local governments issued franchises to attract power companies to their areas. As time went on, these franchises attempted to introduce more control over the companies, but city officials were often inexpert and corruption was frequent. At the turn of the century, there was a widespread cry for reform. Shortly before World War I, most of the states set up public utility commissions with the power to set rates and regulate service, the idea being to transfer control from the local governments to expert commissions. Most public utility regulation is in the hands of state commissions today.

The federal government also has played an important role in regulating the electric power industry since 1935, when the Federal Power Commission (established in 1920) was given power over rates and service in interstate commerce. Also, the commission (now called the Federal Energy Regulatory Commission) was given considerable power over accounting and security issues in the wake of the financial problems of the 1920s and the relative impotence of the state commissions in handling them. Although state commissions still have the principal responsibility for regulating electric power companies, the FERC has introduced many important new policies and methods. It has been stricter in various areas of accounting. Indeed, some firms have tried to get out from under federal regulations by getting rid of their interstate connections. Although conflicts have arisen between the FERC and the state commissions, the FERC's orders generally supplement, rather than override, those of the state commissions.

4 ▪ Does Regulation Affect Prices?

The regulatory commissions and the principles they use have become extremely controversial. *Many observers feel that the commissions are lax, and that they tend to be captured by the industries they are supposed to regulate.* Regulated industries, recognizing the power of such commissions, invest considerable time and money in attempts to influence the commissions. The public, on the other hand, often has only a foggy idea of what the commissions are doing and of whether it is in the public interest. According to come critics like Ralph Nader, "Nobody seriously challenges the fact that the regulatory agencies have made an accommodation with the businesses they are supposed to regulate—and they've done so at the expense of the public." For these and other reasons, some economists believe that regulation has little effect on prices.

It is difficult to isolate and measure the effects of regulation on the average level of prices. Some well-known economists have conducted studies that suggest that regulation has made little or no difference in this regard. Nobel laureate George Stigler and Claire Friedland of the University of Chicago compared the levels of rates charged for electricity by regulated and unregulated electric power companies. They found that there was no significant difference between the average rates charged by the two sets of firms.[1] Other economists challenge Stigler and Friedland's interpretation of their factual findings, and much more research on this topic is needed. Nonetheless, it seems fair to conclude that, although the simple model of the regulatory process presented in Figure 6.1 would predict that regulated prices would be lower, on the average, than unregulated prices (of the same item), the evidence in support of this prediction is much weaker than might be supposed.

5 ▪ Effects of Regulation on Efficiency

Competitive markets provide considerable incentives for a firm to increase its efficiency. Firms that are able to push their costs below those of their competitors reap higher profits than their competitors. As a simple illustration, suppose that firms A and B both have contracts to produce 100 airplanes, and that the price they will get for each airplane is $1 million. Firm A's management, which is diligent, imaginative, and innovative, gets the cost per airplane down to $900,000, and thus makes a healthy profit of $10 million. Firm B's management, which is lazy, unimaginative,

and dull, lets the cost per airplane rise to $1.1 million, and thus loses $10 million. Clearly, firm A is rewarded for its good performance, while firm B is penalized for its poor performance.

One of the primary purposes of regulators is to prevent a monopoly from earning excessive profits. The firm is allowed only a "fair" rate of re-

[1] G. Stigler and C. Friedland, "What Can Regulators Regulate? The Case of Electricity," *Journal of Law and Economics,* 1962. For another point of view, see H. Trebing, "The Chicago School versus Public Utility Regulation," *Journal of Economic Issues,* March 1976.

turn on its investment. One problem with this arrangement is that the firm is guaranteed this rate of return, regardless of how well it performs. If the regulators decide that the Sleepy Hollow Electric and Gas Company should receive a 10 percent rate of return on its investment, this is the rate of return it will receive, regardless of whether the Sleepy Hollow Electric and Gas Company is managed well or poorly. Why is this a problem? Because unlike the competitive firms discussed in the previous paragraph, there is no incentive for the firm to increase its efficiency.

The regulatory process is characterized by long delays. In many regulated industries, a proposed rate increase or decrease may be under consideration for months before a decision is made by the commission. In cases in which such a price change is strongly contested, it may take years for the required hearings to occur before the commission and for appeals to be made subsequently to the courts. Such a delay between a proposed price change and its ultimate disposition is called a **regulatory lag.** Long regulatory lags are often criticized by those who would like the regulatory process to adapt more quickly to changing conditions and to provide more timely decisions. But one advantage of regulatory lags is that they re-

sult in some rewards for efficiency and penalties for inefficiency.

To see why this is so, consider a regulated company whose price is set so that the firm can earn a rate of return of 10 percent (which is what the commission regards as a "fair" rate of return). The firm develops and introduces some improved manufacturing processes which reduce the firm's cost and allow it to earn a 13 percent return. If it takes 18 months for the commission to review the prices it approved before and to modify them to take account of the new (lower) cost levels, the firm earns a higher rate of return (13 percent rather than 10 percent) during these 18 months than if it had not developed and introduced the improved manufacturing processes. This is a reward for efficiency.

Although regulatory lag does restore some of the incentives for efficiency (and some of the penalties for inefficiency), it would be a mistake to believe that it results in as strong a set of incentives as does a competitive market. One of the basic problems with regulation is that, *if a regulatory commission prevents a firm from earning higher-than-average profits, there may be relatively little incentive for the firm to increase its efficiency and innovate.*

6 ▪ The Dawn of a New Competitive Era

In recent years, there have been more and more signs that traditional regulation of the electric power industry is about to be supplanted. For example, in April 1994, the California Public Utilities Commission announced that it was considering a plan whereby all electric consumers, including residential consumers, would be allowed to purchase electricity from the supplier of their choice, not just the local electric utility. For example, power might be obtained from other western states or from Canada or Mexico. The object of this plan was to reduce electric rates by creating a competitive market for electric utilities and independent power producers.

Pacific Gas and Electric, the country's largest private utility, is based in San Francisco. It serves

more than 12 million people distributed over about 90,000 square miles, and has a mix of plants including hydroelectric, fossil fuel, geothermal, and nuclear. During the late 1980s and early 1990s, Pacific Gas and electric made a number of major changes in its operations, with an eye toward preparing for more competition. For one thing, it reduced its work force by about 12 percent during 1992 to 1994, and thus saved about $200 million per year.

In 1992, Pacific Gas and Electric decided not to build new power plants within its service area. Instead, it purchases the extra power it needs from other companies that can provide it cheaply. Further, it has reduced the rates of its 120 largest industrial customers by $100 million per year, and thus lowered the chances that they will switch to rival utilities and other independent power generators.

At the same time, Pacific Gas and Electric (through its subsidiary, the U.S. Generating Company) has built a considerable number of new plants on the East Coast. For example, it has established coal-fired plants at New Bedford, Massachusetts; Northhampton, Pennsylvania; and Jacksonville, Florida. Why? Because returns tend to be higher than in California. When Stanley Skinner became chairman of the firm in 1994, he said, "We're at a critical point of change as the industry becomes unstructured and the pace of competition quickens. Pacific Gas and Electric has stayed ahead of the curve of change, and that has been our source of strength."[2]

7 ▪ Should Indian Point 3 Be Shut Down?

Not all electric power plants are privately owned, as you have already seen. The New York Power Authority, a state-owned utility, runs nuclear power plants, including Indian Point 3, a plant located about 35 miles north of midtown Manhattan. In late 1994, hearings were held to determine the future of the plant, which supplied power to government customers, such as the Metropolitan Transportation Authority and New York City, but which had been closed for almost two years because of safety concerns. Eighteen years old, the plant had been on the Nuclear Regulatory Commission's watch list of least-safe plants for more than a year.

Nuclear power plants have very large fixed costs for capital and maintenance. Thus, it is important that such a plant be reliable. That is, it should be in operation a large percentage of the time. Unfortunately, since it started up in 1976, Indian Point 3 has run only about half the time, its performance in this regard being poorer than any nuclear plant in the New York region. Given its high average fixed costs, it has been estimated that what it charged for power was higher than what Consolidated Edison, the large privately owned New York utility, charged.

Whether to shut down Indian Point 3 was not a simple decision. Much more was involved than a simple comparison of the cost per kilowatt-hour of electricity. As S. David Freeman, president of the New York Power Authority, said, closing a reactor is "like a divorce; not all of your costs go away."[3] For example, when Sacramento closed its biggest nuclear plant, costs were large for many years because of security and maintenance of the facilities required to tend to the spent fuel. As of the beginning of 1997, no decision had been made to close the Indian Point 3 plant.

[2] *New York Times,* June 3, 1994.

[3] *New York Times,* September 26, 1994, p. B6.

8 ▪ Applying Economics: Electricity Demand

The following problem deals with the market for electricity in the United States.

PROBLEM 6.1 D. Chapman, T. Tyrell, and T. Mount estimated that the long-run price elasticity of demand for electricity by all U.S. residential consumers is 1.2, the income elasticity of demand for electricity by such consumers is 0.2, and the cross elasticity of demand for electricity with respect to the price of natural gas is 0.2.

a. If the price of electricity is expected to rise

by 1 percent in the long run, by how much would the price of natural gas have to change to offset the effect of this increase in electricity's price on the quantity of electricity consumed?

b. Among residential consumers in a Chicago suburb, holding other factors constant, there was the following relationship between their aggregate money income and the amount of electricity they consumed.

AGGREGATE INCOME (millions of dollars)	QUANTITY OF ELECTRICITY CONSUMED
100	300
110	303
121	306

Is this evidence consistent with the results by Chapman, Tyrell, and Mount? If not, what factors might account for the discrepancy?

c. Would you expect the income elasticity of demand and the cross elasticity of demand to be higher or lower in the short run than in the long run? Why?

d. According to Lester Taylor of the University of Arizona, the price elasticity of demand for electricity by industry tends to be greater than the price elasticity of demand for electricity by residential consumers. Why do you think this is true?

e. Given the findings in part d, would you expect that the price of electricity to industry would be less than to residential consumers? Why or why not?

9 ▪ Applying Economics: Costs of Electricity

The following two problems deal with the cost of producing electricity in the United States.

PROBLEM 6.2 Laurits Christensen of the University of Wisconsin and William Greene of New York University estimated the long-run cost function for the production of electric power in the United States. Using data for all investor-owned utilities with more than $1 million in revenues, their results for 1955 and 1970 were as shown in Figure 6.2.

a. In Chapter 2, you learned that the long-run average cost curve is U-shaped. That is, as output gets larger and larger, long-run average cost eventually rises. Is this true in Figure 6.2? If not, what factors may help to explain why it is not true?

b. In 1970, what seemed to be the minimum efficient size of a firm in the electric power industry? (The minimum efficient size of a firm is defined as the smallest output at which long-run average cost is at or close to a minimum.)

c. Was the long-run average cost curve in the electric power industry the same in 1970 as in 1955? If not, why was it different?

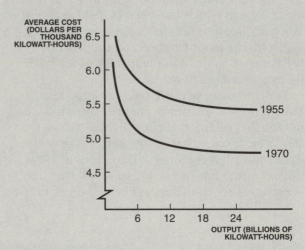

FIGURE 6.2

Long-Run Average Cost of Producing Electric Power

d. Can you use the curves in Figure 6.2 to estimate the long-run average costs of producing electric power in 1996? Why or why not?

PROBLEM 6.3 Environmentalists, economists, and consumers have exhibited great interest in renewable energy sources like solar energy, photovoltaic cells, and wind energy. Hydro-Quebec, a Canadian utility that exports hydro-electric power to the northeastern United States, planned to install about 100 wind machines on the south shore of the St. Lawrence River in 1995 and 1996. This $110 million project was expected to produce enough energy to power 15,000 houses.

California is the biggest user of wind. Windmills produce about 1.2 percent of its electricity. According to Donald Aiken, California could generate one-third of its electricity with wind if every site were used. Moreover, in his view, New York State, which has more wind power available than California, could utilize wind to satisfy half of its electricity requirements if all potential sites were used.[4]

a. Why is wind energy used to produce such a small percentage of electric power in the United States?

b. According to unpublished data obtained by the U.S. Department of Energy, the costs per kilowatt-hour for electricity generated by wind have been as shown in Table 6.1. If the cost of producing power by coal or oil is 6 cents per kilowatt-hour, will the use of wind energy grow rapidly? Why or why not?

c. Bernard Fox, president of Northeast Utilities, which provides electric power for most of Connecticut and large parts of Massachusetts and New Hampshire, has reported that his company is "paying $215 million a year for electricity from plants that burn wood or garbage that it could generate itself for $50 million. The

[4] *New York Times,* April 12, 1994.

▪ TABLE 6.1

Cost of Electricity from Wind in the United States

	EARLY 1980S	1992
Operations and maintenance costs (cents per kilowatt-hour)	4	1
Total costs (cents per kilowatt-hour)	12–37	8
Cumulative industry investment	$10–20 million	$3 billion

SOURCE: OECD, *Projected Costs of Generating Electricity* (Paris: OECD, 1993).

reason is that it priced the power in the early 1980s by comparing it to the cost of oil, which was then high, and the estimated future cost, which was even higher. But the price of oil fell."[5] Does this indicate that changes in the prices of oil, coal, and other inputs, as well as their current levels, will influence the rate at which wind energy is utilized? Why or why not?

d. Considerable research and development is being carried out to improve methods of extracting power from the wind. According to the Organization for Economic Cooperation and Development, the cost per kilowatt-hour for electricity generated from wind in the United States is projected to fall to 4 cents by the year 2000.[6] Does it seem likely that wind energy will become a much more significant source of electric power by the year 2000? Why or why not?

[5] *New York Times,* April 12, 1994, p. B2.

[6] OECD, *Projected Costs of Generating Electricity* (Paris: OECD, 1993), p. 157.

10 ▪ Applying Economics: The Pricing of Electricity

The following two problems deal with ways in which electricity is priced.

PROBLEM 6.4 The demand for electricity varies markedly over time. During the hottest summer days when air conditioners are running full blast, electricity demand is much greater than normal. Also, electricity demand may be higher during the day than at night. Suppose for simplicity that the demand curve for electricity

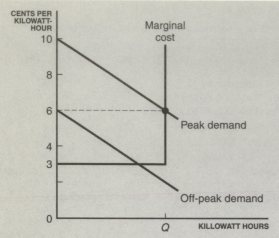

■ **FIGURE 6.3**

Marginal Cost Curve and Peak and Off-Peak Demand Curves: Case I

during periods of peak demand (summer and daytime) is the higher curve in Figure 6.3, and the demand curve for electricity during off-peak periods (winter and nighttime) is the lower curve in Figure 6.3.

Also, assume that, so long as the firm operates within its capacity, the marginal costs of an electric power company are the fuel costs of 3 cents per kilowatt-hour. But once the firm is producing at capacity, the marginal costs in the short run increase indefinitely because no more electricity can be produced, regardless of how much additional fuel the firm uses. The total capacity of all the firms in the electric power industry is *OQ* kilowatt-hours.

a. During the period of peak demand in Figure 6.3, what will be the price of electricity?

b. What is the marginal cost of serving the off-peak customers in Figure 6.3? Is it only the extra fuel needed to produce an extra kilowatt-hour from the existing plant? Why or why not?

c. From the point of view of economic efficiency, would you favor a lower price in the off-peak period than in the peak period in Figure 6.3? If so, what price would you favor for the off-peak period? Why?

d. Suppose that the situation is as shown in Figure 6.4 rather than in Figure 6.3. Is the marginal cost of serving the off-peak customers the extra fuel needed to produce an extra kilowatt-hour from the existing plant? Why or why not?

e. In Figure 6.4, what will be the price of electricity in the peak period?

f. To promote economic efficiency, would you favor a lower price in the off-peak period than in the peak period if the situation is as shown in Figure 6.4? If so, what price would you favor for the off-peak period? Why?

g. In many countries, including the United States, customers pay a price for electricity that is based on the time they use it. Table 6.2 shows some examples. From the point of view of society, does this make sense? Why or why not?

PROBLEM 6.5 Traditionally, electric utilities have charged a lower price for increased consumption. For example, the rate schedule might be:

First 50 kilowatt-hours per month	12¢ per kilowatt-hour
Next 50 kilowatt-hours per month	8¢ per kilowatt-hour
Next 100 kilowatt-hours per month	6¢ per kilowatt-hour
Next 200 kilowatt-hours per month	4¢ per kilowatt-hour

a. Suppose that each consumer purchases 400 kilowatt-hours per month. Why would the local electric utility prefer the above schedule to a flat charge of 4 cents per kilowatt hour?

b. Does the above rate schedule encourage high rates of electricity consumption? Why or why not?

c. In the past several years, there has been a movement away from rate schedules of this sort. Environmentalists and conservationists have been particularly critical of such rate schedules. Why?

d. In 1994, Peco Energy Company, a large Philadelphia electric utility, proposed to the Pennsylvania Public Utility Commission that it

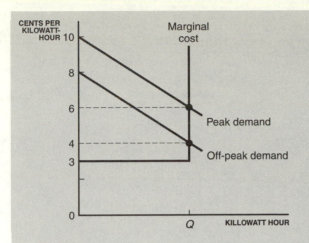

▪ **FIGURE 6.4**

Marginal Cost Curve and Peak and Off-Peak Demand Curves: Case II

▪ **TABLE 6.2**

Effect of Time of Day on Price of Electricity, England, Indonesia, and Kenya

COUNTRY AND TIME OF DAY	(CENTS PER KILOWATT-HOUR)
England	
7 A.M. to midnight	5.91
Midnight to 7 A.M.	2.78
Indonesia	
6 P.M. to 10 P.M.	4.64
10 P.M. to 6 P.M.	3.20
Kenya	
8 A.M. to 10 P.M.	3.75
10 P.M. to 8 A.M.	2.25

SOURCE: E. Mansfield, *Microeconomics* (9th ed.; New York: Norton, 1997).

spend $10 million on energy conservation. For example, it would pay each of its customers up to $100 for energy-efficient home improvements like weather stripping. To help pay the tab, it proposed to add a little more than 25 cents to the average residential electric bill.[7] Why should an electric power company want to promote energy conservation? Why should consumers pay the tab?

[7] *Philadelphia Inquirer,* May 30, 1994.

11 ▪ Applying Economics: Differences among Electric Utilities in Prices Charged

The following two problems deal with the variation among electric utilities in the prices they charge.

PROBLEM 6.6 Enormous differences exist among electric utilities in the prices charged. As shown in Table 6.3 (next page), the price charged by Long Island Lighting Company was over three times that charged by Puget Sound Power and Light Company. These differences influence where firms establish their plants and other facilities. General Motors has estimated that electricity accounts for about $700 of the cost of each auto it makes. In the late 1980s, Air Products and Chemicals closed a plant in New Jersey because electricity prices were too high. According to Peter Sipple of Air Products and Chemicals, "When we site a plant, we not only look for which utility is the low-cost utility today, but which is going to be the low-cost utility for the next 10 to 15 years."[8]

a. Hydroelectric power, which is relatively cheap, is important in the Pacific Northwest. Does this help to explain some of the price differences in Table 6.3? If so, how?

b. Kentucky has abundant coal, whereas utilities in New England, New York City, and

[8] *Philadelphia Inquirer,* May 29, 1994.

■ TABLE 6.3

Ten Utilities with the Highest Prices and Ten Utilities with the Lowest Prices, 1993[a]

UTILITY	LOCATION	PRICE (cents per kilowatt-hour)
HIGHEST PRICES		
Long Island Lighting Co.	Long Beach, N.Y.	17.3
Hawaii Electric Light Co.	Hilo, Hawaii	16.6
Consolidated Edison Co.	New York, N.Y.	16.5
Nantucket Electric Co.	Nantucket, Mass.	16.4
Orange and Rockland Utilities	Middleton, N.Y.	15.8
Commonwealth Electric Co.	New Bedford, Mass.	14.2
Duquesne Light Co.	Pittsburgh, Pa.	13.9
Maui Electric Co.	Wailuku, Hawaii	13.7
Peco Energy Co.	Philadelphia, Pa.	13.7
Cleveland Electric	Cleveland, Ohio	13.5
LOWEST PRICES		
Washington Water Power Co.	Lewiston, Idaho	4.3
Pacific Power and Light Co.	Yakima, Wash.	4.3
Washington Water Power Co.	Spokane, Wash.	4.6
Idaho Power Co.	Boise, Idaho	4.8
Idaho Power Co.	Ontario, Ore.	4.8
Portland General Electric Co.	Portland, Ore.	5.2
Kentucky Utilities	Lexington, Ky.	5.2
Minnesota Power and Light Co.	Duluth, Minn.	5.4
Montana Power Co.	Billings, Mont.	5.5
Puget Sound Power and Light Co.	Bellevue, Wash.	5.5

[a] Note that these prices refer to a later year and to a different country than do those in Table 6.2; hence, they are not comparable without a variety of adjustments.

SOURCE: *Philadelphia Inquirer*, May 29, 1994.

Hawaii use oil that comes from far away. Does this help to explain some of the price differences in Table 6.3? If so, how?

c. According to Irwin Popowsky, the Pennsylvania consumer advocate, Duquesne Light Company "invested in some of the most expensive, least economic nuclear plants in the country."[9] Does this help to explain some of the differences in Table 6.3? If so, how?

[9] Ibid.

PROBLEM 6.7 Long Island Lighting Company (LILCO) began construction of its Shoreham nuclear power plant in 1973. Plagued by work stoppages, low productivity, design changes, theft, defective equipment, and management problems, construction of the plant took 12 years. Its cost, reflecting very large cost overruns, was about $4.5 billion. Moreover, the plant encountered difficulties as soon as it was completed because both county and state officials refused to take part in evacuation plans and one government board denied LILCO a license for the plant.

a. A six-year study by the New York Public Service Commission found that $1.4 billion of the plant's total cost had been spent imprudently. According to New York law, costs found to be imprudent could not be passed on to consumers. Who had to pay these costs?

b. by 1986, 60 percent of the remaining $3.1 billion of Shoreham's costs were included in LILCO's rate base (the investment on which a fair rate of return is to be earned). These costs accounted for 26 percent of the firm's rate of 11.5 cents per kilowatt-hour, which was almost double the national average. (See Table 6.4) What percentage of this disparity between LILCO's price and the national average was due to Shoreham?

c. Even without Shoreham, LILCO's price exceeded the national average, one reason, according to industry observers, being that it relied on oil-burning plants. Why should this result in a relatively high price?

d. Many Long Island residents were concerned about the safety and economic desirability of Shoreham. By late 1985, there was talk of getting rid of LILCO and replacing it with a public power authority. On January 30, 1986, New York Governor Mario Cuomo created a blue-ribbon panel to study "the feasibility and economic viability of replacing the Long Island Lighting Company with a public owned utility."[10] What would be the advantages of creating a public-owned utility? What would be the disadvantages of such a utility?

[10] J. Gomez-Ibanez and J. Kalt, *Cases in Microeconomics* (Englewood Cliffs, N.J.: Prentice-Hall, 1990), p. 201.

▪ TABLE 6.4

Comparison of Rates of Long Island Lighting Company with Average Investor-Owned Utility in the United States, 1984 (cents per kilowatt-hour)

	LONG ISLAND LIGHTING COMPANY	AVERAGE INVESTOR-OWNED UTILITY
Operations and maintenance costs	6.2	3.8
Depreciation	0.4	0.4
Interest and return	2.1	1.1
Income taxes	1.3	0.5
Other taxes	1.5	0.4
Rate	11.5	6.2

SOURCE: J. Gomez-Ibanez and J. Kalt, *Cases in Microeconomics* (Englewood Cliffs, N.J.: Prentice-Hall, 1990).

Subsequently, Governor Cuomo ordered the dismantling of the Shoreham nuclear power plant because an evacuation plan had not been approved and adequate power would eventually be available from Quebec.[11] The company agreed to abandon the plant in exchange for rate increases and other financial compensation. In 1994, the dismantling of the plant was completed; it had taken five years and cost $180 million.[12] In 1994, Governor Cuomo proposed that New York State buy LILCO, but this proposal was rejected. In July 1997, New York State finally agreed to a takeover of most of LILCO, but the deal had to be approved by Federal agencies.[13]

[11] *Regulation*, Winter 1992, p. 12.

[12] *New York Times*, October 13, 1994.

[13] *New York Times*, July 21, 1997.

12 ▪ Applying Economics: The Tennessee Valley Authority

The following problem deals with the Tennessee Valley Authority, a major example of a publicly owned supplier of electric power.

PROBLEM 6.8 During the 1920s and 1930s, there were many proposals that the federal government take responsibility for flood control on the Tennessee River, but local electric utilities feared that by constructing dams, the federal government would provide not just flood control but electric power too. In 1933, the Roosevelt administration created the Tennessee Valley Authority (TVA), which was a construction project designed to control floods, build housing, develop agriculture, and provide electric power. Between 1933 and 1974, the TVA constructed or acquired 29 hydroelectric plants and 11 big steam-generating plants (total capacity more than 20,000 megawatts) at a cost of about $6 billion. Most of its power has been generated in the steam plants.

a. Leonard Weiss of the University of Wisconsin has summarized the case for public power as follows: "Private firms might never have undertaken [public power projects] . . .

because the power produced was not enough to pay for the entire investments but the public gained in many ways where full remuneration was not feasible."[14] In what ways did the public gain?

b. Critics of public power point to the importance and longevity of the pork barrel in Washington and elsewhere. They point out that public funds are likely to go to areas with powerful representatives in Congress. Why is that a problem?

c. In 1954, TVA requested funds from Congress to build a steam-driven electric plant. Congress rejected the proposal. How would you decide whether this was the right decision?

[14] L. Weiss, *Case Studies in American Industry* (3d ed.; New York: Wiley, 1980), pp. 150–51.

13 ▪ Conclusion

Pacific Gas and Electric, LILCO, and the Tennessee Valley Authority are quite different in location, organization, and financial history; yet they all have been part of the market for electricity. To understand this market, you must have a working knowledge of the theory of monopoly, and to understand why the electric power industry has

been regulated, you must know how monopoly differs from perfect competition and with what effects. The material taken up in Chapters 4 and 5 is essential if you want to make sense of the many changes that are likely to occur in the near future in this key industry.

PART THREE

Oligopoly, Monopolistic Competition, and Antitrust Policy

■ CHAPTER 7
Oligopoly and Monopolistic Competition

Essentials of **Oligopoly and Monopolistic Competition**

- Oligopoly is a market structure in which a few firms dominate the market.

- In some cases, oligopolists get together and form a cartel.

- In oligopoly, as in a game, each firm must take account of its rivals' reactions to its actions; thus, economists have used game theory to analyze the behavior of oligopolists.

- Price tends to be higher under oligopoly than under perfect competition, and oligopolistic industries tend to spend more on advertising and style changes than perfectly competitive industries do.

- The key feature of monopolistic competition is product differentiation. Some economists believe that a firm under this form of market organization will tend to operate with excess capacity.

- The firm is likely to produce less and charge a higher price under monopolistic competition than under perfect competition.

1 ■ Oligopoly

Oligopoly (domination by a few firms) is a common and important market structure in the United States; many industries, like steel, automobiles, oil, and electric equipment, are oligopolistic. The key characteristic of oligopoly is **interdependence,** actual and perceived, among firms. Each oligopolist formulates its policies with an eye to their effect on its rivals. Since an oligopoly contains a small number of firms, any change in one firm's price or output influences the sales and profits of its competitors. Moreover, since there are only a few firms, each must recognize that changes in its policies are likely to result in changes in the policies of its rivals as well.

What factors are responsible for oligopoly? First, in some industries, low production costs cannot be achieved unless a firm is producing an output equal to a substantial portion of the total available market. Because of these economies of scale, there will tend to be few firms. Second, there may be economies of scale in sales promotion in certain industries, and this too may promote oligopoly. Third, entry into some industries may be blocked by the requirement that a firm build and maintain a large, complicated, and expensive plant or have access to patents or scarce raw materials. Only a few firms may be in a position to obtain all these necessary prerequisites for membership in the club.

Unlike perfect competition, monopoly, and monopolistic competition, there is no single unified model of oligopoly behavior. Instead, *there are a number of models, each based on a somewhat different set of assumptions concerning the relationships among the firms that make up the oligopoly*. Basically, no single model exists because economists have not yet been able to devise one that would cover all the relevant cases adequately. Economics, like all sciences, continues to grow; perhaps someone —indeed, perhaps someone reading this book— may be able to develop such a model before too long. However, it doesn't exist now.

---

2 ▪ The Kinked Oligopoly Demand Curve

Let's start with a model that sheds light on the stability of oligopolistic prices. Empirical studies of pricing in oligopolistic markets have often concluded that prices in such markets tend to be rigid. A classic example occurred in the sulfur industry. From 1926 to 1938, the price of sulfur remained at $18 a ton, despite great shifts in demand and production costs. This example is somewhat extreme, but it illustrates the basic point. Prices in oligopolistic industries often have remained unchanged for fairly long periods. A well-known model designed to explain this price rigidity was advanced by Paul Sweezy, who asserted that, *if an oligopolist cuts it price, it can be pretty sure that its rivals will meet the reduction. On the other hand, if it increases its price, its rivals may not change theirs.*

Figure 7.1 shows the situation. The oligopolist's demand curve is represented by *DAD'* and the current price is *OP*. There is a "kink" in the demand curve because *under the postulated circumstances the demand curve for the oligopolist's product is much less elastic for price decreases than for price increases.* Why is it less elastic for price decreases than for price increases? Because price decreases will be met by the firm's rivals. This means that the firm will not be able to take any appreciable amount of sales away from its rivals by such de-

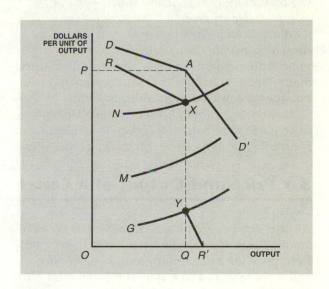

▪ **FIGURE 7.1**

The Kinked Oligopoly Demand Curve

The oligopolist's demand curve is *DAD'*, the current price being *OP*. Because of the kink in the demand curve, the marginal revenue curve consists of two segments, *RX* and *YR'*. Since the marginal cost curve is *M*, the most profitable output is *OQ*. Moreover, it remains the most profitable output—and *OP* the most profitable price—even if the marginal curve shifts to *N* or *G* or if the demand curve shifts considerably (within limits).

creases. The effect of such decreases will be to increase the quantity demanded of the firm's product, since the total quantity demanded of the entire industry's product will increase due to the price reduction. But the increase in the quantity demanded of the firm's product will be relatively modest. On the other hand, if the firm raises its price, it is assumed that its rivals do not follow suit. Thus the quantity demanded of the firm's product will fall considerably if it raises its price.

PREDICTION: RIGID PRICES

Because of the kink in the demand curve, the marginal revenue curve in Figure 7.1 is not continuous. It consists of two segments, *RX* and *YR'*. Given that the firm's marginal cost curve is *M*, the most profitable output is *OQ*, where the marginal cost curve intersects the vertical line, *XY*. Moreover, OQ *remains the most profitable output—and* OP *the most profitable price—even if the marginal cost curve shifts considerably (even to* N *or* G*) or if the demand curve shifts (within limits)*. One would expect price to be quite rigid under these circumstances, since many types of changes in costs and demand will not alter the price that maximizes profits.

This theory, although useful in explaining why price tends to remain at a certain level (*OP* in Figure 7.1), is of no use at all in explaining why

this level, rather than another, currently prevails. It simply takes the current price as given. Thus this theory is an incomplete model of oligopoly pricing. Nonetheless, it seems to explain some of the relevant facts; and for this and other reasons, Sweezy's model has achieved a place in the theory of oligopoly.

 TEST YOUR UNDERSTANDING

True or false?

_____ **1** Prices in oligopolistic markets tend to fluctuate a good deal more than prices under perfect competition.

_____ **2** The theory of the kinked oligopoly demand curve is an incomplete model of oligopoly pricing.

_____ **3** Because of the kink in the demand curve, the marginal cost curve consists of two distinct segments.

3 ▪ Price and Output of a Cartel

A cartel is an open, formal collusive arrangement among firms. If a cartel is established to set a uniform price for a particular product, what price will it charge? As a first step, the cartel must estimate the marginal cost curve for the cartel as a whole. Then it must find the output where its marginal cost equals its marginal revenue, since this output maximizes the total profit of the cartel members. In Figure 7.2 this output is *OQ*. Thus, if it maximizes cartel profits, the cartel will choose a price of *OP*, which is the monopoly price. In short, *the cartel acts like a monopolist with a number of plants or divisions, each of which is a member firm*.

How will the cartel allocate sales among the member firms? If its aim is to maximize cartel profits, it will allocate sales to firms in such a way

that the sum of the firms' costs is minimized. But this allocation is unlikely to occur in reality. The allocation process is a bargaining process, and firms with the most influence and the shrewdest negotiators are likely to receive the largest sales quotas, even though this decreases the total profits of the cartel. Moreover, high-cost firms are likely to receive larger sales quotas than would be the case if total cartel profits were maximized, since they would be unwilling otherwise to stay in the cartel. In practice, it appears that cartels often divide markets geographically or in accord with a firm's level of sales in the past.

There is a constant temptation for oligopolists to cheat on any collusive agreement. If other firms stick to the agreement, any firm that cheats

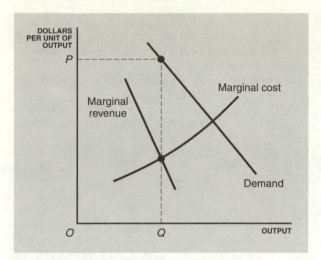

▪ **FIGURE 7.2**

Price and Output of a Cartel

The marginal cost curve shows the marginal cost for the cartel as a whole. On the basis of the demand curve for the industry's product, the cartel can derive the marginal revenue curve. The output that maximizes the total profit of the cartel members is *OQ*. The corresponding price is *OP*.

temptation is particularly great when an industry's sales are depressed and its profits are low. Every firm is hungry for business, and it is difficult to resist. Moreover, one firm may be driven to cheating because it hears that another firm is doing so, with the eventual result that the collusive agreement is torn apart.

In order to coordinate their behavior without outright collusion, some industries contain a **price leader.** It is quite common in oligopolistic industries for one or a few firms to set the price and for the rest to follow their lead. Two types of price leadership are the dominant-firm model and the barometric-firm model. *The **dominant-firm** model applies to cases in which the industry has a single large dominant firm and a number of small firms.* The dominant firm sets the price for the industry, but it lets the small firms sell all they want at that price. *The **barometric-firm** model applies to cases in which one firm usually is the first to make changes in price that are generally accepted by other firms in the industry.* The barometric firm may not be the largest or most powerful firm. Instead, it is a reasonably accurate interpreter of changes in basic cost and demand conditions in the industry as a whole. According to some authorities, barometric price leadership often occurs as a response to a period of violent price fluctuation in an industry, during which many firms suffer and greater stability is widely sought.

—by cutting its price below that agreed to under the collusive arrangement—can take a lot of business away from the other firms and increase its profits substantially, at least in the short run. This

---

 TEST YOUR UNDERSTANDING

True or false?

_____ **1** A cartel may act like a monopolist with a number of plants or divisions, each of which is a member firm.

_____ **2** In practice, it appears that cartels often divide markets geographically or in accord with a firm's level of sales in the past.

_____ **3** Collusion is often difficult to achieve and maintain because an oligopoly contains an unwieldy number of firms, or the product is quite heterogeneous or the cost structures of the firms differ considerably.

Exercises

1 Suppose that a cartel consists of four firms, each of which has a horizontal marginal cost curve. For each firm, marginal cost equals $4. Suppose that the marginal revenue curve for the cartel is $MR = 10 - 2Q$, where MR is marginal revenue (in dollars) and Q is the cartel's output per year (in thousands of units). What output rate will the cartel choose?

2 According to the Senate Subcommittee on Antitrust and Monopoly, "Some system of marketing quotas, whether overt or carefully hidden, must underlie any price-fixing agreement." Comment and evaluate.

3 Discuss the incentives that each firm in Exercise 1 would have to cheat on the collusive agreement described there.

4 The Organization of Petroleum Exporting Countries (OPEC) is a cartel that includes many of the world's leading oil producers, such as Saudi Arabia, Nigeria, Venezuela, Indonesia, and others. Nonetheless, OPEC does not supply all the world's oil. Important oil producers outside OPEC include the United States, Mexico, Canada, Britain, Norway, and Australia. Suppose that the supply curve for non-OPEC oil and the world demand curve for oil are as shown below.

a. If the price of oil is $30 per barrel, what is the quantity demanded of OPEC oil?

b. If the price of oil is $40 per barrel, what is the quantity demanded of OPEC oil?

c. From the above graph, how can you determine the demand curve for OPEC oil?

d. Given the demand curve for OPEC oil, how can you determine the price that would maximize OPEC's profit?

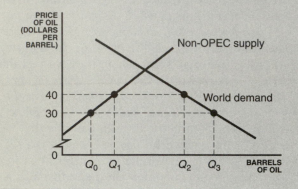

4 ▪ The Theory of Contestable Markets

During the late 1970s and early 1980s, the theory of contestable markets was born. This theory has received considerable attention. Because it is so new, it is very difficult to predict how significant it will eventually turn out to be. But it has had enough influence to warrant discussion.

What is a **contestable market?** It is a market into which entry is absolutely free, *and exit is absolutely costless.* Any firm can leave the market without impediment and can get back whatever costs it incurred in entering. *The key characteristic of a contestable market is its vulnerability to hit-and-run entry.* A firm can enter such a market, make a quick profit, and leave without cost, if this seems to be the most profitable course of action.

Just as a perfectly competitive market is only a model, so the same is true of a contestable market. Nonetheless, models of this sort can be very useful and suggestive. At least three characteristics of a contestable market are worth noting. First, it can be shown that *profits are zero in equilibrium in a contestable market*. If profits were positive, a firm could enter the market, undercut the price of the firm with profits, and make a profit, after which it could leave the market, if this seemed desirable. Thus profits will be eroded by such price cutting until they are zero. This is true regardless of how few firms exist in the contestable market. Because each is subject to such hit-and-run tactics, profits are eliminated.

Second, the organization of a contestable market is efficient in the sense that *the average cost of production is as low as possible.* Again because of the possibility of hit-and-run entry, firms in such a market must maintain their costs at the lowest possible level in the long run. If they do not do so, more efficient firms will enter, undercut their price, and force them to reduce their costs or withdraw from the market.

Third, if a contestable market contains two or more sellers, *their prices, in equilibrium, must equal their marginal costs.* As you will see in the next chapter, there are fundamental reasons why economists favor markets in which price equals marginal cost. One reason that perfect competition is favored by so many economists is that price equals marginal cost. Thus it is very interesting that this desirable feature of perfect competition exists as well in contestable markets.

In the past, it has often been presumed that these three outcomes—zero profits, minimum cost, and price equal to marginal cost—would be very unlikely to occur when there were few sellers. The theory of contestable markets implies that this is not necessarily the case. However, many critics say that this theory is based on very unrealistic assumptions concerning entry and exit. In particular, they point out that entry often is not free and that exit seldom is costless.

 TEST YOUR UNDERSTANDING

True or false?

_____ **1** In a contestable market, the average cost of production is as low as possible.

_____ **2** Profits may or may not be zero in equilibrium in a contestable market.

_____ **3** In a contestable market, exit is costless.

Exercise

1 Explain why the average cost of production will be as low as possible in a contestable market. What is the significance of this fact?

5 ▪ The Theory of Games

As pointed out at the beginning of this chapter, the rivalry among oligopolists has many of the characteristics of a game. As in a game, in oligopoly each firm must take account of its rivals' reactions to its actions. For this reason, an oligopolistic firm cannot tell what effect a change in its output will have on the price of its product and on its profits unless it can guess how its rivals will respond to the change. To understand game theory, you have to know what a **game** is. It is a competitive situation in which two or more persons pursue their own interests and no person can dictate the outcome. Poker is a game, and so is a situation in which two firms are engaged in competitive advertising campaigns. A game is described in terms of its players, rules, payoffs, and information conditions. These elements are common to all conflict situations.

DEFINITIONS OF TERMS

More specifically, a **player,** whether a single person or an organization, is a decision-making unit. Each player has a certain amount of resources, and the **rules of the game** describe how these resources can be used. Thus the rules of poker indicate how bets can be made and which hands are better than others. A **strategy** is a complete specification of what a player will do under each contingency in the playing of the game. Thus a corporation president might tell her subordinates how she wants an advertising campaign to start, and what should be done at subsequent times in response to various actions of competing firms. The game's outcome clearly depends on each player's strategies. A player's **payoff** varies from game to game. It is win, lose, or draw in checkers, and various sums of money in poker.

A SIMPLE TWO-PERSON GAME

For simplicity consider *two-person games*—games with only two players. The relevant features of a two-person game can be shown by constructing a **payoff matrix.** To illustrate, suppose that two big soap producers, Procter & Gamble and Lever Brothers, are about to stage rival advertising campaigns and that each firm has a choice of strategies. Procter & Gamble can choose to concentrate on either television ads or magazine ads; Lever Brothers has the same choice. Table 7.1 shows what will happen to the profit of each firm when each combination of strategies is chosen. If both firms concentrate on TV ads, Procter & Gamble gains $3 million and Lever Brothers gains $2 million. If Procter & Gamble concentrates on TV ads and Lever Brothers concentrates on magazine ads, Procter & Gamble gains $4 million and Lever Brothers gains $3 million. And so on.

PROCTER & GAMBLE'S VIEWPOINT

Given the payoff matrix in Table 7.1, there is a definite optimal choice (called a **dominant strategy**) for each firm. To see that this is the case, begin by looking at the situation from Procter & Gamble's point of view. If Lever Brothers concentrates on TV ads, Procter & Gamble will make more money ($3 million rather than $2 million) if it concentrates on TV rather than magazines. If Lever Brothers concentrates on magazines, Procter & Gamble will make more money ($4 million rather than $3 million) if it concentrates on TV rather than magazines. Thus, regardless of the strategy chosen by Lever Brothers, Procter & Gamble will do best to concentrate on TV.

LEVER BROTHERS' VIEWPOINT

Now look at the situation from the point of view of Lever Brothers. If Procter & Gamble concentrates on TV ads, Lever Brothers will make more money ($3 million rather than $2 million) if it concentrates on magazines rather than TV. If Procter & Gamble concentrates on magazines, Lever Brothers will make more money ($4 million rather than $3 million) if it concentrates on magazines rather than TV. Thus, regardless of the strategy chosen by Procter & Gamble, Lever Brothers will do best to concentrate on magazines.

THE SOLUTION OF THE GAME

At this point, the solution of this game is clear. *Procter & Gamble will concentrate on TV ads and Lever Brothers will concentrate on magazine ads*. This is the best that either firm can do.

NOTEWORTHY FEATURES OF THIS GAME

Several points should be noted concerning this game. First, in this game, both players have a **dominant strategy**—a strategy that is its best choice regardless of what the other player does.

▪ **TABLE 7.1**
Payoff Matrix: Procter & Gamble and Lever Brothers

POSSIBLE STRATEGIES FOR P & G	POSSIBLE STRATEGIES FOR LEVER BROTHERS	
	CONCENTRATE ON TV	CONCENTRATE ON MAGAZINES
Concentrate on TV	P & G's profit: $3 million Lever's profit: $2 million	P & G's profit: $4 million Lever's profit: $3 million
Concentrate on magazines	P & G's profit: $2 million Lever's profit: $3 million	P & G's profit: $3 million Lever's profit: $4 million

Not all games have a dominant strategy for each player.

Second, in this game the best strategy for each player is the same regardless of whether the players choose their strategies simultaneously or one of the players goes first. For example, Procter &

Gamble will choose to concentrate on TV regardless of whether it picks its strategy before, after, or at the same time as Lever Brothers. This is not true for all games. In some games, a player's best strategy depends on the timing of the player's move.

 TEST YOUR UNDERSTANDING

True or false?

_____ **1** In game theory, given the payoff matrix, each firm will always have two equally optimal choices.

_____ **2** A dominant strategy is a strategy that is the firm's best choice regardless of what the other player does.

_____ **3** Every game has a dominant strategy for each player.

Exercises

1 Every week, *Time* and *Newsweek*, two leading news magazines, must each pick a story to emphasize on their covers. Suppose that there are two possibilities for next week's cover: a terrorist attack on a U.S. ambassador or a military agreement between the United States and China. Suppose that the editor of each magazine wants to maximize readership, and that the number of people reading each magazine depends on which story is featured on the cover of each magazine as follows:

| | NEWSWEEK'S CHOICE | |
	TERRORIST ATTACK	U.S.–CHINA AGREEMENT
TERRORIST ATTACK	Newsweek: 6 million readers Time: 10 million readers	Newsweek: 7 million readers Time: 9 million readers
TIME'S CHOICE		
U.S.–CHINA AGREEMENT	Newsweek: 6 million readers Time: 9 million readers	Newsweek: 5 million readers Time: 8 million readers

a. Does *Time* have a dominant strategy? If so, what is it?

b. Does *Newsweek* have a dominant strategy? If so, what is it?

c. If you were *Newsweek*'s editor, which story would you expect Time to put on its cover? Why?

d. Given the answer to part c, which choice would you make if you were the editor of *Newsweek*?

e. What do you think will be on the cover of each magazine? Why?

2 In Table 7.1, suppose that Procter & Gamble's profit if it concentrates on TV and if Lever Brothers concentrates on magazines is $1 million, rather than $4 million. If the rest of the payoff matrix is unchanged, do Procter & Gamble and Lever Brothers still have dominant strategies? Explain.

3 Under the conditions given in Exercise 2, can Procter & Gamble predict which strategy Lever Brothers will adopt? (Hint: Does Lever Brothers have a dominant strategy?) If its prediction is correct, which strategy should Procter & Gamble choose?

6 ■ Comparison of Oligopoly with Perfect Competition

Economists have constructed a number of types of models of oligopoly behavior—the cartel models, price leadership models, contestable market models, various game theoretic models, and others—but there is no agreement that any of these models is an adequate general representation of oligopoly behavior. For this reason, it is difficult to estimate the effects of an oligopolistic market structure on price, output, and profits. Nonetheless, if a perfectly competitive industry were turned overnight into an oligopoly, it is likely that changes would occur.

1 *Price would probably be higher than under perfect competition.* The difference between the oligopoly price and the perfectly competitive price will depend on the number of firms in the industry and the ease of entry. The larger the number of firms and the easier it is to enter the industry, the closer the oligopoly price will be to the perfectly competitive level.

2 If the demand curve is the same under oligopoly as under perfect competition, it also follows that *output will be less under oligopoly than under perfect competition.* However, it is not always reasonable to assume that the demand curve is the same in both cases, since the large expenditures for advertising and product differentiation incurred by some oligopolies may tend to shift the demand curve to the right. Consequently in some cases both price and output may tend to be higher under oligopoly than under perfect competition.

3 *Oligopolistic industries tend to spend more on advertising, product differentiation, and style changes than do perfectly competitive industries.* The use of some resources for these purposes is certainly worthwhile, since advertising provides buyers with information, and product differentiation allows greater freedom of choice. Whether oligopolies spend too much for these purposes is by no means obvious. However, there is a widespread feeling among economists, based largely on empirical studies (and hunch), that in some oligopolistic industries such expenditures have been expanded beyond socially optimal levels.

4 One might expect on the basis of the models presented in this chapter that *the profits earned by oligopolists would be higher, on the average, than the profits earned by perfectly competitive firms.* This conclusion is supported by some statistical evidence. In an early study, Joe Bain of the University of California found that firms in industries in which the largest few firms had a high proportion of total sales tended to have higher rates of return than firms in industries in which the largest few firms had a small proportion of total sales. Nonetheless, this is a controversial topic.

✓ TEST YOUR UNDERSTANDING

True or false?

_____ **1** If a perfectly competitive industry were transformed into an oligopoly, the price of the industry's product would probably go up.

_____ **2** Oligopolistic industries tend to spend more on advertising, product differentiation, and style changes than perfectly competitive industries.

_____ **3** In some cases, both price and output may tend to be higher under oligopoly than under perfect competition.

Exercises

1 One of the biggest legal battles in antitrust history occurred in 1965, when the Ohio Valley Electric Corporation sued Westinghouse and General Electric for damages. According to the Ohio Valley Electric Corporation, it had been overcharged for electric equipment it purchased during the period when the electric equipment producers conspired to raise prices. In the subsequent trial, it built its case in considerable part on the following graph, which shows

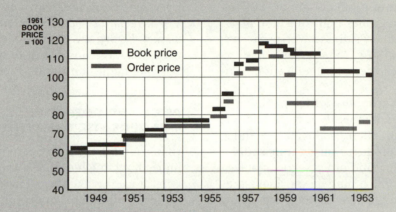

the relationship between average order prices and book prices during 1948 to 1963.

a. The book price was the published price issued by General Electric and other electrical producers. The average order price was the average price actually negotiated for such equipment. Does it appear that this equipment was frequently sold below its book price?

b. There was evidence that the electric equipment producers had held meetings to control prices before 1959. Is the relationship between average order price and book price different in the post-1959 period than in the earlier years? Is this difference what you would expect if the conspiracy ended in 1959?

c. According to the Ohio Valley Electric Corporation, in the absence of a conspiracy, the actual order price would have borne the same relationship to the book price in the early 1950s as in the early 1960s. Specifically, it would have been about 75 percent of the book price. Do you agree? Why or why not?

2 On July 4, 1987, Governor Mario Cuomo of New York, together with the state legislature, put through a bill to terminate a half-century of restriction on milk sales in the state. This bill ended rules that blocked milk dealers in one county from selling in another county, and that denied milk licenses to dealers

whose entry into the state was deemed "destructive" to the New York market. Prior to the passage of the 1987 bill, five major dealers dominated the sale of milk in New York City. According to the *New York Times*, the old state rules were used by state administrators to deny licenses to potential entrants that might reduce price. What precipitated the 1987 bill rescinding these rules was the entrance of a New Jersey firm, Farmland Dairies, into the New York City market in December 1986, after a federal court gave it permission to begin deliveries in the city.

a. After Farmland entered the New York City milk market, do you think that the price of milk changed? If so, how?

b. According to the state attorney general, Robert Abrams, the old rules "encouraged and facilitated" price fixing by the New York dairies. How did the old rules do this?

c. Farmland's president, Marc Goldman, said that Farmland's production costs were only several cents a gallon less than in New York; yet the price dropped between 30 and 71 cents per gallon in New York supermarkets after Farmland's entry. Why did the price drop by so much more than the cost differential?

d. Members of Local 584 of the Teamsters charged that many of their milk truck drivers would lose their jobs because of deregulation of the milk industry. The Milk Industry Council, which represents milk dealers, said that many small milk dealers would be put out of business. Doesn't this mean that it was socially unwise to enact the 1987 bill?

7 ▪ Monopolistic Competition

The key feature of **monopolistic competition** is **product differentiation.** In contrast to perfect competition, under which all firms sell an identical product, under monopolistic competition firms sell somewhat different products. We are talking here about what sometimes may appear to be subtle differences—Macy's dresses versus Stern's dresses, or McDonald's Big Mac versus Burger King's Whopper—but they are significant in economic analysis.

One sector of the economy where product differentiation occurs frequently is retail trade. Producers try to make their product a little different, by altering the product's physical makeup, the services they offer, and other such variables. Other differences—which may be spurious—are based on brand name, image making, advertising claims, and so on. In this way, the producers have some monopoly power, but it usually is small because the products of other firms are very similar.

In perfect competition, the firms included in an industry are easy to determine because they all produce the same product. But if product differentiation exists, it is no longer easy to define an industry, since each firm produces a somewhat different product. Nevertheless, it may be useful to group together firms that produce similar products and call them a **product group.** You can formulate a product group called "toothpaste" or "toilet soap" or "chocolate bars." The process by which firms are combined into product groups is bound to be somewhat arbitrary, since there is no way to decide how close a pair of substitutes must be to belong to the same product group. But it is assumed that meaningful product groups can be established.

Besides product differentiation, other conditions must be met for an industry to qualify as a case of monopolistic competition. First, *there must be a large number of firms in the product group.* In other words, the product must be produced by perhaps 50 to 100 or more firms, with each firm's product a fairly close substitute for the products of the other firms in the product group. Second, *the number of firms in the product group must be large*

enough that each firm expects its actions to go unheeded by its rivals and is unimpeded by possible retaliatory moves on their part. If there is a large number of firms, this condition will normally be met. Third, *entry into the product group must be relatively easy, and there must be no collusion, such as price fixing or market sharing, among firms in the product group.* If there is a large number of firms, collusion generally is difficult, if not impossible.

PRICE AND OUTPUT UNDER MONOPOLISTIC COMPETITION

Under monopolistic competition, what determines how much output a firm will produce, and what price it will charge? If each firm produces a somewhat different product, it follows that the demand curve facing each firm slopes downward to the right. That is, if the firm raises its price slightly, it will lose some, but by no means all, of its customers to other firms. And if it lowers its price slightly, it will gain some, but by no means all, of its competitors' customers. This is in contrast to perfect competition, under which the demand curve facing each firm is horizontal.

Figure 7.3 shows the short-run equilibrium of a monopolistically competitive firm. The firm in the short run will set its price at OP_0 and its output rate at OQ_0, since this combination of price and output will maximize its profits. We can be sure that this combination of price and output maximizes profit because marginal cost equals marginal revenue at this output rate. Economic profits will be earned because price, OP_0, exceeds average total costs, OC_0, at this output rate.

What will the equilibrium price and output be in the long run? One condition for long-run equilibrium is that *each firm be making no economic profits or losses,* since entry or exit of firms will occur otherwise—and entry and exit are incompatible with long-run equilibrium. Another condition for long-run equilibrium is that *each firm be maximizing its profits.* At what price and output will both these conditions be fulfilled?

Figure 7.4 (page 116) shows that the long-run

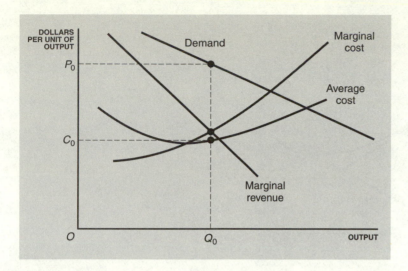

▪ **FIGURE 7.3**

Short-Run Equilibrium: Monopolistic Competition

The firm will set price at OP_0 and its output rate at OQ_0 since marginal cost equals marginal revenue at this output. It will earn a profit of C_0P_0 per unit of output.

equilibrium is at a price of OP_1 and an output of OQ_1. The zero-economic-profit condition is met at this combination of price and output since the firm's average cost at this output equals the price, OP_1. And the profit-maximization condition is met since the marginal revenue curve intersects the marginal cost curve at this output rate.

EXCESS CAPACITY AND PRODUCT DIVERSITY

A famous conclusion of the theory of monopolistic competition is that *a firm under this form of market organization will tend to operate with excess capacity.* In other words, the firm will construct a plant smaller than the minimum-cost size of plant and operate at less than the minimum-cost rate of output. Why? Because, as shown in Figure 7.4, the long-run average cost curve must be tangent in long-run equilibrium to the demand curve. (This tangency condition ensures that, if the firm produces the profit-maximizing output, it obtains a zero economic profit, in accord with the condi-

tions for long-run equilibrium.) Thus, since the demand curve is *downward sloping*, the long-run average cost curve must also be *downward sloping* at the long-run equilibrium output rate. Consequently, the firm's output must be less than OQ_2, the output rate at which long-run average costs are minimized, since the long-run average cost curve slopes downward only at output rates less than OQ_2.

This is an interesting conclusion, since it suggests that monopolistically competitive industries will be overcrowded with firms. There may be too many firms (from society's point of view), each of which is smaller than required to minimize its unit costs. However, one must be careful to recognize that, if there were fewer firms, there would be less diversity of products. Whether the apparently excessive number of firms is really excessive (from society's viewpoint) depends on whether, if there were fewer firms, the reduction in unit costs would outweigh the loss to consumers due to less product diversity.

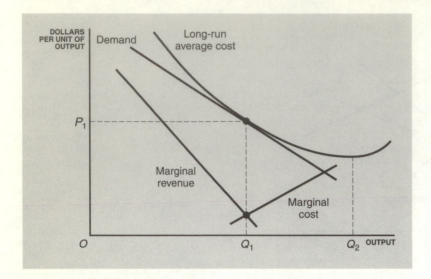

FIGURE 7.4

Long-Run Equilibrium: Monopolistic Competition

The long-run equilibrium is at a price of OP_1 and an output of OQ_1. There are zero profits since long-run average cost equals price. Profits are being maximized since marginal cost equals marginal revenue at this output.

 TEST YOUR UNDERSTANDING

True or false?

_____ **1** A monopolistically competitive firm's short-run demand and cost curves are as follows:

PRICE (dollars)	QUANTITY DEMANDED		TOTAL COST (dollars)	OUTPUT
8	1		5	1
7	2		7	2
6	3		9	3
4	4		11	4
3	5		20	5

This firm, if it maximizes profit, will choose an output rate of 4.

_____ **2** In the previous question, the number of firms in this industry will tend to increase if all firms in the industry are like this one.

_____ **3** In question 1, if the firm's fixed cost rises by $5, the firm's short-run output rate will be unaffected.

_____ **4** In question 1, if the firm's costs rise by $10, the number of firms in this industry will tend to decrease (because of exit) if all firms in the industry are like this one.

Exercises

1 If the demand curve confronting a monopolistically competitive firm is highly elastic, the firm is likely to have less excess capacity than if it is relatively inelastic. Explain why this is true.

2 Explain how a firm's output and price are determined under monopolistic competition in:
   a. The short run.
   b. The long run.

8 ▪ Comparisons with Perfect Competition and Monopoly

Market structure is important because it influences market behavior. We need to know how the behavior of a monopolistically competitive industry differs from that of a perfectly competitive industry or a monopoly. Suppose that there exists a magician who can transform an industry's structure by a wave of a wand. (John D. Rockefeller was a real-life magician who transformed the structure of the oil industry in the late 1800s—but he seemed to favor mergers, mixed with some ungentlemanly tactics, over wands.) Suppose that the magician makes an industry monpolistically competitive, rather than perfectly competitive or monopolistic. What difference would it make in the behavior of the industry? Or, to take a less fanciful case, what difference would it make if government action or technological change resulted in such a change in an industry's market structure? It is difficult to say how the industry's behavior would be affected, because output would be heterogeneous in one case and homogeneous in the other, and its cost curves would probably vary with its organization. But many economists seem to believe that differences of the following kind can be expected.

1 *The firm under monopolistic competition is likely to produce less and charge a higher price than the firm under perfect competition.* The demand curve confronting the monopolistic competitor slopes downward to the right. Consequently, marginal revenue must be less than price. Thus, under monopolistic competition, marginal cost must also be less than price, since marginal revenue must equal marginal cost at the firm's profit-maximizing output rate. But if marginal cost is less than price, the firm's output rate must be smaller—and the price higher—than if marginal cost equals price, which is the case under perfect competition. On the other hand, *relative to monopoly, monopolistically competitive firms are likely to have lower profits, greater output, and lower price.* The firms in a product group might obtain positive economic profits if they were to collude and behave as a monopolist. Such an increase in profits would benefit the

producers. Consumers would be worse off because of the higher prices and smaller output of goods.

2 As noted in the previous section, *a firm under monopolistic competition may be somewhat inefficient because it tends to operate with excess capacity.* Each firm builds a smaller-than-minimum-cost plant and produces a smaller-than-minimum-cost output. More firms exist than if there were no excess capacity; this results in some overcrowding of the industry. Inefficiencies of this sort would not be expected under perfect competition. However, these inefficiencies may not be very great, since the demand curve confronting the monopolistically competitive firm is likely to be highly elastic; and the more elastic it is, the less excess capacity the firm will have.

3 *Firms under monopolistic competition will offer a wider variety of styles, brands, and qualities than firms under perfect competition. Moreover, they will spend much more on advertising and other selling expenses than a perfectly competitive firm would.* Whether this diversity is worth its cost is hard to say. Some economists are impressed by the apparent waste in monopolistic competition. They think it results in too many firms, too many brands, too much selling effort, and too much spurious product differentiation. But if the differences among products are real and are understood by consumers, the greater variety of alternatives available under monopolistic competition may be very valuable to consumers. The proper evaluation of the social advantages and disadvantages of product differentiation is a problem economists have only partially solved.

 TEST YOUR UNDERSTANDING

True or false?

_____ **1** A firm under monopolistic competition may be somewhat inefficient because it tends to operate with excess capacity.

_____ **2** Under perfect competition, firms will offer a greater variety of styles, brands, and qualities than under monopolistic competition.

_____ **3** The firm under monopolistic competition is likely to produce less than the firm under perfect competition.

▪ CHAPTER REVIEW

KEY TERMS

oligopoly

price leader

dominant firm

barometric firm

contestable market

game

player

rules of the game

strategy

payoff matrix

dominant strategy

monopolistic competition

product differentiation

product group

COMPLETION QUESTIONS

1 The demand and cost curves of a monopolistically competitive firm are given below. If the firm charges a price of $4, its profits will equal about _____. If the firm charges a price of $6, its profits will equal about _____. If the firm charges a price of $8, its profits will equal about _____. In the long run, (entry, exit) _____ will occur in this industry.

ANSWERS TO COMPLETION QUESTIONS

−$12

$10

$18

entry

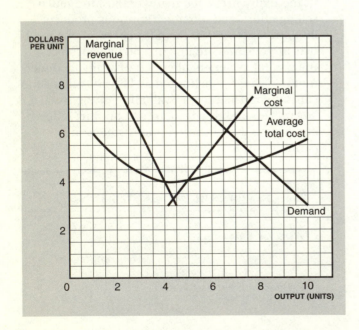

2 A monopolistically competitive firm is in long-run equilibrium. Its marginal revenue equals $5. If its marginal revenue plus its economic profit equal one-half its price, its price equals _____ and its marginal cost equals _____ .

$10
$5

3 All firms in an industry have marginal cost curves that are horizontal lines at $5 per unit of output. If they combine to form a cartel, the cartel's marginal cost (will, will not) _____ be $5 per unit of output. If the cartel maximizes profit, its marginal revenue will be (greater than, smaller than, equal to) _____ $5 per unit of output, and its price will be (greater than, smaller than, equal to) _____ $5 per unit of output.

will

equal to

greater than

4 Under monopolistic competition, the firm is likely to produce (more, less) _____ and charge a (higher, lower) _____ price than under perfect competition.

less
higher

5 Relative to pure monopoly, monopolistically competitive firms are likely to have (greater, lower) _____ profits, (greater, lower) _____ output, and (higher, lower) _____ prices.

lower   greater
lower

6 The demand curve for the oligopolist's product may be less elastic for price _____ than for price _____ .

decreases
increases

7 In some games, a player's best strategy depends on the _____ of the player's move.

timing

8 Not _____ games have a dominant strategy for each player.

all

9 If the demand curve is the same under oligopoly as under perfect competition, then under oligopoly price will tend to be _____ and output _____ than under perfect competition.

higher
lower

10 Oligopoly occurs in markets where there are (few, many) _____ sellers and it has two forms: one in which all sellers produce an identical product and the other in which the sellers produce somewhat different products.

few

11 Under monopolistic competition, the demand curve slopes (downward, upward) _____ to the right. Consequently, marginal revenue must be (less, more) _____ than price. Thus, under monopolistic competition, marginal cost must also be (less, more) _____ than price, since marginal revenue must (equal, exceed) _____ marginal cost at the firms' profit-maximizing output rate. But if marginal cost is (less, more) _____ than price, the firm's output rate must be (less, more) _____ and the price (higher, lower) _____ than if marginal cost equals price, which is the case under perfect competition.

downward

less

less
equal

less
less
higher

12 A _____ is an open, formal, collusive arrangement among firms. In many countries in Europe, _____ have been common and legal. In the United States, most _____ arrangements, whether secret or open, were declared illegal by the Sherman Antitrust Act, which was passed in _____ .

cartel

cartels
collusive

1890

13 There is always a temptation for oligopolists to _____ on any collusive agreement. So long as the other firms stick to the agreement, any firm that _____ its price below that agreed to under the collusive arrangement can take a lot of business away from the other firms and (decrease, increase) _____ its profits substantially, at least in the short run.

cheat

cuts

increase

14 In order to coordinate their behavior without outright collusion, some industries contain a _____ . It is quite common in oligopolistic industries for one or a few firms to _____ the price and for the rest to follow their lead. Two types of _____ leadership are the _____ model and the _____ model.

price leader

set
price
dominant-firm   barometric-firm

NUMERICAL PROBLEMS

1 The cost curves and demand curve of the Jones Manufacturing Company, a monopolistically competitive firm, are shown below.

a What output rate will this firm choose?

b What price will it charge?

c How great will its profits be?

d Is this a long-run equilibrium situation?

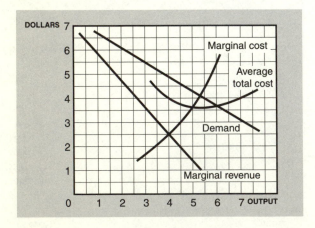

2 The Smith Manufacturing Company is an oligopolist. As perceived by the firm, its demand and cost curves are as shown in the following graph.

a What output rate will this firm choose?

b What price will it charge?

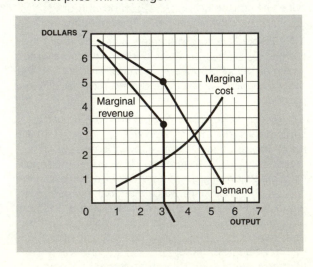

3 Suppose that an industry is composed of 20 firms, each with a horizontal marginal cost curve. In particular, each firm can produce at a marginal cost of $2 per unit of output. Variation in industry output does not affect the cost curves of the individual firms.

a If the industry is cartelized, what will the marginal cost curve of the cartel look like?

b The marginal revenue for the cartel is $3 when it produces 100 units of output, $2 when it produces 200 units of output, and $1 when it produces 300 units of output per month. Will it produce more or less than 100 units of output per month?

c Will it produce more or less than 300 units per month?

d Can you tell what output level it will choose? If so, what is it?

4 The Alpha Corporation, a hypothetical oligopolist, sets its price in the following way. When it operates at 80 percent of capacity, its average total costs are $1.50 per unit of output. Adding a 20 percent markup to this figure, the firm arrives at a price of $1.80. The demand curve for the firm's product follows.

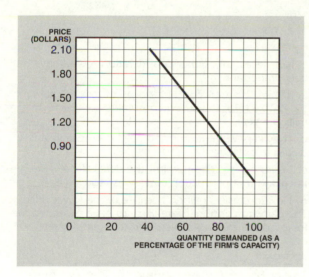

a Can the firm sustain a price of $1.80? Why or why not?

b What does this indicate about this pricing method?

5 An oligopolistic industry selling a homogeneous product is composed of two firms. The two firms set the same price and share the total market equally. The demand curve confronting each firm (assuming that the other firm sets the same price as this firm) and each firm's total cost function are shown above on the right.

PRICE (dollars)	QUANTITY DEMANDED	OUTPUT	TOTAL COST (dollars)
10	5	5	45
9	6	6	47
8	7	7	50
7	8	8	55
6	9	9	65

a Assuming that each firm is right in believing that the other firm will charge the same price that it does, what is the price that each should charge?

b Under the assumption in part a, what output rate should each firm set?

c Is there bound to be entry into this industry in the long run?

d Is there any incentive for each firm to cut its price to somewhat below its rival's price? If so, what is it?

6 Suppose that if industry A sets its price above $5 per unit, a swarm of new firms will enter the industry and take a very large proportion of the sales away from the established firms.

a What effect does this have on the shape of the demand curve confronting the established firms in the industry?

b What effect do you think that this will have on the industry's pricing practices?

7 Suppose that the payoff matrix for a two-person zero-sum game is as follows:

PLAYER B'S POSSIBLE STRATEGIES	PLAYER A'S POSSIBLE STRATEGIES	
	1	2
I	$4,000	$3,000
II	$2,000	$2,500

The two players are A and B. Each has two possible strategies (A's being 1 and 2, and B's being I and II). The values are gains for B (= losses for A).

a Which is A's optimal strategy?

b Which is B's optimal strategy?

c How much will player A lose, according to the solution of the game?

d How much will player B gain, according to the solution of the game?

ANSWERS TO
TEST YOUR UNDERSTANDING

SECTION 1

TRUE OR FALSE: 1. True 2. True 3. True

SECTION 2

TRUE OR FALSE: 1. False 2. True 3. False

SECTION 3

TRUE OR FALSE: 1. True 2. True 3. True

EXERCISES

1. The cartel will choose an output of 3,000 units per year.

2. This seems true.

3. If the other members of the cartel held their prices fixed (in accord with the agreement), each firm would have a strong motive for lowering price, expanding sales, and increasing profits.

4. a. $(OQ_3 - OQ_0)$ barrels of oil.

b. $(OQ_2 - OQ_1)$ barrels of oil.

c. To determine the quantity of OPEC oil demanded at each price, subtract the quantity of non-OPEC oil supplied at that price from the quantity of oil demanded in the world as a whole at that price.

d. Find the marginal revenue curve corresponding to the demand curve for OPEC oil, and determine the output at which this marginal revenue curve intersects OPEC's marginal cost curve. The profit-maximizing price is the one that results in OPEC's selling this quantity of output.

SECTION 4

TRUE OR FALSE: 1. True 2. False 3. True

EXERCISE

1. If firms do not maintain their average costs of production at the lowest possible levels, other firms will under-cut their price.

SECTION 5

TRUE OR FALSE: 1. False 2. True 3. False

EXERCISES

1. a. Yes. Regardless of whether *Newsweek* has the terrorist attack or the U.S.-China agreement on its cover, *Time* has a higher readership if it exhibits the terrorist attack on its cover.

b. No. If *Time* has the terrorist attack on its cover, *Newsweek* will get more readers by putting the U.S.-China agreement on its cover. If *Time* has the U.S.-China agreement on its cover, *Newsweek* will get more readers by putting the terrorist attack on its cover.

c. You would expect *Time* to put the terrorist attack on

its cover because this is its dominant strategy, as pointed out in the answer to part a.

d. Given that you would expect *Time* to put the terrorist attack on its cover (since this is its dominant strategy), you would put the U.S.-China agreement on *Newsweek's* cover, because this would produce a higher readership (7 million versus 6 million).

e. On the basis of the foregoing analysis, *Time* would be expected to have the terrorist attack on its cover, and *Newsweek* the U.S.-China agreement on its cover.

2. Lever Brothers still has a dominant strategy (concentrate on magazines), but Procter & Gamble no longer has a dominant strategy. If Lever Brothers concentrates on TV, Proctor & Gamble should concentrate on TV, but if Lever Brothers concentrates on magazines, Procter & Gamble should concentrate on magazines.

3. Lever Brothers's dominant strategy is to concentrate on magazines; thus, this would seem to be what it will do. If so, Procter & Gamble should concentrate on magazines too.

SECTION 6

TRUE OR FALSE: 1. True 2. True 3. True

EXERCISES

1. a. Yes.

b. Yes. Yes.

c. Not necessarily. Other considerations could have been important.

2. a. Yes. The retail cost of a gallon of milk fell from $2.42 to $1.98; this saved consumers about $100 million a year.

b. They kept out entrants and helped keep only a few dairies in existence.

c. Because the profit margin—the difference between price and unit production cost—was reduced.

d. No. Consumers gained because of the lower price. The gains to consumers are likely to have exceeded the losses to the existing dealers and their employees.

SECTION 7

TRUE OR FALSE: 1. False 2. True 3. True 4. True

EXERCISES

1. As the demand curve becomes closer and closer to horizontal, it is tangent to the long-run average cost curve at a point that is closer and closer to the minimum point.

2. a. See Figure 7.3.

b. See Figure 7.4.

SECTION 8

TRUE OR FALSE: 1. True 2. False 3. True

■ CHAPTER 8

Industrial Concentration and the Antitrust Laws

Essentials of **Industrial Concentration and the Antitrust Laws**

- Monopoly imposes a burden on society by misallocating resources.

- Many economists look with disfavor on serious departures from perfect competition; yet a certain amount of monopoly power is inevitable in practically all real-life situations.

- The market concentration ratio, which shows the percentage of total sales or production accounted for by the four largest firms, is a measure of how concentrated an industry is.

- Three important antitrust laws are the Sherman Act (1890), the Clayton Act (1914), and the Federal Trade Commission Act (1914).

- Two important antitrust cases decided in 1982 were the antitrust suit against the American Telephone and Telegraph Company and that against IBM Corporation.

1 ■ The Case against Monopoly

Many people oppose monopolies on the grounds that they gouge the consumers by charging a higher price than would otherwise exist—a price that can be sustained only because monopolists artificially limit the supply. In other words, these people claim that monopolists reap higher profits than would be possible under perfect competition and that these profits are at the expense of consumers, who pay higher prices than under perfect competition. Is their claim accurate? As you saw in Chapter 5, a monopolist will reap higher profits than firms under perfect competition and consumers will pay higher prices under monopoly than under perfect competition. But is this bad?

To the extent that the monopolist is rich and the consumers are poor, you are likely to answer yes. Also, to the extent that the monopolist is less deserving than the consumers, you are likely to answer the same thing. But suppose the monopolist is a selfless philanthropist who gives to the poor. Is monopoly still socially undesirable? The answer remains yes, because *monopoly imposes a burden on society by misallocating resources. In the presence of monopoly, the price system cannot be relied on to direct the allocation of resources to their most efficient use.*

THE MISALLOCATION OF RESOURCES

To see more precisely how monopoly interferes with the proper functioning of the price system, suppose that all industries other than the shoe industry are perfectly competitive. The shoe industry, however, has been monopolized. How does this cause a misallocation of resources? Under fairly general circumstances, a good's price can be taken as a measure of the social value of an extra unit of the good. Thus, if the price of a pair of socks is $1, the value to the consumer of an extra pair of socks can be taken to be $1.

Moreover, under fairly general circumstances, a good's marginal cost can be taken as a measure of the cost to society of an extra unit of the good. Thus, if the marginal cost of a pair of shoes is $30, the cost to society of producing an extra pair of shoes can be taken to be $30.

In perfectly competitive industries, price is set equal to marginal cost, as you saw in Chapter 4. Thus each of the competitive industries produces up to the point where the social value of an extra unit of the good (which equals price) is set equal to the cost to society of producing an extra unit of the good (which equals marginal cost). This is the amount each of these industries should produce —the output rate that will result in an optimal allocation of resources.

WHY IS THE COMPETITIVE OUTPUT OPTIMAL?

To see that this is the optimal output rate, consider what happens when an industry produces up to the point where the social value of an extra unit of the good is *more* than the cost to society of producing an extra unit. This isn't the socially optimal output rate because a 1-unit increase in the output rate will increase the social value of output by more than the social cost of production; this means that it will increase social welfare. Thus, since a 1-unit increase in the output rate will increase social welfare, the existing output rate cannot be optimal.

Next, consider what happens when an industry produces up to the point where the social value of an extra unit of the good is *less* than the cost to society of producing the extra unit. This isn't the socially optimal output rate because a 1-unit decrease in the output rate will decrease the social value of output by less than the social cost of production; this means that it will increase social welfare. Thus, since a 1-unit decrease in the output rate will increase social welfare, the existing output rate cannot be optimal.

Putting together the results of the previous two paragraphs, it follows that the socially optimal output rate must be at the point where the social value of an extra unit of the good *equals* the so-

cial cost of producing an extra unit of the good. Why? Because if the output rate is not optimal when the social value of an extra unit of the good exceeds or falls short of the cost to society of producing the extra unit, it must be optimal only when the two are equal.

THE MONOPOLIST PRODUCES TOO LITTLE

Now return to the shoe industry—the sole monopolist. Is the shoe industry producing the optimal amount of shoes? The answer is no. Like any monopolist, it produces at the point where marginal revenue equals marginal cost. Thus, since marginal revenue is *less* than price (as was proved in Chapter 5), the monopolist produces at a point where price is *greater* than marginal cost. Consequently, *the monopolistic industry produces at a point where the social value of an extra unit of the good (which equals price) is greater than the cost to society of producing the extra unit (which equals marginal cost).* As you saw in a previous paragraph, this means that the monopolist's output rate is too small. A 1-unit increase in the output of shoes will increase the social value of output by more than the social cost of production.

In summary, *monopoly results in a misallocation of resources since too little is produced of the monopolized good.* Here lies the economist's principal complaint against monopoly: it results in a misallocation of resources. Too little is produced of the monopolized good. Society is less well off—in terms of its own tastes and potentialities—than it could be. The price system, which would not lead to, or tolerate, such waste if all industries were perfectly competitive, is not allowed to perform as it should.

INCOME DISTRIBUTION, EFFICIENCY, AND TECHNOLOGICAL CHANGE

Misallocation of resources is only part of the economist's brief against monopoly. As already has been pointed out, *monopoly redistributes income in favor of the monopolists.* In other words, monopolists can fatten their own purses by restricting their outputs and raising their prices. Admittedly, there is no scientific way to prove that monopolists are less deserving than the rest of the population, but it is also pretty difficult to see why they are more deserving.

In addition, *since monopolists do not have to face direct competition, they are likely to be less diligent in controlling costs and in using resources efficiently.* As Sir John Hicks put it, "The best of all monopoly profits is a quiet life." Certainly we all dream at times of being able to take life easy. It would be strange if monopolists, having succeeded in insulating themselves from direct competition, did not take advantage of the opportunity—not open to firms in perfectly competitive markets—to relax a bit and worry less about pinching pennies. For this reason, economists fear that, to use Adam Smith's pungent phrase, "Monopoly . . . is a great enemy to good management."

Further, *it is often claimed that monopolists are slow to innovate and adopt new techniques and products.* This lethargy stems from the monopolist's freedom from direct competition. Innovation tends to be disruptive, whereas old ways, like old shoes, tend to be comfortable. The monopolist may be inclined, therefore, to stick with "time-honored" practices. Without question, competition is an important spur to innovation and to the rapid diffusion of innovations. But there are well-known arguments on the other side as well. Some economists argue that substantial monopoly power promotes innovation and technological change. Much more will be said on this score below.

COMPLAINTS AGAINST OLIGOPOLY

Although economists are more concerned about monopoly than about oligopoly or monopolistic competition, this does not mean that they give either oligopoly or monopolistic competition a clean bill of health. Even though oligopoly has aroused less public indignation and opposition than out-and-out monopoly, an oligopoly can obviously be just as deleterious to social welfare. After all, *if oligopolists engage in collusion, open or tacit, their behavior with regard to price and output may resemble a monopolist's.* Only if there is real competition among the oligopolists can you expect price to be pushed closer to marginal cost under oligopoly than under monopoly. If oligopolists "cooperate" and "maintain orderly markets," the amount of social waste may be no less than under monopoly.

COMPLAINTS AGAINST MONOPOLISTIC COMPETITION

Monopolistic competition can also be a socially wasteful form of market organization. As you saw above, monopolistically competitive markets may be characterized by overcrowding and excess capacity. In addition, price under monopolistic competition—as well as under monopoly and oligopoly—will exceed marginal cost, although the difference between price and marginal cost may be smaller than it is under monopoly or oligopoly. Thus monopolistic competition, like monopoly and oligopoly, results in a misallocation of resources. The argument leading to this conclusion is exactly like that given above for monopoly. Also, monopolistic competition, as well as oligopoly, may allow waste arising from too much being spent (from society's point of view) on product differentiation, advertising, and other selling expenses. (On the other hand, the diversity of products may benefit consumers enough to offset these disadvantages of monopolistic competition, as pointed out above.)

THE BOTTOM LINE

The moral is that many economists look with disfavor on serious departures from perfect competition, whether these departures are in the direction of monopoly, oligopoly, or monopolistic competition. Judged against the perfectly competitive model, all may lead to social waste and inefficiency. However, monopoly is generally presumed to be the greatest evil, with the result that economists usually look with most disfavor on markets dominated by one or a very few sellers— or buyers.[1]

[1]Monopsony, where a single buyer exists, is taken up in Chapter 10.

TEST YOUR UNDERSTANDING

True or false?

_____ **1** The most important reason why economists oppose monopoly is that monopolists get rich.

_____ **2** Monopoly imposes a burden on society by misallocating resources.

_____ **3** Since monopolists do not have to face direct competition, they are likely to be more diligent in controlling costs and in using resources efficiently.

2 ■ The Defense of Monopoly Power

Not all economists agree that monopoly power is a bad thing. On the contrary, some respected voices in the economics profession have been raised to praise monopoly, not bury it. In discussing the social problems due to monopoly, the rate of technological change was assumed to be independent of an industry's market structure. Some economists, like Joseph Schumpeter, have challenged this assumption. _They assert that the rate of technological change is likely to be higher in an imperfectly competitive industry (for example, monopoly or oligopoly) than in a perfectly competitive industry._ Since the rate of technological change affects productivity and living standards, in their view a perfectly competitive economy is likely to be inferior in a dynamic sense to an economy containing many imperfectly competitive industries.

ARGUMENTS AGAINST PERFECT COMPETITION

These economists point out that firms under perfect competition have fewer resources to devote to research and experimentation than do firms under imperfect competition. Because profits are at a relatively low level, it is difficult for firms under perfect competition to support large expenditures on research and development. Moreover, they argue that unless a firm has sufficient control over the market to reap the rewards from an innovation, the introduction of the innovation may not be worthwhile. If competitors can imitate the innovation very quickly, the innovator may be unable to make any money from it.

REJOINDERS TO THE CRITICS

Defenders of perfect competition retort that there is likely to be less pressure for firms in imperfect markets to introduce new techniques and products, since such firms have fewer competitors. Moreover, firms in imperfect markets are better able to drive out entrants who, uncommitted to present techniques, are likely to be relatively quick to adopt new ones. (Entrants, unlike established producers, have no vested interest in maintaining the demand for existing products and the profitability of existing equipment.) Also, there are advantages in having a large number of independent decision-making units. There is less chance that an important technological advance will be blocked by the faulty judgment of a few men or women.

It is very difficult to obtain evidence to help settle this question if it is posed in this way, since perfect competition is a hypothetical construct that does not exist in the real world. However, it seems unlikely that a perfectly competitive industry (if such an industry could be constructed) would be able in many areas of the economy to carry out the research and development required to promote a high rate of technological change.

Moreover, if entry is free and rapid, firms in a perfectly competitive industry will have little motivation to innovate. Although the evidence is not at all clear-cut, at least this much can be granted the critics of perfect competition.

HOW MUCH MONOPOLY POWER IS OPTIMAL?

The discussion in previous sections makes it clear that the case against monopoly power is not open and shut. On the contrary, a certain amount of monopoly power is inevitable in practically all real-life situations, since perfect competition is a model that can only be approximated in real life. Moreover, a certain amount of monopoly power may be needed to promote desirable technological change. The difficult problem is to determine how much monopoly power is optimal under various circumstances (and how this power is to be measured). Some economists, like John Kenneth Galbraith, are convinced that a great deal of monopoly power is both inevitable and desirable.

Others believe the opposite. And the economic arguments are not strong enough to resolve the differences of opinion.

 TEST YOUR UNDERSTANDING

True or false?

_____ **1** Industrial giants are needed in all industries to ensure rapid technological change and rapid utilization of new techniques.

_____ **2** If entry is free and rapid, firms in a perfectly competitive industry may have little motivation to innovate.

_____ **3** A certain amount of monopoly power is inevitable in practically all real-life situations, since perfect competition is a model that can only be approximated in real life.

3 ▪ Concentration of Economic Power

Some critics of monopoly power and big business are concerned with the centralization of power in the hands of a relatively few firms. Although this is only partly an economic matter, it is obviously relevant to public policymakers. Economic power in the United States is distributed very unevenly; a few hundred corporations control a very large share of the total assets of the nonfarm economy. Moreover, within particular industries, there is considerable concentration of ownership and production, as you will see subsequently. This concentration of power has been viewed with concern by observers like A. A. Berle, who asserted that the largest several hundred firms "each with its own dominating pyramid within it—represent a concentration of power over economies which makes the medieval feudal system look like a Sunday School party. In sheer economic power this has gone far beyond anything we have yet seen."

It is important to note that this distrust of power leads to a distrust of giant firms, whether or not they have substantial monopoly power. Even if General Motors had little power over prices, it would still have considerable economic —and political—power because of its sheer size. Note too that a firm's size is not necessarily a good indicator of the extent of its monopoly power. A small grocery store in a remote community may be a monopolist, but a large merchandising firm with many rivals may have little monopoly power.

Look at the 100 biggest manufacturing firms in the United States. Recognizing that bigness is not the same as monopoly power, what percentage of the country's assets do these firms control, and is this percentage increasing or decreasing over time? According to the latest available figures, the 100 largest manufacturing firms control over half of all manufacturing assets in the United States, and this percentage seems to have increased considerably since the end of World War II.

INDUSTRIAL CONCENTRATION IN THE UNITED STATES

Economists and policymakers are interested in market structure because it influences market performance. But how can one measure an industry's market structure? How can one tell how close an industry is to being a monopoly or a perfectly competitive industry?

The **market concentration ratio,** which shows the percentage of total sales or production accounted for by the four largest firms, is a measure of how concentrated an industry is. The higher the market concentration ratio, the more concentrated the industry is in a very few hands. Basing this measure on four firms is arbitrary. You can use five, six, seven, or any number of firms you like. But the figures issued by the government are generally based on four firms.

It is important to recognize that the concentration ratio is only a rough measure of an industry's market structure. Certainly, to provide a reasonably adequate description, it must be supplemented with data on the extent and type of product differentiation in the industry, as well as on barriers to entry. Moreover, even with these supplements, it is still a crude measure. (Among other things, it takes no account of competition from foreign suppliers.) Nonetheless, the concentration ratio has proved to be a valuable tool to economists.

✓ TEST YOUR UNDERSTANDING

True or false?

_____ **1** Even if General Motors had little power over prices, it would still have considerable economic—and political—power because of its sheer size.

_____ **2** A firm's size is not necessarily a good indicator of the extent of its monopoly power.

_____ **3** The lower the market concentration ratio, the more concentrated the industry is in a very few hands.

Exercises

1 Suppose that an industry is composed of five firms. The market share of each firm is given in the table on the right. What is the concentration ratio for this industry?

FIRM	MARKET SHARE (percent)
A	10
B	10
C	20
D	25
E	35

2 Suppose that firm *E* loses half its sales to firm *C*. If the sales of the other firms remain constant, what is the effect on the concentration ratio in Exercise 1?

---

4 ■ The Antitrust Laws

National policies are too ambiguous and rich in contradictions to be summarized neatly and concisely. Consequently, it would be misleading to say that the United States has adopted a policy of promoting competition and controlling monopoly.

To a large extent, it certainly is true that "competition is our fundamental national policy," as the Supreme Court said in 1963. But it is also true that we have adopted many measures to promote monopoly and to limit competition. On balance, however, we probably have gone further in promoting competition than other major industrialized countries, and the principal pieces of legislation designed to further this objective are the **antitrust laws.**

THE SHERMAN ACT

In 1890, the first antitrust law, the Sherman Act, was passed by Congress. Although the common law had long outlawed monopolistic practices, it appeared to many Americans in the closing years of the nineteenth century that legislation was required to discourage monopoly and to preserve and encourage competition. The formation of "trusts"—monopolistic combines that colluded to raise prices and restrict output—brought the matter to a head. The heart of the Sherman Act lies in the following two sections:

> Sec. 1. Every contract, combination in the form of trust or otherwise, or conspiracy, in restraint of trade or commerce among the several states or with foreign nations, is hereby declared to be illegal. Every person who shall make any such contract or engage in any such combination or conspiracy, shall be deemed guilty of a misdemeanor. . . .

> Sec. 2. Every person who shall monopolize, or attempt to monopolize or combine or conspire with any other person or persons, to monopolize any part of the trade or commerce among the several States, or with foreign nations shall be deemed guilty of a misdemeanor.

THE CLAYTON ACT

The first 20 years of experience with the Sherman Act were not very satisfying to its supporters. The ineffectiveness of the Sherman Act led in 1914 to passage by Congress of two additional laws—the Clayton Act and the Federal Trade Commission Act. The Clayton Act tried to be more specific than the Sherman Act in identifying certain practices that were illegal because they would "substantially lessen competition or tend to create a monopoly." In particular, the Clayton Act outlawed unjustified **price discrimination,** a practice whereby one buyer is charged more than another buyer for the same product. It also outlawed the use of a **tying contract,** which makes the buyers purchase other items to get the product they want. Further, it outlawed mergers that substantially lessen competition; but since it did not prohibit one firm's purchase of a competitor's plant and equipment, it really could not stop mergers. In 1950, this loophole was closed by the Celler-Kefauver Anti-Merger Act.

THE FEDERAL TRADE COMMISSION ACT

The Federal Trade Commission Act was designed to prevent undesirable and unfair competitive practices. Specifically, it created a Federal Trade Commission to investigate unfair and predatory practices and to issue cease-and-desist orders. The act stated that "unfair methods of competition in commerce are hereby declared unlawful." However, the commission—composed of five commissioners, each appointed by the president for a term of seven years—was given the unenviable task of defining exactly what was "unfair." Eventually, the courts took away much of the commission's power; but in 1938, the commission acquired the function of outlawing untrue and deceptive advertising. Also, the commission has authority to carry out economic investigations of the structure and conduct of U.S. business.

✓ TEST YOUR UNDERSTANDING

True or false?

_____ **1** Whether price-fixing is illegal depends on the price fixers' share of the market; if their share is small enough, it is not illegal under U.S. law.

_____ **2** The Celler-Kefauver Act was designed to prohibit all mergers.

_____ **3** A tying contract makes the buyers purchase other items to get the product they want.

Exercises

1 "The antitrust laws effectively protect the large business from social pressure or regulation by maintaining the myth that the market does the regulating instead." Do you agree? Why or why not?

2 "General Motors and Ford are two of the world's largest auto manufacturers. They can acquire whatever firms they want and can afford." Do you agree? Why or why not?

3 In one of the most famous antitrust suits of this century, the government charged Du Pont, the large chemical firm, with "monopolizing, attempting to monopolize and conspiracy to monopolize interstate commerce in cellophane . . . in violation of Section 2 of the Sherman Act." Du Pont produced 75 percent of the cellophane sold in the United States.

a. On the basis of Du Pont's share of the cellophane market, was it clear that Du Pont was in violation of Section 2 of the Sherman Act?

b. The Supreme Court pointed out that, "despite cellophane's advantage, it has to meet competition from other materials in every one of its uses. . . . The overall result is that cellophane accounts for 17.9% of flexible wrapping materials. . . ." How can one tell whether cellophane had to meet competition from other materials, and how stiff this competition was?

c. The Supreme Court also denied that "Du Pont's profits, while liberal . . . demonstrate the existence of a monopoly. . . ." Would a monopoly's profits be expected to be relatively high?

d. The Supreme Court decided that Du Pont was not in violation of the Sherman Act. In reaching this decision it pointed to the high cross elasticity of demand existing between cellophane and other flexible packaging materials like pliofilm. Why is this of relevance?

5 ▪ The Role of the Courts

The antitrust laws, like any laws, are enforced in the courts. Typically, charges are brought against a firm or group of firms by the Antitrust Division of the Department of Justice, a trial is held, and a decision is reached by the judge. In key cases, appeals are made that eventually reach the Supreme Court. The real impact of the antitrust laws depends on how the courts interpret them. And the judicial interpretation of these laws has changed considerably over time.

The first major set of antitrust cases took place in 1911 when the Standard Oil Company and the American Tobacco Company were forced to give up large shares of their holdings of other companies. In these cases, the Supreme Court put forth and used the famous **rule of reason**—that only unreasonable combinations in restraint of trade, not all trusts, required conviction under the Sherman Act. In 1920, the rule of reason was used by the Supreme Court in its finding that U.S. Steel had not violated the antitrust laws even though it had tried to monopolize the industry,

since the Court said it had not succeeded. Moreover, U.S. Steel's large size and its potential monopoly power were ruled beside the point since "the law does not make mere size an offense. It . . . requires overt acts."

During the 1920s and 1930s the courts, including the conservative Supreme Court, interpreted the antitrust laws in such a way that they were as toothless as a new-born babe. Although Eastman Kodak and International Harvester controlled very substantial shares of their markets, the Court, using the rule of reason, found them innocent on the grounds that they had not built up their near-monopoly positions through overt coercion or predatory practices. Moreover, the Court reiterated that mere size was not an offense, no matter how great the unexerted monopoly power might be.

In the late 1930s, this situation changed very greatly, with the prosecution of the Aluminum Company of America (Alcoa). This case, decided in 1945 (but begun in 1937), reversed the decisions in the U.S. Steel and International Harvester cases. Alcoa had achieved its 90 percent of the market by means that would have been considered "reasonable" in the earlier cases—keeping its price low enough to discourage entry, building capacity to take care of increases in the market, and so forth. Nonetheless, the Court decided that Alcoa, because it controlled practically all the industry's output, violated the antitrust laws. Thus, to a considerable extent, *the Court used market structure rather than market conduct as a test of legality.*

 TEST YOUR UNDERSTANDING

True or false?

_____ **1** The antitrust laws have yet had no significant effect on business behavior and markets.

_____ **2** The rule of reason said that only unreasonable combinations in restraint of trade, not all trusts, required conviction under the Sherman Act.

_____ **3** In the Alcoa case, the Supreme Court used market structure as a test of legality.

Exercise

1 Until 1975, resale price maintenance agreements allowed manufacturers of a trademarked item to establish a floor under the retail price of the item. Suppose that the manufacturer of a cosmetic established OP as its minimum retail price, and that D_0 is the demand curve for this cosmetic at a particular drugstore. The drugstore's average costs are also shown in the diagram.

a. Only the solid portion of demand curve D is relevant to the drugstore. Why?

b. Can the drugstore make a profit on the sale of the cosmetic?

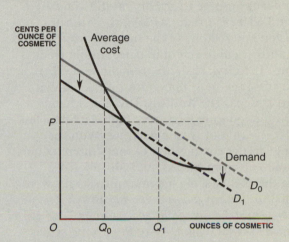

c. Will there be a change in the number of drugstores selling the cosmetic? What sort of a change? Why?

d. As changes occur in the number of drugstores selling the cosmetic, the demand curve eventually moves to D_1. Why? At this point, can a drugstore make a profit on the sale of the cosmetic?

---

6 ▪ The Role of the Justice Department

The impact of the antitrust laws is determined by the vigor with which the Antitrust Division of the Justice Department prosecutes cases. If the Antitrust Division does not prosecute, the laws can have little effect. Like the judicial interpretation of the laws, the extent to which the Justice Department has prosecuted cases has varied from one period to another. Needless to say, the attitude of the political party in power has been an important determinant of how vigorously antitrust cases have been prosecuted. When the Sherman Act was first passed, it was of singularly little value. For example, President Grover Cleveland's attorney general did not agree with the law and would not prosecute under it. Trust-busting was truly a neglected art until President

Theodore Roosevelt devoted his formidable energies to it. In 1903, he established the Antitrust Division of the Justice Department. Moreover, his administration started the major cases that led to the Standard Oil, American Tobacco, and U.S. Steel decisions.

Subsequently, there was a long lull in the prosecution of antitrust cases, reflecting the Supreme Court's rule-of-reason doctrine and a strong conservative tide in the nation. The lull continued for about 25 years, until 1937, when there was a significant upsurge in activity on the antitrust front. Led by Thurman Arnold, the Antitrust Division entered one of the most vigorous periods of antitrust enforcement to date. Arnold went against the glass, cigarette, cement, and other industries, the most important case being that against Alcoa. The Antitrust Division attempted in this period to reopen cases that were hopeless under the rule-of-reason doctrine. With the change in the composition of the Supreme Court, Arnold's activism turned out to be effective.

In the 1980s, some major antitrust suits were settled. *In 1982, a government antitrust suit (begun in 1974) against the American Telephone and Telegraph Company (AT&T) ended.* According to the settlement, AT&T divested itself of 22 companies that provide most of the country's local telephone service and kept its Long Lines division, Western

Electric, and the Bell Laboratories. Although many observers worried that one result was likely to be an increase in local telephone rates, there was also considerable feeling that, after the telephone industry was restricted in this way, AT&T would be a leaner and more dynamic firm. One immediate effect of this divestiture was a great deal of confusion among customers and costly adjustments within AT&T, but subsequently many observers believed that it was resulting in faster introduction of new technologies and services and lower long-distance phone rates.

The Antitrust Division sued IBM Corporation under Section 2 of the Sherman Act in January 1969, thus starting one of the biggest and costliest antitrust cases in history. The government charged that IBM held a monopoly and that the firm's 360 line of computers was introduced in 1965 in a way that eliminated competition. IBM's defense was that its market position stemmed from its innovative performance and economies of scale, that its pricing was competitive, and that its profit rate really had not been high. Once the trial began in 1975, it took the government almost three years to present its case. In early 1982, on the same day that it settled the antitrust case against AT&T, the Reagan administration dropped the IBM case. It said the case was "without merit and should be dismissed."

 TEST YOUR UNDERSTANDING

True or false?

_____ **1** During the late 1930s, there was a substantial upsurge in antitrust activity.

_____ **2** The government dropped the antitrust case against IBM in 1982.

_____ **3** AT&T divested itself of 22 companies that provide most of the country's local telephone service.

Exercises

1 "Perfect competition results in optimal efficiency and an optimal distribution of income. This is why

the United States opts for a perfectly competitive economy." Comment and evaluate.

2 "The real impact of the antitrust laws depends on judicial interpretation." Comment and evaluate.

3 Chief Justice Hughes observed, "Good intentions will not save a plan otherwise objectionable, but knowledge of actual intent is an aid in the interpretation of facts and prediction of consequence." Relate this to the construction of standards for antitrust policy.

▪ CHAPTER REVIEW

KEY TERMS

market concentration ratio
antitrust laws

price discrimination
tying contract
rule of reason

COMPLETION QUESTIONS

1 The government (can, cannot) _____ convict firms of violation of the antitrust laws merely by showing that they fixed prices or attempted to do so. The government (does, does not) _____ have to show how much prices were raised. The government (does, does not) _____ have to show what the effects were.

2 The Standard Oil Case, decided in 1911, resulted in _____. The American Tobacco case, decided in 1911, resulted in _____. The U.S. Steel case, decided in 1920, resulted in _____. All these cases were tried under Section _____ of the _____.

3 The IBM case alleged that IBM had monopoly power in the market for _____. This case was tried under Section _____ of the _____.

4 The market _____ shows the percentage of total sales or production accounted for by the biggest four firms.

5 The _____ outlawed any contract, combination, or conspiracy in restraint of trade and made it illegal to monopolize or attempt to monopolize.

6 If an industry produces up to the point where the social value of an extra unit of the good is more than the cost to society of producing an extra unit, this (is, is not) _____ the socially optimal output rate because a 1-unit (increase, decrease) _____ in the output rate will increase the social value of output by more than the social cost of production.

7 A monopolistic industry produces at a point where the social value of an extra unit of the good (which equals price) is (greater, less) _____ than the cost to society of producing the extra unit (which equals _____ cost).

ANSWERS TO COMPLETION QUESTIONS

can

does not

does not

the dissolution of Standard Oil
the dissolution of American Tobacco
acquittal
2
Sherman Act

electronic computers
2 Sherman Act
concentration ratio

Sherman Act

is not
increase

greater

marginal

8 Some economists, like Schumpeter and Galbraith, have asserted that the rate of technological change is likely to be higher in a(n) _____ competitive industry (for example, monopoly, oligopoly, and so on) than in a(n) _____ competitive industry.

imperfectly

perfectly

NUMERICAL PROBLEMS

1 When the Aluminum Company of America (ALCOA) wanted to acquire the Rome Cable Corporation, this merger was challenged by the government. Here are each firm's market shares, based on alternative market definitions.

DEFINITION	ALCOA	ROME
	(percent)	
Bare aluminum conductor wire and cable	32.5	0.3
Insulated aluminum conductor wire and cable	11.6	4.7
Combined aluminum conductor wire and cable	27.8	1.3
All bare conductor wire and cable (aluminum and copper)	10.3	2.0
All insulated conductor wire and cable	0.3	1.3
Combined insulated and bare wire and cable (all metals)	1.8	1.4

Should this merger have been prevented? Why or why not?

2 Continental Can Company once wanted to merge with the Hazel-Atlas Glass Company. Continental, the second largest producer of tin cans in the United States, sold about one-third of all tin cans, Hazel-Atlas, the third largest bottle maker, sold about one-tenth of all glass bottles. Should this merger have been prevented? Why or why not?

3 a Bethlehem and Youngstown, two major steel producers, accounted for about 21 percent of the national steel market when they proposed to merge. This merger was challenged by the Justice Department. Should the two steel companies have been allowed to merge? Why or why not?

b According to the companies, Bethlehem sold most of its output in the East, whereas Youngstown sold most of its output in the Midwest. Was this fact of relevance? Why or why not?

4 There are several firms that produce left-handed monkey wrenches. Suppose their sales in 1997 were:

FIRM	SALES (millions of dollars)
A	100
B	50
C	40
D	30
E	20
F	5
G	5

a What is the concentration ratio in the left-handed monkey wrench industry?

b Would you regard this industry as oligopolistic? Why or why not?

c Suppose that firm *A* merges with firm *G*. What will be the concentration ratio in this industry now?

d Suppose that, after they merge, firms *A* and *G* go out of business. What will be the concentration ratio in this industry now?

5 Firm *X*, which sells engines, had a uniform price of $500 which it charged all its customers. But after its competitors began to cut their prices in the California market to $400, firm *X* reduced its price to $400.

a Did this tend to violate the Clayton Act?

b If firm *X* had cut its price to $300, might this have tended to violate the Clayton Act?

c Suppose that firm *X* decides to purchase enough of the stock of competing firms so that it can exercise control over them to see to it that the price-cutting in the California market stops. Is this legal? If not, what law does it violate?

6 A number of U.S. laws and a number of antitrust provisions are listed below. In the blank space before each provision, put the letter corresponding to the U.S. law containing this provision.

A. Sherman Act, Section 1

B. Sherman Act, Section 2

C. Clayton Act

D. Federal Trade Commission Act

E. Celler-Kefauver Act

F. Robinson-Patman Act

———— **a** It is illegal to enter into a contract, combination, or conspiracy in restraint of trade.

———— **b** It is illegal to discriminate among purchasers to an extent that cannot be justified by a difference in cost.

———— **c** It is illegal to use unfair methods of competition.

———— **d** It is illegal to attempt to monopolize trade.

———— **e** It is illegal to enter into exclusive and tying contracts.

———— **f** It is illegal to discriminate among purchases, where the effect might be to drive competitors out of business.

———— **g** It is illegal to employ unfair or deceptive acts or practices.

———— **h** It is illegal to acquire the stock of competing corporations.

 ## ANSWERS TO
TEST YOUR UNDERSTANDING

SECTION 1

TRUE OR FALSE: 1. False   2. True   3. False

SECTION 2

TRUE OR FALSE: 1. False   2. True   3. True

SECTION 3

TRUE OR FALSE: 1. True   2. True   3. False

EXERCISES

1. 90 percent.

2. No change.

SECTION 4

TRUE OR FALSE: 1. False   2. False   3. True

EXERCISES

1. The issue is whether firms can escape the discipline of the market. According to this quotation, they can; many (probably most) economists take a different view.

2. Do not agree. Because they are big, it doesn't follow that they are not subject to the antitrust laws.

3. a. No.

b. One can see whether cellophane and other materials are used for the same purposes.

c. Yes.

d. It means that if cellophane's price was raised, the quantity of pliofilm and other materials would increase considerably.

SECTION 5

TRUE OR FALSE: 1. False   2. True   3. True

EXERCISE

1. a. Because the drugstore cannot sell the cosmetic at a price less than OP without running afoul of the resale price maintenance agreements.

b. Yes. If it sells between OQ_0 and OQ_1 ounces of the cosmetic, the price it receives will exceed its average cost.

c. Yes. Because profits are made on this cosmetic, other stores will begin to sell it, the result being that the number of stores selling it will increase.

d. Because more and more stores sell the cosmetic, the total volume is spread more thinly among the stores. In other words, the demand curve facing a particular drugstore shifts to the left. When the demand curve reaches D_1, a drugstore can no longer make a profit from the sale of the cosmetic. Thus entry ceases.

SECTION 6

TRUE OR FALSE: 1. True   2. True   3. True

EXERCISES

1. The statement is incorrect. One cannot prove that perfect competition results in an optimal distribution of income. Also, the United States really has not opted for perfect competition, which is an abstract model.

2. This is true.

3. The answer should touch on the difficulties of establishing intent and, in some circumstances, its irrelevance.

■ CHAPTER 9

Henry Ford Wouldn't Recognize the Auto Industry Today

1 ■ Introduction

The automobile industry is one of the biggest and most important industries in the United States and the world. Since its inception about a century ago, this industry has been marked by considerable change, but in the past 20 years the rate of change has increased dramatically. There has been a transformation of this industry. The present chapter presents eight multipart problems, which analyze selected aspects of this transformation. To provide the background information required to understand and do these problems, it starts with a brief sketch of major developments in the auto industry, beginning in 1905.

In 1905 the average automobile produced in the United States cost more than the average Datsun 70 years later. Many of the firms in the auto industry were warmed-over buggy makers who handcrafted rich men's toys. But change was in the air. *Motor Age*, the industry's first trade magazine, prophesied that "the simple car is the car of the future. A golden opportunity awaits some bold manufacturer of a simple car."

It remained for Henry Ford, the son of a Wisconsin farmer, to translate these words into a car—the Model T. Ford, commenting on his rural youth, declared, "It was life on the farm that drove me into devising ways and means to better transportation." Turning from the kid glove and checkbook set, he saw the potential market—at the right price—for car sales in the agricultural community.

The Model T was introduced in 1909. A few numbers indicate its phenomenal progress.

YEAR	PRICE (dollars)	CARS SOLD
1909	900	58,022
1914	440	472,350
1916	360	730,041

However, all good things come to an end. By the twenties, Ford's unwillingness to alter the Model T in any fashion (cosmetic or mechanical), as well as increased competition from other manufacturers, and the development of trade-in and installment buying (which reduced the price elasticity of demand for automobiles) brought the Model T to an end.

2 ■ General Motors and Alfred P. Sloan

The Model T wasn't the only car on the road. Americans were driving Pierce Arrows, Stutz Bearcats, and Deusenbergs, as well as the Chevrolets, Buicks, Oldsmobiles, and Cadillacs made by Ford's number-one competitor, General Motors, headed by Alfred P. Sloan. Sloan once said, "The primary object of the corporation is to make money, not just to make motor cars. The core of the GM product policy lies in the concept of mass producing a full line of cars graded upward in quality and price." Sloan saw that even if GM could produce for less than Ford, it couldn't *increase* profits by *decreasing* prices. So to do battle with Ford's black Model Ts, GM's massive research and development effort produced a brand for every pocketbook—Chevrolets, Pontiacs, Buicks, and Cadillacs—a color for every taste, and a wish list of options. Every year brought a new edition. GMs were old not when they wore out but when they went out of style.

Any business decision is a kind of gamble. Henry Ford bet that the United States wanted a car that would last forever, was cheap and easy to

fix, and never went out of style. Alfred Sloan bet that there was something more attractive to U.S. drivers than a low price, that they were ready to have some fun with their cars, and that GM advertising could join their desires and GM's cars, at a profit to GM. Henry Ford knew cars, but Alfred Sloan knew the consumer, and he knew the twenties. By the time the Great Depression started in 1929, Henry Ford had yielded to reality and started varying his cars. But he had lost the 50 percent share of the market he had commanded, and had to settle for second place.

3 ▪ Problems of Small Firms: The Case of Studebaker

Another major auto producer was Studebaker, which, after having had its ups and downs before World War II, started off the postwar period in good shape. Flush with cash, Studebaker capitalized on the pent-up demand of the war years by being the first to come out with a new model—a streamlined car of the future. The firm prospered in the late 1940s and early 1950s, and in 1952 it had its best year ever.

As the seller's market of the early postwar years disappeared, however, serious weaknesses in Studebaker's position became obvious. The auto industry was very competitive in the mid-1950s. There were eight major manufacturers (today's Big Three and Studebaker, plus Nash, Hudson, Packard, and Willys). Studebaker suffered from bad management and high-cost labor, but one of its major problems could not have been easily solved by either management or labor—its inability to capture the cost savings that result from a large scale of production.

General Motors and the other large manufac-

turers had begun to introduce new models every year. While these firms could spread the costs of new model development (about $30 million) over the 1 to 2 million units they produced each year, Studebaker was selling fewer than 300,000 cars a year. The company could not reach the minimum cost per car that was possible through large volume. In 1953, it scheduled production of 350,000 cars but built only 186,000. By 1954, Studebaker had set its break-even point at 108,000 per year and was trying to reduce the figure still further.

In 1963, Studebaker's sales dipped to 66,000 as the temporary success of the Lark slowed when the Big Three brought out compacts of their own. If the company had plowed its profits back into expansion in the late 1940s, it might have been able to reach a scale of production that would have enabled it to compete with the larger manufacturers. But its small size made it impossible for Studebaker to weather its other problems, and the company was forced to close in 1964.[1]

4 ▪ The Energy Crisis and the Chrysler Bailout

During the 1970s, the United States experienced an energy crisis. In late 1973, the Organization of Petroleum Exporting Countries (OPEC), a group of major oil-producing countries, including Saudi

[1] E. Mansfield and N. Behravesh, *Economics USA* (5th ed.; New York: Norton, 1998). This text (and others of mine) is the source of some of the material in this chapter.

Arabia, Iran, and Libya, cut back on their oil ex-ports. The result: a quadrupling of the price of oil. In 1979, another massive increase in the price of oil occurred because of the revolution in oil-rich Iran. Consequently, U.S. motorists were confronted with huge increases in the price of gasoline. Whereas the pump price of regular gasoline was $.36 per gallon in 1972, it was around $1.31 per gallon in 1981.

The energy crisis of the 1970s spelled trouble for U.S. automakers, whose production, profits, and employment declined in the late 1970s and early 1980s, while imports of fuel-efficient Japanese cars rose. (See Figures 9.1 to 9.4.) Chrysler, the country's third-largest auto company, was particularly hard hit, its losses being $1.0 billion in 1979 and $1.7 billion in 1980. Where could Lee Iacocca, Chrysler's chairman, look for the money to keep Chrysler afloat? He turned to Douglas Fraser, head of the United Auto Workers (UAW). Fighting for survival, union workers agreed to more than $450 million worth of pay cuts.

Chrysler needed more than cost cuts to design,

build and market the small, stylish cars the United States wanted. It needed credit. But Chrysler's troubles had cut it off from traditional sources of credit and investment. So, like other borrowers with bad credit, Iacocca asked a relative to guarantee a loan: Uncle Sam.

Big-business bailouts had usually gotten short

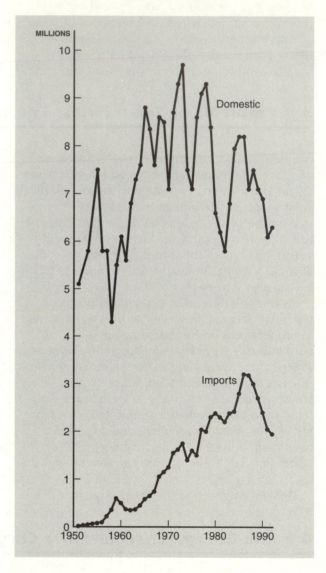

▪ **FIGURE 9.2**

New Passenger Car Sales in the United States, 1951–1992

SOURCE: *AAMA Motor Vehicle Facts and Figures*, p. 14.

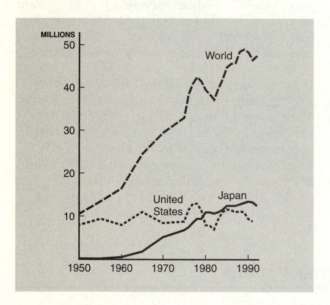

▪ **FIGURE 9.1**

World Motor Vehicle Production, 1950–1992

SOURCE: American Automobile Manufacturers Association, *AAMA Motor Vehicle Facts and Figures* (Washington, D.C.; AAMA, 1993), p. 1.

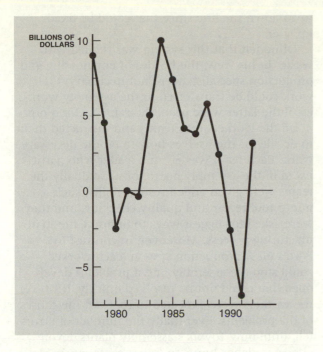

▪ **FIGURE 9.3**

U.S. Motor Vehicle (and Equipment) Manufacturers' Profits, 1978–1992

SOURCE: *AAMA Motor Vehicle Facts and Figures*, p. 76.

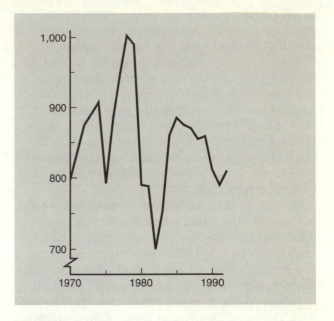

▪ **FIGURE 9.4**

U.S. Motor Vehicle (and Equipment) Employment, 1970–1992

SOURCE: *AAMA Motor Vehicle Facts and Figures*, p. 74.

shrift from Democratic congresses and presidents. But the UAW and Democratic leaders were old allies. When UAW chief Fraser stressed that half a million jobs might be lost in a Chrysler collapse, Capitol Hill listened, and President Jimmy Carter signed Chrysler loan guarantees into law.

By 1984, Chrysler was back in the black and government-guaranteed loans were repaid. The UAW and Chrysler were back on opposite sides of the bargaining table when contract time rolled around again. But something had changed. At Chrysler and around the country, the late 1970s

and the 1980s saw struggling companies and their workers set aside old antagonisms in the common interest of survival.

A business-as-usual wage increase and price hike could have sunk Chrysler, but government loan guarantees, the UAW's agreement to temporary pay cuts, and Chrysler's willingness to give the union unprecedented access to management's top councils kept Chrysler going. A union that was used to asking for more—and a company that was used to giving it—had discovered that staying afloat in a competitive economy could sometimes force two old antagonists to take the same track.

5 ▪ The Japanese Repudiation of Henry Ford

Everyone has heard of Henry Ford, the U.S. manufacturing genius who was responsible for mass production methods in the automobile industry,

but few Americans have heard of Taiichi Ohno, the Japanese manufacturing genius responsible for his country's hugely successful repudiation of many of Ford's teachings. In the 1950s, Ohno concluded that mass production methods were not the optimal techniques for his employer, Toyota, a major automobile producer. Instead, he devised a production system often called "lean production" because, in the words of engineers at the Massachusetts Institute of Technology, "it uses less of everything than a comparable mass-production operation: half the human effort in the factory, half the manufacturing space, half the investment in tools, half the engineering hours to develop a new product."[2]

In Ford's mass-production system, each worker performed only a single task at a station beside a moving assembly line. To complement these narrowly focused production workers on the assembly floor, there was a small army of indirect workers who repaired tools, inspected for quality defects, and fixed up the defects that were identified. The emphasis was on keeping the assembly line moving, since stopping the line would result in delays and lost production which would necessitate expensive overtime work. Moreover, it was felt that little was lost by allowing defective items

[2] J. Womack, D. Jones, and D. Roos, *New York Times*, September 23, 1990.

to go down the line since that could be fixed up later.

Ohno felt that this system was riddled with waste. In his view, the hordes of engineering and production specialists were not necessary; their work could be transferred to the assembly workers if the latter were properly trained. Ohno organized the workers into teams and instructed them to decide for themselves how to do the necessary work. Each team was given a leader who participated in the assembly operations. Gradually the teams were given added responsibility, such as minor tool repair and quality checking, and they were asked to suggest ways to improve the manufacturing process. Moreover, in contrast to Ford's mass-production system, each worker could stop the assembly line if problems developed that could not be resolved quickly. However, the workers were expected to root out the causes of the problems. Eventually the number of errors fell, until now Toyota's assembly plants devote almost no labor hours to fixing mistakes (in contrast to mass production plants where 25 percent of total labor hours may be devoted to such activity). And, ironically, although each worker *can* stop the assembly line, this very seldom occurs.

6 ▪ Import Restriction on Japanese Autos

When the first Japanese cars arrived on the West Coast in the 1970s, no one saw them as a threat to U.S. jobs. Although they were cheaper and more fuel-efficient than U.S.-made cars, most Americans couldn't be bothered; with gasoline at 30 cents a gallon, the difference in cost between a car that got 30 miles per gallon and one that got 10 was not very great, even for someone who drove a lot.

But all this changed with the cutback of OPEC oil exports in 1973. As gas prices climbed, Americans took another look at small foreign cars. With expensive U.S. labor and outmoded facilities on one side, and Japanese efficiency and management techniques on the other, Japan seemed to be winning the war in the showroom.

Although imports may create as many jobs as they consume in the long run, in the short run many smokestack industry workers can be left permanently unemployed or underemployed. Worried U.S. workers wanted protection, and they found a strong advocate in Representative John Dingell, one of the leaders of an emerging protectionist movement in Congress. Dingell spoke with President Reagan and Trade Representative William Brock, and urged that if voluntary restrictions on Japanese auto imports were not adopted, Congress would impose mandatory ones. Faced with this choice, the Japanese agreed in negotiations to voluntary restrictions.

The restrictions worked. As the number of Japanese auto imports dropped between 1981 and 1982, domestic auto industry employment rose. But the cost of saving hundreds of *thousands* of U.S. jobs was restricted choice and higher prices for hundreds of *millions* of U.S. consumers. Hefty dealer markups were imposed on the scarcer but still-popular imports, and as sticker prices rose on Toyotas and Datsuns, General Motors, Ford, and Chrysler found that they could raise prices too.

The combined price paid by consumers for trade restrictions is very high; it has been esti-mated that each job protected from foreign competition with quotas or tariffs costs consumers about $160,000 in higher prices—more than enough to support the holder of that job. Although trade restrictions may save jobs in the short run, they lock inefficiencies into the U.S. economy and merely delay needed efforts to divert people and assets into areas of the economy in which the United States has a competitive advantage—and which therefore offer long-term employment and profit possibilities.

7 ▪ Japanese Transplants and Changes in the Structure of the U.S. Auto Industry

Given the restrictions on how many cars they could export into the U.S. market, Japanese auto producers began to invest in production facilities in the United States. In 1982, Honda's auto assembly plant in Marysville, Ohio, was started up. In 1983, Nissan established a pickup truck assembly plant in Tennessee, which subsequently began producing autos. In 1987, Mazda and Ford (in a joint venture) began assembling cars in Michigan. In 1988, Toyota's new auto plant began operations in Kentucky, and Mitsubishi and Chrysler (in a joint venture) started up production in Illinois. By 1990, these and other Japanese "transplants" had the planned capacity to produce over 2 million cars per year in the United States.

Because they found it difficult to produce a small car profitably in the United States, each major U.S. producer turned to the Japanese for help in learning how to produce such cars. The most publicized case of this sort was General Motors's joint venture with Toyota. "Consummated in 1983, the agreement between the largest auto company in the United States and the largest in Japan provided for U.S. assembly of a derivative of the Toyota Corolla in a recently closed GM plant in California. The plant would be managed by Toyota personnel to ensure operation of the efficient 'Toyota production system' and the vehicle would be sold through GM's Chevrolet dealers as the Nova. The renovated facility

began production in 1985, offering cars that were declared . . . to be the best small cars available in the United States. . . . However, the Nova did not sell well. . . . Whatever the reason, the joint venture experience showed how difficult the comeback would be for the U.S. industry."[3]

Roger Smith, GM's chairman then, also poured money into automated facilities. Between 1980, and 1987, the firm spent over $50 billion on the installation of robots to paint, weld, and move materials in existing plants and to establish new factories employing these automation techniques. One of these showcase factories was its Hamtramck plant, which the *Wall Street Journal* described as follows:

> So far the Hamtramck plant, instead of a showcase, looks more like a basket case. Though the plant has been open for seven months, the automated guided vehicles are sitting idle while technicians try to debug the software that controls their movements. In the ultra modern paint shop, robots at times have spray-painted each other instead of the cars. Some cars have been painted so badly that GM had to ship them to a 57-year-old plant to be repainted. Hamtramck is turning out only 30 to 35

[3] J. Kwoka, "Automobiles: Overtaking an Oligopoly," in L. Deutsch, (ed.), *Industry Studies* (Englewood Cliffs, N.J.: Prentice-Hall, 1993), p. 77.

cars an hour, far less than the 60 an hour it was designed to build.[4]

General Motors eventually became the biggest money-loser in the industry. Trying to turn itself around, it announced 11 plant closings in 1987, 7 additional plant closings in 1990, and 21 further plant closings in 1991. As Jack Smith, GM's chairman in 1994, put it, "We really need to crank up the energy level."[5] The firm that Alfred P. Sloan had managed so well in the 1920s had fallen on hard times, and the structure of the U.S. auto industry had changed enormously. (See Table 9.1.) Nonetheless, the U.S. auto industry was by no means moribund, as you will see below; it was being transformed by fundamental technological and economic changes.

[4] W. Greene, "General Motors Corporation," in J. Pearce and R. Robison (eds.), *Cases in Strategic Management* (2d ed.); (Homewood, Ill.: Irwin, 1991), p. 512.

[5] *Business Week*, November 1, 1993, p. 128.

■ TABLE 9.1

Percentage of U.S. Automobile Sales, by Firm, 1978 and 1991

FIRM	1978	1991
General Motors	47.8	35.4
Ford	23.5	19.9
Chrysler	11.0	8.5
AMC	1.5	—
Volkswagen	2.1	1.1
Toyota	3.9	9.0
Nissan	3.0	5.0
Honda	2.4	9.8
Mazda	0.7	3.3
Mitsubishi	—	2.1
Other	4.1	5.9
Total	100.0	100.0

SOURCE: J. Kwoka, "Automobiles: Overtaking an Oligopoly," in L. Deutsch (ed.), *Industry Studies* (Englewood Cliffs, N.J.: Prentice-Hall, 1993).

8 ■ Applying Economics: Auto Demand

The following two problems deal with the market for automobiles in the United States.

PROBLEM 9.1 Henry Ford believed that "it is better to sell a large number of cars at a reasonably small margin than to sell fewer cars at a larger margin of profit. Bear in mind when you reduce the price of the car without reducing the quality you increase the possible number of purchases. There are many [people] who will pay $360 for a car who would not pay $440. I figure that on the $360 basis we can increase the sales to 800,000 cars for the year. . . . "[6]

a. If sales were about 500,000 per year when the price was $440, what was the price elasticity of demand?

[6] J. Rae (ed.), *Henry Ford* (Englewood Cliffs, N.J.: Prentice-Hall, 1969), p. 112.

b. Is the price elasticity of demand for Ford automobiles the same as the price elasticity of demand for all automobiles? Why or why not? If not, which is likely to be greater, and why?

c. According to Saul Hymans of the University of Michigan, the price elasticity of demand for automobiles in the United States is about 1.2 in the short run (of about one year), but only about 0.75 in the longer run (of about three years).[7] Why is the price elasticity higher in the short run than in the longer run? Is this true of all goods?

d. The income elasticity of demand for automobiles is about 3.00 in the short run (of about

[7] S. Hymans, "Consumer Durable Spending: Explanation and Prediction," *Brookings Papers on Economic Activity* 11 (1971), pp. 173–99.

one year). If a recession occurs and incomes fall by about 4 percent, what will be the effect on auto sales? Does this help to explain why the auto industry is regarded as being very sensitive to business fluctuations?

e. Was Henry Ford's belief in the wisdom of price reductions applicable to all industries? Why or why not?

PROBLEM 9.2 In the 1970s, as the price of gasoline skyrocketed in response to the huge increases in crude oil prices, and U.S. consumers turned in increasing numbers to small Japanese cars that were much more fuel efficient, U.S. auto firms were forced to consider changing their product lines.

> It was all too apparent that Ford, like the others, would have to reduce the size of most of its cars and make its entire line more fuel efficient. The question of how it would downsize dominated the company for two years, starting in 1974. It was a time of total confusion. . . . Detroit seemed to have no idea of what the consumer wanted. Indeed, did the consumer know what he [or she] wanted? But Ford had to make a decision, and it was likely to be the most expensive decision in the company's history. The cost of downsizing, particularly if Ford went to a brand-new line—that is, a new body, new engine, and new transaxle—might be as much as $3 billion. It was in effect the biggest bet on the roll of the market that anyone had ever had to make. It was a figure so large that, as one executive said, either way it was like betting the company.[8]

a. At the beginning of the 1970s, why did U.S. auto firms like Ford produce large, relatively fuel-inefficient cars, rather than smaller ones?

b. According to experts, the price of a used 1973 Dodge Monaco would have been expected to be about $3,314 in December 1973, when

gasoline prices took off. Instead, its price was about $2,650. Was this fact related to its being a large, relatively fuel-inefficient car? Why or why not?

c. In the spring of 1974, the price of a used 1973 Dodge Monaco was $3,200, an increase of about $550 in less than six months. During this period, the price of gasoline fell. Was this price increase related to the fall in the gasoline price? Why or why not?[9]

d. Do increases in the price of gasoline shift the demand curves for fuel-efficient cars to the right and shift those of fuel-inefficient cars to the left? If so, is this because they influence the expectations of consumers as to what gasoline prices will be?

e. Given that there was so much uncertainty, even among experts, concerning the future path of gasoline prices, is it surprising that consumers were not sure of the kinds of cars they wanted in 1974?

f. U.S. producers introduced new lines of smaller, fuel-efficient cars in the fall of 1980. The prices at which they and their Japanese rivals were offered were as follows:

Chevrolet Citation	$6,337
General Motors "J" Cars	6,300
Ford Escort	6,009
Dodge Omni	5,713
Subaru wagon	6,612
Datsun 310	5,439
Subaru hatchback	5,212
Mazda GLC	4,755

According to some observers, "Detroit . . . priced these cars relatively high to replenish its depleted coffers as soon as possible." What assumptions were U.S. auto firms making concerning the cross elasticity of demand between U.S. and Japanese cars? Were these assumptions correct?

[8] David Halberstam, *The Reckoning* (New York: Morrow, 1986), p. 529.

[9] George Daly and Thomas Mayor, "Reason and Rationality During the Energy Crisis," *Journal of Political Economy*, February 1983.

9 ■ Applying Economics: Auto Production

The following two problems deal with the production of automobiles in the United States, Japan, and Germany.

PROBLEM 9.3 To illustrate the differences between mass production and lean production, James Womack, Daniel Jones, and Daniel Roos of Massachusetts Institute of Technology made an intensive study in 1986 of General Motors's assembly plant at Framingham, Massachusetts, and Toyota's assembly plant at Takaoka in Toyota City, Japan. The former was a classic example of mass production; the latter used lean production. They summarized the results of their study as follows:

> The differences between Takaoka and Framingham are striking to anyone who understands the logic of lean production. For a start, hardly anyone was in the aisles. The armies of indirect workers so visible at GM were missing, and practically every worker in sight was actually adding value to the car. . . . Toyota believes in having as little space as possible so that face-to-face communication among workers is easier, and there is no room to store inventories. GM, by contrast, has believed that extra space is necessary to work on vehicles needing repairs and to store the large inventories needed to ensure smooth production. . . .
>
> [At Takaoka,] there were no parts warehouses at all. Instead parts were delivered directly to the line at hourly intervals from the supplier plants where they had just been made. (Indeed, our initial plant survey form asked how many days of inventory were in the plant. A Toyota manager politely asked whether there was an error in translation. Surely we meant *minutes* of inventory.) . . . At the end of the line, the difference between lean and mass production was even more striking. At Takaoka, we observed almost no rework at all. Almost every car was driven directly from the line to the boat or the trucks taking cars to the buyer.[10]

[10] J. Womack, D. Jones, and D. Roos, *The Machine That Changed the World* (New York: Macmillan, 1990), p. 79–80.

■ **TABLE 9.2**

Comparison of General Motors Framingham Assembly Plant and Toyota Takaoka Assembly Plant, 1986

	GENERAL MOTORS FRAMINGHAM	TOYOTA TAKAOKA
Number of labor hours required to assemble a car	31	16
Assembly space per car (square feet)	8.1	4.8
Inventories of parts (average)	2 weeks	2 hours

SOURCE: J. Womack, D. Jones, and D. Roos, *The Machine That Changed the World* (New York: Macmillan Co., 1990), p. 81.

a. Table 9.2 shows the number of hours of labor required to assemble a car at Takaoka and at Framingham. Was the average product of labor higher at one plant than at the other? If so, which plant had the higher average product of labor, and how big was the difference?

b. The number of square feet of assembly space per car at each plant is also shown in Table 9.2. If the amount of capital used in a plant is proportional to the number of square feet of assembly space, was the average product of capital higher at one plant that at the other? If so, which plant had the higher average product of capital, and how big was the difference?

c. Table 9.2 also compares how long the inventory of parts would last at the two plants. Why is this of relevance to a firm? All other things equal, should a firm attempt to keep its inventories high or low? Why?

d. If labor were the only variable input, was average variable cost higher or lower at Takaoka than at Framingham? Is it possible to tell from Table 9.2? Why or why not?

e. Table 9.3 summarizes *Consumer Reports*'s annual compendium of auto repair records for 1979. Do the results indicate that U.S. cars were of equivalent quality to Japanese cars? If not,

▪ TABLE 9.3

Repair Ratings for 1979 Cars Produced in Japan and the United States

RATING	PERCENT OF MODELS IN EACH RATING CATEGORY	
	UNITED STATES	JAPAN
Much better than average	0	94
Better than average	15	6
Average	39	0
Worse than average	18	0
Much worse than average	28	0
Total	100	100

SOURCE: *Consumer Reports*, April 1980, as summarized in Kwoka, "Automobiles," p. 72.

does this mean that the figures in Table 9.2 underestimate or overestimate the advantages of Japanese production methods?

PROBLEM 9.4 During the 1970s and 1980s, it was obvious that Japanese firms could produce autos at a substantially lower cost than their U.S. rivals. But it was far less obvious how great the cost differential was or what factors were primarily responsible. Some observers attributed it largely to differences in the production techniques used in the two countries. (Recall Problem 9.3.) Others said it was due primarily to the relatively high wages paid by U.S. auto firms. Still others cited other possible reasons. A number of studies were carried out to shed light on this topic. One of the most influential was by Clifford Winston and his associates at the Brookings Institution in Washington, D.C.[11]

a. Table 9.4 shows the marginal costs of producing a small car in Japan and the United States during the 1970s and early 1980s, according to A. Aizcorde, C. Winston and A. Friedlander. Does it appear that the differential in costs between Japan and the United States was decreasing during this period?

b. According to Aizcorde, Winston, and Friedlander, if U.S. firms could have increased

[11] C. Winston et al., *Blind Intersection?* (Washington, D.C.: Brookings Institution, 1987).

▪ TABLE 9.4

Marginal Costs of Producing a Small Car in Japan and in the United States, 1970–1983

YEAR	MARGINAL COSTS (1975 dollars)	
	UNITED STATES	JAPAN
1970	3,937	1,543
1975	4,391	1,972
1980	4,428	1.763
1981	3.505	1.800
1982	3,336	1,739
1983	3,333	n./.[a]

SOURCE: A. Aizcorde, C. Winston, and A. Friedlander, "Cost Competitiveness of U.S. Automobile Industry," in C. Winston et al., *Blind Intersection?* (Washington, D.C.: Brookings Institution, 1987), p. 10.

[a] Not available.

their 1982 production by 20 percent, their marginal cost would have been $2,718. Does this indicate that the U.S. auto firms were operating under conditions of increasing, constant, or decreasing returns to scale? Why?

c. If U.S. producers could have paid wages equal to those in Japan, their 1982 marginal cost would have been $2,215, according to Aizcorde, Winston, and Friedlander. What does this indicate about the cause of the cost differential?

d. Is the cost differential dependent on how many Japanese yen exchange for 1 U.S. dollar? If so, has the fact that the dollar exchanged for 227 yen in 1980, but only 111 yen in 1993, raised or lowered the cost differential?

e. In 1993, McKinsey and Company published the results of a study of labor productivity in the auto industry in Germany, Japan, and the United States. According to the study, output per hour of labor in 1990 was 16 percent higher in Japan than in the United States and 76 percent higher in Japan than in Germany. The study notes that "the U.S. is much more exposed to the international productivity leaders from Japan than is Germany."[12] Does this

[12] McKinsey Global Institute, *Manufacturing Productivity* (Washington, D.C.: McKinsey and Company, 1993), p. 5.

help to explain the fact that labor productivity in Germany is so low, relative to that in the United States? If so, why?

f. The McKinsey study concluded that "exposure to competition in the late 1980s has helped reduce the productivity gap [between Japan and the United States]. . . . The U.S. is well on track to virtual parity with the Japa-

nese. . . ."[13] If the U.S. automakers attain parity with the Japanese with regard to output per hour of labor, will this mean that the cost of producing a car will be the same in the two countries? Why or why not?

[13] Ibid., p. 17.

10 ▪ Applying Economics: Pricing and Rivalry

The following three problems deal with pricing and rivalry in the auto industry.

PROBLEM 9.5 Before the explosion of gasoline prices and the Japanese onslaught on the U.S. auto industry, the Big Three used cost-plus pricing to establish prices. For example, General Motors, which had the stated objective of earning a 15 percent profit on its total invested capital, added to its average cost a markup big enough to produce the desired return, the result being the so-called **standard price.** Then the firm's high-level price policy committee took this standard price as a first approximation and made small adjustments to reflect competitive conditions. The result was GM's price.[14]

a. Could General Motors calculate the standard price without making some assumption concerning how many cars it would sell in the coming year? Why or why not?

b. If (as generally was the case) General Motors assumed that it would operate at 80 percent of capacity during the coming year, if its capacity was regarded as 5 million cars per year, and if its total invested capital equaled $40 billion, what would be its standard price if its average cost curve was as shown above on the right?

[14] R. Caves, *American Industry: Structure, Conduct, Performance* (Englewood Cliffs, N.J.: Prentice-Hall, 1967.)

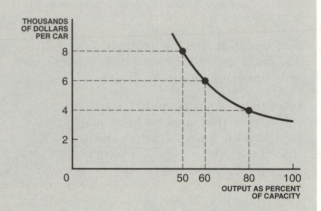

c. In making the final adjustments to arrive at its price, each firm paid close attention to the costs of its rivals and tried to guess what price they were likely to charge. The firm likely to set the lowest price had a disproportionate influence on the level of prices actually charged for a given type of auto. Why?

d. By 1980, the situation in the U.S. auto industry had changed enormously: Consider the pricing of Chrysler's new K car. "On the day in August 1980 when the K car went into production, Chrysler laid off 3,000 of its 6,500 engineers. . . . There was simply no money to pay them. The first K cars came onto the market in October 1980, with 100,000 of the previous year's cars still unsold."[15] What effect did this

[15] Halberstam, *The Reckoning*, p. 557.

inventory of the previous year's cars have on the demand for the new cars?

e. The K car was not the immediate success that Chrysler had hoped for. "[T]he early K cars were loaded with too many options and priced too high. The basic stripped-down K was supposed to sell at $5,800; instead, the average model in the dealers' showroom cost some $2,000 more. Iacocca . . . had opted to go for maximum profit per car."[16] What is wrong with that? Won't the price that maximizes profit per car result in maximum total profit?

PROBLEM 9.6 After the high increases in gasoline prices in the 1970s and the resulting rise in U.S. demand for small, fuel-efficient Japanese cars, U.S. auto firms incurred large losses in 1980, which helped to induce the Reagan administration to impose a quota (misleadingly labeled a "voluntary export restraint") on Japanese auto exports to the United States. As you have seen, this import limitation imposed heavy costs on U.S. consumers. Many economists attacked the quota in the editorial pages of newspapers and in testimony before congressional committees.

a. Figure 9.5 is a simplified representation of the situation in the early 1980s. Suppose that the United States and Japan are the only suppliers of autos. The demand curve for autos in the United States and the supply curve for domestic producers are given. The foreign supply curve in the absence of the quota (of 2.3 million Japanese cars exported to the United States) was S_1; with the quota, it was S_2. Why did the quota push the foreign supply curve upward?

b. By how much did the price of a Japanese car change in the United States due to the imposition of the quota?

c. How many Japanese cars would have been imported into the United States in the absence of the quota?

d. Did U.S. auto makers sell more cars in this country because of the quota? If so, how many more did they sell?

[16] Ibid.

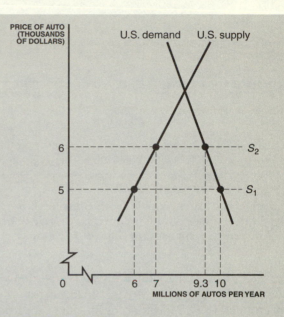

▪ **FIGURE 9.5**

Effect of Quota on Auto Imports

e. Were the U.S. firms able to raise their prices because of the quota? If so, by how much?

f. Is Figure 9.5 based on the assumption that the market for autos in the United States is perfectly competitive? Why or why not?

g. In fact, is the market for autos in the United States perfectly competitive? If not, what sort of a market is it?

PROBLEM 9.7 The auto industry has become highly internationalized. According to Harvard's Kim Clark and Takakiro Fujimoto,

Globalization of competition, a general trend during the 1980s, will continue in the 1990s. Direct product rivalry on an international scale will further intensify as new models penetrate foreign markets and consumers more frequently consider models from different countries. . . . Although some segments [of the market] may remain highly regional—micromini cars in Japan and large road cruisers in the United States, for example—overall the worldwide market of the 1990s will become more crowded with directly competing models from different

▪ **TABLE 9.5**

Profits of Ford and General Motors, Depending on Location of Each Firm's New Plant

POSSIBLE STRATEGIES FOR GENERAL MOTORS	POSSIBLE STRATEGIES FOR FORD			
	LOCATE PLANT IN MEXICO		LOCATE PLANT IN ARGENTINA	
Locate plant in Mexico	Ford's profit:	$300 million	Ford's profit:	$350 million
	GM's profit:	$500 million	GM's profit:	$450 million
Locate plant in Argentina	Ford's profit:	$310 million	Ford's profit:	$250 million
	GM's profit:	$450 million	GM's profit:	$400 million

regions. Customers will become less loyal to particular makes, and producers will have to be even more responsive to changes in customer needs.[17]

a. Some countries have resisted importing foreign cars. For example, in 1962, Mexico prohibited the importation of finished vehicles. There were five auto producers in Mexico (each making about four separate models), and the total national market was about 500,000 cars. Given that an auto assembly plant must produce about 200,000 cars per year to reach minimum efficient size, what problems did this policy cause?[18]

[17] K. Clark and T. Fujimoto, *Product Development Performance* (Boston: Harvard Business School, 1991).

[18] Womack, Jones and Roos, *The Machine That Changed the World*.

b. Suppose that General Motors and Ford are both considering the location of a new plant in either Mexico or Argentina.[19] Suppose that Table 9.5 shows how the profit of each firm depends on which decision each makes. Does General Motors have a dominant strategy? If so, what is it?

c. Does Ford have a dominant strategy? If so, what is it?

d. If you were chairman of Ford, would you expect General Motors to locate its new plant in Mexico or Argentina? Why?

e. Given the answer to part d, what decision would you make if you were chairman of Ford?

f. Where do you think that each firm will locate its new plant? Why?

[19] "New Worlds to Conquer," *Business Week*, February 28, 1994, pp. 50–52.

11 ▪ Applying Economics: Government Regulation

This final problem deals with one aspect of government regulation of the auto industry.

PROBLEM 9.8 In 1975, Congress passed a law establishing corporate average fuel economy (CAFE) standards for new cars sold in the United States. Each auto company's cars had to conform to these standards. Thus, if General Motors sold a car that gets only 15 miles to a gallon, it had to sell enough more-fuel-efficient

cars to bring its average up to the required miles per gallon. If an auto manufacturer did not bring its average up to this figure, it was fined. Thus, General Motors could incur large penalties by falling below the standard by only a mile per gallon.[20]

[20] R. Miller, D. Benjamin, and D. North, *The Economics of Public Issues* (New York: Harper Collins, 1993), p. 194.

a. Should the government insist on very high fuel economy by U.S. cars? What are the benefits to society?

b. What are the costs to society of the CAFE standard?

c. According to Robert Crandall of the Brookings Institution and John Graham of Harvard University, the CAFE standard has prompted the auto industry to make cars that are about 500 pounds lighter than they otherwise would have been. Such a weight reduction would be expected to result in thousands of extra deaths and serious injuries per year. Is this a cost of the CAFE standard? Why or why not?

d. The price of gasoline was much higher when Congress passed the CAFE standard than in 1994. Does this mean that the optimal level of fuel economy was probably lower in 1994 than when Congress passed the CAFE standard? Why or why not?

e. In 1986, Robert Crandall, Howard Gruenspecht, Theodore Keeler, and Lester Lave (all

associated with the Brookings Institution) concluded that ". . . we see no need to compel further improvements in fuel efficiency. Car buyers can be left to choose their own fuel efficiency. If future improvements in fuel efficiency were desired, the most direct way to obtain them would be to raise gasoline prices by increasing the federal tax."[21] Why would increased gasoline prices have this effect?

f. According to Crandall and his colleagues, "Unlike new car standards, an increase in gasoline prices would raise the turnover in the automobile fleet, ridding society of gas-guzzling, polluting and less safe vehicles."[22] Why would increased gasoline prices have this effect, whereas more stringent CAFE standards would not?

[21] R. Crandall, H. Gruenspecht, T. Keeler, and L. Lave, *Regulating the Automobile* (Washington, D.C.: Brookings Institution, 1986), p. 158.

[22] Ibid.

12 ▪ Conclusion

Henry Ford and Alfred Sloan were two of the founders of the auto industry; Lee Iacocca was one of its recent titans. To understand the actions of these industry leaders, as well as those of the many people who worked for and competed with them, it is essential to have some knowledge of the theory of oligopoly and monopolistic competition and the nature of public policy toward industry. Clearly, the Big Three, together with Toyota, Honda, and a few other producers, dominate the U.S. market, and the theories of oligopolistic rivalry and cooperation summarized in Chapter 7 are relevant and useful. And since the U.S. government has had a substantial influence on the industry (for example, the Chrysler bailout, the import restrictions on Japanese autos, and the fuel efficiency standards), the importance of studying public policy in this area is undeniable too. If you want to understand the enormous changes in the auto industry, and their effects, you have to understand these topics in economics.

The Distribution of Income

Wages

1 ■ The Firm's Demand Curve for Labor

Let's begin by discussing the determinants of the price of labor under perfect competition. That is, we assume that firms take the prices of their products, as well as the prices of all inputs, as given; and we assume that owners of inputs take input prices as given. Under these circumstances, what determines how much labor an individual firm will hire (at a specified wage rate)? Once we answer this question, we can derive a firm's demand curve for labor. A **firm's demand curve for labor** is the relationship between the price of labor and the amount of labor utilized by the firm. That is, it shows, for each price, the amount of labor that the firm will use.

THE PROFIT-MAXIMIZING QUANTITY OF LABOR

Let us assume that we know the firm's production function, and that labor is the only variable input. Given the production function, we can determine the marginal product of labor when various quantities are used. The results of such a calculation are as shown in Table 10.1. If the

price of the firm's product is $10, let's determine the value to the firm of each additional worker it hires per day.[1] According to Table 10.1, the firm achieves a daily output of 7 units when it hires the first worker; and since each unit is worth $10, this brings the firm's daily revenues up to $70. By hiring the second worker, the firm increases its daily output by 6 units; and since each unit is worth $10, the resulting increase in the firm's daily revenues is $60. Similarly, the increase in the firm's daily revenues from hiring the third worker is $50, the increase from hiring the fourth worker is $40, and so on.

A firm should hire more workers as long as the extra workers result in at least as great an addition to revenues as they do to costs. Although this is a relatively simple idea, when stated this baldly, it nonetheless is very important. Consider the firm in Table 10.1. If the price of a worker is $50 per day, it is profitable for this firm to hire the first worker

[1] For simplicity, we assume that the number of workers that the firm hires per day must be an integer, not a fraction. This assumption is innocuous, and can easily be relaxed.

■ TABLE 10.1

The Firm's Demand for Labor under Perfect
Competition

NUMBER OF WORKERS PER DAY	TOTAL OUTPUT PER DAY	MARGINAL PRODUCT OF LABOR	VALUE OF MARGINAL PRODUCT (dollars)
0	0		
		7	70
1	7		
		6	60
2	13		
		5	50
3	18		
		4	40
4	22		
		3	30
5	25		

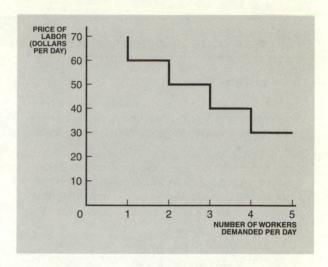

■ FIGURE 10.1

The Firm's Demand Curve for Labor under Perfect
Competition

The firm's demand curve for labor is the firm's value-of-marginal-product curve, which shows the value of labor's marginal product at each quantity of labor used. The data for this figure come from Table 10.1.

since this adds $70 to the firm's daily revenues but only $50 to its daily costs. Also, it is profitable to hire the second worker, since this adds $60 to the firm's daily revenues but only $50 to its daily costs. The addition of the third worker does not reduce the firm's profits. But beyond three workers per day, it does not pay the firm to hire more labor. (The addition of a fourth worker adds $50 to the firm's daily costs but only $40 to its daily revenues.)

THE VALUE OF THE MARGINAL PRODUCT OF LABOR

Thus the optimal number of workers per day for this firm is three. Table 10.1 shows that this is the number of workers at which the value of the marginal product of labor is equal to the price of labor. What is the **value of the marginal product of labor?** It is the marginal product of labor multiplied by the product's price. In Table 10.1, the value of the marginal product of labor is $70 when between 0 and 1 workers are used per day. Why? Because the marginal product of labor is 7 units of output, and the price of a unit of output is $10. Thus this product—7 times $10—equals $70.

To maximize profit, the value of the marginal product of labor must be set equal to the price of labor, because if the value of the marginal product is greater than labor's price, the firm can increase its profit by increasing the quantity used of labor; whereas if the value of the marginal

product is less than labor's price, the firm can increase its profit by reducing the quantity used of labor. Thus *profits must be at a maximum when the value of the marginal product is equal to the price of labor.*

Given the results of this section, it is a simple matter to derive the firm's demand curve for labor. Specifically, its demand curve must be the value-of-marginal-product schedule in the last column of Table 10.1. If the daily wage of a worker is between $51 and $60, the firm will demand two workers per day; if the daily wage of a worker is between $41 and $50, the firm will demand three workers per day; and so forth. Thus *the firm's demand curve for labor is its value-of-marginal-product curve,* which shows the value of labor's marginal product at each quantity of labor used. This curve is shown in Figure 10.1.[2]

---

[2] Strictly speaking, the firm's demand curve is the same as the curve showing the value of the input's marginal product only if this input is the only variable input. For a discussion of the more general case, see my *Microeconomics: Theory and Applications* (9th ed.; New York: Norton, 1997), Chapter 14.

TEST YOUR UNDERSTANDING

True or false?

_____ **1** If the value of the marginal product is greater than the input's price, the perfectly competitive firm can increase its profit by decreasing its utilization of the input.

_____ **2** A firm's demand curve for an input shows the relationship between the input's price and the amount of the input utilized by the firm. That is, it shows, for each price, the amount of the input that the firm will use.

_____ **3** The value of the marginal product must always exceed zero.

Exercise

1 To maximize profit, competitive firms should hire labor up to the point where the value of labor's marginal product is equal to the price of labor. This rule for profit maximization applies to any input, not just to labor. In other words, to maximize profit, competitive firms should hire any input up to the point where the value of the input's marginal product is equal to the input's price.

Water is an important input in California's agricultural industries, particularly during the drought that afflicted the state during 1990 and 1991. The value of the marginal product of an extra acre-foot of water in the production of various California crops has been estimated to be as follows:

Lemons	$62.00	Grain hay	$31.37
Cotton	55.98	Celery	20.77
Onions	51.50	Asparagus	17.40
Oranges	46.86	Peaches	10.59
Tomatoes	32.75	Lima beans	8.83

a. If an extra acre-foot of water were used to produce lemons, what would be the value of the extra lemons produced?

b. If an extra acre-foot of water were used to produce lima beans, what would be the value of the extra lima beans produced?

c. If a firm produces both lemons and lima beans, would the firm increase its profits if it could transfer (at no cost) an acre-foot of water from its lima bean production to its lemon production? Why or why not?

d. If California's agricultural producers are maximizing profit, is the price of water the same for lemon producers as for lima bean producers? Why or why not?

2 ▪ Wages under Perfect Competition

THE MARKET DEMAND CURVE FOR LABOR

In the previous section, the topic was the demand curve of a single firm for labor. But many firms, not just one, are part of the labor market, and the price of labor depends on the demands of all these firms. The situation is analogous to the price of a product, which depends on the demands of all consumers. _The **market demand curve for labor** shows the relationship between the price of labor and the total amount of labor demanded in the market. That is, it shows, for each price, the amount of labor that will be demanded in the entire market._ The market demand curve for labor, like any other input, is quite analogous to the market demand curve for a consumer good, which was discussed in detail in Chapter 1.

But there is at least one important difference. _The demand for labor and other inputs is a **derived demand,** since inputs are demanded to produce other things, not as an end in themselves._ This fact helps to explain why the price elasticity of demand is higher for some inputs than for others. In particular, the larger the price elasticity of demand for the product the input helps produce, the larger the price elasticity of demand for the input. (In addition, the price elasticity of demand for an input is likely to be greater in the long run than in the short run, and greater if other inputs can readily be substituted for the input in question.)

THE MARKET SUPPLY CURVE FOR LABOR

You have already seen that a product's price depends on its market supply curve as well as its market demand curve. This is equally true for labor. *Its* **market supply curve** *is the relationship between the price of labor and the total amount of labor supplied in the market.* When individuals supply labor, they are supplying something they themselves can use, since the time that they do not work can be used for leisure activities. (As Charles Lamb, the English essayist, put it, "Who first invented work, and bound the free and holiday-rejoicing spirit down . . . to that dry drudgery at the desk's dead wood?") Because of this fact, the market supply curve for labor, unlike the supply curve for inputs supplied by business firms, may be **backward bending,** particularly for the economy as a whole. That is, *beyond some point, increases in price may result in smaller amounts of labor being supplied.*

An example of a backward-bending supply curve is provided in Figure 10.2. What factors account for a curve like this? Basically, the reason is that as the price of labor is increased, individuals supplying the labor become richer. And when they become richer, they want to increase their amount of leisure time; this means that they want to work less. Even though the amount of money per hour they give up by not working is greater than when the price of labor was lower, they nonetheless choose to increase their leisure time. This sort of tendency has shown up quite clearly in the last century. As wage rates have increased and living standards have risen, the average work week has tended to decline.

Note that there is no contradiction between the assumption that the supply curve of labor or other inputs *to an individual firm* is horizontal under perfect competition and the fact that the *market* supply curve for the input may not be horizontal. For example, unskilled labor may be

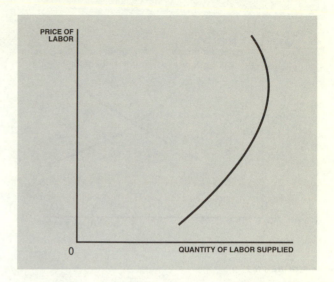

PRICE OF LABOR

0   QUANTITY OF LABOR SUPPLIED

▪ **FIGURE 10.2**

Backward-Bending Supply Curve for Labor

Beyond some point, increases in the price of labor may result in smaller amounts of labor being supplied. The reason for a supply curve of this sort is that, as the price of labor increases, the individuals supplying the labor become richer and want to increase their amount of leisure time.

available to any firm in a particular area at a given wage rate in as great an amount as it could possibly use. But the total amount of unskilled labor supplied in this area may increase relatively little with increases in the wage rate. The situation is similar to the sale of products. As you saw in Chapter 4, any firm under perfect competition believes that it can sell all it wants at the existing price. Yet the total amount of the product sold in the entire market can ordinarily be increased only by lowering the price.

EQUILIBRIUM PRICE AND QUANTITY OF LABOR

Labor's price (or wage rate) is determined under perfect competition in essentially the same way that a product's price is determined—by supply and demand.

The price of labor will tend toward equilibrium at the level where the quantity of labor demanded equals the quantity of labor supplied. Thus, in Figure 10.3,

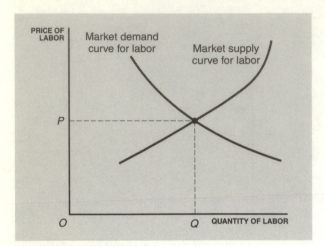

■ **FIGURE 10.3**

Equilibrium Price and Quantity of Labor

The equilibrium price of labor is *OP*, and the equilibrium quantity of labor used is *OQ*.

the equilibrium price of labor is *OP*. If the price were higher than *OP*, the quantity supplied would exceed the quantity demanded and there would be downward pressure on the price. If the price were lower than *OP*, the quantity supplied would fall short of the quantity demanded and there would be upward pressure on the price. By the same token, *the equilibrium amount of labor utilized is also given by the intersection of the market supply and demand curves*. In Figure 10.3, *OQ* units of labor will be utilized in equilibrium in the entire market.

Graphs such as Figure 10.3 are useful, but it is important to look behind the geometry and to recognize the factors that lie behind the demand and supply curves for labor. Consider the market for surgeons and that for unskilled labor. As shown in Figure 10.4, the demand curve for the services of surgeons is to the right of the demand curve for unskilled labor (particularly at high wage rates). Why is this so? Because an hour of a surgeon's services is worth more to people than

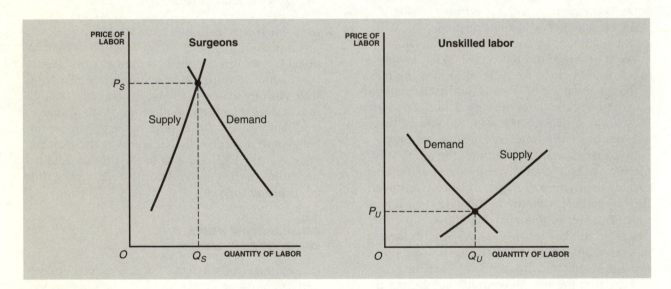

■ **FIGURE 10.4**

The Labor Market for Surgeons and Unskilled Labor

The wage for surgeons is higher than for unskilled labor because the demand curve for surgeons is farther to the right and the supply curve for surgeons is farther to the left than the corresponding curves for unskilled labor.

an hour of an unskilled laborer's services. In this sense, surgeons are more productive than unskilled laborers. Also, as shown in Figure 10.4, the supply curve for the services of surgeons is far to the left of the supply curve for unskilled labor. Why is this so? Because very few people are licensed surgeons, whereas practically everyone can do unskilled labor. In other words, surgeons are much scarcer than unskilled laborers.

For these reasons, surgeons receive a much higher wage rate than unskilled laborers do. As shown in Figure 10.4, the equilibrium price of labor for surgeons is much higher than for un-

skilled labor. If unskilled laborers could quickly and easily turn themselves into competent surgeons, this difference in wage rates would be eliminated by competition, since unskilled workers would find it profitable to become surgeons. But unskilled workers lack the training and often the ability to become surgeons. Thus surgeons and unskilled labor are examples of **noncompeting groups.** Wage differentials can be expected to persist among noncompeting groups because people cannot move from the low-paid to the high-paid jobs. But this is not the only reason for wage differentials, as you will see in the next section.

 TEST YOUR UNDERSTANDING

True or false?

_____ **1** If a technological change occurs which increases the marginal productivity of labor, and if at the same time the supply curve of labor shifts to the right, the price of labor must fall.

_____ **2** Beyond some point, increases in wages may result in smaller amounts of labor being supplied.

_____ **3** The reason for a backward-bending supply curve for labor is that, as the price of labor increases, the individual supplying the labor becomes richer and wants to increase his or her amount of leisure time.

_____ **4** Under perfect competition, the supply of labor to an individual firm is a horizontal line.

Exercises

1 Suppose that a perfectly competitive firm's production function is as follows:

QUANTITY OF LABOR (years)	OUTPUT PER YEAR (thousands of units)
0	0
1	3.0
2	5.0
3	6.8
4	8.0
5	9.0

The firm is a profit maximizer, and the labor market is competitive. Labor must be hired in integer numbers and for a year (no more, no less). If the firm hires four years of labor, and if the price of a unit of the firm's product is $3, you can establish a range for what the annual wage prevailing in the labor market must be.

a. What is the maximum amount it can be?

b. What is the minimum amount? Why?

c. Do these numbers seem realistic? Why or why not?

2 On the basis of the data in Question 1, what is the marginal product of labor when between one and two years of labor are used?

3 ■ Wage Differentials

Everyone realizes that, even in the same occupation, some people get paid more than others. Why is this true?

DIFFERENCES IN ABILITY OR SKILL

One reason for such wage differentials is that people differ in productive capacity; thus each worker differs from the next in the value of his or her output. Under these circumstances, the difference in wages paid to workers equals the difference in their marginal products' value. Consider the case of two lathe operators—Roberta and Leo. Roberta works for firm X and Leo works for firm Y. Roberta (together with the appropriate tools and materials) can produce output worth $2,000 per month and Leo (with the same tools and materials) can produce output worth $1,900 per month. In equilibrium, Roberta will earn $100 more per month than Leo. If the difference in wages were less than $100, Leo's employer would find it profitable to replace Leo with Roberta, since this would increase the value of output by $100 and cost less than $100. If the difference were more than $100, Roberta's employer would find it profitable to replace Roberta with Leo; although this would reduce the value of output

by $100, it would reduce costs by more than $100.

DIFFERENCES IN TRAINING

Besides differences in productive capacity and ability, there are many more reasons for wage differentials. Even if all workers were of equal ability, these differentials would still exist to offset differences in the characteristics of various occupations and areas. Some occupations require large investments in training, whereas other occupations require a much smaller investment in training. Chemists must spend about eight years in undergraduate and graduate training. During each year of training, they incur direct expenses for books, tuition, and the like, and they lose the incomes they could make if they were to work rather than go to school. Clearly, if their net remunerations are to be as high in chemistry as in other jobs they might take, they must make greater wages when they get through than persons of comparable age, intelligence, and motivation whose jobs require no training beyond high school. The difference in wages must be at least sufficient to compensate for the investments in extra training.

 TEST YOUR UNDERSTANDING

True or false?

_____ **1** The differential in wages between skilled and unskilled laborers of the same type will be due, at least in part, to the differential in their marginal products.

_____ **2** The wage for surgeons is higher than for unskilled labor because the demand curve for surgeons is farther to the right and the supply curve for surgeons is farther to the left than the corresponding curves for unskilled labor.

_____ **3** Wage differentials cannot be expected to persist among noncompeting groups because people can move from the low-paid to the high-paid jobs.

Exercises

1 "It is foolish to believe that a bonus payment system can increase a firm's profits. After all, such a system will increase a worker's wage; thus it must increase the firm's costs and reduce its profits." Comment and evaluate.

2 Suppose that the marginal product of skilled labor to a perfectly competitive firm is 2 units and the price of skilled labor is $8 an hour, while the marginal product of unskilled labor is 1 unit and the price of unskilled labor is $5.50 an hour. Is the firm minimizing its costs? (*Hint:* Regard skilled labor and unskilled labor as two separate inputs, and apply the cost-minimization rule in Chapter 2.)

4 ▪ Monopsony

In previous sections, it has been assumed that perfect competition exists in the labor market. In some cases, however, **monopsony** exists instead. *A monopsony is a market structure in which there is a single buyer.* Thus a single firm may hire all the labor in an isolated "company town," such as exists in the coal-mining regions of West Virginia and Kentucky. What determines the price of labor under monopsony? Suppose the firm's demand curve for labor and the supply curve of labor are as shown in Figure 10.5. Because the firm is the sole buyer of labor, it takes into account the fact that to acquire more labor it must pay a higher wage to *all* workers, not just the extra workers. For example, if the firm wants to increase the number of workers it employs from five to six, it may have to pay the sixth an hourly wage of $9. If the supply curve of labor slopes upward to the right, this wage is more than was required to obtain the first five workers. Since the firm must pay all workers the same wage to avoid labor unrest, it must raise the wages of the first five workers to the level of the sixth if it hires the sixth worker. Thus *the cost of hiring the sixth worker exceeds the wage that must be paid this worker*.

The supply curve for labor in Figure 10.5 shows the cost of hiring an additional worker if workers already employed do *not* have to be paid a higher wage when the additional worker is hired. Thus the supply curve does *not* show the true additional cost to the monopsonist of hiring an additional worker, for reasons given in the previous paragraph. Instead, curve *A*, which includes wages that must be paid to the workers already employed, shows the true additional cost.

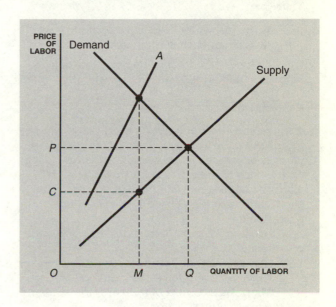

▪ **FIGURE 10.5**

Equilibrium Wage and Quantity of Labor under Monopsony

The monopsonistic firm, if it maximizes profit, will hire laborers up to the point where the extra cost of adding an extra laborer, shown by curve *A*, equals the extra revenue from adding the extra laborer, shown by the demand curve for labor.

For the reasons given above, curve *A* lies above the supply curve.

If profit is maximized, the monopsonistic firm will hire labor up to the point at which the extra cost of adding an additional laborer (shown by curve *A*) equals the extra revenue from adding the additional laborer (shown by the demand curve). Thus the quantity of labor purchased will be *OM* and the price of labor will be *OC* in Figure 10.5. In contrast, under perfectly competitive conditions, the equilibrium quantity and price would be at the intersection of the demand and supply curves. That is, the quantity of labor pur-chased would be *OQ* and the price of labor would be *OP*.

What is the effect of monopsony on the wage rate and the amount of labor hired? In general, the wage rate, as well as the quantity hired, is lower under monopsony than under perfect competition.

 TEST YOUR UNDERSTANDING

True or false?

_____ **1** The market for college professors in New York City is a monopsony.

_____ **2** Under monopsony, the wage rate tends to be higher than under perfect competition.

Exercises

1 In the early days of baseball, every player was free to sign with any team at the end of the season. Owners of baseball teams found themselves bidding up the price of players, and watched stars switch teams. At a secret meeting in 1879, they agreed that each team could protect five of its players from being hired away.

a. Before 1879, what factors governed the wage of a baseball player?

b. After 1879, what factors governed the wage of the five players that a team could protect?

c. What was the effect of the 1879 agreement on the wage of baseball players?

By 1890, the owners had extended their agree-ment to include all baseball players. Every player on every team had to work for the team they signed their first contracts with-or leave baseball. The team could trade a player to another team, but the player could not switch teams. Then, in 1975, two pitchers, Dave McNally of the Montreal Expos and Andy Messersmith of the Los Angeles Dodgers, challenged this arrangement. A legal battle ensued.

d. Eventually, the rules governing the hiring of baseball players were changed. Players were allowed to declare themselves free agents, and other teams were allowed to bid for their services. What was the likely effect of this change on the wage of a baseball player?

e. From the mid-1970s to the early 1980s, the average player's salary more than tripled. Is this in accord with your prediction in part d?

2 Suppose that a perfectly competitive firm suddenly becomes a monopsonist in the market for labor. Do you think that it would pay a lower, a higher, or the same wage rate as it did before?

3 Suppose that you were the president of a small firm that hired nonunion labor. How would you go about estimating the marginal product of a certain worker or of certain types of workers? Would it be easy? If not, does this mean that the theory of wage determination is incorrect or useless?

5 ■ Labor Unions

Over one-tenth of the nonfarm workers in the United States belongs to a union, and the per-fectly competitive model does not apply to these workers any more than it does to monopsonistic labor markets. The biggest unions are the National Education Association, the Teamsters, and the Food and Commercial Workers, each with 1.4 million members or more. Next come the Automobile, Aerospace, and Agricultural Implement Workers; the State, County, and Municipal Employees; and the United Auto Workers, each with over a million members.

The **national unions** are of great importance in the U.S. labor movement.[3] The supreme governing body of the national union is the convention, which is held every year or two. The delegates to the convention have the authority to set policy for the union. However, considerable power is exercised by the national union's officers.

A national union is composed of **local unions,** each in a given area or plant. Some local unions have only a few members, but others have thousands. The local union, with its own president and officers, often plays an important role in collective bargaining. The extent to which the local unions maintain their autonomy varies from one national union to another. In industries where

[3] Sometimes they are called international unions because some locals are outside the United States, for example, in Canada.

markets are localized (like construction and printing), the locals are more autonomous than in industries where markets are national (like steel, automobiles, and coal).

Finally, there is the **AFL-CIO,** a federation of national unions created by the merger of the American Federation of Labor and the Congress of Industrial Organizations in 1955. The AFL-CIO does not include all national unions. The United Mine Workers refused to join the AFL-CIO, and the Auto Workers left it in 1968. (The Teamsters were kicked out in the mid-1950s because of corruption, but in 1987 they were allowed to rejoin.) The AFL-CIO is a very important representative of the U.S. labor movement; but because the national unions in the AFL-CIO have given up relatively little of their power to the federation, its authority is limited.

The AFL-CIO is organized along the lines indicated in Figure 10.6. The constitution of the AFL-CIO puts supreme governing power in the hands of a biennial convention. The national unions are represented at these conventions on the basis of

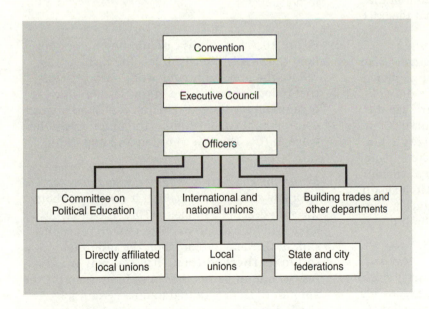

▪ **FIGURE 10.6**

Structure of AFL-CIO

The AFL-CIO, which resulted from a merger of the AFL and CIO in 1955, is organized with the governing power in the hands of a biennial convention.

their dues-paying membership. Between conventions, the AFL-CIO's business is directed by its president (John Sweeney in 1997) and secretary-treasurer, as well as by various committees and councils composed of representatives of various national unions or people elected at the convention. The AFL-CIO contains seven trade and industrial departments, such as building trades, food and beverage trades, maritime trades, and so forth. Also, as indicated by Figure 10.6, a few local unions are not affiliated with a national union, but are directly affiliated with the AFL-CIO.

HOW UNIONS INCREASE WAGES

Unions wield considerable power, and economists must include them in their analyses if they want their models of the labor market to reflect conditions in the real world. To see how this is done, begin by supposing that a union wants to increase the wage rate paid its members. How can it accomplish this objective? In other words, how can it alter the market supply curve for labor or the market demand curve for labor, so that the price of labor—its wage—will increase?

1 *The union may try to shift the supply curve of labor to the left.* It may shift the supply curve as shown in Figure 10.7, with the result that the price of labor will increase from OP to OP_1. How can the union cause this shift in the supply curve? Craft unions have frequently forced employers to hire only union members, and then restricted union membership by high initiation fees, reduction in new membership, and other devices. In addition, unions have favored legislation to reduce immigration, shorten working hours, and limit the labor supply in other ways.

2 *The union may try to get the employers to pay a higher wage, while allowing some of the supply of labor forthcoming at this higher wage to find no opportunity for work.* In Figure 10.8, the union may exert pressure on the employers to raise the price of labor from OP to OP_1. At OP_1, not all the available supply of labor can find jobs. The quantity of labor supplied is OQ_2, while the amount of labor demanded is OQ_1. The effect is the same as in

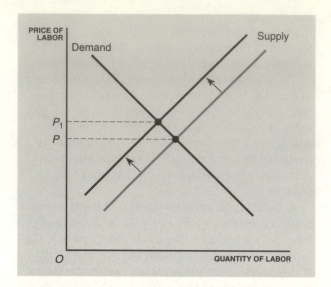

FIGURE 10.7

Shift of Supply Curve for Labor

A union may shift the supply curve to the left by getting employers to hire only union members and then restricting union membership or by other techniques.

Figure 10.7, but in this case the union does not limit the supply directly. It lets the higher wage reduce the opportunity for work. Strong industrial unions often behave in this fashion. Having organized practically all the relevant workers and controlling the labor supply, the union raises the wage to OP_1. This is a common and important case.

3 *The union may try to shift the demand curve for labor upward and to the right.* If it can bring about the shift described in Figure 10.9, the price of labor will increase from OP to OP_2. To cause this shift in the demand for labor, the union may resort to **featherbedding.** That is, it may try to restrict output per worker in order to increase the amount of labor required to do a certain job. (To cite but one case, the railroad unions have insisted on much unnecessary labor.) Unions also try to shift the demand curve by helping the employers compete against other industries or by helping to make Congress pass legislation that protects the employers from foreign competition.

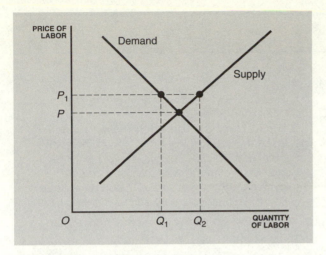

FIGURE 10.8

Direct Increase in Price of Labor

A union may get the employer to raise the wage from *OP* to *OP₁* and let the higher wage reduce the opportunity for work. This is commonly done by strong industrial unions.

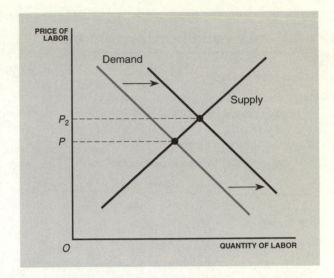

FIGURE 10.9

Shift in Demand Curve for Labor

A union may shift the demand curve for labor to the right by featherbedding or other devices, and thus increase the wage from *OP* to *OP₂*.

COLLECTIVE BARGAINING

Collective bargaining is the process of negotiation between the union and management over wages and working conditions. Representatives of the union and management meet periodically to work out an agreement or contract; this process generally begins a few months before the old labor contract runs out. Typically, each side asks at first for more than it expects to get, and compromises must be made to reach an agreement. The union representatives take the agreement to their members, who must vote to accept or reject it. If they reject it, they may vote to strike or to continue to negotiate.

Collective bargaining agreements vary greatly. Some pertain to only a single plant whereas others apply to an entire industry. However, an agreement generally contains the following elements. It specifies the extent and kind of recognition that management gives the union, the level of wage rates for particular jobs, the length of the work week, the rate of overtime pay, the extent to which seniority will determine which workers will be first to be laid off, the nature and extent of management's prerogatives, and how grievances between workers and the employer will be handled.

Historically, industries and firms have extended recognition to unions by accepting one of three agreements—the closed shop, the union shop, or the open shop. In a **closed shop,** workers must be union members before they can be hired. This gives the union more power than if there is a **union shop,** in which the employer can hire nonunion workers who must then become union members in a certain length of time after being hired. In an **open shop,** the employer can hire union or nonunion labor, and nonunion workers need not, once employed, join the union. The closed shop was banned by the Taft-Hartley Act, passed in 1947. The Taft-Hartley Act also says that the union shop is legal unless outlawed by state laws; and in about 20 states there are "right to work" laws that make the union shop illegal. Needless to say, these right-to-work laws are hated by organized labor, which regards them as a threat to its security and effectiveness.

TEST YOUR UNDERSTANDING

True or false?

_____ **1** In a closed shop, workers must be union members before they can be hired.

_____ **2** If a union shifts the supply curve of labor to the left, and if the price elasticity of demand for labor is infinite, the price of labor will rise.

_____ **3** All unions are organizations of workers in a particular occupation.

Exercises

1 In many isolated areas, a single firm is the only employer of a certain kind of labor. Suppose that a textile firm is in this position, and that its demand curve for labor, as well as the supply curve for labor, are shown below. Curve A shows the extra cost to the firm of adding an extra laborer.

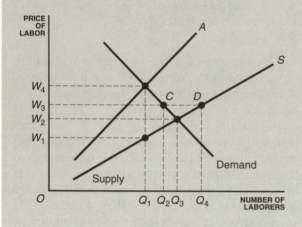

a. How many laborers will the firm hire, and how much will each be paid?

b. Suppose that a union enters the market and that it sets a wage of OW_3. What now is the supply curve for labor?

c. How many laborers will the firm hire now? Is employment higher than before the union entered?

d. Will there be involuntary employment now?

2 "The unions should not be exempt from the antitrust laws." Comment and evaluate.

3 Do you think that labor unions try to maximize the wage rate?

▪ CHAPTER REVIEW

KEY TERMS

firm's demand curve for labor

value of the marginal product of labor

market demand curve for labor

derived demand

market supply curve

backward bending

noncompeting groups

monopsony

national unions

local unions

AFL-CIO

featherbedding

collective bargaining

closed shop

union shop

open shop

COMPLETION QUESTIONS

1 In competitive firm *X*, the marginal product of the first unit of labor is 3 units of output, the marginal product of the second unit of labor is 2 units of output, and the marginal product of the third unit of labor is 1 unit of output. If the price of a unit of output is $15, the firm will demand _____ unit(s) of labor when the price of a unit of labor is $40, _____ unit(s) of labor when the price of a unit of labor is $25, and _____ unit(s) of labor when the price of labor is $20.

2 A perfectly competitive firm's demand curve for labor slopes downward and to the right because of the law of _____. This is because the firm's demand curve for labor is the same as its _____ curve, and the _____ is equal to the price of the product times the marginal product of labor.

3 To a monopsonist, the cost of hiring an additional laborer (decreases, increases) _____ as it hires more and more labor. The cost of hiring an additional laborer (exceeds, equals, is less than) _____ the wage that must be paid this worker. For example, if the monopsonist can hire 10 workers at a daily wage of $35 and 11 workers at a daily wage of $40, the cost of hiring the eleventh worker is _____, as compared with the wage of the eleventh worker, which is _____.

4 The profit-maximizing competitive firm uses each input in an amount such that the input's _____ multiplied by the _____ equals the input's _____.

5 Since inputs are demanded to produce other things, the demand for labor and other inputs is called a(n) _____ demand.

6 Labor's _____ is the relationship between the price of labor and the total amount of labor supplied in the market.

7 _____ is a market structure where there is a single buyer.

8 In the AFL-CIO, the supreme governing power is put in the hands of a _____.

9 Trying to restrict output per worker in order to increase the amount of labor required to do a certain job is called _____.

10 If profit is maximized, the monopsonistic firm will hire labor up to the point at which the extra cost of adding a(n) _____ laborer equals the extra revenue from adding the _____ laborer. The wage rate, as well as the quantity hired, is (higher, lower)

ANSWERS TO COMPLETION QUESTIONS

1
2

2

diminishing marginal returns
value-of-marginal-product
value of the marginal product

increases

exceeds

$90

$40

marginal product
product's price
price

derived

market supply curve

Monopsony

convention

featherbedding

additional
additional

_____ under monopsony than under perfect competition.   lower

11 In a(n) _____ shop a worker must be a union member before he or she can be hired. This gives the union more power than a(n) _____ shop, in which the employer can hire nonunion workers who must then become union members in a certain length of time after being hired. In a(n) _____ shop, the employer can hire both union and nonunion workers, and the latter need not join a union once employed.

closed

union

open

NUMERICAL PROBLEMS

1 Suppose that the demand curve for lawyers is as follows:

ANNUAL WAGE (thousands of dollars)	QUANTITY OF LABOR DEMANDED (thousands of person-years)
30	200
45	180
60	160
75	140
90	120
105	100
120	80

a Draw the demand curve for lawyers.

b Suppose that the supply curve for lawyers is as follows:

ANNUAL WAGE (thousands of dollars)	QUANTITY OF LABOR SUPPLIED (thousands of person-years)
30	80
45	100
60	120
75	140
90	160
105	180
120	200

Draw the supply curve for lawyers on the graph for part a.

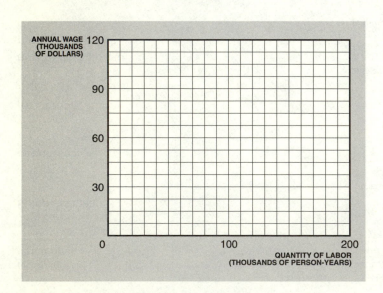

c What is the equilibrium wage for lawyers if the market is perfectly competitive?

d Suppose that lawyers form a union, and that the union forces the wage up to $105,000 a year. How many person-years of labor will be supplied but will be unable to find work?

2 Suppose that the relationship between the number of laborers employed per day in a car wash and the number of cars washed per day is as follows:

NUMBER OF LABORERS	CARS WASHED
1	15
2	40
3	50
4	55

a Suppose that the owner of the car wash receives $2 for each car wash, and that the price of labor is $20 per day. How many laborers will the owner hire per day?

b What is the value of the marginal product of labor when between one and two laborers per day are used? When between two and three laborers per day are used? When between three and four laborers per day are used?

c If the owner of the car wash hires three laborers per day, does the value of the marginal product of labor equal the wage?

3 Suppose that the Ace Manufacturing Company is a member of a perfectly competitive industry. Suppose that the relationship between various amounts of labor input and output is as shown below.

PRODUCT PRICE (dollars)	UNITS OF LABOR	UNITS OF OUTPUT	MARGINAL PRODUCT OF LABOR	VALUE OF MARGINAL PRODUCT (dollars)
10	0	0		
10	1	2½	_____	_____
10	2	5	_____	_____
10	3	7	_____	_____
10	4	8	_____	_____

a Fill in the blanks.

b If you are told that the Ace Manufacturing Company is hiring 3 units of labor, you can establish a range for

the value of the wage rate prevailing in the labor market (assuming that the firm maximizes profit). What is this range? Specifically, what is the maximum value that the wage (for a unit of labor) may be? What is the minimum value? Why?

c Suppose that the Ace Manufacturing Company must pay $20 for a unit of labor. How many units of labor will it hire? Why?

d In the graph below, draw the Ace Manufacturing Company's demand curve for labor.

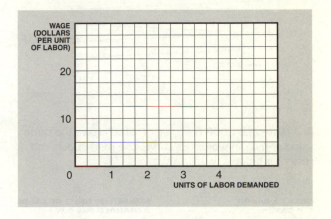

e Suppose that the Ace Manufacturing Company were a monopsonist rather than a perfectly competitive firm. Do you think it would pay a higher, a lower, or the same wage? Why?

4 The demand and supply curves for musicians in a particular area in 1996 are as shown below.

a If a union makes the users of musicians demand 50 percent more hours per week of musicians' time than in 1996 at each wage rate, draw the new demand curve in the graph.

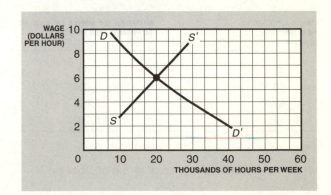

b After the union shifts the demand curve, perhaps due to featherbedding, what will be the new equilibrium wage? What will be the new equilibrium quantity employed?

5 A perfectly competitive firm has the following value-of-marginal-product curve:

NUMBER OF UNITS OF LABOR PER DAY	VALUE OF MARGINAL PRODUCT (dollars)
1	52
2	47
3	42
4	37
5	32
6	

(The lines connect the number of units of labor to the value of marginal product in a crisscross pattern.)

a If there are 1,000 firms, all of which have the same value-of-marginal-product curve, the market demand curve for labor is as follows:

PRICE OF LABOR PER DAY (dollars)	NUMBER OF UNITS OF LABOR DEMANDED PER DAY
50	_____
45	_____
40	_____
35	_____

Fill in the blanks above. (Assume that only integer numbers of units of labor can be used.)

b The supply curve for labor is as follows:

PRICE OF LABOR PER DAY (dollars)	NUMBER OF UNITS OF LABOR SUPPLIED PER DAY
35	3,000
40	4,000
45	5,000
50	6,000

What is the equilibrium price of a unit of labor per day?

c What will be the total amount of labor demanded in the market? What will be the amount demanded by each firm?

d What will be the extra cost that a firm would incur if it added an extra unit of labor per day?

e What will be the value of the marginal product of labor for this firm?

f If a minimum wage of $45 per day were established, what would be the total amount of labor demanded in the market?

6 Firm *R*, a monopsonist, confronts the supply curve for labor shown below:

WAGE RATE PER HOUR (dollars)	NUMBER OF UNITS OF LABOR SUPPLIED PER HOUR	COST OF ADDING AN ADDITIONAL UNIT OF LABOR PER HOUR (dollars)
3	1	_____
4	2	_____
5	3	_____
6	4	_____
7	5	_____
8	6	_____

a Fill in the blanks. (Assume that only integer numbers of units of labor can be used.)

b Firm *R*'s demand curve for labor is a horizontal line at a wage rate of $8 per hour. What quantity of labor will firm *R* demand?

c What will be the equilibrium wage rate?

d If this were a perfectly competitive labor market, what would be the equilibrium quantity of labor demanded? What would be the equilibrium price?

7 Firm *Z*, a monopsonist, confronts the supply curve for labor shown below; its demand curve for labor is as shown below:

SUPPLY CURVE OF LABOR		DEMAND CURVE FOR LABOR	
WAGE RATE PER HOUR (dollars)	NUMBER OF UNITS OF LABOR SUPPLIED PER HOUR	WAGE RATE PER HOUR (dollars)	NUMBER OF UNITS OF LABOR DEMANDED PER HOUR
5	1	9	1
6	2	8	2
7	3	7	3
8	4	6	4
9	5	5	5

a Firm *Z* is organized by a union, which demands a wage rate of $9 per hour. Firm *Z* agrees because it cannot afford a strike. What amount of labor will firm *Z* demand? What will be the equilibrium wage rate?

b In the absence of the union, what amount of labor would firm *Z* demand? What would be the equilibrium wage rate?

 ANSWERS TO
TEST YOUR UNDERSTANDING

SECTION 1

TRUE OR FALSE: 1. False   2. True   3. False

EXERCISE

1. a. $62.

b. $8.83.

c. Yes. The extra acre-foot of water would result in an extra $62 worth of lemons. By reducing the amount of water devoted to lima beans by 1 acre-foot, the value of the lima bean production would fall by $8.83. Thus the net effect would be an increase in profit of $62.00 − $8.83 = $53.17. (Note that this assumes that the firm can *costlessly* divert an acre-foot of water from lima bean production to lemon production. This may not be true. For example, the firm's lemons may be grown in an area far removed from its lima beans.)

d. No. As pointed out above, if firms are maximizing profit (and if they are perfectly competitive), they are purchasing water up to the point where the value of water's marginal product is equal to the price of water. Thus, since the value of water's marginal product differs between lemons and lima beans, one would expect that the price of water to lemon producers is different from the price of water to lima bean producers.

SECTION 2

TRUE OR FALSE: 1. False   2. True   3. True   4. True

EXERCISES

1. a. The maximum is $3,600, since if the wage exceeded this amount, the firm would hire three, not four, years of labor.

b. The minimum is $3,000, since if the wage were below this amount, the firm would hire five, not four, years of labor.

c. These wage rates seem unrealistically low for the United States at present.

2. 2,000 units of output per year of labor.

SECTION 3

TRUE OR FALSE: 1. True   2. True   3. False

EXERCISES

1. If a bonus payment system results in a worker's working harder, thus increasing the firm's sales or productivity, it may increase the firm's profits even though the worker may get paid more because of the bonus.

2. No.

SECTION 4

TRUE OR FALSE: 1. False   2. False

EXERCISES

1. a. Supply and demand.

b. The situation was a monopsony.

c. Wages tended to be depressed.

d. Wages would tend to increase.

e. Yes.

2. A lower wage.

3. This is not an easy task, as you would need data relating output responses to changes in various types of labor. No, the theory is not useless. Employers must form judgments of some sort on this score.

SECTION 5

TRUE OR FALSE: 1. True   2. False   3. False

EXERCISES

1. a. The firm will hire OQ_1 laborers and pay a wage of OW_1, in accord with the discussion of monopsony.

b. It is W_3DS, because the firm cannot pay a wage below OW_3 under the assumed circumstances.

c. The firm will hire OQ_2 workers, since the extra cost of hiring an extra worker equals OW_3 so long as less than OQ_4 workers are hired. Employment is higher than before the union entered (when it was OQ_1).

d. Yes. At a wage of OW_3, OQ_4 workers will seek employment but only OQ_2 workers will be hired. Thus $(OQ_4 − OQ_2)$ workers will be involuntarily unemployed.

2. The focus of the answer should be on whether the unions can be considered as monopolizers of a service.

3. No.

■ CHAPTER 11

Interest, Rent, and Profits

Essentials of **Interest, Rent, and Profits**

- The demand curve for loanable funds shows the quantity of loanable funds demanded at each interest rate; the supply curve for loanable funds is the relationship between the quantity of loanable funds supplied and the interest rate. In equilibrium the interest rate is at the intersection of the demand and supply curves.

- The interest rate for an asset enables you to determine the value of the asset over time. For instance, with an interest rate of r percent per year, a dollar received now is worth $(1 + r)$ dollars a year from now, $(1 + r)^2$ dollars two years from now, and so on.

- Land is any input that is fixed in supply, its limits established by nature. Rent, its price, is above the minimum necessary to attract whatever amount of the input is offered.

- Profits are due to innovation, uncertainty, and monopoly power. Profits and losses are mainsprings of a capitalistic system; they signal where resources are needed and where they are too abundant.

1 ■ The Demand and Supply of Loanable Funds

THE DEMAND FOR LOANABLE FUNDS

The rate of interest is the amount of money you must pay for the use of a dollar for a year. Thus, if the interest rate is 6 percent, you must pay 6 cents for the use of a dollar for a year. Since the interest rate is the price paid for the use of loanable funds, it—like any price—is determined by demand and supply. The **demand curve for loanable funds** shows the quantity of loanable funds demanded at each interest rate. The demand for loanable funds is a demand for what these funds will buy. Money is not wanted for its own sake, since it cannot build factories or equipment. Instead, it can provide command over resources—labor and equipment and materials—to do things like build factories or equipment.

As shown in Figure 11.1, the demand curve slopes downward to the right, indicating that more loanable funds are demanded at a lower rate of interest than at a higher rate of interest. A

very large demand for loanable funds stems from firms that want to borrow money to invest in capital goods like machine tools, buildings, and so forth. At a particular point in time a firm has available a variety of possible investments, each with a certain rate of return, which indicates its profitability or net productivity. At higher interest rates, a firm will find it profitable to borrow money for fewer of these projects than at lower interest rates.

To be more specific, *an asset's* **rate of return** *is the interest rate earned on the investment in the asset.* Suppose that a piece of equipment costs $10,000 and yields a permanent return to its owner of $1,500 per year.[1] (This return allows for the costs of maintaining the machine.) The rate of return on this piece of capital is 15 percent. Why?

---

[1] It is unrealistic to assume that the yield continues indefinitely, but it makes it easier to understand the principle involved.

Because if an investment of $10,000 yields an indefinite annual return of $1,500, the interest rate earned on this investment is 15 percent.

If a firm maximizes profit, it will borrow to carry out investments where the rate of return, adjusted for risk, exceeds the interest rate. For example, it is profitable for a firm to pay 10 percent interest to carry out a project with a 12 percent rate of return, but it is not profitable to pay 15 percent interest for this purpose. (More will be said on this score in a subsequent section.) Consequently, the higher the interest rate, the smaller the amount that firms will be willing to borrow.

Large demands for loanable funds are also made by consumers and the government. Consumers borrow money to buy houses, cars, and many other items. The government borrows money to finance the building of schools, highways, housing, and many other types of public projects. As in the case of firms, the higher the interest rate the smaller the amount that consumers and governments will be willing to borrow. Adding the demands of firms, consumers, and government together, you will find the aggregate relationship at a given point in time between the interest rate and the amount of funds demanded—which is the demand curve for loanable funds. For the reasons given above, this demand curve looks like a demand curve should. It is downward sloping to the right.

THE SUPPLY OF LOANABLE FUNDS

The **supply curve for loanable funds** is the relationship between the quantity of loanable funds supplied and the interest rate. The supply of loanable funds comes from households and firms that find the available rate of interest sufficiently attractive to get them to save. In addition, the banks play an extremely important role in influencing the supply of loanable funds. Indeed, banks can create or destroy loanable funds (but only within limits set by the Federal Reserve System, the central bank.)

The equilibrium value of the interest rate is given by the intersection of the demand and

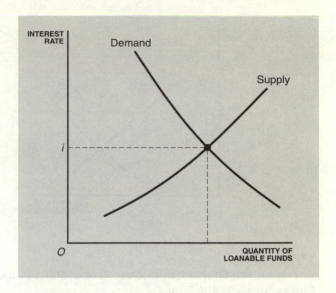

▪ **FIGURE 11.1**

Determination of Equilibrium Rate of Interest

The interest rate is determined by the demand and supply of loanable funds, the equilibrium level of the interest rate being Oi.

supply curves. In Figure 11.1 the equilibrium rate of interest is *Oi*. Factors that shift the demand curve or supply curve for loanable funds tend to alter the interest rate. If people become more willing to postpone consumption to future time periods, the supply curve for loanable funds will shift to the right, and the interest rate will decline. Or if inventions result in very profitable new investment possibilities, the demand curve will shift to the right and the interest rate will increase. (See Figure 11.2, next page.)

However, this is only part of the story. Because of the government's influence on both the demand and supply sides of the market for loanable funds, the interest rate at any point in time is to a considerable extent a matter of public policy. A country's monetary policy can have a significant effect on the level of the interest rate. More specifically, when the Federal Reserve pursues a policy of easy money, this generally means that interest rates tend to fall in the short run because the Fed is pushing the supply curve for loanable

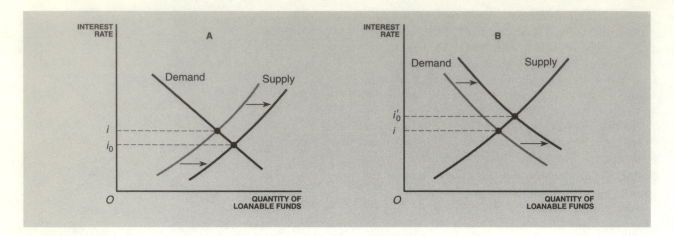

■ **FIGURE 11.2**

Effects on the Equilibrium Interest Rate of Shifts in the Demand or Supply Curves for Loanable Funds

If people become more willing to postpone consumption to future time periods, the supply curve will shift to the right, and the equilibrium interest rate will fall from i to i_0.

If very profitable new investment opportunities are opened up, the demand curve will shift to the right, and the equilibrium interest rate will rise from i to i_0'.

funds to the right. On the other hand, when the Federal Reserve pursues a policy of tight money, interest rates generally tend to rise in the short run because the Fed is pushing the supply curve for loanable funds to the left. (See Figure 11.3.)

The government is also an important factor on the demand side of the market for loanable funds, because it is a big borrower. During the 1980s and 1990s, it borrowed huge amounts to finance the mammoth federal deficits.

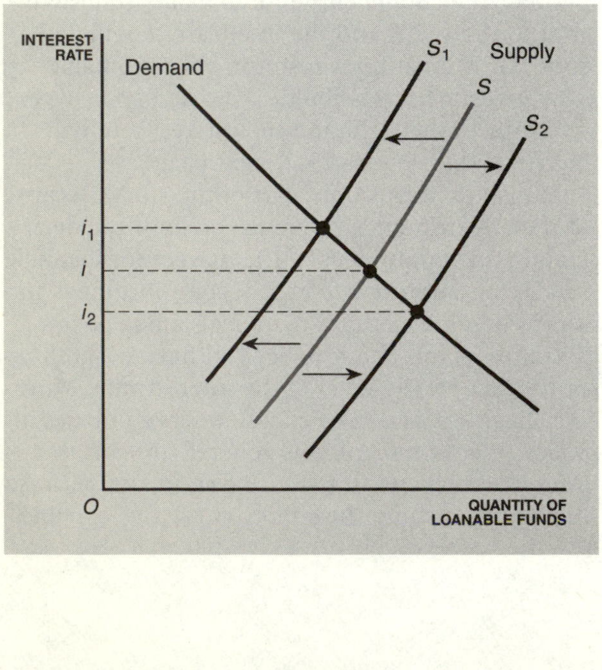

■ **FIGURE 11.3**

Effects on the Equilibrium Interest Rate of Federal Reserve Policies Influencing the Supply Curve for Loanable Funds

When the Federal Reserve pushes the supply curve to the right (from S to S_2), the equilibrium interest rate falls from i to i_2. When the Federal Reserve pushes the supply curve to the left (S to S_1), the equilibrium interest rate increases from i to i_1.

TEST YOUR UNDERSTANDING

True or false?

_____ **1** If Pennsylvania has a usury law that puts a limit of 10 percent on interest rates, and if a bond yielding $100 per year indefinitely is selling for $800 on Wall Street, the quantity of loanable funds supplied is likely to be less than the quantity of loanable funds demanded in Pennsylvania.

_____ **2** If the Federal Reserve pursues a policy of easy money, and at the same time profitable new investment opportunities open up, the equilibrium quantity of loanable funds will increase.

_____ **3** A very large demand for loanable funds stems from firms that want to borrow money to invest in capital goods like machine tools, buildings, and so forth.

_____ **4** An asset's rate of return is the interest rate earned on the investment in the asset.

Exercises

1 Suppose that the demand curve for loanable funds is as follows:

QUANTITY DEMANDED (billions of dollars)	INTEREST RATE (percent)
50	4
40	6
30	8
20	10

Plot the demand curve on a graph. Describe the various kinds of borrowers that are on the demand side of the market for loanable funds.

2 Suppose that the supply curve for loanable funds is as follows:

QUANTITY SUPPLIED (billions of dollars)	INTEREST RATE (percent)
20	4
25	6
30	8
35	10

Plot the supply curve on the same graph you used to plot the demand curve. What is the equilibrium rate of interest? If usury laws do not permit interest rates to exceed 6 percent, what do you think will happen in this market?

2 ▪ Functions of the Interest Rate

Interest has often been a relatively unpopular and somewhat suspect form of income. Even Aristotle, who was hardly noted for muddle-headedness, felt that money was "barren" and that it was improper to charge interest. And in the Middle Ages, church law outlawed usury, even though interest continued to be charged. In real life and in fiction, the money lender is often the villain, almost never the hero. Yet it is perfectly clear that _interest rates serve a very important function. They allocate the supply of loanable funds._

At a given point in time, funds that can be used to construct new capital goods are scarce, and society faces the problem of allocating these scarce funds among alternative possible uses. One way to allocate the loanable funds is through freely fluctuating interest rates. When such funds are relatively scarce, the interest rate will rise, with the result that only projects with relatively high rates of return will be carried out since the others will not be profitable. On the other hand, when such funds are relatively plentiful, the interest rate will fall, and less-productive projects will be carried out because they now become profitable.

CAPITALIZATION OF ASSETS

Capital goods are produced for the purpose of creating other goods. Factory buildings, equipment, inventories—all are various types of capital. In a capitalist economy, each capital good has a market value. How can you determine what this value is? How much money is a capital good worth? To keep things reasonably simple, suppose that you can get 5 percent on various investments open to you; specifically, you can get 5 percent by investing your money in the stock of a local firm. That is, for every $1,000 you invest, you will receive a permanent return of $50 a year—and this is the highest return available. Now suppose that you have an opportunity to buy a piece of equipment that will yield a permanent return of $1,000 per year. This piece of equipment is worth $1,000 ÷ .05 = $20,000 to you. Why? Because this is the amount you would have to pay for any other investment open to you that yields an

equivalent amount—$1,000—per year. (If you must invest $1,000 for every $50 of annual yield, $20,000 must be invested to obtain an annual yield of $1,000.)

In general, if a particular asset yields a permanent amount—X dollars—each year, how much is this asset worth? In other words, how much should you be willing to pay for it? If you can get a return of $100 \times r$ percent per year from alternative investments, you would have to invest $X \div r$ dollars in order to get the same return as this particular asset yields. Consequently, this asset is worth

$$\frac{\$X}{r}.$$

This process of computing an asset's worth is called **capitalization.**

Thus, if the rate of return on alternative investments had been 3 percent rather than 5 percent in the example above, the worth of the piece of equipment would have been $1,000 ÷ .03 = $33,333 (since $X = 1,000$ and $r = .03$). This is the amount you would have to pay for any other investment open to you that yields an equivalent amount—$1,000—per year. To see this, note that, if you must invest $1,000 for every $30 (not $50, as before) of annual yield, $33,333 (not $20,000, as before) must be invested to obtain an annual yield of $1,000.

 TEST YOUR UNDERSTANDING

True or false?

_____ **1** The government is an important factor on the demand side of the market for loanable funds, because it is a big borrower.

_____ **2** In the Middle Ages church law outlawed usury, even though interest continued to be charged.

_____ **3** Although interest is sometimes represented as a product of greedy capitalists, even socialist and Communist economies have had to use something like an interest rate to help allocate funds.

Exercises

1 Describe the social functions of the interest rate.

2 Suppose that you can get 10 percent per year from alternative investments and that, if you invest in a particular business, you will get $1,000 per year indefinitely. How much is this investment worth to you?

3 If a firm can borrow money at 10 percent per year and will accept only (riskless) investments that yield 12 percent per year or more, is the firm maximizing profit?

3 ▪ The Present Value of Future Income

In the previous section, you determined the value of an asset that yields a perpetual stream of earnings. Now consider a case in which an asset will provide you with a single lump sum at a certain time in the future. Suppose that you are the heir to an estate of $100,000, which you will receive in two years. How much is that estate worth now?

To answer this question, the first thing to note is that a dollar now is worth more than a dollar later. Why? Because you can always invest money that is available now and obtain interest on it. If the interest rate is 6 percent, *a dollar received now is equivalent to $1.06 received a year hence.* Why? Because if you invest the dollar now, you'll get $1.06 in a year. Similarly, *a dollar received now is equivalent to (1.06)² dollars two years hence.* Why? Because if you invest the dollar now, you'll get 1.06 dollars in a year; and if you reinvest this amount for another year at 6 percent, you'll get $(1.06)^2$ dollars.

With this in mind, let's determine how much an estate of $100,000 (to be received two years hence) is worth now. If the interest rate is 6 percent, each dollar received two years hence is worth $1 \div (1.06)^2$ dollars now. Thus, if the interest rate is 6 percent, the estate is worth $100,000 ÷ $(1.06)^2$ dollars now. Since $(1.06)^2 = 1.1236$, it is worth

$$\frac{\$100,000}{1.1236} = \$89,000.$$

In general, *if the interest rate is 100 × r percent per year, a dollar received now is worth $(1 + r)^2$ dollars*

two years from now. Thus, whatever the value of the interest rate may be, the estate is worth

$$\frac{\$100,000}{(1 + r)^2}.$$

The principle that a dollar now is worth more than a dollar later is of fundamental importance. If you don't understand it, you don't understand a basic precept of the world of finance. Although the example considered in previous paragraphs pertains only to a two-year period, this principle remains valid no matter how long the period of time we consider. Table 11.1 shows the present value of a dollar received at various points of time in the future. As you can see, its present value declines with the length of time before the dollar is received (so long as the interest rate remains constant).

▪ **TABLE 11.1**

Present Value of a Future Dollar (cents)

NUMBER OF YEARS HENCE (that dollar is received)	INTEREST RATE (percent)			
	4	6	8	10
1	96.2	94.3	92.6	90.9
2	92.5	89.0	85.7	82.6
3	89.0	83.9	79.4	75.1
4	85.5	79.2	73.5	68.3
5	82.3	74.7	68.1	62.0
10	67.6	55.8	46.3	38.5
15	55.5	41.7	31.5	23.9
20	45.6	31.1	21.5	14.8

TEST YOUR UNDERSTANDING

True or false?

_____ **1** If the interest rate is 4 percent, a dollar received three years from now is worth 89 cents now.

_____ **2** If the interest rate is 8 percent, a dollar received now is worth $(1.08)^2$ dollars two years from now.

Exercises

1 Assume that you inherit $1,000, which will be paid to you in two years. If the interest rate is 8 percent, how much is this inheritance worth now?

2 The Martin Tool and Die Company is deciding whether to buy a numerically controlled machine tool or a conventional machine tool. The price of the numerically controlled machine tool is $100,000, while the price of the conventional machine tool is $40,000. Each machine tool is estimated to have a life of five years, after which the scrap value is zero. Each machine tool produces the same quantity (and quality) of output, but the numerically controlled machine tool requires $15,000 less labor per year. In all other respects, the cost of the two machines are the same.

a. If the Martin Tool and Die Company buys the numerically controlled machine tool (rather than the conventional machine tool), how much more or less will its cash inflow be now, one year from now, and so on? Fill in the blanks below.

NUMBER OF YEARS HENCE	DIFFERENCE IN CASH INFLOW
0	_____
1	_____
2	_____
3	_____
4	_____
5	_____

b. On the basis of the above information, can we be sure that the Martin Tool and Die Company should purchase either machine tool? Why or why not?

4 ▪ Rent: Nature and Significance

Besides interest, another type of property income is rent. To understand rent, one must understand what economists mean by land. **Land** is defined by economists as *any input that is fixed in supply, its limits established by nature.* Thus, since certain types of minerals and natural resources are in relatively fixed supply, they are included in the economist's definition of land. Suppose that the supply of an input is completely fixed. Increases in its price will not increase its supply and decreases in its price will not decrease its supply. Following the terminology of the classical economists of the nineteenth century, *the price of such an input is* **rent.** Note that rent means something quite different to an economist than to the man in the street, who considers rent the price of using an apartment or a car or some other object owned by someone else.

If the supply of an input is fixed, its supply curve is a vertical line, as shown in Figure 11.4. Thus the price of this input, its rent, is determined entirely by the demand curve for the input. If the demand curve is D_0, the rent is OP_0; if the demand curve is D_1, the rent is OP_1. Since the supply of the input is fixed, the price of the input can be lowered without influencing the amount

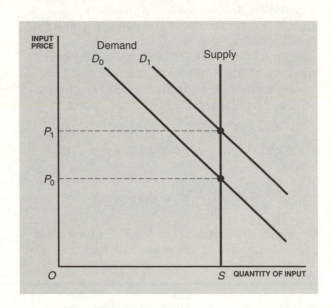

▪ **FIGURE 11.4**

Rent

Rent is the price of an input in fixed supply. Since its supply curve is vertical, the price of such an input is determined entirely by the demand curve for the input. If the demand curve is D_0, the rent is OP_0; if the demand curve is D_1, the rent is OP_1.

supplied. Thus *a rent is a payment above the minimum necessary to attract this amount of the input.*[2]

Why is it important to know whether a certain payment for inputs is a rent? Because a reduction of the payment will not influence the availability and use of the inputs if the payment is a rent; whereas if it is not a rent, a reduction of the payment is likely to change the allocation of resources. If the government imposes a tax on rents, there will be no effect on the supply of resources to the economy.

[2] In recent years, there has been a tendency among economists to extend the use of the word "rent" to encompass all payments to inputs above the minumum required to make these inputs available to the industry or to the economy. To a great extent these payments are costs to individual firms; the firms must make such payments to attract and keep these inputs, which are useful to other firms in the industry. But if the inputs have no use in other industries, these payments are not costs to the industry as a whole (or to the economy as a whole) because the inputs would be available to the industry whether or not these payments were made.

 TEST YOUR UNDERSTANDING

True or false?

_____ **1** Land is fixed in supply.

_____ **2** A rent is a payment below the minimum required to obtain the service of an input.

Exercises

1 "The supply curve for iron ore is horizontal, so its price is a rent." Comment.

2 D. Allan Bromley, President Bush's science adviser, pointed out that, in mathematics, physics, and engineering, many college teachers have been leaving their jobs to work in industry.
  a. Why do you think that this has been occurring?
  b. What might be the effect of such a trend on the size and quality of *future* supplies of scientists and engineers?
  c. If society feels that more scientists of a particular type are needed, one way of achieving an increase in supply is to shift the supply curve for this type of scientist to the right, as shown in the graph on the right. How can the government effect such a shift?

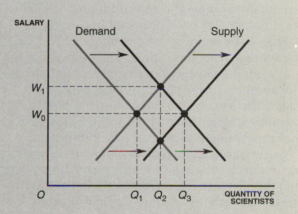

  d. Suppose that the supply curve does not shift to the right. If the demand curve for this type of scientist shifts to the right, as shown in the graph, does this result in some scientists of this sort receiving a higher salary than the minimum for which they would be willing to work? If so, is this a rent?

---

5 ▪ Profits

Besides interest and rent, another important type of property income is profit. According to accountants, profit is the amount of money the owner of a firm has left after paying wages, interest, and rent—and after providing proper allowance for the depreciation of buildings and equipment. Economists dissent from this view; their position is that the opportunity costs of the labor, capital, and land contributed by the owner should also be deducted.

Why do profits—as economists define them—exist? Three important factors are innovation, uncertainty, and monopoly power. Suppose that an economy was composed of perfectly competitive industries, that entry was completely free, and that no changes in technology—no new processes, no new products, or other innovations—were permitted. Moreover, suppose that everyone could predict the future with perfect accuracy. Under these conditions, there would be no profits, because people would enter industries where profits exist, and thus reduce these profits eventually to zero, and leave industries where losses exist and thus reduce these negative profits eventually to zero. This sort of no-profit equilibrium has already been discussed in Chapter 4.

But in the real world, innovations of various kinds are made. For example, Du Pont introduces a new product like nylon, Henry Ford introduces the assembly line, or Marconi introduces the radio. The people who carry out these bold schemes are the **innovators,** those with vision and the daring to back it up. The innovators are not necessarily the inventors of new techniques or products, although in some cases the innovator and the inventor are the same. Often the innovator takes another's invention, adapts it, and introduces it to the market. According to economists like the late Joseph Schumpeter, profits are the rewards earned by innovators. The profits derived from any single innovation eventually erode with competition and imitation, but other innovations replace them, with the result that profits from innovation continue to be made.

In the real world, uncertainty also exists. Indeed, one of the real hazards in attempting to be an innovator is the **risk** involved. According to a theory set forth several decades ago by Frank Knight of the University of Chicago, all economic profit is due to uncertainty. Profit is the reward for risk bearing. Assuming that people would like to avoid risk, they will prefer relatively stable, sure earnings to relatively unstable, uncertain earnings—*if the average level of earnings is the same*. Consequently, to induce people to take the risks involved in owning businesses in various indus-

tries, a profit—a premium for risk—must be paid to them. This is similar to the higher wages that often must be paid to workers for jobs for which earnings are unstable or uncertain (to compensate them for risk).

Still another reason for the existence of profits is the fact that markets are not perfectly competitive. Under perfect competition, there will be a tendency in the long run for profits to disappear. But, as you have seen, this will not be the case if an industry is a monopoly or oligopoly. Instead, profits may well exist in the long run in such imperfectly competitive industries. And, as you know from Chapter 8, much of the economy is composed of imperfectly competitive industries. Monopoly profits are fundamentally the result of "contrived scarcities." Since a firm's demand curve is downward sloping if competition is imperfect, it pays the firm to take account of the fact that the more it produces, the smaller the price it will receive. In other words, the firm realizes that it will spoil the market if it produces too much. Thus it pays firms to limit their output, and this contrived scarcity is responsible for the existence of the profits they make as a consequence.

PROFITS AND LOSSES: MAINSPRINGS OF A CAPITALISTIC SYSTEM

Profits and losses are mainsprings of any capitalistic system. They signal where resources are needed and where they are too abundant. When there are economic profits in an industry, this is the signal for resources to flow into it; when economic losses exist in an industry, this is the signal for resources to leave it. In addition, profits are very important incentives for innovation, for betting on the future, and for efficiency.

The importance of profits in a free-enterprise economy is clear enough. However, this does not mean that all profits are socially justified or that the system as a whole cannot be improved. Monopoly profits may not be socially justified, and a competitive system, despite its advantages, may produce many socially undesirable effects—for example, an undesirable income distribution. Much more will be said on this score in Chapter 14.

☑ TEST YOUR UNDERSTANDING

True or false?

_____ **1** Clearly, monopoly profits are socially justified.

_____ **2** One reason for the existence of profits is "contrived scarcity" due to monopoly power.

_____ **3** Profits may be due to innovation.

_____ **4** Profits may be due to uncertainty.

Exercise

1 Suppose that a candidate for president proposes that all profits be taxed away. Would you support this proposal? Why or why not?

▪ CHAPTER REVIEW

KEY TERMS

demand curve for loanable funds

rate of return

supply curve for loanable funds

capitalization

land

rent

innovators

risk

COMPLETION QUESTIONS

1 Mr. Smith buys a bond for $1,000. If the bond pays interest of $50 per year indefinitely, the interest rate is _____ percent. If the price of the bond increases to $1,500, the interest rate is _____ percent. If the price of the bond falls to $500, the interest rate is _____ percent.

2 If the interest rate is 10 percent, a dollar received a year from now is currently worth _____, and a dollar received two years from now is currently worth _____. Thus, a business venture that will pay you both a dollar a year from now and a dollar two years from now is currently worth _____.

3 If the present value of a dollar received two years from now is 85.7 cents, the interest rate must be _____ percent. If the present value of $2 received three years from now is $1.78, the interest rate must be _____ percent. If the interest rate is more than _____ percent, 1 dollar received 20 years from now is worth less than 15 cents now.

4 Interest rates vary as a functon of the loan's _____, its _____, and the cost of _____.

ANSWERS TO COMPLETION QUESTIONS

5

$3\frac{1}{3}$

10

90.9 cents

82.6 cents

173.5 cents

8

4

10

riskiness   term
bookkeeping and collection

5 The equilibrium interest rate is given by the intersection of the _____ and _____ curves for loanable funds.

demand   supply

6 Holding an asset's annual returns constant, the asset's worth is higher, the (lower, higher) _____ the rate of return available on other investments.

lower

7 _____ is a process of computing an asset's worth.

Capitalization

8 The _____ for loanable funds is the relationship between the quantity of loanable funds supplied and the interest rate.

supply curve

9 Increases in the interest rate tend to (increase, reduce) _____ aggregate investment, and thereby (increase, reduce) _____ national output.

reduce
reduce

10 The price of an input which has a fixed supply is _____. (A(n) _____ is a payment above the minimum necessary to attract this amount of the input.

rent   rent

11 Were the government to impose a tax on rents, there would be (some, no) _____ effect on the supply of resources to the economy.

no

12 If land can be improved, the supply of land (is, is not) _____ completely price inelastic.

is not

13 In the accountant's definition, the money the owner of a firm has left after paying wages, interest, and rent and after providing proper allowance for the depreciation of buildings and equipment is _____. The economist's definition differs in that he or she would also deduct the _____ costs of the labor, capital, and land contributed by the owner.

profit
opportunity

NUMERICAL PROBLEMS

1 Suppose that the demand curve for loanable funds in the United States is as follows:

INTEREST RATE (percent)	QUANTITY OF LOANABLE FUNDS (billions of dollars)
4	60
6	50
8	40
10	30
12	20

a Draw the demand curve:

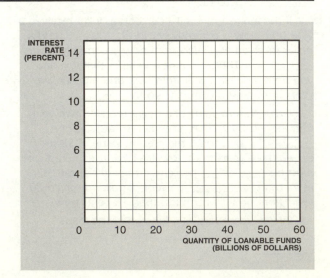

b Suppose that the existing supply of loanable funds in the United States is $40 billion. What is the equilibrium interest rate, given the data presented above?

c If the interest rate is the one indicated in part b, what is the worth of an asset that yields $1,000 a year permanently?

d If the interest rate is the one indicated in part b, and if you are considering investing your money in an investment with a rate of return of 7 percent, should you accept the investment? Why or why not?

2 What is the present value of a dollar received 15 years hence if the interest rate is 10 percent?

3 Suppose that the supply curve for a particular type of mineral is as follows:

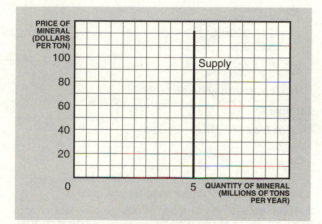

a Is the price of this mineral a rent?

b Suppose that a tax of $2 per ton is imposed on the producers of this mineral. What effect will this have on the quantity supplied? Does the answer depend on the demand curve for the mineral?

4 Suppose that the Jones Construction Company can borrow money at 15 percent per year and that it is willing to accept only those (riskless) investments that yield 20 percent per year or more. Is this firm maximizing profit?

5 Suppose that the Jones Construction Company has the following investment opportunities:

RATE OF RETURN (percent)	AMOUNT OF MONEY THE FIRM CAN INVEST AT THE GIVEN RATE OF RETURN (millions of dollars)
35	5
30	10
25	8
20	9
17	4

a If it has to pay 15 percent interest, which investment opportunities should it accept?

b How much less should it invest in these projects if it has to pay 18 percent interest?

6 Mr. Smith buys a very long-term bond that pays annual interest of $50 per year. It is a 5 percent bond that has a face value of $1,000. Mr. Smith bought it in 1955 when the prevailing interest rate was 5 percent, and he paid $1,000 for it. In 1982, the prevailing interest rate was about 10 percent. Approximately how much was the bond worth then?

7 a Suppose that you will receive $10,000 in three years. How much is it worth now? (Assume that the interest rate is 6 percent).

b How much is it worth to you to get the $10,000 one year earlier—that is, in two years, not three?

8 Mr. Q owns 100 acres of farm land which he rents at $100 per acre.

a If the interest rate is 10 percent, how much is Mr. Q's land worth?

b Because of a fall in the price of wheat, Mr. Q can rent his land for only $75 per acre. Now how much is Mr. Q's land worth?

c Oil is found on Mr. Q's property, the result being that he can rent his land for $400 an acre. Now how much is Mr. Q's land worth?

9 Ms. Q, if she does not undergo any further training, can expect to earn $25,000 per year for the indefinite future. If she takes this year off and goes to school rather than works, she can expect to earn $26,000 a year for the indefinite future. The school is free, but she will not be able to work at all while going to school.

a If Ms. Q expects to live and work forever, what rate of return will she earn from this investment in her own education?

b Suppose that Ms. Q can obtain 10 percent on alternative investment opportunities. Is this investment worthwhile?

c To make this investment worthwhile, how much must she be able to earn per year after the year in school?

10 Firm X must choose between investing in machine A and machine B. The machines do exactly the same work but their purchase and maintenance costs differ. The purchase price of machine A is $10,000, while the purchase price of machine B is $5,000. The maintenance cost each year with machine A is $1,000, while the maintenance cost each year with machine B is

$1,600. Both machines last so long that it is reasonable to assume (for simplicity) that they last forever.

a If the interest rate is 5 percent, which machine should firm *X* buy? Why?

b If the interest rate is 10 percent, which machine should firm *X* buy? Why?

c If the interest rate is 15 percent, which machine should firm *X* buy? Why?

d At what interest rate would firm *X* be indifferent between the two machines? Why?

 ANSWERS TO
TEST YOUR UNDERSTANDING

SECTION 1

TRUE OR FALSE: 1. True   2. True   3. True   4. True

EXERCISES

1. Borrowers might include consumers purchasing durable goods, businesses financing inventories, and local, state, and federal governments financing expenditures.

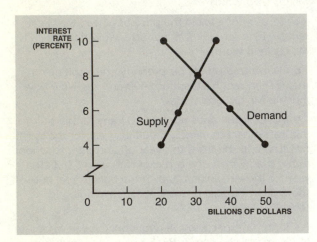

2. Eight percent is the equilibrium interest rate. If ursury laws put a 6 percent ceiling on interest rates, the demand for loanable funds would exceed the supply.

SECTION 2

TRUE OR FALSE: 1. True   2. True   3. True

EXERCISES

1. Interest rates allocate the supply of loanable funds.

2. $10,000.

3. No.

SECTION 3

TRUE OR FALSE: 1. True   2. True

EXERCISES

1. $857.

2. a. −$60,000
　+$15,000
　+$15,000
　+$15,000
　+$15,000
　+$15,000

b. No. Neither may be profitable.

SECTION 4

TRUE OR FALSE: 1. True   2. False

EXERCISES

1. This is false.

2. a. Because new PH.D.s have been offered higher salaries by industry rather than by universities.

b. If the quality and number of college teachers were reduced, there might well be an adverse effect on the size and quality of future supplies of scientists and engineers.

c. By scholarship and other programs subsidizing the training of such scientists,

d. If the supply curve does not shift to the right, the equilibrium salary increases from OW_0 to OW_1, and those scientists who were willing to work for a salary of OW_0 receive a windfall of $(OW_1 - OW_0)$. Thus it is a rent in the sense that it is a payment above the minimum necessary to attract this amount of this input. But it is not a rent in the sense that the supply curve is vertical.

SECTION 5

TRUE OR FALSE: 1. False   2. True   3. True   4. True

EXERCISE

1. If you want to maintain a capitalist system, you should not be for this proposal.

■ CHAPTER 12

A Woman's Work Is Never Done

1 ■ The Growing Role of Women in the Labor Force

Not too many decades ago, the prevailing view was that women belonged in the home. Things certainly have changed. Today most adult U.S. women (two-thirds of those between the ages of 25 and 54) work outside the home. One reason why more women enter the labor force today than in the early twentieth century (when only about 20 percent of adult U.S. women worked outside the home) is that household management requires less time than it did then. Technological advances have resulted in a variety of labor-saving devices in the home. In addition, the decline in the birth rate has provided women with more time for work, while the demand for women's services has increased as physical strength has become less important in many jobs and the service sectors of the economy have grown. Also, prevailing attitudes toward the proper role of women have changed; women now are encouraged to enter the labor force.

Despite the tremendous growth in the participation of women in the labor force, women's earnings tend to be considerably lower than men's. Among workers between the ages of 20 and 24, the gap in earnings averages about 15 percent; among workers between 45 and 54, it averages about 40 percent. This pay differential can be attributed to many factors. For example, as pointed out by the Council of Economic Advisers, the "average employed man has more work experience, fewer interruptions in that work experience, and longer tenure with his current employer than does his female counterpart of a comparable age."[1] Econometric evidence suggests that these factors explain some but not all of the earnings gap. It is not always clear which way the causality runs, either; to some extent, low earnings may encourage interrupted work lives, since the opportunity cost of leaving the work force is low.

[1] *Economic Report of the President* (Washington, D.C.: U.S. Government Printing Office, 1987), p. 220.

2 ■ Sex Discrimination

Although Congress has passed laws, such as the Equal Pay Act of 1964, that prohibit discrimination against women, many observers believe that this pay differential is due partly to discrimination. If there were only one employer of a particular type of labor, it is easy to see how discrimination of this sort might occur. Even if men and women are equally productive, a monopsonist can increase its profits if it separates the labor supply into two groups—men and women—and pays different wages to each group. To see this, recall from Chapter 10 that a monopsonist will maximize profit by setting the extra cost of adding an additional worker equal to the extra revenue from adding this worker. Suppose that, as shown in Figure 12.1, the supply curve for labor is less elastic for women than for men because women have fewer opportunities other than this type of work. Thus the extra cost of adding an additional worker is shown by curve E_M for men and E_W for women. If the extra revenue from adding a worker (male or female) equals OX, the wage will be OP_M for men and OP_W for women. Clearly, men are paid more than women.

However, this model supposes that labor markets are monopsonies, which is seldom the case. If labor markets are competitive and if men and women are hired for the same jobs, there are limitations on the extent to which firms can discriminate. Assume, for example, that male lawyers earn $70,000 and (equally talented and productive) female lawyers earn $60,000. Under these circumstances, an employer can make $10,000 (that is, $70,000 − $60,000) by hiring a female lawyer rather than a male. As more and more employers respond in this way to the profit motive, the wage of female lawyers will be bid up and the wage of male lawyers will go down until the wage differential between them tends to disappear.

Of course, discrimination of this sort can be due to the preferences of consumers not employers. For example, the clients of some law firms

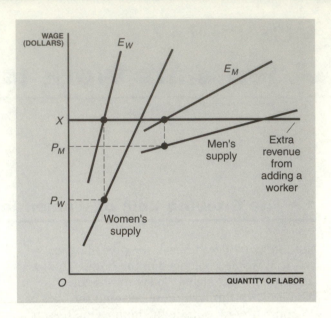

■ **FIGURE 12.1**

Sex Discrimination under Monopsony

may not trust female lawyers as much as male lawyers. Also, other employees of law firms (including male lawyers) may prefer not to work with female lawyers. If prejudice and discriminatory attitudes are sufficiently widespread, and if people are willing to absorb significant costs rather than change their attitudes, women will be paid less than men, even for equal performance.

3 ■ Affirmative Action

Since 1972, all federal contractors (and first-tier subcontractors) with 50 or more employees or a contract worth $50,000 or more have had to have affirmative action plans for women. Federal contractors are supposed to "take affirmative action to ensure that applicants are employed, and that employees are treated during employment without regard to their race, color, religion, sex or national origin."

Affirmative action plans are controversial. Opponents argue that such plans unfairly exclude people with superior qualifications and harm the intended beneficiaries more than they help them.

Supporters say that they are a useful device to reduce discrimination. To illustrate, consider a case involving the Transportation Department of Santa Clara County in California, in which a woman had never been appointed to the job of dispatcher (or to any of the several hundred jobs in its category). When a woman with the required experience applied and the interviewing committee rated a man as marginally more qualified, the committee was overruled under an affirmative action plan and the job went to the woman. Saying that he was the victim of discrimination, the man sued, but the Supreme

Court ruled that the affirmative action plan was acceptable and that the woman could remain in the job.[2]

It is difficult to measure how much effect affirmative action programs have had. According to a study by James Smith of the RAND Corporation and Michael Ward of Unicon Research Corporation,

> The overall impact of affirmative action on the average woman was quite small. However, there were some winners and unfortunately some losers

[2] B. Bergmann, "Does the Market for Women's Labor Need Fixing?" *Journal of Economic Perspectives,* Winter 1989.

as well. Black women have been the primary beneficiaries, most likely because they allow firms to fill two quotas for the price of one. To a lesser extent college-educated white women gained as firms covered by affirmative action placed women in managerial and professional jobs where they have been previously quite scarce. In contrast, covered firms also responded by reducing their employment of white women in traditionally female occupations, particularly clerical jobs. The new result was a wash with no significant employment effect for the average working woman.[3]

[3] J. Smith and M. Ward, "Women in the Labor Market and in the Family," *Journal of Economic Perspectives,* Winter 1989: 15–16.

4 ▪ Comparable Worth

Women tend to be found in a relatively small cluster of occupations. Recently, women have constituted about 94 percent of registered nurses, 98 percent of secretaries, and 85 percent of waiters and waitresses in the United States. Some believe that these jobs are underpaid because they tend to be filled by women, and to eliminate what they regard as a major inequity, they argue for "equal pay for work of comparable worth." The idea is to compare the worth of one occupation with that of another occupation and to press for equal wage rates for them if they are judged to be of equal worth. Thus, if a nurse does work that is of equal worth to that of a stevedore, nurses should get the same wage as stevedores.

How do the proponents of "comparable worth" propose to measure the worth of an occupation? A common answer is to use a job evaluation point system. In 1983, a federal court found the state of Washington guilty of discrimination because it paid male-dominated occupations more than "comparable" female-dominated occupations. To determine what occupations were comparable, every state job was evaluated in terms of "accountability," "knowledge and skills," "mental demands," and "working conditions." A committee decided how many points to give each occupation on each of these criteria, and two occupations were regarded of comparable worth if they got the same total number of points.

This decision by the federal court, which said

that Washington should raise women's wages and grant restitution for past injuries to them (cost to the state: $800 million), caused a great deal of controversy. So did the law enacted in Ontario, Canada, in 1989 that said that employers with more than ten workers must assess jobs in which at least 60 percent of the employees are women and use such a job evaluation system to determine how much women should be paid. In the York (Ontario) Region Board of Education, this has meant that the wage rate for switchboard receptionists has had to be raised to equal that of grass cutters, since these jobs have been determined to be comparable.

Many economists have criticized the idea that an occupation's wage rate should be determined in this way by "comparable worth." For example, Rutgers's Mark Killingsworth is reported to have said that "The solution is worse than the disease."[4] Nonetheless, this idea has not gone away. Although higher courts reversed the Washington decision described above, a considerable number of states have implemented policies based on "comparable worth," and leading politicians have espoused the idea. Whether this concept should be employed more widely in the public and private sectors of the economy is a lively issue.

[4] *New York Times,* May 31, 1990.

5 ■ Applying Economics: Female Participation in the Labor Force

This section contains a problem regarding the participation of females in the labor force (outside the home).[5]

PROBLEM 12.1 Suppose that Sally and John Barton can devote their time to the production of market goods (goods and services produced outside the home) or home goods (goods and services provided inside the home). Sally's production possibilities curve is shown in the top panel of Figure 12.2; John's production possibilities curve is shown in the bottom panel of Figure 12.2. (The production possibilities curve

■ TABLE 12.1

Alternative Production Possibilities, Sally and John Barton

SALLY		JOHN	
MARKET GOODS	**HOME GOODS**	**MARKET GOODS**	**HOME GOODS**
(dollars)			
100	0	150	0
75	50	112	25
50	100	75	50
25	150	38	75
0	200	0	100

shows the maximum amount of market goods that can be produced, given each amount of home goods produced.) The numbers on which these curves are based are presented in Table 12.1.

a. What is the maximum quantity of market goods Sally and John can jointly produce, given that they produce $200 of home goods? What is the maximum quantity they can produce, given that they produce $100 of home goods?

b. Draw the production possibilities curve for Sally and John taken together. Use the grid below.

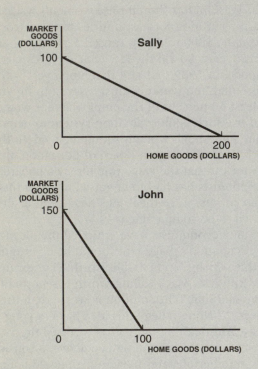

■ FIGURE 12.2

Production Possibilities Curves, Sally and John Barton

[5] For further discussion of these topics, see F. Blau and M. Ferber, *The Economics of Women, Men, and Work* (2d ed.; Englewood Cliffs, N.J.: Prentice-Hall, 1992).

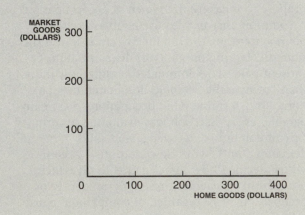

6 ▪ Applying Economics: The Effect of Taxes and Subsidies on Female Labor Force Participation

The following three problems are concerned with the effects of taxes and subsidies on female labor force participation.[6]

PROBLEM 12.2 Mary and Bill earn $30,000 each and produce $5,000 worth of goods and services in their household. (The $5,000 worth of goods and services include cooking, cleaning, and related activities.) Jane and Ken are in a different situation. Ken earns $45,000 and Jane, a full-time homemaker, produces $20,000 worth of goods and services in their home.

a. Is there any difference between the total income of Mary and Bill and the total income of Jane and Ken? Why or why not?

b. Suppose that everyone pays 30 percent of his or her income in income taxes. How much will Mary and Bill pay in such taxes? How much will Jane and Ken pay in such taxes?

c. Some observers argue that the income tax creates a disincentive for married women to participate in the labor force. Do you agree? Why or why not?

d. Would you be in favor of taxing household production? Why or why not?

e. Sweden taxes each person as an individual, regardless of his or her marital status. Would two-earner families benefit? Would one-earner families benefit?

PROBLEM 12.3 The federal welfare program Aid to Families with Dependent Children (AFDC) provided subsidies for many women with dependent children. To qualify for this program, a family had to contain dependent children who were without the support of a parent (usually the father) through death, disability, or absence

(and in some states, through unemployment as well). The amount paid to a family under this program varied from state to state, since each state administered its own program and set its own schedule of payments.

a. Suppose that the AFDC program was structured so that a female-headed family received $8,000 when the mother was not employed, and that this payment was cut by whatever amount she earned if she took a job. How much would she receive in income (labor market earnings plus government welfare payment) if her labor market earnings were $1,000? If her labor market earnings were $3,000?

b. Recognizing that there are job-related expenses like commuting costs and child care, is it possible under these circumstances that a woman might receive less in income if she worked than if she did not work?

c. In contrast, suppose that the reduction in welfare payments is less than the amount a woman receives in labor market earnings. Specifically, assume that the situation is as shown in Table 12.2. By how much is the welfare payment reduced when a woman's labor market earnings increase from $4,000 to $6,000?

▪ **TABLE 12.2**

Relationship between a Family's Labor Market Earnings and the Government Welfare Payment It Receives

LABOR MARKET EARNINGS	GOVERNMENT WELFARE PAYMENTS	TOTAL FAMILY INCOME
	(dollars)	
0	5,000	5,000
4,000	2,000	6,000
6,000	1,000	7,000
8,000	0	8,000

[6] For further discussion, see Blau and Ferber, *The Economics of Women, Men, and Work,* and Victor Fuchs, *Women's Quest for Economic Equality* (Cambridge, Mass.: Harvard University Press, 1988).

d. Is there more incentive for women under the AFDC program to go to work under the situation in part c than in part a? Why or why not?

e. Prior to 1967, welfare payments were reduced by the full amount earned. In 1967, welfare recipients were permitted to keep $30 per month, plus one-third of their earnings. Was this likely to increase the incentive for women under the AFDC program to go to work?

PROBLEM 12.4 In 1996, Aid to Families with Dependent Children was replaced by a system of block grants and much greater authority for the states.

a. The states have considerable latitude in how they use these grants. What are the pros and cons of this latitude?

b. Work requirements are established for most people seeking welfare or other benefits. What are the pros and cons of this provision?

7 ▪ Applying Economics: Poverty and Age-Earnings Profiles

The following two problems deal with the feminization of poverty and with age-earnings profiles.

PROBLEM 12.5 Table 12.3 shows the percentage of men and women who, according to definitions used by J. Smith and M. Ward, were in families that were poor in various years in the past.

a. Between 1940 and 1980, did women increase as a percentage of the people who were poor?

b. In 1940, over 90 percent of all families included a husband and wife. Did this tend to reduce the extent to which the percent of women who were poor could differ from the percent of men who were poor? Why or why not?

c. The fraction of female-headed families rose during this period. By 1980, women headed almost one in seven families. (In the African American population, they headed more than four out of ten families.) Did this help to account for the growing feminization of poverty during this period? Why or why not?

d. What factors have been responsible for the rising incidence of families headed by women?

▪ **TABLE 12.3**

Percent of Women and Men Who Were Poor and Percent of Poor Who Were Women, United States, 1940–1980

| YEAR | PERCENT WHO WERE POOR | | PERCENT OF POOR WHO WERE WOMEN |
	WOMEN	MEN	
1940	34	34	50
1950	23	22	51
1960	15	13	55
1970	11	8	60
1980	11	7	62

SOURCE: J. Smith and M. Ward, "Women in the Labor Market and in the Family," *Journal of Economic Perspectives*, Winter 1989, pp. 15–16.

PROBLEM 12.6 Figure 12.3 shows the age-earnings profiles of females and males with four years of high school and four years of college. An age-earnings profile shows how earnings vary with a person's age. Of course, each earnings figure in Figure 12.3 is an average; for example, females with four years of high school earn, on the average, about $16,000 when they

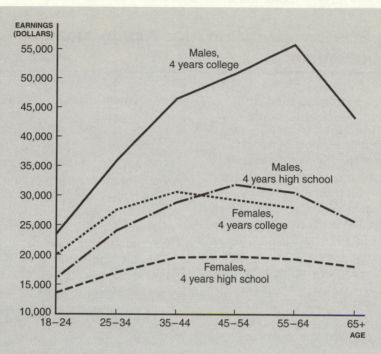

▪ FIGURE 12.3

Age-Earnings Profiles by Gender and Education, 1990

SOURCE: F. Blau and M. Ferber, *The Economics of Women, Men, and Work* (2d ed.; Englewood Cliffs, N.J.: Prentice-Hall, 1992.

are 25 to 34 years old. The data in Figure 12.3 pertain to 1990.

a. Because of women's greater likelihood of work force interruptions, they tend to have less labor market experience than men, at any given age. Does this tend to explain the results in Figure 12.3? If so, in what respect?

b. Because women's employment has been more likely to be relatively short and interrupted (because of childbirth and other factors), the payoff to women from on-the-job training has often been less than to men. Does this tend to explain the results in Figure 12.3? If so, in what respect?

c. To the extent that families have placed more emphasis on the husband's career (rather than the wife's career), the wife's earnings are likely to be lowered because the best job for both may not be in the same geographical area. Does this tend to explain the results in Figure 12.3? If so, in what respect?

d. If women place more emphasis than men on child rearing and other family matters, they may limit the hours they will work and the amount of travel they will do. Does this tend to explain the results in Figure 12.3? If so, in what respect?

8 ■ Applying Economics: Affirmative Action and Comparable Worth

The final two problems are concerned with affirmative action and comparable worth.

PROBLEM 12.7 Affirmative action as mandated by executive orders of the President applies only to federal contractors. Jonathan Leonard of the University of California at Berkleley compared the share of total employment comprised of women in comparable firms with and without federal contracts in 1974 and 1980. The results are shown in Table 12.4.

a. Did the female share of employment increase more among federal contractors than among noncontractors? If so, is this what you would expect if affirmative action programs tended to raise the employment of women? Why or why not?

b. If the difference between contractors and noncontractors in the change in the female employment share is regarded as a measure of the effect of affirmative action, does it appear that affirmative action had more effect on the employment of African American women than white women? Why or why not?

PROBLEM 12.8 Proponents of comparable worth often argue that a job evaluation point system should be used to measure the worth of an occupation. Recall that, in the case of the state of Washington, each job was evaluated in terms of accountability, knowledge and skills, mental demands, and working conditions. Two occupations were regarded as of comparable worth if they received the same total number of points from a committee which decided how many points to give each occupation on each of these criteria.

a. How can you determine how many points to give a particular occupation with regard to mental demands? Are the four criteria given above the only ones that could be used? How can you determine the proper weights to apply to various criteria? Is a point system of this sort largely arbitrary?

b. According to the point system described above, the value of each occupation can be determined from its characteristics alone. But the marginal product of workers in a particular occupation decreases as more and more of them are hired. Can one legitimately determine the value of an occupation to society without specifying how many people are in this occupation?

c. Suppose that the doctrine of comparable worth is accepted by Boston's municipal government and that a study concludes that the value of a typist's job is comparable to that of an electrician, the result being that the wage of typists is raised from $8 to $12 an hour. Will this result in more and better applicants for the city's typing jobs?

d. If skilled typists not working for Boston's

■ **TABLE 12.4**

Female Employment as a Percent of Total Employment, Federal Contractors and Noncontractors, 1974 and 1980

	1980	1974	CHANGE
White Female			
Contractor	28.8	27.6	1.2
Noncontractor	40.0	39.4	0.6
Black Female			
Contractor	4.5	3.0	1.5
Noncontractor	5.9	4.7	1.2
Other Female			
Contractor	2.8	1.6	1.2
Noncontractor	3.6	2.4	1.2

SOURCE: J. Leonard, "Women and Affirmative Action," *Journal of Economic Perspectives*, Winter 1989, pp. 65, 74.

municipal government can displace the typists currently working there, is such a displacement likely to occur (under the conditions described in part c)? Will the increase in the wage rate be of benefit to the typists currently working there in the short run? In the long run?

e. The doctrine of comparable worth has received more serious attention and has been put into effect more often in government agencies than in business firms. (A majority of state governments have studied the idea, and some have begun to apply it.) Why would such a scheme be more likely to encounter resistance among firms than government agencies?

f. Is the adoption of the idea of comparable worth the only way that women can improve their access to high paid jobs? If not, what are some other important ways? According to Chicago's Nobel laureate, Gary Becker, "Changes in the earnings and occupations of women in this country are much more closely related to changes in their productivity than to government action."[7] Do you agree?

[7] *Business Week,* April 27, 1987, p. 18.

9 ▪ Conclusion

According to the Book of Leviticus in the Bible, the value of maidservants should be three-fifths the value of manservants. Regardless of their religious beliefs, few women are likely to subscribe to this view. But to go beyond this to an informed analysis of the labor market for women, both men and women need to know some economics. As we have seen, concepts like production possibilities curves, as well as the theory of monopsony, are useful in this regard. But they are just a sample of the relevant concepts and theories. Economics is essential to understand a wide variety of controversial issues, such as affirmative action and comparative worth, which are presently at the heart of this area.

PART FIVE

Resource Allocation and the Government

CHAPTER 13 (Optional*)

Optimal Resource Allocation

Essentials of **Optimal Resource Allocation**

There are three necessary conditions for optimal resource allocation:

1 The ratio of the marginal utilities of any two goods must be the same for any two consumers who use both goods.

2 The ratio of the marginal products of two inputs must be the same for any pair of producers that use both inputs.

3 Any commodity's output level must be such that the marginal social benefit from an extra unit of the commodity is equal to its marginal social cost.

▪ A perfectly competitive economy satisfies these conditions for welfare maximization. This is one principal reason why many economists are so enamored of perfect competition and so wary of monopoly and other market imperfections.

▪ However, these conditions are incomplete, since they say nothing about the optimal income distribution; the judgment of whether one distribution of income is better than another must be made on ethical, not scientific, grounds.

1 ▪ Welfare Economics

One of the great goals of economics is to determine how best to allocate society's scarce resources. Questions concerning the optimal allocation of inputs among industries and the optimal distribution of commodities among consumers can be difficult, since the optimal usage of any input cannot be determined by looking at the market for this input alone, and the optimal output of any commodity cannot be determined by looking at the market for this commodity alone. On the contrary, the **optimal resource allocation** between two products depends on the relative strength of the demands for the products and their relative production costs.

The term **welfare economics** covers the branch of economics that studies policy issues concerning the allocation of resources. It should be stressed from the start that welfare economics, although useful, is certainly no panacea. By itself,

welfare economics can seldom provide a clear-cut solution to issues of public policy. But in combination with other disciplines, it can frequently show useful ways to structure and analyze these issues.

INTERPERSONAL COMPARISONS OF UTILITY

Perhaps the most important limitation of welfare economics stems from the fact that *there is no scientific way to compare the utility levels of different individuals*. There is no way to show scientifically that a bottle of Château Haut-Brion will bring you more satisfaction than it will me, or that your backache is worse than mine. This is because there is no scale on which you can measure pleasure or pain so that interpersonal comparisons can be made scientifically. For this reason, the judgment of whether one distribution

---

* This brief chapter, somewhat more advanced than the others, is optional. It can readily be skipped.

of income is better than another must be made on ethical, not scientific, grounds. If you receive twice as much income as I do, economists cannot tell us whether this is a better distribution of income than if I receive twice as much income as you do. This is an ethical judgment.

However, most problems of public policy involve changes in the distribution of income. A decision to increase the production of jet aircraft and to reduce the production of railroad locomotives may mean that certain stockholders and workers will gain, while others will lose. Because it is so difficult to tell whether the resulting change in the distribution of income is good or bad, it is correspondingly difficult to conclude whether such a decision is good or bad.

Faced with this problem, economists have adopted a number of approaches, all of which have significant shortcomings. Some economists have simply paid no attention to the effects of proposed policies on the income distribution. Others have taken the existing income distribution as optimal, while still others have asserted that less unequal income distributions are preferable to more unequal ones. Purists have argued that you cannot be sure a change is for the better unless it hurts no member of society, while others have suggested that you must accept the judgment of Congress (or the public as a whole) on what is an optimal distribution of income.

For now, the major thing to note is that the conditions for an optimal allocation of resources, described in the following sections, are incomplete, since they say nothing about the optimal income distribution. Whatever the income distribution you or I may consider best on ethical or some other (nonscientific) grounds, the conditions in Section 2 must be met if resources are to be allocated optimally. Remember, however, that there may be many allocations of resources that meet these conditions, and the choice of which is best will depend on your feelings about the optimal income distribution.

 TEST YOUR UNDERSTANDING

True or false?

_____ **1** If you receive twice as much income as I do, economics cannot tell us whether this is a better distribution of income than if I receive twice as much income as you do.

_____ **2** Welfare economics is concerned with how resources should be allocated.

_____ **3** The conditions for optimal resource allocation in the following sections are incomplete.

2 ■ Conditions for Optimal Resource Allocation

CONDITION 1

Fundamentally, there are three necessary conditions for optimal resource allocation. The first pertains to the optimal allocation of commodities among consumers and states that *the ratio of the marginal utilities of any two goods must be the same for any two consumers who consume both goods*. That is, if the marginal utility of a good *A* is twice that of good *B* for one consumer, it must also be twice that of good *B* for any other consumer who consumes both goods. The proof that this condition is necessary to maximize consumer satisfaction is quite simple. You need only note that, if this ratio

were unequal for two consumers, both consumers could benefit by trading.

Thus assume that the ratio of the marginal utility of good *A* to that of good *B* is 2 for one consumer, but 3 for another consumer. This means that the first consumer regards an additional unit of good *A* as having the same utility as 2 extra units of good *B*, whereas the second consumer regards an additional unit of good *A* as having the same utility as 3 extra units of good *B*. Then, if the first consumer trades 1 unit of good *A* for 2.5 units of good *B* from the second consumer, both are better off. (Why? Because the first consumer receives 2.5 units of good B, which he prefers to 1 unit of good A, and the second consumer receives 1 unit of good A, which she prefers to 2.5 units of good B.)

CONDITION 2

The second condition, which pertains to the optimal allocation of inputs among producers, states that *the ratio of the marginal products of two inputs must be the same for any pair of producers that use both inputs.* That is, if the marginal product of input 1 is twice that of input 2 in one firm, it must also be twice that of input 2 in any other firm that uses both inputs. If this condition does not hold, total production can be increased merely by reallocating inputs among firms.

To illustrate this, suppose that for the first producer the marginal product of input 1 is twice that of input 2, whereas for the second producer the marginal product of input 1 is 3 times that of input 2. Then, if the first producer gives 1 unit of input 1 to the second producer in exchange for 2.5 units of input 2, both firms can expand their output. To see this, suppose that the marginal product of input 1 is M_1 for the first producer and M_2 for the second producer. Then the output of the first producer is reduced by M_1 units because of its loss of the unit of input 1, but it is increased

by $2.5 \times M_1/2$ units because of its gain of the 2.5 units of input 2, so that on balance its output increases by $M_1/4$ units because of the trade. Similarly, the output of the second producer is increased by M_2 units because it gains the 1 unit of input 1, but it is decreased by $2.5 \times M_2/3$ units because it loses the 2.5 units of input 2, with the consequence that on balance its output increases by $M_2/6$ units because of the trade.

CONDITION 3

The third condition pertains to the optimal output of a commodity. It states that *any commodity's output level, if it is optimal, must be such that the marginal social benefit from an extra unit of the commodity is equal to its marginal social cost.* If this condition is violated, social welfare can be increased by altering the output level of the commodity. Specifically, if the marginal social benefit from an extra unit of the commodity exceeds it marginal social cost, an increase in the output of the commodity will increase social welfare. (Why? Because the extra social benefit resulting from an extra unit of the commodity outweighs the extra social cost.) And if the marginal social benefit from an extra unit of the commodity is less than marginal social cost, a decrease in the output of the commodity will increase social welfare.

 TEST YOUR UNDERSTANDING

True or false?

_____ **1** For optimal resource allocation, the ratio of the marginal utilities of any two goods must be the same for any two consumers who consume both goods.

_____ **2** For optimal resource allocation, the ratio of the marginal products of two inputs must not be the same for any pair of producers that use both inputs.

_____ **3** The marginal social benefit always equals the marginal private benefit.

Exercises

1 According to some kinds of agricultural price supports, each firm is allowed to produce only a certain quota. For example, the Chidester farm may be able to produce no more than *OX* bushels of corn per year. Is this likely to result in optimal resource allocation?

2 In the situation described in Exercise 1, would there be social advantages if farms with low marginal costs were permitted to produce more and if farms with high marginal costs produced less? Why or why not?

3 ▪ Optimal Resource Allocation: A Case Study

Turn now to a case study of how these conditions can be applied to one of the most important commodities—water. If the first condition is to hold, the ratio of the marginal utility of water to that of any other good must be the same for all consumers. To be specific, suppose that the other good is money. Then the ratio of the marginal utility of water to the marginal utility of money must be the same for all consumers. That is, if resources are allocated optimally, *the amount of money a consumer will give up to obtain an extra unit of water must be the same for all consumers.* This follows because the ratio of the marginal utility of good *A* to the marginal utility of good *B* equals the number of units of good *B* that the consumer will give up to get an extra unit of good *A*.

The common sense underlying this condition has been described well in a study of water resources done at the RAND Corporation:

> Suppose that my neighbor and I are both given rights (ration coupons, perhaps) to certain volumes of water, and we wish to consider whether it might be in our mutual interest to trade those water rights between us for other resources—we might as well say for dollars, which we can think of as a generalized claim on the other resources like clam chowders, babysitting services, acres of land, or yachts. . . . Now suppose that the last acre-foot of my periodic entitlement is worth $10 at most to me, but my neighbor would be willing to pay anything up to $50 for the right. . . . Eventually, if I transfer the right to him for any compensation between $10 and $50, we will both be better off in terms of our own preferences. . . . But this is not yet the end. Having given up one acre-foot, I will not be inclined to give up another on such easy terms (and) my neighbor is no longer quite so anxious to buy as he was before, since his most urgent need for one more acre-foot has been satisfied. . . . Suppose he is now willing to pay up to $45 (for another acre-foot), while I am willing to sell for anything over $15. Evidently, we should trade again. Obviously, the stopping point is where the last (or marginal) unit of water is valued equally (in terms of the greatest amount of dollars we would be willing to pay) by the two of us. . . . At this point no more mutually advantageous trades are available—and efficiency has been attained.[1]

If people can trade water rights freely—as in this hypothetical case—an efficient allocation of water rights will be achieved. But what if water rights cannot be traded freely, because certain kinds of water uses are given priority over other types of uses, and it is difficult, even impossible, for a low-priority user to purchase water rights from a high-priority user? The effect is to prevent water from being allocated so as to maximize consumer satisfaction. Unfortunately, this question is not merely an academic exercise. If focuses attention on a very practical problem. In fact, there has been a wide variety of limitations on the free exchange of water rights in the United States. Thus some legal codes have granted certain types of users priority over other types of users, and the free exchange of water has been limited. Experts believe that these limitations have been a serious impediment to the optimal allocation of water resources.

[1] J. Hirshleifer, J. Milliman, and J. DeHaven, "The Allocation of Water Supplies," in E. Mansfield (ed.), *Microeconomics, Selected Readings* (4th ed.; New York: Norton, 1982.)

 TEST YOUR UNDERSTANDING

True or false?

_____ **1** If resources are allocated properly, the price of water must be the same for all consumers, regardless of where they live.

_____ **2** If water rights can be traded freely, an efficient allocation of water rights can be achieved.

4 ▪ Perfect Competition and Welfare Maximization

One of the most fundamental findings of economic theory is that a perfectly competitive economy satisfies the three sets of conditions for **welfare maximization** set forth in previous sections. An argument for competition can be made in various ways. Some people favor it simply because it prevents the undue concentration of power and the exploitation of consumers. But to the economic theorist, the basic argument for a perfectly competitive economy is that such an economy satisfies these three conditions. In this section that is proved.

Condition 1—The Ratio of the Marginal Utilities of Any Pair of Commodities Must Be the Same for All Consumers Buying Both Commodities. Recall that under perfect competition consumers choose their purchases so that the marginal utility of a commodity is proportional to its price. Since prices, and thus price ratios, are the same for all buyers under perfect competition, it follows that the ratio of the marginal utilities between any pair of commodities must be the same for all consumers. If every consumer can buy bread for $.50 a loaf and butter for $1 a pound, each one will arrange his or her purchases so that the ratio of the marginal utility of butter to that of bread is 2. Thus the ratio will be the same for all consumers: 2 for everyone.

To make sure you understand this point, consider any two goods, *A* and *B*. On the basis of the discussion in Chapter 1, you know that each consumer will buy amounts of these goods so that

$$\frac{MU_A}{P_A} = \frac{MU_B}{P_B},$$

where MU_A is the marginal utility of good *A*, MU_B is the marginal utility of good *B*. P_A is the price of good *A*, and P_B is the price of good *B*. Multiplying both sides of this equation by $P_A \div MU_B$, you get

$$\frac{MU_A}{MU_B} = \frac{P_A}{P_B}.$$

Since $P_A \div P_B$ is the same for all consumers, $MU_A \div MU_B$ must also be the same for all of them; this means that condition 1 is satisfied.

Condition 2—The Ratio of the Marginal Products of Any Pair of Inputs Must Be the Same for All Producers Using Both Inputs. You have already seen in Chapter 2 that under perfect competition producers will choose the quantity of each input so that the ratio of the marginal products of any pair of inputs equals the ratio of the prices of the pair of inputs. Since input prices, and thus price ratios, are the same for all producers under perfect competition, it follows that the ratio of the marginal products must be the same for all producers. If every producer can buy labor services for $8 an hour and machine tool services for $16 an hour, each one will arrange the quantity of its inputs so that the ratio of the marginal product of machine tool service to that of labor is 2. Thus the ratio will be the same for all producers: 2 for each.

To make sure you understand this point, consider any two inputs, *X* and *Y*. On the basis of the discussion in Chapter 2, you know that each firm will buy amounts of these inputs so that

$$\frac{MP_X}{P_X} = \frac{MP_Y}{P_Y},$$

where MP_X is the marginal product of input X, MP_Y is the marginal product of input Y, P_X is the price of input X, and P_Y is the price of input Y. Multiplying both sides of this equation by $P_X \div MP_Y$, it follows that

$$\frac{MP_X}{MP_Y} = \frac{P_X}{P_Y}.$$

Since $P_X \div P_Y$ is the same for all firms, $MP_X \div MP_Y$ must also be the same for all of them; this means that condition 2 is satisfied.

Condition 3—The Marginal Social Benefit from an Extra Unit of Any Commodity Must Be Equal to Its Marginal Social Cost. Recall from Chapter 4 that under perfect competition firms will choose their outputs so that price equals marginal cost. If a commodity's price is an accurate measure of the marginal social benefit from producing an extra unit of it, and if its marginal cost is an accurate measure of the marginal social cost of producing an extra unit of it, the fact that price is set equal to marginal cost ensures that this condition will be met.

Thus, in summary, *all three conditions for optimal resource allocation are satisfied under perfect competition*. This is one principal reason why many economists are so enamored of perfect competition and so wary of monopoly and other market imperfections. If a formerly competitive economy is restructured so that some industries become mo-

nopolies, these conditions for optimal resource allocation are no longer met. As we know from Chapter 5, each monopolist produces less than the perfectly competitive industry that it replaces would have produced. Thus too few resources are devoted to the industries that are monopolized, and too many resources are devoted to the industries that remain perfectly competitive. This is one of the economist's chief charges against monopoly. It wastes resources because it results in overallocation of resources to competitive industries and underallocation of resources to monopolistic industries. The result is that society is less well off. Similarly, oligopoly and monopolistic competition are charged with wasting resources, since the conditions for optimal resource allocation are not met there either.

However, in evaluating this result and judging its relevance, you must be careful to note that it stems from a very simple model that ignores such things as technological change and other dynamic considerations, risk and uncertainty, and external economies and diseconomies (which are discussed in Chapter 14). Also, there is the so-called **theory of the second best** which states that unless *all* the conditions for optimal resource allocation are met, it may be a mistake to increase the number of such conditions that are fulfilled. Thus piecemeal attempts to preserve or impose competition may do more harm than good.

 TEST YOUR UNDERSTANDING

True or false?

____ **1** The marginal social cost always equals the marginal private cost.

____ **2** Some people favor competition because it prevents the undue concentration of power.

____ **3** Optimal resource allocation will occur if only two of the three sets of conditions described in this chapter are satisfied.

____ **4** The discussion of optimal resource allocation in this chapter ignores technological change and other dynamic considerations.

____ **5** If a formerly competitive economy is restruc-

tured so that some industries become monopolies, the conditions for optimal resource allocation are no longer met.

Exercise

1 The Hoover Commission, a high-level commission established to analyze the performance of the federal government, concluded that, "in come cases, the federal subsidy [to water users in irrigation projects] amounts to some 95 percent of capital cost plus interest." Does this conform to the principles of optimal resource allocation described above?

▪ CHAPTER REVIEW

KEY TERMS

optimal resource allocation

welfare economics

welfare maximization

theory of the second best

COMPLETION QUESTIONS

1 There is no way to compare the _____ of different individuals.

2 A _____ economy satisfies the three sets of conditions for welfare maximization.

3 If resources are allocated optimally, the _____ of the marginal utilities of any two goods must be the same for any two _____ who _____ both goods.

4 If resources are allocated optimally, the _____ of the marginal products of any two inputs must be the same for any two _____ that _____ both inputs.

5 If resources are allocated optimally, any commodity's output level must be such that the _____ equals the _____ .

6 One of the most important limitations of welfare economics is the fact that there is no scale on which to compare the _____ levels of different individuals. _____ comparisons cannot be made scientifically.

7 If resources are allocated optimally, the amount of money a consumer will give up to obtain an extra unit of water must be (different, the same) _____ for all consumers. This follows because the ratio of the marginal utility of good *A* to the marginal utility of good *B* (equals, does not equal) _____ the number of units of good *B* that the consumer will give up to get an extra unit of good *A*.

8 Since prices, and thus price ratios, are the same for all buyers under perfect competition, it follows that the ratio of the marginal utilities between any pair of commodities must be (different, the same) _____ for all consumers. For example, if every consumer can obtain one item for $.25 and another for $1, each consumer will arrange his or her purchases so that the ratio of the marginal utility of the second item to the first is _____ .

9 Since input prices, and thus price ratios, are the same for all producers under perfect competition, it follows that the ratio of the marginal products must be

ANSWERS TO COMPLETION QUESTIONS

utilities

perfectly competitive

ratio

consumers

consume

ratio

producers

use

marginal social benefit from an extra unit of the commodity

marginal social cost

utility

Interpersonal

the same

equals

the same

4

(different, the same) _____ for all producers. For example, if every producer can buy one input for $4 and another for $8, each producer will arrange the quantity of its inputs so that the ratio of the marginal product of the second input to that of the first is

_____ .

10 Monopoly results in (overallocation, underallocation) _____ of resources to competitive industries and (overallocation, underallocation) _____ of resources to monopolistic industries. The result is that society is (less, more) _____ well off.

the same

2

overallocation
underallocation

less

NUMERICAL PROBLEMS

1 If the marginal cost of producing a bicycle is $50 per bicycle, will resources be allocated optimally if the price of a bicycle is $40? If not, should the price be raised or lowered?

2 If the marginal cost of producing a piano is $1,000 per piano, will resources be allocated optimally if the price of a piano is $1,500? If not, should the price be raised or lowered? Why?

3 The market for screwdrivers is monopolized. At present, 1 million screwdrivers are produced per year.

If all other industries are perfectly competitive, is the optimal annual production of screwdrivers greater than or less than 1 million? Why?

4 Suppose that the ratio of the marginal utility of jam to that of jelly is 3 for Sam but 2 for Linda. Are resources allocated optimally? Why or why not?

5 Suppose that the ratio of the marginal product of labor to that of capital is 3 for the Ajax Company but 2 for the Perfecto Company. Are resources allocated optimally? Why or why not?

 ANSWERS TO
TEST YOUR UNDERSTANDING

SECTION 1

TRUE OR FALSE: 1. True   2. True   3. True

SECTION 2

TRUE OR FALSE: 1. True   2. False   3. False

EXERCISES

1. No.

2. Yes. This would lower the total costs of production.

SECTION 3

TRUE OR FALSE: 1. False   2. True

EXERCISES

1. Farmers are likely to use water in applications where the returns are less than in the manufacturing industry.

2. Yes.   Yes.

SECTION 4

TRUE OR FALSE: 1. False   2. True   3. False   4. True
5. True

EXERCISES

1. No.

CHAPTER 14

The Economic Role of the Government

Essentials of **Economic Role of the Government**

■ Despite its many advantages, the price system suffers from limitations: The distribution of income may not be fair, public goods may not be provided in the right amounts, and the price system may not operate effectively if the production or consumption of a good by one firm or consumer has adverse or beneficial uncompensated effects on other firms or consumers.

■ Both conservatives and liberals agree that the government should establish a proper legal, social, and competitive framework, keep markets reasonably competitive, help the poor, and keep the country reasonably stable.

■ Government expenditures have grown much faster than output in the United States in the past 70 years. This is because of increased military responsibilities as well as a long-term increase in the demand for services provided by government.

■ At the federal level, the biggest money raiser is the personal income tax; at the local level, it is the property tax; and at the state level, it is the sales (and excise) tax.

1 ■ The United States: A Mixed Capitalist System

To state that the United States is a mixed capitalist system, in which both government decisions and the price system play important roles, is hardly to provoke a controversy. But going a step beyond takes us into areas where viewpoints often diverge. The proper functions of government and the desirable size and kinds of government expenditures and taxes are not matters on which all agree. Indeed, the question of how big government should be and what its proper functions are, are hotly debated by conservatives and liberals throughout the land.

LIMITATIONS OF THE PRICE SYSTEM

Despite its many advantages, the price system suffers from limitations. Because these limitations are both prominent and well known, no one believes that the price system, left to its own de-

vices, can be trusted to solve all society's basic economic problems. To a considerable extent, the government's role in the economy has developed in response to the limitations of the price system, which are described below.

DISTRIBUTION OF INCOME   There is *no* reason to believe that the distribution of income generated by the price system is *fair* or, in some sense, *best*. Most people feel that the distribution of income generated by the price system should be altered to suit humanitarian needs, in particular, that help should be given to the poor. Both liberals and conservatives tend to agree on this score, although there are arguments over the extent to which the poor should be helped and the conditions under which they should be eligible for help. But the general principle that the government should step in to redistribute income in favor of the poor is generally accepted in the United States today.[1]

PUBLIC GOODS   Some goods and services *cannot be provided through the price system because there is no way to exclude citizens from consuming the goods whether they pay for them or not.* For example, there is no way to prevent citizens from benefiting from national expenditures on defense, whether they pay money toward defense or not. Consequently, the price system cannot be used to provide such goods; no one will pay for them since they will receive them whether they pay or not. Further, these goods, like the quality of the environment and national defense (and others cited below), *can be enjoyed by one person without depriving others of the same enjoyment.* Such goods are called **public goods.** The government provides many public goods. Such goods are consumed collectively or jointly, and it is inefficient to try to price them in a market. They tend to be indivisible; thus they frequently cannot be split into pieces and be bought and sold in a market.

EXTERNAL ECONOMIES AND DISECONOMIES   In cases in which *the production or consumption of a good by one firm or consumer has adverse or beneficial uncompensated effects on other firms or consumers, the price system will not operate effectively.* An **external econ-**

[1] Also, because the wealthy have more "dollar votes" than the poor, the sorts of goods and services that society produces will reflect this fact. Thus luxuries for the rich may be produced in larger amounts and necessities for the poor may be produced in smaller amounts than some critics regard as sensible and equitable. This is another frequently encountered criticism of the price system.

omy is said to occur when consumption or production by one person or firm results in uncompensated benefits to another person or firm. A good example of an external economy exists where fundamental research carried out by one firm is used by another firm. (To cite one such case, there were external economies from the Bell Telephone Laboratories' invention of the transistor. Many electronics firms, such as Texas Instruments and Fairchild, benefited considerably from Bell's research.) Where external economies exist, it is generally agreed that the price system will produce too little of the good in question and that the government should supplement the amount produced by private enterprise. This is the basic rationale for much of the government's huge investment in basic science. An **external diseconomy** is said to occur when consumption or production by one person or firm results in uncompensated costs to another person or firm. A good example of an external diseconomy occurs when a firm dumps pollutants into a stream and makes the water unfit for use by firms and people downstream. Where activities result in external diseconomies, it is generally agreed that the price system will tolerate too much of the activity and that the government should curb it. For example, the government, in keeping with this doctrine, has involved itself in environmental protection and the reduction of air and water pollution.[2]

[2] The effects of external economies and diseconomies can also be taken care of by legal arrangements that assign liabilities for damages and compensate for benefits. However, such arrangements often are impractical or too costly to be used.

 TEST YOUR UNDERSTANDING

True or false?

_____ **1** The research activities of industrial firms often result in external economies.

_____ **2** Public goods frequently are sold in the private market.

_____ **3** The government should discourage the production of goods and services that entail external economies.

Exercise

1 During the past 40 years, the federal government has promoted and encouraged the redevelopment of the inner core of major U.S. cities. Consider two adjacent urban properties. Suppose that the two owners, Mr. Lombardi and Mr. Moore, are each trying to determine whether to invest $100,000 to redevelop his property. If he does not invest the $100,000 in redevelopment, each can get a 10 percent return from other forms of investment. The rate of return on the $100,000 investment by each owner (which depends on whether the other owner redevelops his property as well) is shown below:

	RATE OF RETURN (percent)	
	OTHER OWNER REDEVELOPS	OTHER OWNER DOES NOT REDEVELOP
Redevelop	12	5
Do not redevelop	15	10

a. If Mr. Lombardi redevelops his property, is Mr. Moore better off by redeveloping his property as well?

b. If Mr. Lombardi does not redevelop his property, is Mr. Moore better off by redeveloping his property?

c. Will either owner redevelop his property?

d. In a situation of this sort, can social gains be achieved by government intervention?

2 ■ What Functions Should the Government Perform?

There are wide differences of opinion on the proper role of government in economic affairs. Although it is generally agreed that the government should redistribute income in favor of the poor, provide public goods, and offset the effects of external economies and diseconomies, there is considerable disagreement over how far the government should go in these areas and what additional areas the government should be responsible for. Some people feel that "big government" is already a problem, that government is doing too much. Others believe that the public sector of the economy is being undernourished and that government should be allowed to do more. This is a fundamental question, and one that involves a great deal more than economics.

CONSERVATIVE VIEW

On the one hand, conservatives such as Stanford University's Nobel laureate Milton Friedman, believe that the government's role should be limited severely. They feel that economic and politi-

cal freedom is likely to be undermined by excessive reliance on the state. Moreover, they tend to be skeptical about the government's ability to solve the social and economic problems at hand. They feel that the prevailing faith in the government's power to make a substantial dent in these problems is unreasonable, and they call for more and better information concerning the sorts of tasks government can reasonably be expected to do—and do well. They point to the slowness of the government bureaucracy, the difficulty in controlling huge government organizations, the inefficiencies political considerations can breed, and the difficulties in telling whether government programs are successful. On the basis of these considerations, they argue that the government's role should be carefully circumscribed.

LIBERAL VIEW

To such arguments, liberals like Nobel laureate Paul Samuelson of the Massachusetts Institute of Technology respond with telling salvos of their own. Just as conservatives tend to be skeptical about the government's ability to solve important social and economic problems, so liberals tend to be skeptical about the price system's ability to solve these problems. They point to the limitations of the price system, discussed previously, and they assert that the government can do a great deal to overcome these limitations, by regulating private activity and by subsidizing and providing goods and services that the private sector produces too little of. Liberals tend to be less concerned than conservatives about the effects on personal freedom of greater governmental intervention in the economy. They point out that the price system also involves coercion, since the fact that the price system awards the available goods and services to those who can pay their equilibrium price can be viewed as a form of coercion. In their view, people who are awarded only a pittance by the price system are coerced into discomfort and malnutrition.

ESTABLISHING "RULES OF THE GAME"

Although there is considerable disagreement over the proper role of the government, both conservatives and liberals agree that it must do certain things. The first of these is to establish the "rules of the game"—that is, a legal, social, and competitive framework enabling the price system to function as it should. Specifically, *the government must see to it that contracts are enforced, that private ownership is protected, and that fraud is prevented.* Clearly, these matters must be tended to if the price system is to work properly. Also, *the government must maintain order (through the establishment of police and other forces), establish a monetary system (so that money can be used to facilitate trade and exchange), and provide standards for the weight and quality of products.*

As an example of this sort of government intervention, consider the Pure Food and Drug Act. This act, originally passed in 1906 and subsequently amended in various ways, protects the consumer against improper and fraudulent activities on the part of producers of foods and drugs. It prohibits the merchandising of impure or falsely

labeled food or drugs, and it forces producers to specify the quantity and quality of the contents on labels. These requirements strengthen the price system. Without them, the typical consumer would be unable to tell whether food or drugs are pure or properly labeled. Unless consumers can be sure that they are getting what they pay for, the basic logic underlying the price system breaks down. Similar regulation and legislation have been instituted in fields other than food and drugs—and for similar reasons.

MAINTAINING A COMPETITIVE FRAMEWORK

Besides establishing a legal and social framework that will enable the price system to do its job, *the government must also see to it that markets remain reasonably competitive.* Only if they are, will prices reflect consumer desires properly. If markets are dominated by a few sellers (or a few buyers), prices may be rigged by these sellers (or buyers) to promote their own interests. For example, if a single firm is the sole producer of aluminum, it is a safe bet that this firm will establish a higher price than if there were many aluminum producers competing among themselves.

As previous chapters have indicated, the unfortunate thing about prices determined in noncompetitive markets—rigged prices, if you will—is that they give incorrect signals concerning what consumers want and how scarce resources and commodities are. Producers, responding to these incorrect signals, do not produce the right things in the right quantities. Consumers respond to these incorrect signals by not supplying the right resources in the right amounts and by not consuming the proper amounts of the goods that are produced. Thus the price system is not permitted to function properly in the absence of reasonable competition.

To try to encourage and preserve competition, the Congress, as you have seen, has enacted a series of **antitrust laws,** such as the Sherman Antitrust Act and the Clayton Act, and it has established the Federal Trade Commission. The antitrust laws make it illegal for firms to collude or to attempt to monopolize the sale of a product. Both conservative and liberal economists, with some notable exceptions, tend to favor the intent and operation of the antitrust laws.

REDISTRIBUTION OF INCOME

There is general agreement that the government should redistribute income in favor of the poor. In other words, *it is usually felt that help should be given to people who are ill, handicapped, old and infirm, disabled, and unable for other reasons to provide for themselves*. To some extent, the country has decided that income—or at least a certain minimum income—should be divorced from productive services. Of course, this doesn't mean that people who are too lazy to work should be given a handout. It does mean that people who cannot provide for themselves should be helped. To implement this principle, various payments are made by the government to needy people—including the aged, the handicapped, the unemployed, and pensioners.

These **welfare programs** are to some extent a "depression baby," for they grew substantially during the Great Depression of the 1930s, when relief payments seemed to be a necessity. But they also represent a feeling shared by a large segment of the population that human beings should be assured that, however the wheel of fortune spins and whatever number comes up, they will not starve and their children will not be deprived of a healthy environment and basic schooling. Of course, someone has to pay for all this. Welfare payments allow the poor to take more from the country's output than they produce. In general, the more affluent members of society contribute some of their claims on output to pay for these programs, their contributions

being in the form of taxes. By using its expenditures to help certain groups and by taxing other groups to pay for these programs, the government accomplishes each year, without revolt and without bayonets, a substantial redistribution of income.

STABILIZING THE ECONOMY

It is also generally agreed that *the government should promote the maintenance of reasonably full employment with reasonably stable prices*. Capitalist economies have tended to alternate between booms and depressions in the past. The Great Depression of the 1930s hit the U.S. economy—and the world economy—a particularly devastating blow, putting millions of people out of work and in desperate shape. There are important differences of opinion among economists regarding the extent to which the government can stabilize the economy. But it is generally agreed that the government should do what it can to avoid serious recessions and to maintain employment at a high level.

Also, the government must try to maintain a reasonably stable price level. No economy can function well if prices are gyrating wildly. Through its control of the money supply and its decisions regarding expenditures and taxation, the government has considerable impact on the price level, as well as on the level of employment. Unfortunately, during the 1970s in particular, the government was not very successful in maintaining price stability. According to many economists, the government's own policies contributed to this inflation.

 TEST YOUR UNDERSTANDING

True or false?

_____ **1** The government relies on the legitimate and systematic use of force.

_____ **2** Prices determined in noncompetitive markets provide incorrect signals regarding what con-

sumers want and how scarce resources and commodities are.

_____ **3** To be equitable, each and every citizen should pay an equal amount to the government in taxes.

Exercise

1 Decisions concerning government expenditures and taxes are political decisions. In democracies, such decisions are made by majority rule. Kenneth Arrow, a Nobel laureate at Stanford University, has carried out some fundamental studies of majority rule and social choice. To illustrate simply the sorts of results obtained by Arrow and other economists, suppose that a society consists of three members, Jane Blue, William Gray, and Joan Green. Suppose too that each member of society must vote on three possible levels of the government budget in this simple society: high, medium, and low. Each person's vote has equal weight in determining the outcome. Further, suppose that the preferences of the three people with respect to budget levels are as indicated below:

	BLUE	GRAY	GREEN
First preference	High	Low	Medium
Second preference	Medium	High	Low
Third preference	Low	Medium	High

a. Suppose that the choice is between a high budget and a low one. Which will be chosen?

b. Suppose that the choice is between a low budget and a medium one. Which will be chosen?

c. Given the results of parts a and b, what seems to be the level of the government budget that will win with majority rule?

d. What if the sequence in which the choices are made is altered? Suppose that the choice first is between a medium and a low budget, and that the winner is then compared with a high budget. What seems to be the level of the government budget that will win with majority rule? Is your answer the same as in part c?

3 ▪ Providing Public Goods

As has been indicated, the government provides many public goods. Here public goods are considered in more detail.

WHAT IS A PUBLIC GOOD?

One hallmark of a public good is that it can be consumed by one person without diminishing the amount that other people consume of it. Public goods tend to be relatively indivisible, they often come in such large units that they cannot be broken into pieces that can be bought or sold in ordinary markets. *Once such goods are produced, there often is no way to bar certain citizens from consuming them.* Whether or not citizens contribute toward their cost, they benefit from them. This means that the price system cannot be used to handle effectively the production and distribution of such goods.

NATIONAL DEFENSE: A PUBLIC GOOD

National defense is a public good. The benefits of expenditure on national defense extend to the entire country. Extension of the benefits of national defense to an additional citizen does not mean that any other citizen gets less of these benefits. Also, there is no way of preventing citizens from benefiting from them, whether they contribute to their cost or not. Thus there is no way to use the price system to provide for national defense. Since it is a public good, national defense, if it is to reach an adequate level, must be provided by the government. Similarly with flood control, environmental protection, and a host of other services.

DECISION MAKING REGARDING PUBLIC GOODS

Essentially, deciding how much to produce of a public good is a political decision. The citizens of the United States elect senators and members of Congress who decide how much should be spent on national defense, and how it should be spent. These elected representatives are responsive to special-interest groups, as well as to the people as a whole. Many special-interest groups lobby hard for the production of certain public goods. For

example, an alliance of military and industrial groups presses for increased defense expenditures, and other interested groups promote expenditures on other functions.

The tax system is used to pay for the production of public goods. In effect, the government says to each citizen, "Fork over a certain amount of money to pay for the expenses incurred by the government." The amount a particular citizen is assessed may depend on his or her income (as in the income tax), the value of all or specific types of his or her property (as in the property tax), the amount he or she spends on certain types of goods and services (as in the sales tax), or on still other criteria.

 TEST YOUR UNDERSTANDING

True or false?

_____ **1** Public goods frequently are sold in the private market.

_____ **2** Once a public good is produced, it is easy to bar citizens from consuming it.

_____ **3** National defense is not a public good.

Exercises

1 "I believe the government should do only that which private citizens cannot do for themselves, or which they cannot do so well for themselves." Interpret and comment. Indicate how you might determine in practice what the legitimate functions of government are, according to this proposition.

2 "The ideal public policy, from the viewpoint of the state, is one with identifiable beneficiaries, each of whom is helped appreciably, at the cost of many unidentifiable persons, none of whom is hurt much." Do you agree?

3 Explain why national defense is a public good but a rifle is not a public good.

4 "I cannot get the amount of national defense I want and you, a different amount." Is this true of all public goods?

5 The federal government spends billions of dollars on general science, space, and technology. Why should the government support each of these activities?

---

4 ▪ Externalities

It is generally agreed that *the government should encourage the production of goods and services that entail external economies and discourage the production of those that entail external diseconomies*. Take the pollution of air and water. When a firm or individual dumps wastes into the water or air, other

firms or individuals often must pay all or part of the cost of putting the water or air back into a usable condition. Thus the disposal of these wastes entails external diseconomies. Unless the government prohibits certain kinds of pollution, enforces air and water quality standards, or charges polluters in accord with the amount of waste they dump into the environment, there will be socially undesirable levels of pollution.

EFFECTS OF EXTERNAL DISECONOMIES

To see how such externalities affect the social desirability of the output of a competitive industry, consider Figure 14.1, where the industry's demand and supply curves are contained in the left-hand panel. As shown there, the equilibrium output of the industry is OQ_0. If the industry results in no external economies or diseconomies, this is likely to be the socially optimal output. But what if the industry results in external diseconomies, such as the pollution described above? Then the industry's supply curve does not fully reflect the true social costs of producing the product. The supply curve that reflects these social costs is S_1, which, as shown in the middle panel of Figure 14.1, lies to the left of the industry's supply curve. The optimal output of the good is OQ_1, which is less than the competitive output, OQ_0.

What can the government do to correct the situation? There are a variety of ways that it can intervene to reduce the industry's output from OQ_0 to OQ_1. For example, it can impose taxes on

the industry. If these taxes are of the right type and amount, they will result in the desired reduction of output.

EFFECTS OF EXTERNAL ECONOMIES

What if the industry results in external economies? For example, what if the manufacturer of one industrial product makes it cheaper to produce other products? Then the industry's demand curve underestimates the true social benefits of producing the product. The demand curve that reflects these social benefits correctly is D_1, which, as shown in the right-hand panel of Figure 14.1, lies to the right of the industry's demand curve. The optimal output of the good is OQ_2, which is greater than the competitive output, OQ_0.

As in the case in which the industry results in external diseconomies, the government can intervene in various ways to change the industry's output. But in this case, the object is to increase, not decrease, its output. To accomplish this, the government can, among other things, grant subsidies to the industry. If they are of the right type and amount, they can be used to increase the industry's output from OQ_0 to OQ_2.

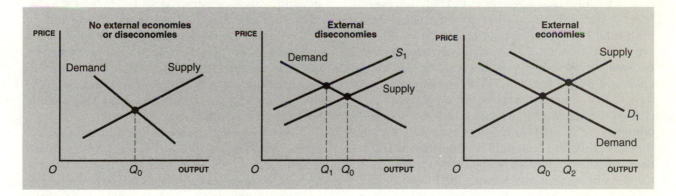

▪ **FIGURE 14.1**

Effect of External Economies and Diseconomies on the Optimal Output of a Competitive Industry

The optimal output is OQ_0 if neither external economies nor diseconomies are present. If there are external diseconomies, curve S_1 reflects the true social costs of producing the product, and OQ_1 is the optimal output. If there are external economies, curve D_1 reflects the true social benefits of producing the product, and OQ_2 is the optimal output.

TEST YOUR UNDERSTANDING

True or false?

____ **1** If an industry results in external economies, the government might grant subsidies to the industry.

____ **2** The government should impose taxes on

goods that result in external economies in order to promote an optimal allocation of resources.

____ **3** An industry's supply curve may not fully reflect the social costs of producing the product.

5 ■ Size and Nature of Government Activities

HOW BIG IS THE GOVERNMENT?

Up to this point, the primary concern has been with the reasons why the government must intervene in our economy—and the types of roles it should play—but little or no attempt has been made to describe its role in quantitative terms. It is time now to turn to some of the relevant facts. One useful measure of the extent of the government's role in the U.S. economy is the size of government expenditures, both in absolute terms and as a percent of total output.

The sum total of government expenditures—federal, state, and local—has grown much faster than total U.S. output in the past 70 years. There are several reasons. First, *the United States did not maintain anything like the kind of military force in pre-World War II days that it does now.* In earlier days, when weapons were relatively simple and cheap, and when military and political responsibilities were viewed much more narrowly than they are now, the U.S. military budget was relatively small. The cost of being a superpower in the days of nuclear weaponry is high by any standards. Second, *there has been a long-term increase in the demand for the services provided by government,* like more and better schooling, more extensive highways, more complete police and fire protection, and so forth. As incomes rise, people want more of these services. Third, **government transfer payments**—*payments in return for no products or services*—*have grown very substantially.*

For example, various types of welfare payments have risen, and Social Security payments have increased substantially.

WHAT THE FEDERAL, STATE, AND LOCAL GOVERNMENTS SPEND MONEY ON

There are three levels of government in the United States—federal, state, and local. The state governments spend the least, and the federal government spends the most. This was not always the case. Before World War I, the local governments spent more than the federal government. In those days, the federal government did not maintain the large military establishment it does now, nor did it engage in the many programs in health, education, welfare, and other areas that it currently does. Federal spending is now a much larger percentage of the total than it was almost a century ago.

Much of federal expenditures goes for defense and other items connected with international relations and national security. An even larger share goes for Social Security, Medicare, welfare (and other income security) programs, health, and education. The rest goes to support farm, transportation, housing, and other such programs, as well as to pay interest on the federal debt and to run Congress, the courts, and the executive branch of the federal government.

What about the local and state governments? On what do they spend their money? *The biggest expenditure of the state and local governments is on schools.* Traditionally, schools in the United States have been a responsibility of local governments— cities and towns. *State governments spend most of their money on education; welfare, old age, and unemployment benefits; and highways.* (Besides supporting education directly, they help localities to cover the cost of schooling.) In addition, the local and state governments support hospitals, redevelopment programs, courts, and police and fire departments.

 TEST YOUR UNDERSTANDING

True or false?

_____ **1** Government expenditures in the United States have grown much more rapidly than total output in this century.

_____ **2** The biggest expenditure of the state and local governments is on schools.

_____ **3** The government produces most of the goods and services it provides. For example, the federal government supports over half of the research and development carried out in the United States, and practically all of it is carried out in government laboratories.

6 ▪ What the Federal, State, and Local Governments Receive in Taxes

To get the money to cover most of the expenditures discussed in previous sections, governments collect taxes from individuals and firms. *At the federal level the* **personal income tax** *is the biggest single money raiser.* It brings in almost half the tax revenue collected by the federal government. The next most important taxes at the federal level are the social insurance (Social Security) taxes. Other noteworthy taxes are the corporation income tax, excise taxes (levied on the sale of tobacco, liquor, imports, and certain other items), and death and gift taxes. (Even when the Grim Reaper shows up, the Tax Man is not far behind.)

At the local level, on the other hand, the most important form of taxation and source of revenue is **the property tax.** This is a tax levied primarily on real estate. Other important local taxes—although dwarfed in importance by the property tax—are local sales taxes and local income taxes. Many cities—for example, New York City—levy a sales tax, equal to a certain percent—4 percent in New York City—of the value of each retail sale. The tax is simply added on to the amount charged the customer. Also, many cities—for example, Philadelphia and Pittsburgh—levy an income (or wage) tax on their residents and even on people who work in the city but live outside it. *At the state level,* **sales (and excise) taxes** *are the biggest money raisers,* followed by income taxes and highway-user taxes. The latter includes taxes on gasoline and license fees for vehicles and drivers. Often they exceed the amount spent on roads, and the balance is used for a variety of nonhighway uses.

 TEST YOUR UNDERSTANDING

True or false?

_____ **1** At the federal level the personal income tax is the biggest single money raiser.

_____ **2** At the local level, the most important source of revenue is the sales tax.

_____ **3** At the state level, the most important source of revenue is sales (and excise) taxes.

■ CHAPTER REVIEW

KEY TERMS

public goods
external economy
external diseconomy

antitrust laws
welfare payments
government transfer payments
personal income tax

property tax
sales (and excise) taxes

COMPLETION QUESTIONS

1 The _____ make it illegal for firms to collude or to attempt to monopolize the sale of a product.

2 The government often tries by establishing _____ to control the activities of firms in markets where competition cannot be expected to prevail.

3 Public goods are generally paid for by _____.

4 At the federal level the biggest money raiser is _____ tax.

5 Some _____ cannot be provided through the price system because there is no way to _____ a citizen from consuming the good. For example, there is no way to _____ a citizen from benefiting from national expenditures on defense, whether he or she _____ money toward defense or not. Consequently, the _____ cannot be used to provide such goods.

6 A(n) _____ is said to occur when consumption or production by one person or firm results in uncompensated benefits to another person or firm. A good example of a(n) _____ exists where fundamental research carried out by one firm is used by another firm.

7 Where external economies exist, it is generally agreed that the price system will produce too (little, much) _____ of the good in question and that the government should _____ the amount produced by private enterprise. This is the basic rationale for much of the government's huge _____ in basic science.

8 A(n) _____ is said to occur when consumption or production by one person or firm results in uncompensated costs to another person or firm. A good example of a(n) _____ occurs when a firm dumps pollutants into a stream and makes the water unfit for use by firms and people downstream.

ANSWERS TO COMPLETION QUESTIONS

antitrust laws

regulatory commissions

taxes

personal income

goods and services
exclude

prevent

pays
price system

external economy

external economy

little
supplement

investment

external diseconomy

external diseconomy

9 Local governments now spend (less, more)
_____ than the federal government, although
before World War I, they spent (less, more)
_____ .

less

more

NUMERICAL PROBLEMS

1 The paper industry has the demand and supply
curves shown below:

PRICE OF PAPER (dollars per ton)	QUANTITY DEMANDED	QUANTITY SUPPLIED
	(millions of tons)	
2	80	40
3	70	50
4	60	60
5	50	70

a Suppose that this industry results in substantial external diseconomies. What can be said about its optimal
output rate?

b In the graph below, draw the supply and demand
curves for paper. Does the supply curve reflect the true
social costs of producing the product? If not, will a
supply curve reflecting the true social costs lie above or
below the supply curve you have drawn?

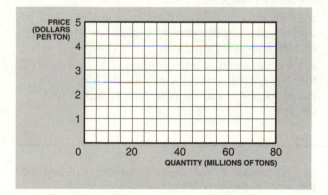

c What is the equilibrium price of paper? From the
point of view of reflecting the true social costs, is this
price correct, too low, or too high?

2 Suppose that for the past decade the United States
has been faced with apple crops far in excess of de-

mand. As Secretary of Agriculture, it is your job to
present to Congress a bill to provide price supports for
apples. In presenting your case, you assume that the
support price for apples will be *OP*, and that output
will be restricted to 1,000 million bushels of apples.

a If the demand curve for apples is as shown, how
much will the government have to purchase?

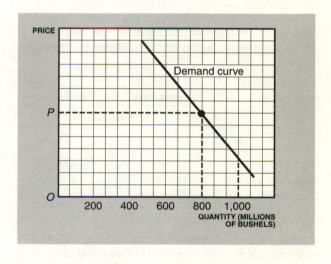

b If farmers sold the 1,000 million bushels of apples
for the best price they could get in the open market,
what price would they get?

c By how much would the demand curve have to
shift, and in what direction, in order to eliminate the
surplus if the government supports the price of a
bushel of apples at *OP*?

3 The town of Lucretia is faced with a serious smog
problem. The smog can be dispelled if an air treatment
plant is installed at an annual cost of $1 million. There
is no way to clean up the air for some but not all of
the town's population. Each of the town's families acts
independently, and no single family can afford to carry
out the project by itself. Why doesn't a private firm
build the air treatment plant and sell its services to the
town's families (acting individually)?

4 Indicate the economic rationale for the government's carrying out the following functions:

a Regulating the sale and development of drugs

b Maintaining an army

c Establishing a monetary system

d Supporting agricultural experiment stations

e Establishing the Antitrust Division of the Department of Justice

f Imposing an income tax

g Establishing unemployment insurance

5 In the United States, what processes are used to reallocate resources from the private sector (firms and individuals) to the government?

6 Besides its smog problem, the town of Lucretia has a transportation problem which it hopes can be solved by building a new road through the center of town. There are three types of roads that can be built, their annual costs and benefits to the townspeople being as follows:

ROAD	TOTAL COST	TOTAL BENEFIT
	(dollars)	
No road	0	0
Road 10 miles long	5 million	8 million
Road 20 miles long	12 million	16 million
Road 30 miles long	20 million	20 million

a What is the extra annual cost of building a 20-mile road rather than a 10-mile road? What is the extra annual cost of building a 30-mile road rather than building a 20-mile road?

b What is the extra annual benefit from building a 20-mile road rather than a 10-mile road? What is the extra annual benefit from building a 30-mile road rather than building a 20-mile road?

c Should the town build one of these roads? If so, which one?

7 Suppose that the demand and supply curves for good *X* are as follows:

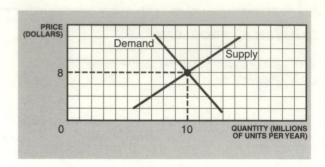

a If the market for good *X* is in equilibrium, how much would consumers be willing to pay for an additional unit of good *X*?

b The supply curve shows the extra cost of producing an extra unit of good *X*. If the market for good *X* is in equilibrium, how much would it cost to produce an extra unit of good *X*?

c If the social costs of producing good *X* exceed the private costs, will the social cost of producing an extra unit of good *X* be equal to the amount consumers would be willing to pay for this extra unit? If not, will the social cost of the extra unit be greater or less than the amount consumers would pay for it? Why?

d Under the circumstances described in part c, indicate why the socially optimal output of good *X* is less than 10 million units per year.

e If the social cost of producing good *X* were *less* than the private costs, indicate why the optimal output of good *X* would be more than 10 million units per year.

 ANSWERS TO
TEST YOUR UNDERSTANDING

SECTION 1

TRUE OR FALSE: 1. True   2. False   3. False

EXERCISE

1. a. No, because the rate of return Mr. Moore receives if he redevelops is 12 percent, whereas the rate of re-

turn he receives if he does not redevelop is 15 percent (because his property benefits from Mr. Lombardi's investment in redevelopment even though he pays nothing).

b. No, because the rate of return Mr. Moore receives if he redevelops is only 5 percent (because little is accomplished so long as Mr. Lombardi does not redevelop too), whereas the rate of return he receives if he does not redevelop is 10 percent (which is what he can obtain from other investments).

c. No. Consider Mr. Moore. As pointed out in a and b, whether or not Mr. Lombardi redevelops, Mr. Moore receives a higher return if he does not redevelop than if he does. Thus he will not redevelop. Neither will Mr. Lombardi, for the same reasons.

d. Yes. From society's point of view or from the point of view of the two owners acting together as a unit, redevelopment may be desirable. If carried out properly, government intervention may bring this about.

SECTION 2

TRUE OR FALSE: 1. True 2. True 3. False

EXERCISE

1. a. A low budget.

b. A medium budget.

c. A medium budget.

d. High budget. No.

SECTION 3

TRUE OR FALSE: 1. False 2. False 3. False

EXERCISES

1. It is very difficult in many cases to know whether a certain activity can be performed better by government than by private citizens. But the first half of this chapter indicates a number of areas where most economists believe the government has legitimate functions.

2. Many observers agree with this statement.

3. You can consume the services provided by national defense without depriving another person of also doing so simultaneously. Also, citizens cannot be prevented from benefiting from national expenditures on defense, whether or not they pay money toward defense. A rifle is not a public good; the hallmark of a public good is that it is consumed collectively or jointly.

4. Yes.

5. Such activities result in external economies.

SECTION 4

TRUE OR FALSE: 1. True 2. False 3. True

SECTION 5

TRUE OR FALSE: 1. True 2. True 3. False

SECTION 6

TRUE OR FALSE: 1. True 2. False 3. True

■ CHAPTER 15

Will Pollution Make Caviar Extinct?

1 ■ The Plight of the Beluga

Caviar, which can sell for as much as $100 an ounce in New York or Paris restaurants, is one of the most celebrated and expensive foods available. But how long it will be available is a matter of controversy. More than 95 percent of all black caviar comes from the Caspian Sea (on the southern coast of Russia), where there are beluga, the largest members of the sturgeon family. A full-grown beluga can weigh a ton and carry more than 2 million eggs; these eggs are called caviar.

In 1994, only about 5,000 tons of sturgeon were caught in the Caspian Sea, less than 1 percent of the annual catch about half a century ago.

One of the principal reasons is environmental pollution. Because the area close to the Caspian Sea has been rich in oil, thousands of derricks have been erected nearby, and a layer of oil, about $1/4$ inch thick, has formed on the Caspian Sea. Also, the Volga river contains tens of thousands of tons of pollutants. The sturgeon cannot swim hundreds of miles up the Volga and other rivers, as they have in the past, to spawn; and when they try to do so, they seldom get back alive.[1]

[1] For further discussion, see the *New York Times*, June 7, 1994.

2 ■ Why Environmental Pollution?

Environmental pollution is not confined to the Caspian Sea; for example, in the hot summer of 1988, beaches were closed in New Jersey and New York because syringes, dead fish, and human wastes washed up on the shore. Why does the economic system tolerate such pollution of the environment? To answer this question, you must understand the nature and effects of external diseconomies. As pointed out in Chapter 14, an *external diseconomy* occurs when one person's (or firm's) use of a resource damages other people who cannot obtain proper compensation. When this occurs, a market economy is unlikely to function properly. The price system is based on the supposition that the full cost of using each re-

source is borne by the person or firm that uses it. If this is not the case and if the user bears only part of the full cost, then the resource is not likely to be directed by the price system into the socially optimal use.

Consider electric power companies (discussed in Chapter 6), which frequently have not paid the full cost of disposing of wastes in the atmosphere. They have charged an artificially low price, and the public has been induced to use more electric power than is socially desirable. Similarly, since the owners of automobiles (discussed in Chapter 9) have not paid the full cost of disposing of exhaust and other wastes in the atmosphere, they have paid an artificially low price for operating an automobile and have been induced to own more automobiles and use them more than is socially desirable.

To see why divergences between private and social costs can cause the price system to malfunction, you must understand how resources are allocated in the market economy. The basic idea is that resources will be used in their socially most valuable way because they are allocated to the people and firms who find it worthwhile to bid most for them, assuming that prices reflect true social costs. Under these circumstances, a firm that maximizes its profits will produce the socially desirable output and use the socially desirable amount of labor, capital, and other resources. Under these circumstances, there is no problem.

Suppose, however, that because of the presence of external diseconomies, people and firms do not pay the true social costs for resources. For example, suppose that some firms or people can use water and air for nothing, but that other firms or people incur costs as a consequence of this prior use. In this case, the **private costs** of using air and water differ from the **social costs:** *the prices paid by the users of water and air is less than the true costs to society.* In a case like this, users of water and air are guided in their decisions by the private costs of water and air—by the prices they pay. Since they pay less than the true social costs, water and air are artificially cheap to them, so that they will use too much of these resources, from society's point of view.

Note that the divergence between private and social costs occurs if and only if the use of water or air by one firm or person imposes costs on other firms or persons. Thus, if a paper mill uses water and then treats it to restore its quality, there is no divergence between private and social costs. But when the same mill dumps harmful wastes into streams and rivers (the cheap way to get rid of its by-products), the towns downstream that use the water must incur costs to restore its quality. The same is true of air pollution. If an electric power plant uses the atmosphere as a cheap and convenient place to dispose of wastes, people living and working nearby may incur costs as a result, since the incidence of respiratory and other diseases may increase. In such cases, there may be a divergence between private and social costs.

As noted, pollution-causing activities that result in external diseconomies represent a malfunctioning of the market system. At this point, the nature of this malfunctioning should be clear. *Firms and people dump too much waste material into the water and the atmosphere. The price system does not provide the proper signals because the polluters are induced to use the streams and atmosphere in this socially undesirable way by the artificially low price of disposing of wastes in this manner. Moreover, because the polluters do not pay the true costs of waste disposal, their products are artificially cheap, so that too much of them is produced.*

3 ▪ Direct Regulation by Government

Pollution is caused by defects in institutions, not by malicious intent, greed, or corruption. In cases in which waste disposal causes significant external diseconomies, economist generally agree that government intervention may be justifiable. But how can the government intervene? Perhaps the simplest way is **direct regulation,** through the issuance of certain enforceable rules for waste disposal. For example, the government can prohibit the burning of trash in furnaces or incinera-

tors, or the dumping of certain materials in the ocean, and can make any person or firm that violates these restrictions subject to a fine, or perhaps even imprisonment. Also, the government can ban the use of chemicals like DDT or require that all automobiles meet certain regulations for the emission of air pollutants. Further, the government can establish quality standards for air and water.

At present, the United States relies heavily on

direct regulation to reduce pollution. However, economists agree that direct regulation suffers from some serious disadvantages:

1 Such regulations have generally taken the form of general, across-the-board rules. For example, if two factories located on the same river dump the same amount of waste material into the river, such regulations would probably call for each factory to reduce its waste disposal by the same amount. Unfortunately, although this may appear quite sensible, it may in fact be very inefficient. Suppose that it is much less costly for one factory to reduce its waste disposal than for the other. In such a case, it would be more efficient to ask the factory that could reduce its wastes more cheaply to cut down more on its waste disposal than the other factory. For reasons of this sort, *pollution reductions are likely to be accomplished at more than minimum cost if they are accomplished by direct regulation.*

2 *To formulate such regulations in a reasonably sensible way, the responsible government agencies must have access to much more information than they are likely to obtain or assimilate.* Unless the government agencies have a detailed and up-to-date familiarity with the technology of hundreds of industries, they are unlikely to make sound rules. Moreover, unless the regulatory agencies have a very wide jurisdiction, their regulations will be evaded by the movement of plants and individuals from localities where regulations are stiff to localities where they are loose. In addition, the regulatory agencies must view the pollution problem as a whole, since piecemeal regulation may simply lead polluters to substitute one form of pollution for another. For example, New York and Philadelphia attempted to reduce water pollution by more intensive sewage treatment. However, one result was the production of a lot of biologically active sludge that was (until 1988) being dumped into the ocean—and perhaps causing problems there.

4 ▪ Effluent Fees

The government can also intervene by establishing effluent fees. An **effluent fee** is a fee a polluter must pay to the government for discharging waste. In other words, a price is imposed on the disposal of wastes into the environment; and the more that firms or individuals pollute, the more they must pay. The idea behind the imposition of effluent fees is that they can bring the private costs of waste disposal closer to the true social costs. Faced with a closer approximation to the true social costs of their activities, polluters will reduce the extent to which they pollute the environment. Needless to say, many practical difficulties are involved in carrying out this seemingly simple scheme, but many economists believe that this is a better way than direct regulation to deal with the pollution problem.

The use of effluent fees has the following advantages over direct regulation. First, *it obviously is socially desirable to use the cheapest way to achieve any given reduction in pollution. A system of effluent fees is more likely to accomplish this objective than direct regulation, because the regulatory agency cannot have all the relevant information* (as noted above), *whereas polluters, reacting in their own interest to effluent fees, will tend to use the cheapest means to achieve a given reduction in pollution.*

To see why this is the case, consider a particular polluter. Faced with an effluent fee—that is, a price it must pay for each unit of waste it discharges—the polluter will find it profitable to reduce its discharge of waste so long as the cost of doing so is less than the effluent fee it saves. Thus, if this firm can reduce its discharge of wastes relatively cheaply, it will be induced to make such a reduction by the prospect of increased profits. On the other hand, if it cannot reduce its discharge of wastes at all cheaply, it will not make such a reduction, since the costs will exceed the saving in effluent fees. Thus a system of effluent fees induces firms that can reduce waste disposal more cheaply to cut down more on their waste disposal than firms where such a reduction is more expensive. This means that a given reduction of pollution will occur at a relatively low cost.

Another advantage of effluent fees is that they do not require government agencies to have the detailed technological expertise often required by direct regulation. After all, when effluent fees are used, all the government has to do is meter the amount of pollution a firm or household produces (which admittedly is sometimes not easy) and charge accordingly. It is left to the firms and households to figure out the most ingenious and effective ways to cut down on their pollution and save on effluent fees. This too is a spur to inventive activities aimed at developing more effective ways to reduce pollution. Also economists favor the use of effluent fees because financial incentives are likely to be easier to administer than direct regulation.

Although economists tend to favor the use of effluent fees, they are not always against direct regulation. Some ways of disposing of certain types of waste are so dangerous that the only sensible thing to do is to ban them. For example, a ban on the disposal of mercury or arsenic in places where human beings are likely to consume them—and die—seems reasonable enough. In effect, the social cost of such pollution is so high that a very high penalty—imprisonment—is put on it. In addition, of course, economists favor direct regulation when it simply is not feasible to impose effluent fees—for example, in cases in which it would be prohibitively expensive to meter the amount of pollutants emitted by various firms or households.

5 ▪ Transferrable Emissions Permits

Another way that the government can reduce pollution is to issue **transferable emissions permits.** These permits, each of which allows the holder of the permit to generate a certain amount of pollution, are limited in total number. They are sold to the highest bidders. Thus the price of a permit is set by supply and demand. If there is a great demand for such permits, and if the total number is small, the price of a permit will be high. If there is a weak demand for such permits, and if the total number is large, the price of a permit will be low.

One advantage of transferable emissions permits is that the authorities can predict how much pollution there will be. After all, the total amount of pollution cannot exceed the amount authorized by the total number of permits issued. In contrast, if an effluent fee is adopted, it is difficult to predict how much pollution will result, since this depends on how polluters respond to the particular level of the effluent fee that is chosen. For this reason, transferable emissions permits are often preferred over effluent fees.

6 ▪ Tax Credits for Pollution-Control Equipment

Still another way for the government to intervene is to establish **tax credits** for firms that introduce pollution-control equipment. There are, of course, many types of equipment that a plant can introduce to cut down on pollution—for example, "scrubbers" for catching poisonous gases, and electrostatic precipitators for decreasing dust and smoke. But such pollution-control equipment

costs money, and firms are naturally reluctant to spend money on purposes where the private rate of return is so low.

To reduce the burden, the government can allow firms to reduce their tax bill by a certain percentage of the amount they spend on pollution-control equipment. A typical suggestion is that the government offer a *tax credit* equal to 20 percent of the cost of pollution-control equipment. In this way, the government would help defray some of the costs of the pollution-control equipment by allowing a firm that installed such equipment to pay less taxes than if no such tax inducements existed.

However, such schemes have a number of disadvantages:

1 *Subsidies to promote the purchase of particular types of pollution-control equipment may result in relatively inefficient and costly reductions in pollution.* After all, other methods that don't involve special pollution-control equipment—such as substituting one type of fuel for another—may sometimes be a more efficient way to reduce pollution.

2 *Subsidies of this sort may not be very effective.* Even if the subsidy reduces the cost to the firm of re-

ducing pollution, it may still be cheaper for the firm to continue to pollute. In other words, subsidies of this sort make it a little less painful for polluters to reduce pollution; but unlike effluent fees, they offer no positive incentive.

3 *It seems preferable on grounds of equity for the firms and individuals that do the polluting—or their customers—to pay to clean up the mess that results.* Effluent fees work this way, but with tax credits for pollution-control equipment, the government picks up part of the tab by allowing the polluter to pay lower taxes. In other words, the general public, which is asked to shoulder the additional tax burden to make up for the polluters' lower taxes, pays part of the cost. But is this a fair allocation of the costs? Why should the general public be saddled with much of the bill?

7 ▪ How Clean Should the Environment Be?

One of the most fundamental questions about pollution control is: How clean do you want the air, water, and other parts of our environment to be? At first glance, it may seem that you should want to restore and maintain a pristine pure environment, but this is not a very sensible goal, since the costs of achieving it would be enormous. The Environmental Protection Agency has estimated that the cost of achieving zero discharge of pollutants would be hundreds of billions of dollars—a truly staggering sum.

Fortunately, however, there is no reason to aim at so stringent a goal. *It seems obvious that, as pollution increases, various costs to society increase as well.* For example, increases in air pollution result in increased deaths, and increases in water pollution reduce the recreational value of rivers and streams. Suppose that you could get accurate data on the cost to society of various levels of pollution. Of course, it is extremely difficult to get such data, but if you could, you could determine the relationship between the amount of these costs and the level of pollution. It would look like the hypothetical curve in Figure 15.1. The

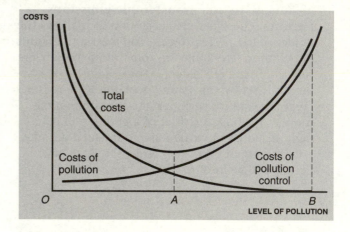

▪ **FIGURE 15.1**

Determining the Optimal Level of Pollution

The optimal level of pollution is at point *A*, since this is where the total costs are a minimum. Below point *A*, the cost to society of more pollution is less than the cost of preventing it. Above point *A*, the cost to society of more pollution is greater than the cost of preventing it.

greater the level of pollution, the higher these costs will be.

But these costs are not the only ones that must be considered. *You must also take into account the costs of controlling pollution.* In other words, you must look at the costs to society of maintaining a certain level of environment quality. These costs are not trivial, as you saw at the beginning of this section. To maintain a very low level of pollution, it is necessary to invest heavily in pollution-control equipment and to make other economic sacrifices. If you could get accurate data on the cost to society of controlling pollution, you could find the relationship between the amount of these costs and the level of pollution. It would look like the hypothetical curve in Figure 15.1; the lower the level of pollution, the higher these costs will be.

8 ▪ A Goal of Zero Pollution?

At this point, it should be obvious why you should not try to achieve a zero level of pollution. *The sensible goal for a society is to minimize the sum of the costs of pollution and the costs of controlling pollution.* In other words, you should construct a graph, as shown in Figure 15.1, to indicate the relationship between the sum of these two types of costs and the level of pollution. Then you should choose the level of pollution at which the sum of these two types of costs is a minimum. Thus, in Figure 15.1, you should aim for a pollution level of *A*. There is no point in trying for a lower level; such a reduction would cost more than it would be worth. For example, the cost of achieving a zero pollution level would be much more than it would be worth. Only when the pollution level exceeds *A* is the extra cost to society of the additional pollution greater than the cost of preventing it. For example, the cost of allowing pollution to increase from *A* to *B* is much greater than the cost of prevention.

It is easy to draw hypothetical curves, but not so easy actually to measure these curves. Unfortunately, no one has a very clear idea of what the curves in Figure 15.1 really look like—although you can be sure that their general shapes are like those shown there. Thus no one really knows just how clean you should try to make the environment. Under these circumstances, expert opinion differs on the nature and extent of the programs that should be carried out. Moreover, political considerations and pressures enter in. But one thing is for sure: you will continue to live with some pollution—and that, for the reason just given, will be the rational thing to do.

9 ▪ The Ban on Ocean Dumping

To illustrate the political factors involved, return to the summer of 1988 when garbage and filth washed up on New Jersey and New York beaches in such amounts that the beaches were closed. What was the political outcome? Congress voted unanimously to impose a ban on the dumping of sewage into the ocean. However, many knowledgeable observers argue that the real cause of the beach closing was New York City's antiquated sewage system. Whenever there is a heavy storm, so much water goes into this system—which handles both rainwater and sewage—that treatment plants are overwhelmed and raw sewage flows out into rivers and the sea. While the ban on ocean dumping resulted in additional costs of more than $2 billion, it had only a secondary effect on the problem it was meant to solve.

According to Alan Rubin, a senior official at

the Environmental Protection Agency (the federal agency that oversees environmental quality and devises policies to improve it), "By 1988, ocean dumping had become taboo, about as politically incorrect as any disposal of waste can be. Maybe it was a good thing that happened. Maybe not. But is was not decided on the merits. Congress acted on emotion, not data."[2] Albert Appleton, commissioner of New York City's Department of Environmental Protection, has commented: "Am I sad that we no longer dump sludge in the Atlantic Ocean? Absolutely not. In a perfect world we simply wouldn't dump our waste at sea. But is that how I would have spent our next $2 billion? Never in a million years."[3]

[2] *New York Times*, March 22, 1993.

[3] Ibid.

10 ▪ Global Warming

Finally, let's turn to a topic of major international concern. According to many world political leaders, there is an urgent need to take action to halt global warming. Scientists have long known that certain gases, notably carbon dioxide, in the atmosphere trap solar energy and heat the planet. (See Figure 15.2.) Many leading scientists now believe that these gases are being generated faster than the biosphere can neutralize their effects, and that as a consequence the global climate is warming up. Because of this "greenhouse effect," it has been estimated that the Earth's global mean temperature could increase by about 5 degrees by the end of the century, with the result that the sea level may increase by about 2 feet.

Faced with this situation, 68 countries (including the United States, Japan, and Russia) agreed in late 1989 that carbon dioxide emissions would have to be curbed, and a United Nations report called for a 60 percent cut in "greenhouse" gas emissions. Because fuel combustion is the primary source of carbon dioxide emissions, lower energy consumption would probably be required to curb carbon dioxide resulting from fossil fuel consumption.

Scientists are sharply split in their views concerning the likelihood of global warming. Some scientists, like Richard Lindzen of Massachusetts Institute of Technology, argue that current forecasts of global warming "are so inaccurate and fraught with uncertainty as to be useless to policymakers."[4] Given these uncertainties, the Bush

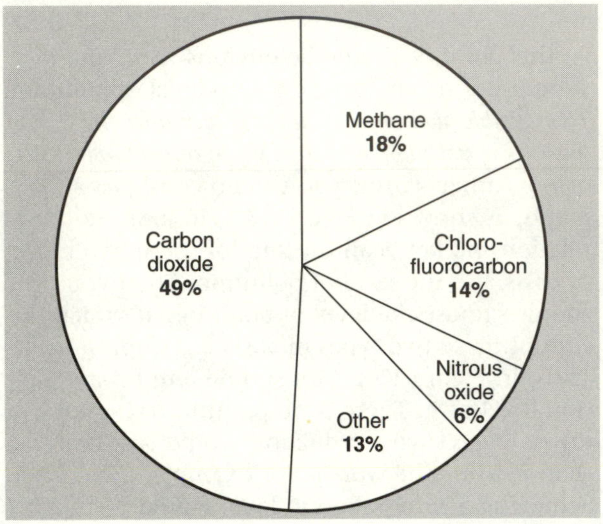

▪ **FIGURE 15.2**

Gases Creating the Greenhouse Effect

SOURCE: *New York Times*, November 19, 1989.

administration adopted a "no regrets" policy. In other words, it was willing to act to cut greenhouse gas emissions only if those actions could be justified on other grounds (even if these emissions were determined ultimately to be unrelated to climatic changes). In contrast, the Clinton administration "sees cost-effective policies to reduce greenhouse gas emissions as appropriate insurance against the threat of climate change."[5]

[4] *New York Times*, December 13, 1989.

[5] *Economic Report of the President* (Washington, D.C.: Government Printing Office, 1994), p. 184.

11 ▪ Applying Economics: Global Warming

The following two problems deal with global warming, which was just discussed briefly.

PROBLEM 15.1 In 1988, the Intergovernmental Panel on Climate Change, a committee of distinguished scientists, was established to provide information to help international negotiations on policies regarding global warming. Figure 15.3 shows this panel's forecasts of future changes in mean temperature on Earth if mankind proceeds on a business-as-usual basis. In June 1992, most members of the United Nations agreed to a Convention on Climate Change, but the Bush administration insisted that parties not be obligated to any particular policy actions. In April 1993, the Clinton administration changed U.S. policy on this issue.

a. How much of an increase in mean temperature does this panel expect by 2100 (relative to 1900)?

b. Isn't it obvious that a change in climate of this magnitude must be prevented? According to many observers, human behavior that may change the Earth's climate is likely to foul our nest in a fundamental way; thus, it should be stopped regardless of the cost. Do you agree? Why or why not?

c. According to Yale's William Nordhaus, the impact on U.S. incomes of a 2.5 to 3 degree increase in mean temperature would be:[6]

SECTOR OF ECONOMY	BILLIONS OF DOLLARS
Agriculture	1.0
Coastal areas	10.7
Energy	0.5
Other	38.1
Total	50.3

[6] W. Nordhaus, "Reflections on the Economics of Climate Change," *Journal of Economic Perspectives*, Fall 1993.

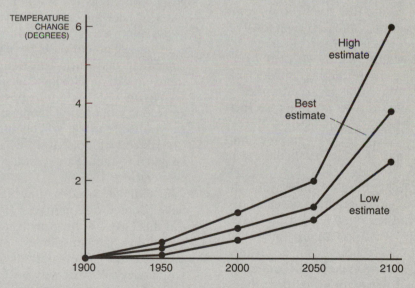

▪ **FIGURE 15.3**

Projections of Global Temperature Increase, Intergovernmental Panel on Climate Change

SOURCE: W. Nordhaus, "Reflections on the Economics of Climate Change," *Journal of Economic Perspectives*, Fall 1993, p. 13.

Why are agricultural and coastal areas affected?

d. Curve *C* in Figure 15.4 shows the marginal cost of reducing the emission of green house gases by various amounts. For example, if the level of emission of such gases is reduced by *U*, the marginal cost to society of reducing the emissions by an extra unit equals *X*. Why is this curve upward sloping to the right?

e. Curve *B* in Figure 15.4 shows the marginal benefit of reducing the emission of greenhouse gases by various amounts. For example, if the level of emission of such gases is reduced by *U*, the marginal benefit to society of reducing the emissions by an extra unit equals *Z*. Why is this curve downward sloping to the right?

f. On the basis of Figure 15.4, can you tell how much reduction there should be in the emission of greenhouse gases? If so, how big should it be? Why?

PROBLEM 15.2 If there were agreement as to how much the emission of greenhouse gases should be reduced, there still would be the question of how such a reduction should be achieved. One measure that has been suggested is a carbon tax, which is a tax on each fossil fuel in proportion to the amount of carbon dioxide emitted when it is burned. Thus, because coal produces more carbon dioxide per unit of energy than natural gas or oil, coal would have a higher carbon tax rate than these other two fuels.

a. In Figure 15.4, if a tax were imposed on each unit of greenhouse gases emitted, how big should the tax be? Why?

b. According to Stanford's John Weyant, the cost of a long-run global program designed to limit emissions to their 1990 level would be about 2.5 percent of world GDP by the year 2043—or about 2.25 trillion dollars per year.[7] What percentage of the present GDP of the United States does this amount to? Does the likelihood of adoption of such a program de-

■ **FIGURE 15.4**

Marginal Social Cost and Benefit from Reduction of Greenhouse Gas Emissions

pend on how these costs are distributed among various countries? Why or why not?

c. In the developing countries, the rate of growth of energy use is double the world average. Consider the case of China. As its economy grows and uses its large coal reserves, China's emissions of greenhouse gases in about 50 years will equal total world emissions today.[8] (For the trends in carbon dioxide emissions by region, see Figure 15.5.) Will it be possible to reduce emissions without the cooperation of China? Do you think that it will be difficult to obtain China's cooperation? If so, what steps might be taken to reduce the cost to China of cooperating?

d. Finland, Sweden, and the Netherlands have adopted carbon taxes.[9] How much effect can this have on the growth rate of global greenhouse gas emissions? If other countries do not do the same, does this seem to be a wise policy? Why or why not?

e. Most experts expect little substantial climate change in the next decade or two. Indeed,

[7] J. Weyant, "Costs of Reducing Global Carbon Emissions," *Journal of Economic Perspectives*, Fall 1993.

[8] Ibid.

[9] J. Poterba, "Global Warming Policy: A Public Finance Perspective," *Journal of Economic Perspectives*, Fall 1993.

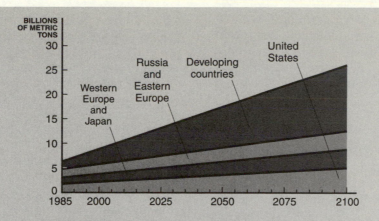

Carbon Dioxide Emissions by Region

SOURCE: Environmental Protection Agency, *Policy Options for Stabilizing Global Climate* (Rapidly Changing World Scenario).

it may be much longer (if ever) before any significant change occurs. If people are much more concerned about hardships and costs incurred now and in the near future than about hardships and costs incurred in the distant future (in part because they are likely to be dead then), will this affect the policies that will be adopted? If so, in what way?

12 ▪ Applying Economics: Water Pollution

The following two problems are concerned with water pollution.

PROBLEM 15.3 The paper industry has been a notable source of water pollution. Suppose that every ton of paper produced imposes costs on others (for example, on people using local rivers for recreation and fishing) of $5. The supply and demand curves for paper (SS' and DD') are given on the right.

   a. Assuming no government intervention, what will be the output of the paper industry?

   b. Does curve S_1S_1' show the marginal cost of producing each level of output? Why or why not?

   c. If a product's price were a reasonable measure of the social value of an extra unit of output, what would be the socially optimal level of output of the paper industry?

   d. Assuming no government intervention, would the output of the paper industry be too large or too small? Why?

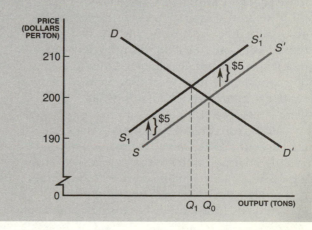

PROBLEM 15.4 According to estimates made by Allen Kneese and Charles Schultze, the cost of achieving a 1-pound reduction in the amount of pollutants emitted at a petroleum refinery and a beet-sugar plant are as shown below:

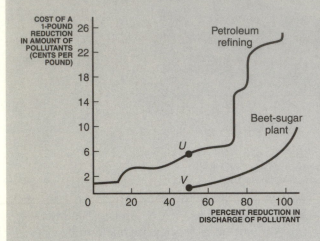

a. Suppose that it is decided that the total amount of pollutants discharged by both plants should be reduced by 50 percent. If the government decrees that each plant should cut its discharge by 50 percent, what would be the cost of a 1-pound reduction at each plant?

b. Can you suggest a way in which this total reduction in pollution can be achieved more efficiently?

c. To achieve this reduction most efficiently, which plant (the petroleum refinery or the beet-sugar plant) should reduce its discharge by the greater percentage?

d. Would an effluent fee achieve this reduction at less cost than the regulation in a?

13 ▪ Applying Economics: Air Pollution

The next two problems are concerned with air pollution.

PROBLEM 15.5 In the late 1970s, the Environmental Protection Agency (EPA) began to experiment with market-like schemes for pollution control. Rather than directly controlling the behavior of each source of pollution, these schemes introduced financial incentives for firms to use their own expertise to achieve air quality levels relatively cheaply. The EPA moved very cautiously in this direction; direct regulation was not abandoned. Only limited use of financial incentives was approved. Three incentive schemes—bubbles, offsets, and banks—were developed.

a. The concept of a **bubble** was meant to take account of the fact that the costs of controlling pollution differ among processes within a particular plant and among plants and firms. A "bubble" is put around the entire plant or area, which is then viewed as a single source of

pollution rather than several distinct sources. Regulators establish emission limits for a plant (or area) as a whole, and managers can allocate pollution abatement in any way they like as long as the overall emission target is attained. The bubble concept could only be applied to existing firms, not to potential sources of pollution. Why would the bubble concept be expected to reduce the cost of controlling pollution?

b. The concept of an **offset** was developed to permit new plants to open and old ones to expand in areas that did not meet the national environmental standards, while at the same time ensuring that air quality did not get worse. Whereas bubbles applied only to existing sources of pollution, offsets applied to new sources. Offsets permitted the construction of new pollution sources (and enlargement of existing sources) if the resulting new emissions were *less than* the reduction in emission from existing sources. The offset program allowed firms that wanted to introduce new sources of pollution to negotiate with existing firms to purchase emission reductions from them. Also, firms could offset the increases in pollution stemming from their new sources by reducing the emissions from other sources that they owned in the area. Why would the offset concept be expected to reduce the cost of controlling pollution?

c. The concept of a **bank** is an extension of an offset, the idea being to promote greater flexibility with regard to the timing of the trade of emission reductions. If a firm pushed its daily emissions below the mandated standards, it could hold these reductions in reserve at a clearinghouse, and it could trade them at some date in the future. In other words, if could "bank" these reductions. Would the bank concept be expected to reduce the cost of controlling pollution?

PROBLEM 15.6 On July 16, 1991, the Chicago Board of Trade voted to create a private market for rights to emit sulfur dioxide. This was made possible by the Clean Air Act of 1990, which gave polluters the right to meet sulfur dioxide standards by buying and selling pollution emissions permits that the Environmental Protection Agency would issue to electric utilities. Moreover, individuals can speculate on the rise or fall in the price of such pollution permits, in essentially the same way that they have speculated on bonds or stocks. The Clean Air Act established a particular limit on total emissions of sulfur dioxide from 110 power plants beginning in 1995. In the year 2000, this limit will be reduced substantially (to less than half the 1991 level). One object of this program is to reduce acid rain.

a. Firms finding it relatively expensive to cut down on their sulfur dioxide emissions are likely to buy pollution permits. Why?

b. Firms finding it relatively cheap to cut down on their sulfur dioxide emission are likely to sell their pollution permits. Why?

c. What determines the price of the right to emit a ton of sulfur dioxide?

d. Why would you expect this scheme to lower the cost of reducing the total emission of sulfur dioxide?

14 ▪ Applying Economics: Tax Relief, Economic Development, and the Environment

The final two problems are concerned with tax relief, economic development, and the environment.

PROBLEM 15.7 A government agency is considering imposing an effluent fee on pollutants discharged by the chemical industry into local waterways. The revenue obtained from this effluent fee may be used to cut the taxes of the general public or it may be used to compensate water users for the industry's pollution of water. The demand curve for chemicals is DD'. The supply curve for chemicals is SS' (assumed for simplicity to be horizontal). The pollution damage imposed on water users by each ton of chemical output is OH and the effluent fee for each ton of output is ST, where $ST = OH$.

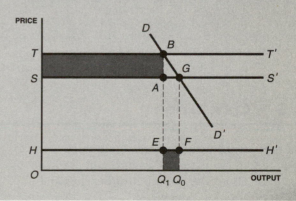

a. If the effluent fee is used to reduce the taxes of the general public, how much will the general public gain? How much will water users gain?

b. If the effluent fee is used to compensate water users, how much will water users gain?

c. In your view, is it more equitable to use the effluent fee to compensate water users than to reduce the taxes of the general public? Why or why not?

PROBLEM 15.8 In 1968, the Department of the Interior made a study of four alternative sites for a dam on the Middle Snake River in Idaho. The estimated costs and benefits of establishing a dam at each site are as follows:

	ALTERNATIVE SITES			
	APPALOOSA AND LOW MOUNTAIN SHEEP	**HIGH MOUNTAIN SHEEP AND CHINA GARDENS**	**HIGH MOUNTAIN SHEEP ONLY**	**PLEASANT VALLEY AND LOW MOUNTAIN SHEEP**
Benefits (millions of dollars)				
Power	49.3	60.7	35.9	44.2
Fish and Wildlife	6.6	None	None	None
Recreation	0.4	0.3	0.3	0.3
Flood Control	0.2	0.2	0.2	0.1
Total[a]	56.5	61.3	36.5	44.5
Costs (millions of dollars)				
Total	20.8	24.3	13.6	19.0
Benefit-cost ratio	2.72	2.53	2.69	2.35

[a] Individual figures may not sum to total because of rounding errors.

SOURCE: Lawrence Hines, *Environmental Issues* (New York: Norton, 1973).

a. What was the principal benefit of such a dam?

b. Did the estimated benefits exceed the estimated costs at each site?

c. According to a number of conservationists and economists, the Department of Interior's analysis was faulty because it took no account of fish and wildlife destruction. Do you agree that this factor should be taken into account? Why or why not?

d. The staff of the Federal Power Commission (now the Federal Energy Regulatory Commission) concluded that, when fish and wildlife destruction and other costs were included, the estimated benefits were less than the estimated costs at each of the sites. On the basis of this conclusion, was the construction of a dam at any of these sites economically justified? Why or why not?

15 ▪ Conclusion

Whether or not you are much concerned about the potential extinction of caviar, you are likely to be uneasy about the pollution of beaches and rivers, the threats to clean air, and the possibility of global warming. Human beings must be stupid indeed if they are not concerned about the world they live in. To understand the reasons for environmental pollution, you must know such elementary economic concepts as external diseconomies; and to help formulate rational responses to pollution, you must have a working knowledge of the principles set forth in this and previous chapters. These are essential elements in dealing with the world around us.

Answers to Odd-Numbered Numerical Problems

1. $-\dfrac{(Q_2 - Q_1)}{(Q_1 + Q_2)/2} \div \dfrac{(P_2 - P_1)}{(P_1 + P_2)/2}$

$= -\dfrac{(7 - 8)}{(8 + 7)/2} \div \dfrac{(2 - 1)}{(1 + 2)/2} = \dfrac{3}{15} = 0.20.$

$-\dfrac{(Q_2 - Q_1)}{(Q_1 + Q_2)/2} \div \dfrac{(P_2 - P_1)}{(P_1 + P_2)/2}$

$= -\dfrac{(4 - 5)}{(5 + 4)/2} \div \dfrac{(5 - 4)}{(4 + 5)/2} = \dfrac{9}{9} = 1.00.$

3. The quantity of automobiles demanded will increase by 3 percent in the United Kingdom and by 5 percent in the United States (assuming other factors are constant).

5. a. $-\dfrac{200 - 100}{150} \div \dfrac{1,500 - 2,000}{1,750}$

$= \dfrac{100}{150} \div \dfrac{500}{1,750}$

$= \dfrac{2}{3} \div \dfrac{2}{7} = \dfrac{2}{3} \times \dfrac{7}{2} = \dfrac{7}{3} = 2\frac{1}{3}.$

b. $-\dfrac{500 - 300}{400} \div \dfrac{500 - 1,000}{750} = \dfrac{200}{400} \div \dfrac{500}{750}$

$= \dfrac{1}{2} \div \dfrac{2}{3} = \dfrac{1}{2} \times \dfrac{3}{2} = \dfrac{3}{4}.$

c. As indicated in part b, the price elasticity of demand is less than 1 in this range. Thus, an increase in price should increase the total expenditure on the product. Looking at the figures, this is the case. When the price is $500, total expenditure is $250,000; when it is $1,000, total expenditure is $300,000.

d. As indicated in part a, the price elasticity of demand is greater than 1 in this range. Thus, an increase in price should decrease the total expenditure on the product. Looking at the figures in the table, this is the case. When the price is $1,500, total expenditure is $300,000; when it is $2,000, total expenditure is $200,000.

7. Expressed in terms of calculus, the price elasticity of demand is $-dQ/dP \times P/Q$. If the demand curve is D_1, $dQ/dP = -1$; thus,

$-\dfrac{dQ}{dP} \times \dfrac{P}{Q} = \dfrac{P}{Q} = \dfrac{P}{5 - P}.$

If the demand curve is D_2, $dQ/dP = -2$; thus,

$-\dfrac{dQ}{dP} \times \dfrac{P}{Q} = \dfrac{2P}{Q} = \dfrac{2P}{10 - 2P} = \dfrac{P}{5 - P}.$

Since the price elasticity of demand equals $P/(5 - P)$ in each case, it must be the same for both demand curves if the price is the same.

9. About 95.

11. a. The cost of the first alternative would be 10 million × $2.50, or $25 million. The cost of the second alternative would be 100 million × $1, or $100 million. Thus, the second alternative would be more expensive.

b. If the demand for labor were price elastic, the answer would be the opposite. Let Q_1 be the quantity of labor demanded (in millions of hours) when the wage is $2.50. Under the first alternative, the cost to the government is $2.5 × (100 − Q_1). Under the second alternative, the cost is $100 million. If 2.5 × (100 − Q_1) > 100, the cost under the first alternative would be higher. In other words, if Q_1 < 60, this is the case. If the demand for labor is price elastic, Q_1 will be less than 60, because an increase in the wage rate will reduce the total amount spent on labor.

13. a. 5 utils, 4 utils.

b.

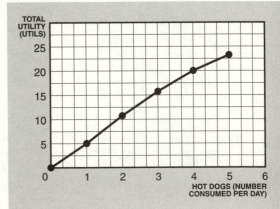

c. Four hot dogs.

d. Five hot dogs.

e. Three hot dogs.

15. It does not, because not all people have the same demand curve for hamburger.

CHAPTER 2

1. a. 50 bushels of wheat per person-year of labor.

b. 30 bushels of wheat.

c. Yes, because as more labor is used, the marginal product of labor declines.

3. a.

MARGINAL PRODUCT OF LABOR	TOTAL PRODUCT PER DAY
3	0
5	3
8	8
7	16
2	23
	25

b. Yes, because marginal product eventually falls as more labor is applied.

5. a. 6.

b. 6.

c. 1,200.

d. 600.

e. No, because the marginal product of labor is the same regardless of how much labor is used.

f. No, because it violates the law of diminishing marginal returns.

7. a. You cannot tell because not enough information is given.

b. No, because, since the prices of capital and labor are the same at both plants, the ratio of the marginal product of labor to the marginal product of capital must be the same at both plants if each plant is minimizing cost.

c. 100.

d. No.

e. 3/20.

9. a. $20,000.

b. $500.

c. $300.

d. Yes. The law of diminishing marginal returns.

11. a.

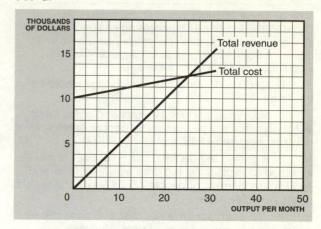

b. $10,000 + 100X = 500X$

$10,000 = 400X$

$25 = X.$

The break-even point is 25 rugs per month.

13. a.

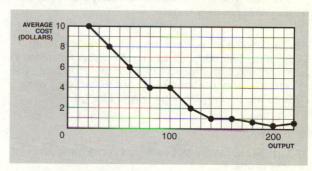

b. $.40.

15. a.

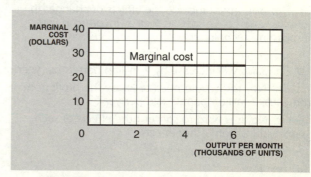

b. Infinite.

CHAPTER 3

1. a. These changes will shift the market demand curve to the left because people aged 20 to 44, the age group with the most people drinking beer, will decrease from 40 percent to 36.3 percent of the population, according to Table 3.4.

b. It seems doubtful that the change would be this large.

c. No. Among adults 35 years and older, Table 3.3 shows that the percentage of people drinking beer declined between 1985 and 1992.

d. It shifted the demand curve for beer to the left. It helped to explain the big drop between 1985 and 1992 in the percent of people 18–24 years of age that drank beer. See Table 3.3.

e. No. Such tax increases raise the price of beer, which reduces the quantity of beer consumed.

3. a. Consumers said the beer labeled M was best because they were told it was a high-priced brand.

b. No, because consumers thought that the brands were qualitatively different.

c. Yes.   Yes.

d. No. Milk is regarded as relatively homogeneous, whereas beer is not.

5. a. Since a 67 percent increase in income (from $15,000 to $25,000) results in a 24 percent increase in beer consumption (from 34 percent to 42 percent), the income elasticity is about 24/67 = .36, which is quite close to the finding by Fogarty and Elzinga.

b. Yes.

c. Yes.

d. No. Data are not provided concerning amount of beer drunk.

e. 15 percent × .4 = 6 percent increase.

f. In making such a long-run forecast, you might multiply the percent change in income in the long run by the income elasticity of demand for beer.

g. You might include the effects of changes in whiskey and cola prices, as well as income, in your forecasting techniques.

7. a. Sales will increase by 2 million barrels per year.

b. No. You would need to know the profit from the extra 2 million barrels sold per year.

c. No. It is hard to sort out the effects of such sponsorships from other effects.

d. $700 million per year.

e. Yes.

f. Because tastes have changed.

CHAPTER 4

1. a. 3 or 4 units of output per period of time.

b, c, and d.

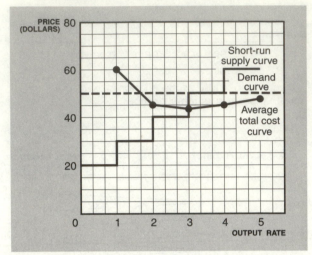

e. $20.

3. Yes. Because you will lose less money ($800 rather than $1,000) if you cease production than if you continue.

5. a.

PRICE OF A TON OF PEANUT BRITTLE	TOTAL REVENUE	PROFIT	MARGINAL COST
		(dollars)	
	0	−100	
			100
200	200	0	
			110
200	400	90	
			190
200	600	100	
			200
200	800	100	
			300
200	1,000	0	

b. It will shut down.

c. $100.

d. Either 3 or 4 tons per day. Yes; as shown in the answer to part a, marginal cost is $200 when output is between 3 and 4 tons per day. Price too equals $200.

7. a. 1. 2. 3. 4.

b. −$9. −$6. −$1. +$6.

c. **QUANTITY SUPPLIED**

1,000

2,000

3,000

4,000

d. $5.

e. 2.

f. −$6.

g. They will leave it.

9.

P	Q	TR	TC	TFC	TVC	ATC	AVC	MC	RE-SPONSE
10	80	800	800	500	300	10	3.75	10	1
4	100	400	200	100	100	2	1	5	5
3	10	30	23	20	3	2.3	.30	.25	4
10	100	1,000	1,200	200	1,000	12	10	10	6
6	50	300	350	100	250	7	5	7	5

CHAPTER 5

1. a.

TOTAL REVENUE	MARGINAL REVENUE
(dollars)	

30	
40	10
30	−10
24	−6
5	−19

b. The second unit of output will add $9 to its costs and $10 to its revenue. Yes.

c. $20.

d. Two units of output a day.

e. $22.

f. No. Yes. It will decrease its profit by $10.

3. a. Demand curve.

b. Marginal revenue.

c. Marginal cost curve.

d. It will choose an output of OQ and a price of OP.

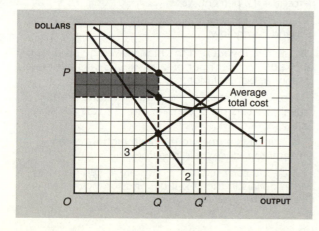

e. No. Yes.

f. The shaded area in the graph in the answer to part d equals this profit.

g. OQ' in the graph in the answer to part d.

5. a. The marginal revenue from the fifth unit in market A is zero. The marginal revenue from the first unit in market B is $50. Thus, it should sell the unit in market B.

b. The marginal revenue from the fifth unit in market B is −$20. The marginal revenue from the first unit in market A is $70. Thus, it should sell the unit in market A.

c. If the marginal revenue in one market is less than in the other, it will pay the monopolist to allocate 1 more unit to the latter market and 1 less to the former market. Thus, the monopolist will be maximizing profit only when the marginal revenue in each market is equal.

7. a. Yes, because long-run average cost falls continually as output increases.

b. The firm's long-run total cost equals $Q(5 + 3/Q) = 3 + 5Q$. Thus, its long-run marginal cost equals $5. Since marginal revenue equals marginal cost if the monopolist maximizes profit, long-run marginal revenue equals $5.

c. Price exceeds $5, because price exceeds marginal revenue so long as the product's demand curve is downward sloping to the right.

9. a. Since marginal revenue = marginal cost,

$$1,000 − 20Q = 100 + 10Q$$
$$30Q = 900$$
$$Q = 30.$$

Since $PQ = 1,000Q − 10Q^2$, the demand curve must be

$$P = 1,000 − 10Q.$$

And since $Q = 30$, P must equal 700.

b. Since the industry's supply curve would be the same as the monopolist's marginal cost curve, the supply curve would be

$$P = 100 + 10Q.$$

As pointed out in part a, the demand curve is

$$P = 1,000 − 10Q.$$

Thus, in a competitive market,

$$100 + 10Q = 1,000 − 10Q$$
$$20Q = 900$$
$$Q = 45.$$

And $P = 1,000 − 10(45) = 550$.

CHAPTER 6

1. a. The 1 percent rise in the price of electricity will reduce the quantity of electricity demanded per year by 1.2 percent; to offset this, the price of natural gas will have to rise by 6 percent.

b. The evidence seems to indicate that the income elasticity of demand for electricity in this suburb equals 0.1, not 0.2. This may be because the income level or tastes of the population are different from elsewhere.

c. Lower, because it takes time to adjust.

d. Industry is more sensitive to price changes of this sort than consumers.

e. This may be true.

3. a. It is relatively costly.

b. Because it is relatively costly, its use would not be expected to grow rapidly.

c. Yes.

d. If its costs fall, it will become a more significant source of power.

5. a. The electric utility receives 12(50) + 8(50) + 6(100) + 4(200) = 2400 cents, or $24. With a flat charge of 4 cents per kilowatt hour, it would receive 4(400) = 1600 cents, or $16.

b. Yes, since the price goes down as consumption increases.

c. These groups emphasize energy conservation.

d. The company would argue that this was in the public interest.

7. a. The owners of LILCO.

b. Shoreham's costs = .26 × 11.5 cents per kilowatt hour = 2.99 cents per kilowatt hour. The national average was about 6.2 cents per kilowatt hour (Table 6.4). Hence, 2.99 ÷ (11.5 − 6.2)—or about half—of the disparity was due to Shoreham.

c. If such plants are relatively high-cost, this obviously could result in a relatively high price.

d. Whether a public-owned utility would be better managed than a privately owned utility is an important factor here, and one that is difficult to evaluate.

CHAPTER 7

1. a. 4 units of output.

b. $5.

c. $4.

d. No.

3. a. A horizontal line at $2 = MC.

b. More.

c. Less.

d. Yes. 200 units of output if it maximizes profit.

5. a. $9.

b. 6.

c. Not necessarily; it depends on the extent of the barriers to entry.

d. Yes; its demand curve is likely to be very elastic if the other firm does not match its price cut.

7. a. Strategy 2.

b. Strategy I.

c. Yes. Player *A* adopts strategy 2; and player *B* adopts strategy I.

d. $3,000.

e. $3,000.

CHAPTER 8

1. The Supreme Court ruled against the merger, whereas the district court permitted it.

3. a. The district court ruled against the merger.

b. The court held that transportation costs were small enough so that competition on a national basis was practical.

5. a. No.

b. It might be charged that firm *X* was discriminating to a greater degree than was justified to meet competition.

c. No. The Celler-Kefauver Act.

CHAPTER 9

1. a. $-\dfrac{800,000 - 500,000}{650,000} \div \dfrac{360 - 440}{400} = 2.3$

b. No, because there are other autos besides Fords. The price elasticity of demand for Fords is likely to be higher.

c. People can postpone buying a car, but in the long run this is hard to do. No.

d. Auto sales would fall by about 3 × 4 percent = 12 percent. Yes.

e. No. In some industries, the price elasticity of demand is very low.

3. a. Yes. Toyota had the higher average product of labor (.06 cars per hour of labor vs. .03 cars per hour of labor at General Motors).

b. Yes. Toyota had the higher average product of capital (.21 cars per square foot vs. .12 cars per square foot at General Motors).

c. It costs money to maintain high inventories. Firms try to reduce their inventories.

d. You can't tell, since costs are in yen in Japan and in dollars in the U.S. It depends on how many yen can be exchanged for a dollar.

e. No. The figures in Table 9.2 underestimate the advantage of Japanese production methods.

5. a. No, because average cost depended on how many cars were sold.

b. At 80 percent of capacity, average cost equaled $4,000 per car. If General Motors earned a 15 percent profit on $40 billion, it earned $6 billion; this was $6 billion ÷ 4 million = $1,500 per car. Thus, standard price equaled $4,000 + $1,500 = $5,500 per car.

c. Because no firm wanted its price to be well above the lowest price for a comparable car.

d. The new cars had to compete with the unsold previous year's cars.

e. No.

7. a. Auto producers in Mexico tended to be below minimum efficient size.

b. Yes. The dominant strategy is to locate the plant in Mexico.

c. No.

d. Mexico, since this is General Motors' dominant strategy.

e. Locate the plant in Argentina, since this is best for Ford, assuming that General Motors adopts its dominant strategy.

f. The General Motors plant would be expected to be in Mexico and the Ford plant would be expected to be in Argentina, for the reasons given above.

CHAPTER 10

1. a.

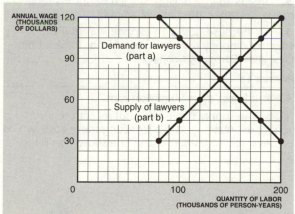

b. See the answer on the graph for part a.

c. $75,000.

d. 80,000.

3. a.

MARGINAL PRODUCT OF LABOR	VALUE OF MARGINAL PRODUCT (dollars)
2½	25
2½	25
2	20
1	10

b. The wage must be between $10 and $20, because if it were more than $20, the firm would hire only 2 units of labor, and if it were less than $10, the firm would hire 4 units of labor.

c. 3 units of labor or 2 units of labor. Because this will maximize its profit.

d.

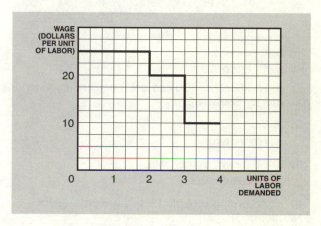

e. A lower wage, for reasons given in the section of Chapter 10 on monopsony.

5. a.

NUMBER OF UNITS OF LABOR DEMANDED PER DAY
2,000
3,000
4,000
5,000

b. $40.

c. 4,000 units, 4 units.

d. $40.

e. $42.

f. 3,000 units.

7. a. 1 unit of labor per hour. $9.

b. 2 units of labor per hour. $6.

CHAPTER 11

1. a.

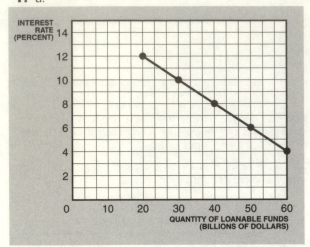

b. 8 percent.

c. $12,500.

d. No. Because you can get 8 percent if you lend your money elsewhere.

3. a. Yes.

b. None. No.

5. a. All shown in the table.

b. $4 million less.

7. a. According to Table 11.1, it is worth .839 × $10,000, or $8,390.

b. According to Table 11.1, it is worth .89 × $10,000, or $8,900, to get it in two years. Thus, it is worth $510 more than if you got the money in three years.

9. a. $1,000 ÷ $25,000 = 4 percent.

b. No.

c. $27,500.

CHAPTER 12

1. a. $150 worth of market goods. $200 worth of market goods.

b.

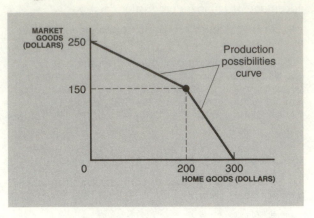

3. a. $8,000. $8,000.

b. Yes.

c. $1,000.

d. Yes. Total family income is higher if the woman works than if she does not work.

e. Yes.

5. a. Yes.

b. Yes.

c. Yes.

d. A host of factors, including changing attitudes toward marriage and the family.

7. a. Yes.   Yes.

b. No.

CHAPTER 13

1. No. The price should be raised.

3. Greater than 1 million, since monopolies tend to produce less than the optimal amount.

5. No, because both can expand output if the Perfecto Company trades 1 unit of labor for 2.5 units of the Ajax Company's capital.

CHAPTER 14

1. a. It is less than 60 million tons.

b. The supply curve does not reflect the true social costs. A supply curve reflecting these costs would be above and to the left of the one shown on page 237.

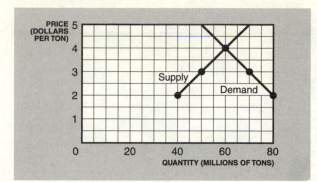

c. $4. Too low.

3. If any family buys smog-free air, it automatically buys it for others too, regardless of whether the others pay for it or not. And since no family can afford the cost, so long as families act independently, it will be unprofitable for a private firm to carry out this project.

5. Taxes and government borrowing.

7. a. $8.

b. $8.

c. No. It will be greater than the amount that consumers would be willing to pay for it, since consumers would be willing to pay only $8 for it, but its social cost exceeds $8.

d. The optimal output of good X is less than 10 million units per year because the optimal output is at the intersection of the demand curve with the supply curve reflecting social costs. Because this supply curve lies to the left of the industry's supply curve (in the diagram), the optimal output must be less than 10 million units per year.

e. If the social costs of producing good X were less than the private costs, the supply curve reflecting social costs would lie to the right of the industry's supply curve. Thus, the intersection of the supply curve reflecting social costs with the demand curve would be at an output exceeding 10 million units per year.

CHAPTER 15

1. a. An increase of between 3 and 4 degrees.

b. The cost of stopping this change in climate must be taken into account.

c. Because they obviously are heavily dependent on climate.

d. Because the marginal social cost of reducing pollution by an extra unit increases as more and more pollution is reduced.

e. Because, as the reduction in pollution gets bigger and bigger, the marginal benefit to society from reducing the emission by another unit gets smaller.

f. The reduction should equal OV because marginal social cost equals marginal social benefit from emission of greenhouse gases at this point.

3. a. $0Q_0$.

b. Yes, but this curve includes costs to others.

c. $0Q_1$.

d. Too large.

5. a. Because the emission limits pertain to a plant (or area) as a whole, it is often less expensive to control pollution than if the limits pertained to narrower areas.

b. Because it is often cheaper to find and close an existing source of pollution than to reduce the pollution from a new plant.

c. Yes.

7. a. The general public gains an amount equal to rectangle $SABT$ since this is the amount of the revenue from the effluent fee. Water users gain rectangle Q_1Q_0FE, since this is the reduction in the amount of pollution damage caused by the industry.

b. If the effluent fee is used to compensate water users, they gain both rectangle Q_1Q_0FE and rectangle $SABT$.

c. If one believes that water users are entitled to clean water, they are also entitled to compensation for its loss if such a loss occurs.

GLOSSARY OF TERMS

Alternative cost the value of what certain resources could have produced had they been used in the best alternative way; also called **opportunity cost.**

American Federation of Labor-Congress of Industrial Organizations (AFL-CIO) a federation of national labor unions formed in 1955 by the merger between the American Federation of Labor (originally a federation of unions organized along craft lines) and the Congress of Industrial Organizations (originally a federation of unions organized along industrial lines).

Antitrust laws legislation (such as the Sherman Act, the Clayton Act, and the Federal Trade Commission Act) intended to promote competition and control monopoly.

Asymmetric information situation in which all participants in a market do not have the same information (for example, sellers may know more about the quality of a product than do potential buyers).

Average fixed cost the firm's total fixed cost divided by its output.

Average product of an input total output divided by the amount of the input used to produce this amount of output.

Average product of labor total output per unit of labor.

Average total cost the firm's total cost divided by its output; equal to average fixed cost plus average variable cost.

Average variable cost the firm's total variable cost divided by its output.

Backward-bending supply curve for labor a supply curve for labor inputs showing that, beyond some point, increases in price may result in smaller amounts of labor's being supplied.

Balance sheet an accounting statement showing the nature of a firm's assets, the claims by creditors on those assets, and the value of the firm's ownership at a certain point in time.

Barometric firm in an oligopolistic industry, any

single firm that is the first to make changes in prices, which are then generally accepted by other firms.

Bond a debt (generally long term) of a firm or government.

Break-even chart a chart that plots a firm's total cost and total revenue and shows the output level that must be reached if the firm is to avoid losses.

Budget line a line showing the market baskets that the consumer can purchase, given his or her income and prevailing prices.

Capital resources (such as factory buildings, equipment, raw materials, and inventories) that are created within the economic system for the purpose of producing other goods.

Capitalism an economic system characterized by private ownership of the tools of production, freedom of choice and of enterprises whereby consumers and firms can pursue their own self-interest, competition for sales among producers and resource owners, and reliance on the free market.

Capitalization of assets a method of computing the value of an asset by calculating the present value of the expected future income this asset will produce.

Cartel an open, formal collusive arrangement among firms.

Closed shop a situation in which firms can hire only workers who are already union members.

Collective bargaining a process of negotiation between a union and management over wages and working conditions.

Collusion a covert arrangement whereby firms agree on price and output levels in order to decrease competition and increase profits.

Common stock a certificate of ownership of a corporation. Holders of common stock are owners of the corporation.

Comparative advantage the law that states that a country should produce and export goods in which its efficiency *relative to other countries* is highest; specialization and trade depend on comparative, not absolute, advantage.

Complements commodities that tend to be consumed together, i.e., commodities with a negative cross elasticity of demand such that a decrease in the price of one will result in an increase in the quantity demanded of the other.

Constant returns to scale a long-run situation in which, if the firm increases the amount of all inputs by the same proportion, output increases by the same proportion as each of the inputs.

Consumer an individual or household that purchases the goods and services produced by the economic system.

Consumer's surplus the difference between the maximum amount that a consumer would pay for a good or service and what he or she actually pays.

Corporation a fictitious legal person separate and distinct from the stockholders who own it, governed by a board of directors elected by the stockholders.

Cost function the relationship between cost and a firm's level of output, i.e., how much cost a firm will incur at various levels of output.

Council of Economic Advisers a group established by the Employment Act of 1946, whose function is to help the president formulate and assess the economic policies of the government.

Craft union a labor union that includes workers in a particular craft (such as machinists or carpenters).

Cross elasticity of demand the percentage change in the quantity demanded of one commodity resulting from a 1 percent change in the price of another commodity; it may be either positive or negative.

Decreasing returns to scale a long-run situation in which, if the firm increases the amount of all inputs by the same proportion, output increases by a smaller proportion than each of the inputs.

Demand curve for loanable funds a curve showing the quantity of loanable funds that will be demanded at each interest rate.

Depreciation the value of the capital (plant, equipment, and structures) that is worn out in a year; also called a **capital consumption allowance.**

Derived demand the demand for labor and other inputs not as ends in themselves, but as means to produce other things.

Differentiated oligopoly a market structure (such as those for automobiles and machinery) in which there are only a few sellers of somewhat different products.

Direct regulation government issue of enforceable rules concerning the conduct of firms.

Dominant firm in an oligopolistic industry, a single large firm that sets the price for the industry but lets the small firms sell all they want at that price.

Dominant strategy a strategy that is best for a player regardless of what the other player's strategy may be.

Economic profits the excess of a firm's profits over what it could make in other industries.

Economic resources resources that are scarce and thus command a nonzero price.

Economics the study of how resources are allocated among alternative uses to satisfy human wants.

Economies of scale efficiencies that result from carrying out a process (such as production or sales) on a large scale.

Efficiency wage a wage rate that is higher than the perfectly competitive wage. Firms may pay such a wage to reduce shirking and raise worker productivity.

Effluent fee a fee that a polluter must pay to the government for discharging waste.

Equilibrium a situation in which there is no tendency for change.

Equilibrium price a price that shows no tendency for change, because it is the price at which the quantity demanded equals the quantity supplied; the price toward which the actual price of a good tends to move.

Excise tax a tax imposed on each unit sold of a particular product, such as cigarettes or liquor.

Explicit cost the cost of resources for which there is an explicit payment.

Exports the goods and services that a country sells to other countries.

External diseconomy an uncompensated cost to one person or firm resulting from the consumption or output of another person or firm.

External economy an uncompensated benefit to one person or firm resulting from the consumption or output of another person or firm.

Featherbedding a practice whereby a union restricts output per worker in order to increase the amount of labor required to do a certain job.

Firm an organization that produces a good or service for sale in an attempt to make a profit.

Firm's demand curve for labor a curve showing the relationship between the price of labor and the amount of labor demanded by a firm; that is, the amount of labor that will be demanded by a firm at various wage rates.

Firm's supply curve a curve, usually sloping upward to the right, showing the quantity of output a firm will produce at each price.

Fixed input a resource used in the production process (such as plant and equipment) whose quantity cannot be changed during the particular period under consideration.

Food programs federal antipoverty programs that distribute food to the poor, either directly from surpluses produced by farm programs or indirectly via stamps that can be exchanged for food.

Free resources resources (such as air) that are so abundant that they can be obtained without charge.

Game a competitive situation in which two or more players pursue their own interest and no player can dictate the outcome.

Historical cost of assets what a firm actually paid for its assets.

Implicit cost the cost (for which there is no explicit payment) of the resources that are provided by the owner of a firm, measured by what these resources could bring if they were used in their best alternative employment.

Imports the goods and services that a county buys from other countries.

Income effect the change in the quantity demanded by the consumer of a good due to the change in the consumer's level of utility resulting from a change in the price of the good.

Income elasticity of demand the percentage change in the quantity demanded of a commodity resulting from a 1 percent increase in total money income (all prices being constant).

Income statement an accounting statement showing a firm's sales, costs, and profits during a particular period (often a quarter or a year).

Income tax a federal, state, or local tax imposed on personal income and corporate profits.

Increasing returns to scale a long-run situation in which, if a firm increases the amount of all inputs by the same proportion, output increases by a larger proportion than each of the inputs.

Indifference curve a curve representing market baskets among which the consumer is indifferent.

Indirect business taxes taxes (such as general sales taxes, excise taxes, and customs duties) that are imposed not directly on the business itself but on its products or services, and hence are treated by firms as costs of production.

Individual demand curve a curve showing the relationship between individual consumer demand and prices; it shows how much of a good an individual consumer will demand at various prices.

Industrial union a labor union that includes all the workers in a particular plant or industry (such as autos or steel).

Inflation an economywide increase in the general level of prices.

Innovation the first commercial application of a new technology.

Innovator a firm that is the first to apply a new technology.

Input any resource used in the production process.

Interest the payment of money by borrowers to suppliers of money capital.

Interest rate the annual amount that a borrower must pay for the use of a dollar for a year.

Isocost curve a curve showing the input combinations the firm can obtain for a given expenditure.

Isoquant a curve showing all possible efficient combinations of inputs capable of producing a certain quantity of output.

Labor human effort, both physical and mental, used to produce goods and services.

Labor force the number of people employed plus the number of those unemployed (actively looking for work, not having a job, and willing to take a job if one were offered).

Labor productivity the average amount of output that can be obtained for every unit of labor.

Land natural resources, including minerals as well as plots of ground, used to produce goods and services.

Law of diminishing marginal returns the principle that if equal increments of a given input are added (the quantities of other inputs being held constant), the resulting increments of product obtained from the extra unit of input (the marginal product) will begin to decrease beyond some point.

Law of diminishing marginal utility the principle that if a person consumes additional units of a given commodity (the consumption of other commodities being held constant), the resulting increments of utility derived from the extra unit of the commodity (the commodity's marginal utility) will begin to decrease beyond some point.

Law of increasing cost the principle that as more and more of a good is produced, the production of each additional unit of the good is likely to entail a larger and larger opportunity cost.

Liabilities the debts of a firm.

Local unions labor unions, organized around either craft or industrial lines, that are set up in particular geographical areas or plants and may or may not belong to a larger national union.

Long run the period of time during which all of a firm's inputs are variable, that is, during which the firm could completely change the resources used in the production process.

Long-run average cost function a representation of the minimum average cost of producing various output levels when any desired type or scale of plant can be built.

Marginal cost the addition to total cost resulting from the addition of the last unit of output.

Marginal cost pricing a pricing rule whereby the price of a product is set equal to its marginal cost.

Marginal product of an input the addition to total output that results from the addition of an extra unit of a particular input (the quantities of all other inputs being held constant).

Marginal product of labor the additional output resulting from the addition of an extra unit of labor.

Marginal revenue the change in total revenue that results from the addition of 1 unit to the quantity sold.

Marginal tax rate the proportion of an extra dollar of income that must be paid in taxes.

Marginal utility the additional satisfaction derived from consuming an additional unit of a commodity.

Market a group of firms and individuals that are in touch with each other in order to buy or sell some good or service.

Market demand curve a curve, usually sloping downward to the right, showing the relationship between a product's price and the quantity demanded of the product.

Market demand curve for labor a curve showing the relationship between the price of labor and the total amount of labor demanded in the market.

Market period the relatively short period of time during which the supply of a particular good is fixed and output is unaffected by price.

Market structure the type or organization of a market. Markets differ with regard to the number and size of buyers and sellers in the market, the ease with which new firms can enter, the extent of product differentiation, and other factors.

Market supply curve a curve, usually sloping upward to the right showing the relationship between a product's price and the quantity supplied of the product.

Market supply curve for labor a curve showing the

relationship between the price of labor and the total amount of labor supplied in the market.

Model a theory composed of assumptions that simplify and abstract from reality, from which conclusions or predictions about the real world are deduced.

Monopolistic competition a market structure in which there are many sellers of somewhat differentiated products, entry is easy, and there is no collusion among sellers. Retailing seems to have many of the characteristics of monopolistic competition.

Monopoly a market structure (such as those for public utilities) in which there is only one seller of a product.

Monopsony a market structure (such as that for the single firm that employs all the labor in a company town) in which there is only a single buyer.

Multinational firm a firm that makes direct investments in other countries, and produces and markets its products abroad.

Natural monopoly an industry in which the average costs of producing the product reach a minimum at an output rate large enough to satisfy the entire market, so that competition among firms cannot be sustained and one firm becomes a monopolist.

Normative economics economic propositions about what ought to be or about what a person, organization, or country ought to do.

Old-age insurance benefits paid under the Social Security program to retired workers, from taxes imposed on both workers and employers.

Oligopoly a market structure (such as those for autos and steel) in which there are only a few sellers of products that can be either identical or differentiated.

Open shop a situation in which a firm can hire both union and nonunion workers with no requirement that nonunion workers ever join a union.

Opportunity cost the value of what certain resources could have produced had they been used in the best alternative way; also called **alternative cost.**

Partnership a form of business organization whereby two or more people agree to own and conduct a business, with each party contributing some proportion of the capital and/or labor and receiving some proportion of the profit or loss.

Payoff matrix a table showing each player's payoff (often profit) if various strategies are chosen by each player.

Perfect competition a market structure in which there are many sellers of identical products, no one seller or buyer has control over the price, entry is easy, and resources can switch readily from one use to another. Many agricultural markets have many of the characteristics of perfect competition.

Positive economics descriptive statements, propositions, and predictions about the economic world that are generally testable by an appeal to the facts.

Price discrimination the practice whereby one buyer is charged more than another buyer for the same product.

Price elastic the demand for a good if its price elasticity of demand is greater than 1.

Price elasticity of demand the percentage change in quantity demanded resulting from a 1 percent change in price; by convention, always expressed as a positive number.

Price elasticity of supply the percentage change in quantity supplied resulting from a 1 percent change in price.

Price inelastic the demand for a good if its price elasticity of demand is less than 1.

Price leader in an oligopolistic industry, a firm that sets a price that other firms are willing to follow.

Price supports price floors imposed by the government on a certain good.

Price system a system under which every good and service has a price and which in a purely capitalistic economy carries out the basic functions of an economic system (determining what goods and services will be produced, how the output will be produced, how much of it each person will receive, and what the country's growth of per capita income will be).

Primary inputs resources (such as labor and land) that are produced outside of the economic system.

Principal-agent problem the problem that arises because managers or workers may pursue their own objectives, even though this reduces the profits of the owners of the firm.

Prisoners' dilemma a situation in which two persons (or firms) would both do better to cooperate than not to cooperate, but each feels it is in his or her interests not to do so; thus each fares worse than if they cooperated.

Private cost the price paid by the individual user for the use of a resource.

Product differentiation the process by which producers create real or apparent differences between products that perform the same general function.

Product group a group of firms that produce similar products that are fairly close substitutes for one another.

Product market a market in which products are bought and sold.

Production function the relationship between the quantities of various inputs used per period of time and the maximum quantity of output that can be produced per period of time; it shows the most output that existing technology permits the firm to produce from various quantities of inputs.

Production possibilities curve a curve showing the combinations of amounts of various goods that a society can produce with given (fixed) amounts of resources.

Profit the difference between a firm's revenue and its costs.

Progressive tax a tax whereby the rich pay larger proportions of their incomes for the tax than do the poor.

Property tax a tax imposed on real estate and/or other property.

Proprietorship a firm owned by a single individual.

Public goods goods and services which can be consumed by one person without diminishing the amount of them that others can consume and for which there is no way to prevent citizens from consuming them whether they pay for them or not.

Public sector the governmental sector of the economy.

Pure rate of interest the interest rate on a riskless loan.

Quota a limit imposed on the amount of a commodity that can be imported annually.

Rate of return the annual profit per dollar invested that a business can obtain by building new structures, adding new equipment, or increasing its inventories; the interest rate earned on the investment in a particular asset.

Regressive tax a tax whereby the rich pay smaller proportions of their incomes for the tax than do the poor.

Rent in the context of Chapter 11, the return derived from an input that is fixed in supply.

Reproduction cost of assets what a firm would have to pay to replace its assets.

Resource market a market in which resources are bought and sold.

Resources inputs used to produce goods and services.

Retained earnings the total amount of profit that the stockholders of a corporation have reinvested in the business, rather than withdrawn as dividends.

Rule of reason the idea that not all trusts, but only unreasonable combinations in restraint of trade, require conviction under the antitrust laws.

Sales tax a tax imposed on the goods consumers buy (with the exception, in some states, of food and medical care).

Short run the period of time during which at least one of a firm's inputs (generally its plant and equipment) is fixed.

Social Security a program that imposes taxes on wage earners and employers and provides old-age, survivors, disability, and medical benefits to workers covered under the Social Security Act.

Substitutes commodities with a positive cross elasticity of demand (a decrease in the price of one commodity will result in a decrease in the quantity demanded of the other commodity).

Substitution effect the change in the quantity demanded (by a consumer) of a commodity resulting from a change in the commodity's price if the consumer's level of utility is held constant.

Supply curve for loanable funds a curve showing the relationship between the quantity of loanable funds supplied and the interest rate.

Tariff a tax imposed by the government on imported goods (designed to cut down on imports and thus protect domestic industry and workers from foreign competition).

Tax avoidance legal steps taken by taxpayers to reduce their tax bill.

Tax evasion misreporting of income or other illegal steps taken by taxpayers to reduce their tax bills.

Technological change new methods of producing existing products, new designs that make it possible to produce new products, and new techniques of organization, marketing, and management.

Technology society's pool of knowledge concerning how goods and services can be produced from a given amount of resources.

Total cost the sum of a firm's total fixed cost and total variable cost.

Total fixed cost a firm's total expenditure on fixed inputs per period of time.

Total revenue a firm's total dollar sales volume.

Total variable cost a firm's total expenditure on variable inputs per period of time.

Trading possibilities curve a curve showing the various combinations of products that a country can get if it specializes in one product and trades that specialty for foreign goods.

Tying contract an agreement that a buyer must purchase other items from the seller in order to get the product it wants from the seller.

Unemployment according to the definition of the Bureau of Labor Statistics, joblessness among people who are actively looking for work and would take a job if one were offered.

Unemployment rate the number of people who are unemployed divided by the number of people in the labor force.

Union shop a situation in which firms can hire nonunion workers who must then become union members within a certain length of time after being hired.

Unitary elasticity a price elasticity of demand equal to 1.

Utility a number representing the level of satisfaction that a consumer derives from a particular market basket.

Value of the marginal product of labor the marginal product of labor (the additional output resulting from the addition of an extra unit of labor) multiplied by the product's price.

Variable input a resource used in the production process (such as labor or raw material) whose quantity can be changed during the particular period under consideration.

Wage rate the price of labor.

INDEX

Page numbers in **bold type** indicate definitions.

ability, wage differentials and, 158
Abrams, Robert, 113
Adams, Henry, 10
Adams, W., 48n
advertising, 137
    of beer, 40, 41, 42, 45–46, 51–52
    children and, 46
    demand curve and, 83n
    exclusives and, 45
    game theory and, 109–11
    in monopolistic competition, 114, 117
aerospace industry, input prices in, 62
affirmative action, 184–85, 190
AFL, *see* American Federation of Labor
AFL-CIO:
    formation of, 161
    structure of, 161–62
age:
    of beer drinkers, 46, 47
    earnings profiles and, 188–89
    of U.S. population, 1990 and 2000, 46, 47
agriculture:
    perfect competition in, 56, 57
    see also wheat
Aid to Families with Dependent Children (AFDC),
        187–88
Aiken, Donald, 97
air pollution, 203, 208–9, 217, 226–27
    social cost of, 220–21
Air Products and Chemicals, 99
Aizcorde, A., 145
alcohol, *see* beer, beer industry
alternative (opportunity) cost doctrine, **26,** 177–78
aluminum, 205
Aluminum Company of America (Alcoa), 74, 130–31,
        132
AMC, 142
American Automobile Manufacturers Association, 138n

American Federation of Labor (AFL), 161
American Telephone and Telegraph Company (AT&T),
        132
American Tobacco Company, 130, 132
Anheuser, Eberhard, 41
Anheuser-Busch Brewing Company, 41–47
    advertising of, 41, 45, 51–52
    concentration and, 43–44
    economies of scale and, 51–52
    history of, 41
    income statement of, 41
    pricing policy of, 44, 49–50
antitrust laws, 128–32, **205**–6
    aluminum and, 74
    beer industry and, 44
    Clayton Act and, 44, 129, 205
    courts and, 128, 130–31, 132
    electric equipment industry and, 112–13
    Federal Trade Commission Act and, 129
    Justice Department and, 130, 131–32
    Sherman Act and, 129, 130, 131, 205
    tungsten carbide and, 84
Appleton, Albert, 222
Argentina, 148
Aristotle, 173
Arnold, Thurman, 132
assembly line, in auto industry, 140, 178
assets:
    capitalization of, **174**
    present value of future income from, 175–76
    rate of return of, **170**–71
    valuation of, 92
Australia, 108
Austria, market demand in, 3
Automobile, Aerospace, and Agricultural Implement
        Workers, 161
automobiles, automobile industry:
    conclusion about, 149
    cost of, 26, 99, 136, 137, 140, 141, 145
    external diseconomies and, **216**–17

price elasticity of demand for, **7,** 136, 142
production of, 136–37, 139–41, 144–46
regulation of, 148–49
world production of, 1950–1992, 138
automobiles, automobile industry, Japanese, 139–42, 144–47
Ford repudiated by, 139–40
U.S. import restriction on, 140–41
U.S. joint ventures with, 141–42
U.S. production facilities of, 141
automobiles, automobile industry, U.S., 104, 136–49
Chrysler bailout and, 138–39
energy crisis and, 137–38, 140, 143
introduction to, 136
Model T Ford and, 136, 137
new passenger car sales and, 138
percentage of sales by firms in 1978 and 1991, 142
Studebaker and, 137
see also General Motors
average cost, average cost curve:
in long run, **30**–32, 51, 66–67, 75, 96, 115, 116
in monopolistic competition, 115, 116
in short run, 28–29, 60, 64, 67
average fixed cost, **28,** 29–30, 61
average product, **22**
of labor, 22, 144
average total cost, **28,** 29–30
in monopolistic competition, 114
in perfect competition, 60, 61, 66
regulation and, 91, 92
average variable cost, **28,** 29–30
in perfect competition, 60, 61

backward-bending supply curve, 155
Bain, Joe, 112
bank, concept of, 226, **227**
bank loans, 171
barometric-firm model, **107**
barriers to entry, oligopoly and, 104
Bartlett, H., 42*n*
bauxite, monopoly of, 74
Beckenstein, A., 51*n*
beer, beer industry, 40–53
adult drinkers of, by sex, age, and race, 46, 47
advertising of, 40, 41, 42, 45–46, 51–52
concentration in, 43
conclusions about, 53
economies of scale in, 51–52
in foreign countries, 40, 53
in historical perspective, 40
home brewers of, 48
light, 41, 42, 43, 45, 47–48

national output of, 1947–1990, 43, 44
production of, 43
see also specific beers and companies
Beer Institute, 46
Behravesh, N., 137*n*
Belgium, 75
Bellegante, D., 43*n*
Bell Telephone Laboratories, 203, 132, 203
beluga, pollution and, 216
Benjamin, D., 148*n*
Bergmann, B., 185*n*
Berle, A. A., 127
black women:
affirmative action and, 185, 190
as heads of families, 188
Blatz Brewing Company, 44, 48
Blau, F., 186*n*, 187*n*, 189*n*
bonds, interest on, 26
Brock, William, 140
Bromley, D. Allan, 177
Brookings Institution, 145, 149
bubble, **226**
Bud Light, 41, 47
Budweiser, 41, 47
advertising of, 52
alcohol content of, 43
pricing of, 44, 49
Bureau of Mines, U.S., 63
Busch (beer), 41, 44, 45
Busch, Adolphus, 41
Busch, August A., III, 41, 45
Bush administration, 222, 223
Business Week, 48–49, 142*n*, 191*n*
butter, price of, 10
Byars, L., 42*n*

CAFE (corporate average fuel economy) standards, 148–49
California:
affirmative action in, 184–85
auto industry in, 141
beer market in, 44
electricity in, 94, 95
wind energy in, 97
California Public Utilities Commission, 94
Callinicos, B., 47*n*
Canada, 94, 108
comparable worth in, 185
labor unions in, 161*n*
monopoly in, 74
wind energy in, 97
capital, return on, 81

capital goods, 174
capitalism:
　mixed, 202–4
　profits and losses in, 178
capitalization, **174**
carbon dioxide, greenhouse effect and, 222–25
carbon tax, 224
cartels, **106**–8, 112
Carter, Jimmy, 139
Caspian Sea, pollution in, 216
Caves, R., 146*n*
caviar, pollution and, 216
Celler-Kefauver Anti-Merger Act (1950), 44, 129
Chapman, D., 95–96
Chevrolet, 141
Chevrolet Citation, 143
Chevrolet Nova, 141
Chicago Board of Trade, 227
children, beer advertising and, 46
China, greenhouse effect and, 224
chlorofluorocarbon, 222
Christensen, Laurits, 96
Chrysler, 141, 142
　bailout of, 138–39
　K car of, 146–47
cigarette industry, 42, 45
Clark, Kim, 147–48
Clayton Act (1914), 44, 129, 205
Clean Air Act (1990), 227
Cleveland, Grover, 131
Cleveland Electric, 100
climate, global warming and, 222–25
Clinton administration, 222, 223
closed shop, **163**
cola drinks, demand for, 50
collective bargaining, **163**
collusion:
　cartels and, 106–8
　monopolistic competition and, 114
　oligopoly and, 106–8, 125
　prevention of, *see* antitrust laws
commerce, interstate, 92–93
Commerce Department, U.S., 46
commodities, **11**
　demand curve for, *see* market demand curves
　income elasticity of demand for, **9,** 50, 142–43
　marginal utility of, **11**–15
　optimal resource allocation of, *see* optimal resource
　　allocation
　pairs of, *see* complements; substitutes
　price elasticity of demand for, *see* price elasticity of
　　demand

price inelasticity of demand for, **7**–8
production function of, **21**
unitary elasticity of demand for, **7**, 8
Commonwealth Electric Company, 100
comparable worth, 185, 189–90
competition:
　in automobile industry, 136–37, 139–42, 147–48
　in beer industry, 44, 45
　efficiency and, 93
　in electric industry, 94–95
　innovation and, 178
　labor unions and, 162
　monopolistic, *see* monopolistic competition
　perfect, *see* perfect competition
　production cost declines and, 75
　promotion of, 128–29, 205–6; *see also* antitrust laws
complements, **10**
Congress, U.S., 162, 195, 208
　antitrust law and, 129
　auto industry and, 139, 140, 148, 149
　pollution control and, 221, 222
　sex discrimination and, 183
　see also House of Representatives, U.S.; Senate, U.S.,
　　Subcommittee on Antitrust and Monopoly of
Congress of Industrial Organizations (CIO), 161
Connecticut, 97
Conrad, Carl, 41
conservatives, government role as viewed by, 202, 204,
　　205–6
Consolidated Edison, 95, 100
constant returns to scale, **31**
Consumer Reports, 144–45
consumers, consumption:
　auto industry and, 7*n*, 137, 141, 143, 147
　of beer, 40, 46
　behavior model of, 10–13
　demand for loanable funds of, 171
　health and appearance concerns of, 40
　income level of, 3, 9, 13, 20
　market demand curve and, 3
　monopolistic competition and, 117
　monopoly and, 123
　optimal resource allocation and, 195–96, 198
　perfect competition and, 123
　price elasticity of demand and, 7
　rational, 13–14
　satisfaction of, *see* utility
　tastes of, 3, 10–11, 13, 184
contestable markets, **108**–9, 112
contracts, 205
　tying, **129**
Convention on Climate Change, 223

Coors (beer), 42, 43
Coors, William, 42
Adolph Coors Company, 42–45, 51–52
    pricing policy of, 44–45
Coors Light, 42
corn, price of, 3
corporate average fuel economy (CAFE) standards,
        148–49
cost, cost functions, 24–32
    of automobiles, 26, 99, 136, 137, 140, 141, 145
    average fixed, **28,** 29–30, 61
    average total, *see* average total cost
    average variable, **28,** 29–30, 60, 61
    defined, **26**
    of electricity, 96–97
    in long run, 30–32, 51, 66–67, 75, 91, 96
    marginal, *see* marginal cost, marginal cost curve
    minimizing of, 24–25
    in monopoly, 75, 78–80, 83
    in short run, 26–30, 60, 64, 67
    total, 26, **27,** 28, 57–61, 78, 79
    total fixed, **26,** 27, 28, 57–58, 60, 78
    total variable, 26, **27,** 28, 57–58, 78
cost-plus pricing, 146
costs:
    historical, **92**
    opportunity (alternative), **26,** 177–78
    of pollution control, 221
    private, **217**
    production, *see* production cost
    reproduction (replacement), **92**
    social, 196, 199, 209, **217,** 220–21, 224
    transaction, 51
Council of Economic Advisers, 183
Crandall, Robert, 149
cross elasticity of demand, **10**
    for beer, 50
    for electricity, 95–96
Cuomo, Mario, 101, 113

Daly, George, 143*n*
Datsun, 136, 141, 143
decreasing returns to scale, **31**
defense, national, 210
    as public good, 207–8
DeHaven, J., 197*n*
demand, demand theory, 2–19
    cross elasticity of, **10,** 50, 95–96
    derived, **154**–55
    essentials of, 2
    income elasticity of, **9,** 50, 95–96, 142–43
    market, 2–9; *see also* market demand curves

price elasticity of, *see* price elasticity of demand
    price inelasticity of, **7**–8
    unitary elasticity of, **7,** 8
demand curves:
    for labor, **152**–54, 159
    for loanable funds, **170**–71, 172
    market, *see* market demand curves
Democrats, Democratic party, 139
Denmark, 75
Depression, Great, 137, 206
derived demand, **154**–55
Deutsch, L., 42*n*, 44*n*, 141*n*
diminishing marginal returns, law of, **23**–24, 28, 29
diminishing marginal utility, law of, **12**
Dingell, John, 140
Disclosure Information Service, 41*n*
discrimination, sex, 183–84
Dodge Monaco, 143
Dodge Omni, 143
dominant-firm model, **107**
dominant strategy, **110**–11
drinking:
    national age for, 40, 46–47
    underage, 46
drunk-driving laws, 40
DuPont, 130, 178
Duquesne Light Company, 100
durable goods, price elasticity of demand for, 7*n*

Eastman Kodak, 130
easy money, 171–72
economic power, concentration of, 127–28
Economic Report of the President, 183*n*, 222*n*
economic profits, **66**
    in monopolistic competition, 115–16, 117
    in monopoly, 82
    in perfect competition, 66–67
economies of scale:
    in beer industry, 51–52
    oligopoly and, 104
efficiency:
    in auto industry, 140, 141, 143, 147, 148–49
    contestable markets and, 109
    minimum size and, 96
    monopolistic competition and, 115, 117
    monopoly and, 125
    regulation and, 93–94, 148–49
    of U.S. economy, 141
effluent fees, **218**–19, 227–28
Egypt, ancient, beer in, 40
elasticity of demand:
    beer industry and, 49–50

elasticity of demand (*continued*)
   cross, **10,** 50, 95–96
   income, **9,** 50, 95–96, 142–43
   price, *see* price elasticity of demand
electric equipment industry, 104, 113
electricity, electric industry, 91–102, 216
   competition in, 94–95
   conclusions about, 102
   cost of, 96–97
   demand for, 95–99
   introduction to, 91
   nuclear power plants and, 95, 100–101
   price differences in, 99–101
   pricing of, 93, 97–99
   regulation of, 91–94
   renewable energy sources for, 97
   Tennessee Valley Authority and, 101–2
electronics firms, 203
Elzinga, Kenneth, 48*n*, 49, 50
employment, 206
   in auto industry, 137–41, 144, 145, 146
   see also labor; labor force, women in; labor unions
energy:
   conservation of, 99
   renewable, 97
   see also electricity, electric industry
energy crisis, 137–38, 140, 143
Energy Department, U.S., 97
engineering, in auto industry, 140, 146
England, *see* Great Britain
environmental pollution, *see* pollution
environmental protection, 203, 217–25
   ban on ocean dumping and, 221–22
   bubbles, offsets, and banks and, **226–27**
   direct regulation and, **217**–18
   effluent fees and, **218**–19, 227–28
   global warming and, 222–25
   social costs and, 220–21
   tax credits and, **219**–20
   transferable emissions permits and, **219**
   zero pollution and, 221
Environmental Protection Agency (EPA), 220, 222, 225*n*, 226, 227
Equal Pay Act (1964), 183
equilibrium market basket, 13–**14**
equilibrium output:
   externalities and, 209
   in monopolistic competition, 114–15
   in monopoly, 80, 83
   in perfect competition, 64–67, 83
equilibrium price:
   in contestable markets, 109
   interest, 171, 172

   in monopolistic competition, 114–15
   in monopoly, 80, 83
   in perfect competition, 64–67, 83
   quantity of labor and, 155–57, 159
   in short run, 64–65, 80
excess capacity, in monopolistic competition, 115, 117, 125
excise taxes, **211**
exclusives, 45
external diseconomy, 199, **203,** 208–9
   pollution and, 216–17
external economy, 199, **203,** 209

Fairchild, 203
Farmland Dairies, 113
featherbedding, **162**
Federal Communications Commission, 91
Federal Energy Regulatory Commission (FERC), 91, 92–93
Federal Power Commission, 92, 228
Federal Reserve System, 171–72
Federal Trade Commission, 50, 205
Federal Trade Commission Act (1914), 129
Ferber, M., 186*n*, 187*n*, 189*n*
Finance Ministry, Japanese, 53
Finland, 224
firms:
   barometric, **107**
   demand for loanable funds by, 170–71
   dominant, **107**
   labor demand curve of, **152**–54, 159
   law of diminishing marginal returns and, 23–24
   in long run, 22, 26, 30–32, 66–68, 82
   minimum efficient size of, 96
   monopolist, *see* monopoly
   monopsonistic, *see* monopsony
   motivation of, 20
   in oligopoly, *see* oligopoly
   optimal input decision of, 24–26
   perfectly competitive, *see* perfect competition
   profit maximization of, 20, 24–25
   in short run, 22, 26–30, 57–65, 78–81
   supply curve of, 61–63
   technology and, **20**–21, 24, 51, 56–57
   see also cost, cost functions; inputs; production, production theory; *specific firms*
fixed costs:
   average, **28,** 29–30, 61
   of nuclear power plants, 95
   total, *see* total fixed cost
fixed inputs, **21,** 22, 24, 26, 57, 64
   rent and, **176**–77
Fogarty, Thomas, 49, 50

Food and Commercial Workers, 160
Ford, Henry, 136, 137, 142, 143, 178
    Japanese repudiation of, 139–40
Ford Escort, 143
Ford Motor Company, 139–43, 148
    mass production system of, 139, 140
    Model T and, 136, 137
Fox, Bernard, 97
Fox, Karl, 5
Framingham, Mass., GM assembly plant in, 144
franchises, 74–75, 92
Fraser, Douglas, 138–39
fraud, prevention of, 205
Freeman, S. David, 95
Friedland, Claire, 93
Friedlander, A., 145
Friedman, Milton, 204
Fuchs, Victor, 187n
fuel efficiency, 140, 143, 147, 148–49
Fujimoto, Takakiro, 147–48

Galbraith, John Kenneth, 127
Gallagher, J., 41n, 44n
game theory, **109**–12
gasoline, price of, 95–96, 138, 140, 143, 147
General Electric, 84, 112–13
General Motors (GM), 99, 127, 141, 148
    Framingham assembly plant of, 144
    "J" cars of, 143
    percentage of sales of, 1978 and 1991, 142
    pricing policy of, 146
    Sloan and, 136–37, 142
    Toyota's joint venture with, 141–42
Germany:
    auto industry of, 145–46
    beer sales in, 40, 53
gin, price of, 10
global warming, 222–25
GM, see General Motors
Golden Rule of Output Determination:
    for monopoly, 78–80
    for perfect competition, 58–61, 80
Goldman, Marc, 113
Gomez-Ibanez, J., 101n
goods:
    capital, 174
    durable, 7n
    luxury, **9**, 203n
    public, **203**, 207–8
government, U.S.:
    conservative view of role of, 202, 204, 205–6
    demand for loanable funds by, 171
    economic functions of, 204–7

economic role of, 202–15
    economic stabilization and, 206
    expenditures of, 210–11
    external economies and diseconomies and, **203**, 208–9
    income distribution and, 202–3, 206
    liberal view of role of, 202, 204–6
    mixed capitalism and, 202–4
    monetary policy and, 171–72, 206
    monopoly created by, 74–75
    price system limitations and, 202, 203n, 205
    public goods and, **203**
    regulation by, 75, 91–94, 148–49, 217–20
    rules of the game and, 205
    size of, 210
    see also specific branches and agencies
government transfer payments, **210**
Graham, John, 149
Great Britain, 108
    electricity prices in, 99
Greece, ancient, beer in, 40
Greene, William, 96, 142n
greenhouse effect, 222–25
Greer, D., 42n, 44n
Gruenspecht, Howard, 149

Halberstam, David, 143n, 146n
Hamms (beer), 44
Hamtramck plant, 141–42
Hawaii, energy in, 100, 101
Hawaii Electric Light Company, 100
Haymer and Urban Brewery, 41
Health and Human Services Department, U.S., 47
Heileman, 45, 48, 51
Henry, Bill, 42
Hicks, Sir John, 125
Hines, Lawrence, 228n
Hirshleifer, J., 197n
historical cost, **92**
home brewers, 48
Honda, 141, 142
Hoover Commission, 199
House of Representatives, U.S., 32
Howell, William, 42
Hudson, 137
Hughes, 132
Hunger, J. D., 43n, 44n
hydroelectric power, 99, 102
Hydro-Quebec, 97
Hymans, Saul, 142

Iacocca, Lee, 138
IBM Corporation, 132

Idaho, electricity in, 100
Idaho Power Company, 100
Illinois, 3
  auto industry in, 141
imports:
  Mexico's restriction of, 148
  U.S. restriction of, 140–41, 147
income, income level:
  beer drinking and, 50
  of consumers, 3, 9, 13, 20, 50
  future, present value of, 175–76
  market demand and, 3
  monopoly and, 124–25
income distribution, 151–91
  female labor force and, *see* labor force, women in
  government role in, 202–3, 206
  interest rate and, 170–76
  profits and, 177–78
  redistribution and, 124–25, 202–3, 206
  rent and, **176**–77
  welfare economics and, 194–95
  see also wages
income elasticity of demand, **9**
  for automobiles, 142–43
  for beer, 50
  for electricity, 95–96
income statement, of Anheuser-Busch, 41
income tax, personal, **211**
increasing returns to scale, **31**
Indiana, 3
Indian Point 3, 95
Indonesia, 108
  electricity prices in, 99
industrial concentration, 123–35
  antitrust laws and, 128–32; *see also* antitrust laws
  case against monopoly and, 123–26
  defense of monopoly and, 126–27
  economic power and, 127–28
  in United States, 128
industry demand curve, *see* market demand curve
inflation, 206
innovation, innovators, **178**
  monopoly and, 125
  perfect competition and, 126
  profits and, 178
inputs, 20–27
  average product of, **22,** 144
  defined, **21**
  fixed, **21,** 22, 24, 26, 57, 64, 176–77
  law of diminishing marginal returns and, **23**–24
  marginal product of, **22**–25, 196, 198–99
  market supply curve and, 62

  monopoly of, 74
  optimal, 24–26
  prices of, 62, 63
  production function and, **21**
  variable, **21**–22, 27, 30, 57
interdependence, oligopoly and, **104**
interest rate, **170**–76
  on bonds, 26
  demand for loanable funds and, 170–71
  equilibrium, 171, 172
  functions of, 173–74
Intergovernmental Panel on Climate Change, 223
Interior Department, U.S., 228
International Harvester, 130, 131
International Nickel Company, 74
international unions, 161*n*
Interstate Commerce Commission, 91
inventors, 178
investment, rate of return on, 91–94
investor-owned utilities, 91
Iran, 138

Jacksonville, Fla., 95
Japan, 222
  automobile industry of, *see* automobiles, automobile industry, Japanese
  beer sales in, 40, 53
job evaluation point system, 185
Jones, D., 140*n*, 144, 148*n*
Justice Department, U.S., 44
  Antitrust Division of, 130, 131–32

Kalt, J., 101*n*
Kansas, 2
Kaufer, E., 51*n*
Keeler, Theodore, 149
Kelly, Tom, 49
Kendall, David, 43
Kendix, M., 47*n*
Kentucky:
  auto industry in, 141
  energy in, 99, 100
  monopsony in, 159
Kentucky Utilities, 100
Kenya, electricity prices in, 99
Keynes, John Maynard, 32
Kiely, Lee, 42
Killingsworth, Mark, 185
kinked demand curve, 105–6
Kirin, 53
Kneese, Allen, 226
Knight, Frank, 178
Kwoka, J., 141*n*, 142*n*

LA (beer), 41, 43
labor:
    automobile industry and, 137–41, 144, 145, 146
    average product of, 22, 144
    equilibrium price of, 155–57, 159
    firm's demand curve for, **152**–54, 159
    as input, 21–25, 27
    marginal product of, 22–25, **153**
    market demand curve for, **154**–55, 156–62, 163
    market supply curve for, **155,** 156, 159, 162, 184
    profit maximization and, 152–53
    unskilled, 155, 156–57
labor force, women in, 183–91
    affirmative action and, 184–85, 189
    age and, 188–89
    comparable worth and, 185, 189–90
    conclusion about, 191
    growing role of, 183
    poverty and, 188
    sex discrimination and, 183–84
    subsidy effects on, 187–88
    tax on, 187
labor unions, 160–64
    auto industry and, 138–39, 161
    closed shop and, **163**
    collective bargaining and, **163**
    featherbedding and, **162**
    local, **161,** 162
    national, **161**–62
    open shop and, **163**
    union shop and, **163**
    wage increases and, 162
Lamb, Charles, 155
land, **176**
    as input, 21, 25, 176
Lave, Lester, 149
law of diminishing marginal returns, **23**–24
    average variable cost and, 28
    marginal cost and, 29
law of diminishing marginal utility, **12**
lawyers, earnings of, 184
Lee, B., 50
Leonard, Jonathan, 190
Lever Brothers, 110–11
Levin, R., 47n
liberals, government role as viewed by, 202, 204–5
Libya, 138
Lindzen, Richard, 222
loanable funds, 170–74
    allocation of, 173–74
    demand curve for, **170**–71, 172
    supply curve for, 171–72

local government:
    expenditures of, 210–11
    tax receipts of, 211
local unions, **161,** 162
Long Island Lighting Company (LILCO), 100–101
long run, **22,** 26, 66
    average cost in, **30**–32, 51, 66–67, 75, 96, 115, 116
    demand for automobiles in, 142
    equilibrium in, 66–68, 82, 114–15, 116
    monopolistic competition in, 114–15, 116
    monopoly in, 82
    perfect competition in, 57, 66–68
    as planning horizon, 22, 30
    price and output in, 66–68, 82
luxury goods, 203n
    elasticity of demand for, **9**

McConnell, J. D., 48
McGuinness, T., 50
McKinsey and Company, 51, 53, 145–46
McKinsey Global Institute, 40n, 51n
Mansfield, E., 99n, 137n, 153n, 197n
manufacturing, 127–28
    of automobiles, 136–42
Marconi, Guglielmo, 178
margarine, demand for, 10
marginal cost, marginal cost curve, **29**
    average cost functions and, 29–30
    of electricity company, 98, 99
    firm supply curve and, 61, 63
    in long run, 66–67, 115, 116
    market supply curve derived from, 62–63
    in monopolistic competition, 114–17, 125
    in monopoly, 78–80, 83, 92, **125**
    in oligopoly, 105, 106, 125
    in perfect competition, 58–64, 66–67, 80, 109, 124
    in short run, 58–64, 67, 78–80
marginal product:
    of an input, **22**–25, 196, 198–99
    optimal input decision and, 24–25
    optimal resource allocation and, 196, 198–99
marginal revenue, marginal revenue curve:
    in monopolistic competition, 114–17
    in monopoly, **76**–80, 83, 92, 124
    in oligopoly, 105, 106, 107
    in perfect competition, 80
marginal utility, **11**–15
    diminishing, law of, **12**
    equilibrium market basket and, 13–15
    optimal resource allocation and, 195–96, 197, 198
market basket, equilibrium, 13–14
market concentration ratio, **128**

market demand, 2–19
  see also cross elasticity of demand; income elasticity of demand
market demand curves, **2**–5
  for automobiles, 147
  for beer, 46–49
  for labor, **154**–55, 156, 162, 163
  in monopolistic competition, 114, 115, 117
  in monopoly, 75, 76–77, 83
  in oligopoly, 105–6, 112
  in perfect competition, 64, 83, 112
  price elasticity of demand and, 4, 5
  slope of, 3
  for wheat, 2–3, 5
markets:
  in agriculture, 56, 57
  contestable, **108**–9
market sharing, 114
market structure:
  market behavior and, 82–83
  types of, *see* monopolistic competition; monopoly; monopsony; oligopoly; perfect competition
market supply curves:
  for automobiles, 147
  backward-bending, **155**
  derivation of, 62–63
  determining location and shape of, 62–63
  for labor, **155,** 156, 159, 162, 184
  in perfect competition, **62**–66, 83, **155,** 156
  in short run, 62–65
Marysville, Ohio, Honda in, 141
Massachusetts, energy in, 95, 97, 100
mass production, of automobiles, 136–37, 139–40, 144
Maui Electric Company, 100
Mayor, Thomas, 143*n*
Mazda, 141, 142, 143
Meister Brau, 45
men, as beer drinkers, 46, 47–48
mergers:
  in beer industry, 42, 44
  in oil industry, 117
  of unions, 161
methane, 222
Metropolitan Transportation Authority, 95
Mexico, 94, 108
  automobiles in, 148
Michelob, 41, 44
Michelob Classic Dark, 41
Michelob Light, 41
Michigan, auto industry in, 141, 143
microbrewers, 43
Microeconomics: Theory and Applications (Mansfield), 153*n*

Middle Ages, 173
Middle Snake River, dam study on, 228
milk, sale of, 113
Milk Industry Council, 113
Miller, Frederick, 42
Miller, R., 148*n*
Miller Brewing Company, 42–46
  advertising of, 42, 45, 51–52
  concentration and, 43–44
  pricing policy of, 44–45
Miller High Life, 42, 45
Miller Lite, 42, 45
Millman, J., 197*n*
Milwaukee's Best, 45
Minnesota Power and Light Company, 100
Mitsubishi, 141, 142
Model T Ford, 136, 137
monetary policy, 206
  interest rates and, 171–72
monopolistic competition, **114**–18
  complaints against, 125
  conditions for, 114
  excess capacity in, 115, 117, 125
  monopoly compared with, 117
  number of firms in, 114, 117
  oligopoly compared with, 104, 125
  perfect competition compared with, 114, 117
  price and output under, 114–15, 117
  product diversity in, 115, 117, 125
  product group in, **114**
  resource allocation in, 199
monopoly, **74**–94, 123–35
  case against, 123–26
  causes of, 74–76
  control of, 128–32; *see also* antitrust laws
  control of input in, 74
  defense of, 126–27
  equilibrium and, 80, 82
  Golden Rule of Output Determination for, 78–80
  government action and, 74–75
  income redistribution and, 124–25
  inefficiency and, 125
  lack of innovation and technological change in, 125
  in long run, 82
  marginal cost in, 78–80, 83, 92, 125
  marginal revenue in, **76**–80, 83, 92, 124
  market demand curve in, 75, 76–77, 83
  mergers and, 44
  misconceptions about, 81
  monopolistic competition compared with, 117
  natural, **75**
  oligopoly compared with, 104, 125

optimal, 127
patents and, 74
perfect competition compared with, 80, 82–85,
    123–24, 126
price and output in, 78–84, 117, 123
production cost declines and, 75
profits in, 78–82, 123–78
regulation of, 75, 91–94
resource allocation in, 82, 84, 123–24, 199
in short run, 78–81
shutting down of, 80
total revenue in, 76, 78–80
monopsony, 125n, **159**–60
    sex discrimination and, 183–84
Montana, 3
Montana Power Company, 100
Motor Age, 136
Mount, T., 95–96
Murphy, R., 51n

Nader, Ralph, 93
Nantucket Electric Company, 100
Nash, 137
National Bureau of Economic Research, 47
national defense, *see* defense, national
National Education Association, 160
National Institute of Alcohol Abuse and Alcoholism,
    45–46
national unions (international unions), **161**–62
natural Light, 41, 45
natural monopoly, **75**
Nebraska, 3
necessities, **9**
Neil, T., 42n
Netherlands, 224
New Bedford, Mass., 95
New Hampshire, 97
New Jersey:
    electricity prices in, 99
    pollution in, 216, 221
New York, N.Y.:
    Department of Environmental Protection of, 222
    energy in, 95, 99–100
    pollution in, 218
    sales tax in, 211
New York Power Authority, 95
New York Public Service Commission, 101
New York State:
    energy in, 95, 97, 99–100
    milk sales in, 113
    pollution in, 216, 218, 221
New York Times, 95n, 97n, 101n, 140n, 216n, 222n

nickel monopoly, 74
Nigeria, 108
Niskanen, W., 50
Nissan, 141, 142
nitrous oxide, 222
noncompeting groups, **157**
Nordhaus, William, 223
North, D., 148n
North Dakota, 2
Northeast Utilities, 97
Northhampton, Pa., 95
Norway, 108
nuclear power plants, 95, 100–101
Nuclear Regulatory Commission, 95
nurses, 185

ocean dumping, ban on, 221–22
offset, **226**–27
Ohio, 3
    auto industry in, 141
    electricity in, 100
Ohio Valley Electric Corporation, 112–13
Ohno, Taiichi, 139–40
oil, oil industry:
    energy crisis and, 137–38, 140, 143
    mergers in, 117
    as oligopoly, 104, 108
    pollution and, 216
    price elasticity of, demand for, 6, 7
    price of, 97, 108, 138
Oklahoma, 2
Old Milwaukee, 42, 45
Old Milwaukee Light, 42
oligopoly, **104**–13
    cartels and, **106**–8, 112
    causes of, 104
    complaints against, 125
    contestable markets and, **108**–9, 112
    game theory and, **109**–12
    interdependence and, **104**
    kinked demand curve in, 105–6
    lack of unified model for, 104–5
    monopolistic competition compared with, 104, 125
    monopoly compared with, 104, 125
    perfect competition compared with, 104, 109,
        112–13, 126
    price leader and, **107**, 112
    profits and, 104, 106–8, 178
    resource allocation in, 109, 112, 199
open shop, **163**
opportunity (alternative) cost doctrine, **26**, 177–78
optimal resource allocation, **194**–201

optimal resource allocation (*continued*)
    case study of, 197–98
    conditions for, 195–96
    theory of the second best and, **199**
    welfare economics and, **194**–95
Orange and Rockland Utilities, 100
Oregon, electricity in, 100
Organization for Economic Cooperation and
    Development, 97
Organization of Petroleum Exporting Countries
    (OPEC), 108, 137–38, 140
output:
    average costs and, 28–31
    average product and, 22
    of beer, 1947–1990, 43, 44
    cartels and, 106–8
    equilibrium, *see* equilibrium output
    Golden Rule of determination of, 58–61, 78–80
    in long run, 57, 66–68
    marginal cost and, 29–30
    marginal product and, 22
    oligopoly and, 104, 106–7, 112
    optimal, 124, 209
    optimal input decision and, 24–26
    optimal resource allocation and, 196, 199
    in perfect competition, 57–68, 80, 83–84, 112
    production function and, 21
    in short run, 57–65
    total costs and, 26–27, 57–58
    see also price and output

Pabst Brewing Company, 44, 45, 48
Pacific Gas and Electric, 94–95
Pacific Power and Light Company, 100
Packard, 137
paper industry, 217, 225
patents, 74, 104
payoff, **110**
payoff matrix, **110**
Pearce, J., 142*n*
Peco Energy Company, 98–99, 100
Pennsylvania, 211, 218
    energy in, 95, 98–99, 100
Pennsylvania Public Utility Commission, 98–99
perfect competition, **56**–73, 152–57
    in agriculture, 56, 57
    arguments against, 126
    conditions for, 56–57
    defense of, 126
    determinants of price of labor under, 152–54
    and discontinuing production, 60–61, 80
    equilibrium in, 64–67, 83
    firm supply curve in, 61–63

Golden Rule of Output Determination in, 58–61, 80
in long run, 57, 66–68
marginal cost in, 58–64, 66–67, 80, 109, 124
marginal revenue in, 80
market demand curve in, 64, 83, 112
market supply curves in, **62**–66, 83, **155,** 156
monopolistic competition compared with, 114, 117
monopoly compared with, 80, 82–85, 123–24, 126
monopsony compared with, 160
number of firms in, 56, 63
oligopoly compared with, 104, 109, 112–13, 126
output in, 57–68, 80, 83–84, 112
price and output in, 64–68, 83–84, 112, 117
product homogeneity in, 56, 114
profits in, 78–82, 123, 178
resource allocation in, 56–57, 84, 112, 123–24,
    198–99
in short run, 57–65
technology and, 125, 126
wages under, 154–57, 160
welfare maximization and, 198–99
Philadelphia, Pa.:
    pollution in, 218
    taxes in, 211
Philadelphia Inquirer, 48*n*, 99*n*, 100*n*
Philip Morris, 42, 45, 52
Pittsburgh, Pa., taxes in, 211
planning horizon, long run as, 22, 30
plant and equipment:
    as fixed input, 22, 26, 64
    oligopoly and, 104
player, **109**
poker, game theory and, 109, 110
pollution, 216–29
    air, 203, 208–9, 217, 220–21, 226–27
    causes of, 216–17
    conclusion about, 228–29
    direct regulation of, **217**–18, 219
    effluent fees and, **218**–19, 227–28
    global warming and, 222–25
    optimal level of, 220–21
    transferable emissions permits and, **219**
    water, *see* water pollution
    zero, 221
pollution-control equipment, tax credits for, **219**–20
Popowsky, Irwin, 100
population, market demand curve and, 3
Porter, D., 43*n*
Portland General Electric Company, 100
Poterba, J., 224*n*
poverty, the poor:
    government role in, 202–3, 206
    of men vs. women, 188

preferences, consumer, *see* tastes, consumer
present value, of future income, 175–76
price and output:
    of cartels, 106–8
    in long run, 66–68, 82
    in monopolistic competition, 114–15, 117
    in monopoly, 78–84, 117, 123
    in perfect competition, 64–68, 83–84, 112, 117
    in short run, 64–65, 78–81
price discrimination, **76, 129**
price elasticity of demand, **4**–9
    for automobiles, **7,** 136, 142
    for beer, 49
    calculation of, 5
    consumers' budgets and, 7
    derived demand and, **154**–55
    determinants of, 6–7
    for electricity, 95–96
    length of time interval and, 7
    in oligopoly, 105
    substitutes and, 6, 7
    total money expenditure and, 7–9
    for wheat, 5, 6
price fixing, 114
price inelasticity, **7**–8
price leader, **107,** 112
price makers, 56
prices, pricing, price system:
    of automobiles, 137, 141, 142, 143, 146–47
    in beer industry, 44–45, 48–50
    cost-plus, 146
    of electricity, 93, 97–99
    equilibrium, *see* equilibrium price
    external diseconomies and, **216**–17
    of gasoline, 95–96, 138, 140, 143, 147
    kinked demand curve and, 105–6
    limitations of, 202, 203*n,* 205
    marginal cost and, 58–61, 109, 117, 124, 125
    market demand curve and, 2, 3
    of oil, 97, 108, 138
    in oligopoly, 104–9, 112, 113
    regulation of, 91–92, 93
    relative vs. absolute change in, 4
    rent as, **176**–77
    rules of the game and, 205
    stability of, 206
    standard, **146**
    see also interest rate
price takers, 56
private costs, **217**
private ownership, 205
Procter & Gamble, 110–11
product, diversity of, 115, 117, 125

product differentiation, 112
    in monopolistic competition, **114,** 117
product group, **114,** 117
production, production theory, 20–39
    of automobiles, 136–37, 139–41, 144–46
    of beer, 43
    cost functions and, *see* cost, cost functions
    discontinuing, 60–61, 80
    function, **21,** 22, 31
    inputs and, *see* inputs
    lean, 140, 141, 144
    mass, 136–37, 139–40, 144
production cost:
    for automobiles, 26, 99, 136, 137, 138, 140, 141, 145
    decline in, 75
    oligopoly and, 104, 109
    optimal resource allocation and, 194
production possibilities curve, 186
profit maximization, 20
    in monopolistic competition, 114–15, 117
    in monopoly, 78–82
    in monopsony, 159–60, 183–84
    optimal input decision and, 24–25
    in perfect competition, 57–61, 64, 67, 80
    quantity of labor and, 152–53, 159–60
profits, **20**
    accountants' vs. economists' view of, 177–78
    in auto industry, 136, 137, 138, 142, 146, 147
    capitalistic system and, 178
    economic, **66**–67, 82, 115–16, 117
    income distribution and, 177–78
    innovation and, 178
    in monopolistic competition, 114–17
    in monopoly, 78–82, 123, 178
    oligopoly and, 104, 106–8, 178
    in perfect competition, 57–62, 64–67, 123, 178
    risk taking and, 178
    total, 57–58, 78–79
property taxes, 26, 211
protectionism:
    imports and, 140–41, 147, 148
    labor unions and, 162
public goods, **203,** 207–8
    decision making about, 208
    national defense as, 207–8
Puget Sound Power and Light Company, 99, 100
Pure Food and Drug Act (1906), 205

quotas, automobile, 140–41, 147

Rae, J., 142*n*
railroad unions, 162
Ramses III, 40

Rand Corporation, 197
rate of return, **170**–71
  fair, 91–94
raw materials:
  as input, 21, 22, 27
  oligopoly and, 104
Reagan, Ronald (Reagan administration), 40, 132, 140, 147
regulation:
  of auto industry, 148–49
  direct, **217**–18, 219
  efficiency and, 93–94
  effluent fees and, **218**–19, 227–28
  of electric industry, 91–94
  pollution and, 217–20, 227–28
  price effects of, 91–92, 93
  public, **91**–94
  tax credits and, **219**–20
  transferrable emissions permits and, **219**
regulatory commissions, 91–93
regulatory lag, **94**
renewable energy, 97
rent, **176**–77
reproduction (replacement) cost, **92**
research and development, 126, 137
resource allocation:
  game theory and, 109
  misallocation in, 123–24
  in monopoly, 82, 84, 123–24, 199
  in oligopoly, 109, 112, 199
  optimal *see* optimal resource allocation
  in perfect competition, 56–57, 84, 112, 123–24, 198–99
  private vs. social costs and, 217
retail trade, product differentiation in, 114
returns to scale:
  constant, **31**
  decreasing, **31**
  increasing, **31**
revenue:
  marginal, *see* marginal revenue, marginal revenue curve
  total, 57–61, **76,** 78–80
right-to-work laws, 163
risk, 199
  profits and, 178
Robison, R., 142*n*
robots, 141
Rockefeller, John D., 117
Romans, ancient, beer of, 40
Roos, D., 140*n*, 144, 148*n*
Roosevelt, Theodore, 132

Rubin, Alan, 221–22
rule of reason, **130**–31, 132
rules of the game, **109,** 205
Russia, 222
Ruttan, V., 5*n*

Sacramento, Calif., 95
sales tax, **211**
Samuelson, Paul, 204–5
San Francisco, Calif., 94
satisfaction, consumer, *see* utility
Saudi Arabia, 108, 137–38
Scherer, F. M., 51–52
Schipper, M., 43*n*
Joseph Schlitz Brewing Company, 42, 43, 44, 48
Schultze, Charles, 226
Schumpeter, Joseph, 126, 178
second best, theory of the, **199**
secretaries, 185
Senate, U.S., Subcommittee on Antitrust and Monopoly of, 107
sewage treatment, 218, 221
sex, of beer drinkers, 46, 47–48
sex discrimination, 183–84
Sherman Act (1890), 129, 130, 131, 132, 205
shoe industry:
  as monopolist, 123–24
  patents and, 74
Shoreham nuclear plant, 100–101
short run, **22, 64**
  average costs in, 28–29, 60, 64, 67
  demand for automobiles in, 142–43
  equilibrium in, 64–65, 80, 114, 115
  interest rates in, 171–72
  marginal costs in, 29–30
  market supply curve in, 62–65
  monopolistic competition in, 114, 115
  monopoly in, 78–81
  perfect competition in, 57–65
  price and output in, 64–65, 78–81
  total costs in, 26–27
Simmons Market Research Bureau, 46, 50
Sipple, Peter, 99
skill, wage differentials and, 158
Skinner, Stanley, 95
slingshots, price elasticity of demand for, 4
Sloan, Alfred P., 136–37, 142
Smith, Adam, 84, 125
Smith, Jack, 142
Smith, James, 185, 188
Smith, Roger, 141

social cost:
of pollution, **217,** 220–21, 224
social benefit vs., 196, 199, 209, 224
social welfare, 124, 125
specialization, increasing returns to scale and, 31
sports, beer advertising and, 40, 45–46, 52
Standard Oil Company, 130, 132
standard price, **146**
State, County and Municipal Employees, 161
state government:
expenditures of, 210–11
tax receipts of, 211
steel industry, 104
antitrust law and, 130, 131, 132
Stigler, George, 93
strategy, **109–10**
dominant, **110**–11
Stroh, Peter, 49
Stroh Brewing Company, 42, 44, 45, 51–52
Studebaker, 137
Studebaker Lark, 137
sturgeon, pollution and, 216
Subaru, 143
subsidies, female labor force and, 187–88
substitutes, 3, **10**
price elasticity of demand and, 6, 7
Suits, Daniel, 61
sulfur dioxide, 227
sulfur industry, as oligopoly, 105
supply curves:
of firm, 61–63
for loanable funds, 171–72
market, *see* market supply curves
Supreme Court, U.S., 48, 74
affirmative action and, 184–85
antitrust law and, 128, 130–31, 132
surgeons, labor market for, 156–57
Sweden, 224
Sweeney, John, 162
Sweezy, Paul, 105–6

Taft-Hartley Act (1947), 163
Takaoka assembly plant, 144
tariffs, 141
tastes, consumer, 3
assumptions about, 11
sex discrimination and, 184
transitive, 11
tax credits, **219**–20
taxes, 206, 208, 209
beer consumption and, 47
carbon, 224

excise, **211**
female labor force and, 187
government receipts from, 211
property, 26, **211**
sales, **211**
Taylor, Lester, 96
Teamsters, 160, 161
Local 584 of, 113
technology, **20,** 199
in beer industry, 51
law of diminishing marginal returns and, 24
monopoly and, 125, 126
perfect competition and, 56–57, 126–27
production function and, **21**
profit maximization and, 20
Tennessee, auto industry in, 141
Tennessee Valley Authority (TVA), 101–2
Texas, 3
beer market in, 44
Texas Instruments, 203
tight money, 172
tonic, demand for, 10
total cost, 26, **27,** 28
in monopoly, 78, 79
in perfect competition, 57–61
total fixed cost, **26,** 27, 28
in monopoly, 78
in perfect competition, 57–58, 60
total money expenditure, price elasticity and, **7**–9
total profit:
in monopoly, 78–79
in perfect competition, 57–58
total revenue, **57–61, 76**
in monopoly, 76, 78–80
total utility, 11, 12, 14
total variable cost, 26, **27,** 28
in monopoly, 78
in perfect competition, 57–58
Toyota, 140, 141, 142
Takaoka assembly plant of, 144
Toyota Corolla, 141
trade:
reduction of barriers to, 75
restriction of, 140–41, 147, 148
retail, 114
training, wage differentials and, 158
transaction costs, advertising and, 51
transferable emissions permits, **219**
transfer payments, government, **210**
transistors, 203
Transportation Department, Santa Clara County, 184–85

Trebing, H., 93*n*
Tremblay, V., 50
Tullberg-Kelly, Lori, 48
tungsten carbide, monopoly of, 84
tying contract, **129**
Tyrell, T., 95–96

uncertainty, 199
  profits and, 178
unemployment, 140
unions, *see* labor unions
union shop, **163**
unitary elasticity, **7,** 8
United Auto Workers (UAW), 138–39, 161
United Mine Workers, 161
United Nations, 222, 223
United Shoe Machinery Company, 74
United States:
  concentration of economic power in, 127–28
  government of, *see* government, U.S.; *specific branches and agencies*
  industrial concentration in, 128
  Japanese auto imports restricted by, 140–41
  labor unions in, 138–39, 160–64
  market demand curve for wheat in, 2–3
  military budget of, 210
  mixed capitalism in, 202–4
  natural monopoly in, 75
  new passenger car sales in, 1951–1992, 138
  oil of, 108
  patent laws of, 74
  see also specific cities, states, and topics
U.S. Generating Company, 95
U.S. Steel, 130, 131, 132
util, **11**
utilities, investor-owned, 91
utility, **11**
  interpersonal comparisons of, 194–95
  marginal, *see* marginal utility
  maximizing of, 13–14
  total, 11, 12, 14

variable input, **21**–22, 27, 30, 57
Venezuela, 108
Volga River, pollution in, 26
Volkswagen, 142

wage differentials, 157, 158–59
  women and, 183, 184, 185
wages, 152–69
  ability or skill difference and, 158

equilibrium, 155–57, 159
  firm's demand curve for labor and, **152**–54, 159
  labor unions and, 160–64
  market demand curve for labor and, **154**–55, 156, 162, 163
  market supply curve for labor and, **155,** 156, 159, 162
  monopsony and, **159**–60
  noncompeting groups and, **157**
  under perfect competition, 154–57, 160
  of surgeons vs. unskilled labor, 156–57
  training difference and, 158
  see also income, income level
waiters and waitresses, 185
Wall Street Journal, 141–42
Ward, Michael, 185, 188
Warner, Kenneth, 6
Washington, 3
  comparable worth in, 185, 190
Washington Water Power Company, 100
water pollution, 203, 208–9, 225–26
  ban on ocean dumping and, 221–22
  plight of the beluga and, 216
  reduction of, 218
  social cost of, 220–21
water resources, optimal allocation of, 197
Wealth of Nations (Smith), 84
Weiss, Leonard, 102
welfare, social, 124, 125
welfare economics, **194**–95
welfare maximization, perfect competition and, 198–99
welfare program, 187–88, 206
Western Electric, 132
Westinghouse, 112–13
West Virginia, monopsony in, 159
Weyant, John, 224
wheat:
  average and marginal products of labor and, 22
  market demand curve for, 2–3, 5
  optimal input decision for, 25
  price elasticity of demand for, 5, 6
Wheelen, T., 41*n*, 43*n*, 47*n*
whiskey, demand for, 50
Willys, 137
wind energy, 97
windmills, 97
Winston, Clifford, 145
Wisconsin, beer market in, 44
Witt, L., 5*n*
Womack, James, 140*n*, 144, 148*n*

women:
    as beer drinkers, 46, 47–48
    black, 185, 188, 190
    in labor force, *see* labor force, women in
Wood, R., 43*n*
World War II, 137

Yamada, T., 47*n*
York (Ontario) Region Board of Education, 185

zero economic profit:
    in monopolistic competition, 114–15
    in perfect competition, 66–67